The Authoritative Source on Gaming Destinations in America

GAMBLER'S
DIGEST

Edited by Dennis Thornton

Published by

Please, call or write us for our free catalog of publications.
Our toll-free number to place an order or obtain a free catalog is 800-258-0929 or please use our regular business telephone 715-445-2214.

ISBN: 0-87349-422-9
Library of Congress Number: 2002105083
Printed in the United States of America

Acknowledgments

We recruited a host of gambling experts and prize-winning writers to share their knowledge with Gambler's Digest readers. They combined to write more than a dozen feature articles that cover the broadening spectrum of gaming.

Frank Scoblete, whose dozen books on gambling have sold more than a million copies, shared his inside tips on the exciting, fast-paced table games of blackjack and craps. The articles tell you which bets are best and which are long-odds losers to avoid.

Another seasoned gambling writer, Andrew Glazer has written a well-respected book on gambling as well as a weekly column in the Detroit Free Press and regular features in Poker Digest magazine. He shares tips on how to cash in on your time in the casino by earning comps from free meals to free hotel stays. And he also analyzes the online casinos and sports books that have grown in popularity as the Internet has spread.

Howard Herz, of Nevada's Gaming Archaeology, brought more than four decades of expertise in collecting to his article on gambling collectibles, such as casino chips, slot machines and matchbooks.

We also would like to acknowledge the superior reporting and writing skills brought by authors on topics from Indian casinos to Mississippi riverboats. Craig Cooper wrote articles on riverboats, sports books, Las Vegas, pari-mutuel wagering and Deadwood, S.D. Craig DeVrieze added an article describing the poker parlors of riverboats. Mike Hlas brought out the camaraderie present as players root for their numbers at a craps table. Sean Schultz described the inner workings of a typical Indian casino as well as interviewing the current and past chairmen of the National Indian Gaming Association. Tony Boylan's article said that minding your manners can pay off at the gaming tables. And Felicia Lowenstein told how casinos pumped new life into America's playground, Atlantic City.

A round of applause also goes out to the operators of casinos, dog and horse tracks, riverboats and cruise ships for providing photos and information about their establishments.

Also, Gambler's Book Shop in Las Vegas provided its list of thousands of books on gambling topics, while Gamblers General Store, another Las Vegas institution, contributed information on home gaming equipment.

We'd also like to acknowledge help and guidance from the following:

Debbie Bradley	Rick Lodholz
Bill Hahn	Steve Massie
Cheryl Hayburn	Gena Pamperin
Kay Sanders	Bill Krause
Gordon Ullom	Greg Krueger
Kevin Ulrich	

— Dennis Thornton, Editor

The Las Vegas Strip

Las Vegas News Bureau

3

Table of Contents

Great Gaming Spots

Sure Bets

Play In Paradise

Caesars Tahoe

Atlantic City Convention & Visitors Bureau

Ameristar Casino St. Charles

Tribal Treasures

Part 2: Gaming Guide

Oneida Casino

Introduction

A game of chance. That means every time you put a quarter in a slot machine or every time you place a wager on a blackjack hand, you have a chance to win. You could even win the BIG SCORE – hundreds, thousands, maybe even a million dollars.

It's that excitement that draws people to casinos, race tracks and riverboats. Even if they don't always come out ahead, they keep coming back to try their luck, or skill, against the dealers or the machines

Gambling has been around as long as mankind. But it's become more popular and prevalent than ever in the United States during the last decade. Not so long ago, the only legal games were in Nevada, unless you had the major bankroll to visit an exotic locale like Monte Carlo. Then along came Atlantic City and Donald Trump's Taj Mahal.

State lotteries and Indian casinos spread like wildfire in the 1990s, until there was gaming of some sort in more than 30 states. That trend continues, with tribes and private businesses racing to build the biggest and best casino-resort-hotel complexes around.

Now visitors to Las Vegas can view the best features of Paris, New York, Rio, Egypt or Venice. Or they can witness a volcanic eruption, a clash of pirate ships or live lions, or take a thrill ride up the side of a skyscraper or aboard a roller coaster.

Now couples and families can spend weekends and vacations enjoying the plush amenities of gambling resorts not far from their homes. When they're not playing the slots or table games, they can soak in a pool or spa, enjoy a gourmet meal, play a round of golf or enjoy a first-rate live performance without ever leaving the resort.

Gambler's Digest is designed to be a guide to the nation's gambling scene. You'll find comprehensive listings for every casino, horse or dog track, riverboat, cruise ship and jai-alai site in the United States. Included are addresses, phone numbers, restaurants, entertainment and games that each establishment features.

There's also a mix of informative articles ranging from tips on how to play winning blackjack or craps to a rundown of the newest casinos emerging on construction sites. And there are suggestions on how to claim those valuable "comps," including free meals and hotel rooms, that casinos hand out to their customers.

Use the resources in Gambler's Digest to enhance your gaming fun and find the casino or race track that best suits your interests. Then step up to the table or the slot machine and try to win that BIG SCORE.

Best of luck to you.

Gambling's Glitter Spreads Across America

▌*New Casinos, Hotels, and Riverboats Popping Up from Coast to Coast*

By Dennis Thornton

Multi-million dollar casinos, hotels, and riverboats opening from Connecticut to California mean gambling is a growth industry. It also means gambling enthusiasts have more opportunities than ever before to enjoy games of chance in ever-more luxurious surroundings and many more locations.

The biggest project that gamblers can look forward to seeing in the next few years will be Le Reve, a Las Vegas megaresort scheduled to cost more than $1.6 billion. It is expected to open in 2004.

Atlantic City won't be far behind in the parade of megaresorts. The Borgata, which is scheduled to open in 2003, will have more than 2,000 rooms, a 135,000 square foot casino, and 11 restaurants.

Aztar Corp. has acquired the full Tropicana Resort & Casino property in Las Vegas and has plans to develop adjoining Strip space into another one or two casinos.

This $28 million expansion will result in an enclosed walkway connecting Bally's Atlantic City to the Claridge between Pacific Avenue and Brighton Park, along Park Place. The project also includes approximately 10,000 square feet of retail space on the second floor, and a 12,000 square foot ballroom that will be accessible from the sixth floor of Bally's Atlantic City.

Caesars Atlantic City is sporting a new Baccarat Pit and also has added the Palace Court Arena of Slots. Both were completed in mid-2002.

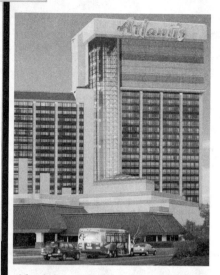

Atlantis Resort Casino in Reno sports a new 27-story tower with 392 additional rooms. Below is Atlantis' pyramid-shaped Sky Terrace.

And major projects are under way or have just been completed in 16 states.

Long gone are the days when anyone interested in dropping a quarter in a slot machine or being dealt a hand of blackjack had to travel to Las Vegas or Reno. Atlantic City, seeing the need to attract more tourists, was the next to join Nevada as a gambling destination.

By the mid-1990s, the trickle of gaming opportunities became a gusher as more states started lotteries, Indian tribes got the green light to open casinos in many states, and riverboat casinos reappeared on the mighty Mississippi River for the first time in a century.

Although Las Vegas casinos suffered through hard times in the wake of the Sept. 11 tragedies, when vacationers and conventioneers stopped flying to the Nevada resorts, other gaming locations across the country benefited when tourists stayed closer to home and visited their local or regional casinos.

The high costs of cleanup and rebuilding after Sept. 11 led the state of New York to expand its gaming sites to create new revenue sources. The New York Legislature passed legislation in 2001 permitting as many as six new Indian casinos in the state as well as allowing video lottery terminals at horse racing tracks. Lawmakers said the additional gaming could raise $1 billion annually in revenues for the cash-strapped state.

Another barrier was broken when South Carolina began selling lottery tickets in January 2002, making it the 38th state with a lottery. The lottery had been authorized by voters in November 2000. Nevada politicians are pushing for a lottery, Tennessee voters were to vote on a lottery plan in November 2002, and Ohio's legislature voted to join the multi-state Powerball lottery. Nevada is also considering legalizing online gambling, currently illegal in the U.S. and limited to off-shore Internet operations.

Here are some of the new or expanded casinos and riverboats that opened in 2001 or 2002, as well as a few that are in the planning stages.

Las Vegas

The biggest project in the planning stages is **Le Reve**, the megaresort dreamed up by Steve Wynn, who earlier developed Bellagio while working for Mirage Resorts. The Desert Inn was imploded at its Strip location in 2001 to make room for the new resort.

An artist's drawing shows the new high limit slot parlor that opened in June 2002 at Bally's Atlantic City. The collection of premium slots contains 148 slot machines in $5 to $100 denominations.

Wynn says Le Reve, French for "the dream," will have 2,455 rooms in a 42-story hotel tower and should be ready to open by September 2004.

Three other casinos joined the Las Vegas scene late in 2001. **Tuscany Suites** opened its 1,000-room Flamingo Road hotel-casino, featuring a 60,000 square foot casino with 1,000 slot machines. The $265 million **Palms**, also on Flamingo Road, debuted in November 2001, featuring a 42-story hotel tower with 455 rooms and a 95,000 square foot casino. And **Green Valley Ranch Resort & Spa** opened in December 2001 with a party and fireworks display. The $300 million project offers 201 rooms, 45 suites, and a 50,000 square foot casino on a 40-acre property.

That's not all that's happening in Las Vegas. Aztar Corp. announced plans early in 2002 to acquire the rest of the **Tropicana Resort and Casino** property with the intention of developing 34 acres of Strip space into one or two major casino resorts in future years. Park Place planned to open a 4,000 seat Coliseum concert venue at **Caesars** in 2003. And the lenders for the **Aladdin Hotel and Casino** planned to sell the bankrupt resort, just a year old, later in 2002.

Mandalay Bay is adding a convention center which, at 1.4 million square feet, will be among the five largest in the nation. The facility, scheduled to open in January 2003, is being constructed on 16.5 acres adjacent to the existing 190,000 square foot Mandalay Bay Conference Center.

Meanwhile, **Bellagio** and **The Mirage** proved that Las Vegas cuisine has advanced far beyond the traditional casino buffet. Bellagio won the AAA Five Diamond Award for its Picasso restaurant as well as for its hotel. The Renoir restaurant in The Mirage also received the Five Diamond Award.

Reno

A new 27-story hotel tower added 392 rooms to the **Atlantis Casino Resort** in Reno, for a total of 982 rooms. The resort, in a $60 million project, also added 20,000 square feet of convention, meeting and special event space including a Grand Ballroom expansion, and added 16,000 square feet of casino space with 500 new slot machines and 10 new table games.

The Borgata Resort, costing $1 billion, will tower over Atlantic City when it's completed in 2003.

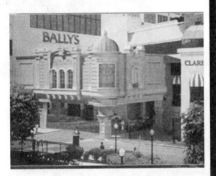

Bally's Atlantic City and the Claridge will be brought closer together with a $28 million concourse.

A 96-room Hilton Garden Inn and an additional 50,000 square feet of casino and restaurant space were added at Win-River Casino in California.

The new arena at the Mohegan Sun in Connecticut can seat 10,000 for basketball games, boxing matches or concerts.

A new 34-story hotel tower with 1,200 rooms is a part of the Mohegan Sun's major expansion project, completed in early 2002.

Atlantic City

The $1 billion **Borgata Resort**, on a 27-acre site, is in the spotlight in Atlantic City, but that's not the only project under way.

Harrah's is working on an $80 million expansion of **Harrah's Atlantic City** to complement a $113 million hotel tower, with 452 rooms, that opened in the spring of 2002. The 50,000 square foot expansion will include 28,000 square feet of new casino space as well as an addition to the lobby and expansion of the Fantasea Reef buffet.

Construction was also under way on a $28 million concourse between **Bally's Atlantic City** and the **Claridge**. The project includes 10,000 square feet of retail space and a 12,000 square foot ballroom.

Connecticut

The **Mohegan Sun** opened its 34-story, 1,200-room hotel in April 2002, enhancing the New England resort. The hotel opening marked completion of the Mohegan Sun's $1.1 billion "Project Sunburst" expansion. The new Casino of the Sky opened in September 2001, expanding casino space to 315,000 square feet. The project also included a 10,000 seat Mohegan Sun Arena and 300-seat Cabaret, as well as 16 additional restaurants and a shopping mall.

The Trump 29 Casino, formerly Spotlight 29, opened in 2002 in Coachella, Calif., offering new gaming, dining, and entertainment opportunities

New York

One of the new casinos authorized by the New York state Legislature will be a 750-room hotel and 130,000 square foot casino in the Catskills owned by the **Saint Regis Mohawk Tribe** and managed by Park Place. An agreement was signed in November 2001 to develop the project, pending government approval.

Other tribes were negotiating in 2002 to develop casinos under the expansion plan authorized by the Legislature.

Monticello Raceway was authorized to install video lottery terminals and plans were being made to locate a casino at the site.

A bill was also signed in 2001 that will help reopen the **Batavia Downs Racetrack**. The legislation allowed Western Regional Off-Track Betting Corp. to apply for a license to operate the track, which went out of business in 1998.

North Carolina

A 15-story hotel and conference center opened at **Harrah's Cherokee** in Cherokee, N.C., in the spring of 2002. The project includes 250 rooms and eight suites as well as an indoor pool, 15,000 square foot conference center, and two new restaurants. The casino added 800 video slots.

Florida

The Seminole Tribe is working on one of several expansion phases at the **Coconut Creek Casino.** A temporary addition opening in March 2002 will add 5,200 square feet of casino space, 279 more video pull tab machines and 350 parking spaces. A future addition of 50,000 square feet is planned that would provide more casino space and add three restaurants.

The Hyatt Regency Resort & Casino has completed a $27 million renovation to restore its 1920s "grand lodge" look and construction on a new spa was under way in 2002.

A series of three photos shows the new Black Hawk Casino in Black Hawk, Colo. At top, the 55,000 square foot facility includes two restaurants and a Starbucks coffee shop. Above, the casino features 1,332 slot and video machines as well as blackjack and poker tables. Below, a chef prepares a buffet.

Illinois

Hollywood Casino is constructing a $70 million dockside riverboat casino in Aurora. The project will include a 53,000 square foot casino.

Indiana

The Chicago area got an additional luxury hotel when **Harrah's East Chicago** opened a 293-room hotel tower in December 2001. The hotel complements the riverboat casino.

Missouri

Isle of Capri Casinos opened a new $75 million, 72,000 square foot riverboat casino in Boonville, Mo., in December 2001. The casino features 900 slot machines and 28 gaming tables as well as three restaurants.

Expansion of the **Ameristar Casino** in St. Charles was scheduled for completion in mid-2002. The project will increase the casino to 115,000 square feet with 3,000 slot machines and 104 table games. A steakhouse, buffet, lounge, arcade and gift shop are planned.

Louisiana

Delta Downs Racetrack in Vinton, La., near Houston has undergone extensive renovations and improvements. The grandstand areas have been renovated and a new buffet restaurant added. And a casino has been constructed on the 220-acre site, which features thoroughbred and quarter horse racing.

The State Gaming Control Board also granted its 15th and final riverboat gaming license to **Pinnacle Entertainment**, which has proposed a $220 million casino resort on 175 acres in Lake Charles. The resort is expected to open in 2004.

Minnesota

One new resort casino was under way in 2002 in Minnesota and two expansions had just been completed. The Upper Sioux Community held a groundbreaking in the fall of 2001 for its new **Prairie's Edge Casino Resort**.

The **Treasure Island Resort & Casino** in southeastern Minnesota completed a 58,000 square foot addition with space for 800 more slot machines and eight blackjack tables. And **Shooting Star Casino** in Mahnomen, Minn., completed a $26 million project adding 110 hotel rooms, a poker room, a restaurant, expanded gift shop and new Event Center holding up to 1,000 people.

Colorado

The $150 million **Black Hawk Casino** in Black Hawk opened in late 2001 with a casino that features 1,332 slot and video machines, 16 blackjack tables and six poker tables. The 55,000 square foot facility also includes two restaurants and a Starbucks coffee shop. Plans call for a Hyatt Hotel to be built adjacent to the casino.

Arizona

The Pascua Yaqui Tribe opened its **Casino Del Sol** in Tucson in October 2001. The first phase of a $65 million project includes 70,000 square feet of space for 500 slot machines, a dozen poker tables and a restaurant as well as the 4,400-seat Anselmo Valencia Tori Amphitheater.

New Mexico

Santa Ana Star Hotel Casino was in the first phase of an elaborate expansion project in 2002. Included in the Bernalillo, N.M., facilities will be a 288-room hotel, three new restaurants, a 3,000-seat special events center and a 36-lane bowling center.

California

Donald Trump, owner of Atlantic City's Taj Mahal, is among the players in the expanding gaming scene in California. Work was under way in 2002 on a $60 million expansion at **Trump 29 Casino** in Coachella that will include a new casino wing, renovated showroom, 200-room hotel and several restaurants. The expansion will triple the size of the existing 75,000 square foot casino.

Expansion of the **Barona Valley Ranch Resort & Casino** near San Diego was expected to be completed in 2002. Included in the $225 million project were a new casino, a hotel, a wedding chapel and the Barona Creek Golf Club, an 18-hole championship course.

The **Pechanga Entertainment Center** in Temecula was scheduled to open in the summer of 2002. Featured is a 522-room Four Star Hotel & Casino with a 1,300-seat theater, seven restaurants and 75,000 square feet of casino space. The casino will feature 2,000 slots, 60 table games and 23 poker tables.

Located in the heart of Los Angeles is the new **Crowne Plaza Hotel**, which opened in October 2001. The nine-story hotel includes 200 rooms and suites. The 24-hour Commerce Casino, which was already open at the site, features 250 poker tables.

Harrah's and the **Rincon Band** of Indians are building a $125 million resort hotel and casino in Pauma Valley, about 25 miles from San Diego. The hotel will include 200 rooms and suites and six restaurants, while the casino will have 45,000 square feet of gaming space. Expected opening was in the fourth quarter of 2002.

And in northern California, the **Win-River Casino** is adding a 96-room Hilton Garden Inn to its casino in Redding. The casino will also add 50,000 square feet, including space for 750 new slot machines, a restaurant and a lounge.

Washington

Chehalis Tribes began construction in December 2001 on a 15,000 square foot addition to the **Lucky Eagle Casino** in Rochester. Included in the project are a new buffet restaurant and enhanced banquet and entertainment facilities.

Delta Downs, shown in an architect's drawing, has renovated the grandstand at the horse track. It also added a casino featuring slot machines.

A 15-story hotel and conference center is the centerpiece of Harrah's Cherokee in North Carolina. The 250-room hotel opened in 2002.

An architect's sketch shows plans for the Santa Ana Star Hotel Casino in New Mexico. It will include a 288-room hotel, three new restaurants, a special events center, and a bowling center.

Players Once Again Are Rolling Down The River

▌ *Mark Twain Era Returns on the Mississippi, Ohio*

BY Craig Cooper

Bernie Goldstein is Isle of Capri chairman and CEO.

Isle of Capri Casinos Inc.

> **There was a mystical magnetism of the river 400 years ago that remains today.**

Classic literature has been written about the Mississippi River and its cities. Songs have told stories about the river for generations. Photographers and artists have been inspired by the great river.

The art of the river describes and portrays large paddlewheel boats belching smoke, the gray-bearded captains of those boats standing in the wheelhouse overlooking the miles ahead of them and the smoky poker tables busy with games of stud and draw. There was a mystical magnetism of the river 400 years ago that remains today.

From the clear, cold waters running out of Lake Itasca in Minnesota, where thousands of tourists walk in bare feet across the headwaters every summer, to the Gulf of Mexico, the river winds past large and small communities that depend on the river for so many things.

Riverboat revival

Bernie Goldstein understood the attraction of the river. He loved the river. He had grown up discovering the river. His successful business was moving product down the river with barges. He also built a scrap metal business on the riverfront of the Quad-Cities area on the border of Iowa and Illinois.

In the late 1980s, Goldstein read about legislators in Iowa who were suggesting that thousands of tourists would enjoy the river experience if there was

Isle of Capri executives include, from left, Allan Solomon, executive vice president, Bernard Goldstein, CEO and chairman, and John M. Gallaway, president.

Isle of Capri Casinos Inc.

something to bring them to the river. There would have to be an attraction. Maybe low-stakes gaming on boats that resembled those in the art history f the river and in Mark Twain's stories would bring visitors to the river cities.

Goldstein was already in the barge business. He was involved in the lobbying efforts that resulted in the passing of legalized riverboat gaming in 1990. Iowa became only the fourth state in the country, following Nevada, New Jersey and South Dakota, to allow casino gaming.

On April 1, 1991, beating his competition by 1 hour, 45 minutes, Goldstein's Diamond Lady opened on the riverfront of Bettendorf, Iowa, to become the first modern-day riverboat casino. Television letter-turner Vanna White and movie actor Howard Keel were among the celebrity guests for the opening.

Only a few miles away in Davenport, the President Casino, a lumbering, old St. Louis excursion boat that had been retrofitted as a casino, was opening on the same day.

Eleven years later there are nearly 60 riverboat casinos operating on the Mississippi and Missouri Rivers. Goldstein, who at 73 is the chairman and chief executive officer of the Isle of Capri, the seventh largest gaming company in the United States, is betting that expansion of riverboat gambling will continue.

Smaller scale than Vegas

Riverboat gambling has a different niche than Las Vegas or Atlantic City. That seems to be part of the attraction of the boats.

Las Vegas and Atlantic City are gambling destinations with huge hotels, casinos and elaborate stage shows. Riverboats offer the same games and same amenities, but on a smaller scale.

The riverboats do offer fine dining, hotels, entertainment and sports bars. Gaming has been introduced to major markets like Kansas City, Omaha, Chicago, St. Louis and New Orleans because of riverboat gambling.

Originally, cruising the river was billed as part of the riverboat experience. These days the casino structures are built on large barges and do not cruise at all. The games, not the rivers, are the draw. Critics expected that from the start.

Goldstein was one of the pioneers of modern riverboat gambling. He wasn't sure how long he would last in the business. The excitement of having one of the first riverboat casinos didn't last long for Goldstein.

Illinois soon followed Iowa with its own riverboat gaming laws. The differences in the gaming laws between the two states nearly killed Iowa riverboats.

Players crowd around table games in the casino aboard the riverboat Ameristar Casino St. Charles.

The land-based exterior in Bossier City is the entrance to the riverboat.

Isle of Capri Casinos Inc.

> *Riverboat gambling has a different niche than Las Vegas or Atlantic City. That seems to be part of the attraction of the boats.*

The Ameristar Casino Vicksburg is one of the riverboats that has opened along the Mississippi River.

Illinois operators were not limited by the $5 table limit and the $200 maximum loss Iowa law stipulated.

"The Iowa law was written to bring tourists to the state," said Goldstein. "Originally in Iowa we had the loss limits and only 30 percent of the space on our boats could be devoted to gambling. The boats were not designed for gambling. They were excursion boats that offered a little gambling."

Laws in both states required the boats to cruise except in the winter and when the weather was considered unsafe. There were admission fees and in busy periods, bettors could only stay on the boat for one cruising session.

"Illinois changed everything. It was awful. The restrictions we had in Iowa were horrible. We were losing our shirts. We owed everyone money," Goldstein said. "It was so bad that we could have claimed bankruptcy. Legally we could have but we just weren't going to do that."

With a series of right moves, favorable changes in the Iowa law and the expansion of riverboat gaming into other states, Goldstein's company survived. In 2002 the publicly traded Isle of Capri (NASDAQ: ISLE) will top $1 billion in revenue. Isle of Capri was one of the gaming companies that successfully fought through the economic downturn of tourist-based companies after the terrorism attacks of Sept. 11, 2001.

When the stocks of other gaming companies were tumbling, Isle of Capri shares were showing significant gains late in 2001.

Isle of Capri expands

Goldstein still isn't certain how he has gone from having two boats in Iowa that were on the brink of bankruptcy to overseeing a company with 15 gaming venues. The Isle of Capri's 12 riverboats, two land-based casinos and Florida's only harness racing track are holding their own against "name" gaming companies like Harrah's, MGM, and Caesars.

One of the right moves Goldstein made, as much as it hurt him personally, was to move his two boats in Iowa to Mississippi when that state approved riverboat gambling.

"We hated to move our two boats to Mississippi because I had grown up in Rock Island and still live in Bettendorf part of the year; but we had to because of the Iowa law and the competition from Illinois," Goldstein said. "When we got to Biloxi, there were people waiting four or five hours in 95-degree heat for us to open. It was amazing.

"Our situation was that we could either stay in Iowa and go bankrupt, or move and make some money."

Isle of Capri's niche in the gaming industry is primarily its riverboats in Mississippi, Louisiana, Missouri, and back in Iowa, where Goldstein returned

> *"When we got to Biloxi, there were people waiting four or five hours in 95-degree heat for us to open. It was amazing."*
> — Bernie Goldstein

The Lake Charles Grand Palais has the classic look of a Mississippi Rover riverboat.

Isle of Capri Casinos Inc.

when laws were changed to level the gambling playing field in the Quad-Cities area. Ironically, when Iowa changed its law so that the boats didn't have to cruise as much, then it was the Illinois border boats that took the hit.

"I think what happened to our company is that we were among the first to get into riverboat casinos and we were riding the wave as riverboat gaming expanded," Goldstein said of his company's success.

Riverboats are no fad

When Iowa first allowed casinos in 1991, casino mogul Steve Wynn called the boats a fad. "He (Wynn) said the boats would float away," Goldstein recalls. "It wasn't long before he was building the Beau Rivage in Mississippi."

Goldstein believes Wynn and others in the land-based casino industry underestimated the potential of riverboat casinos by not foreseeing that the riverboats would make the action geographically convenient compared to trips to Las Vegas or Atlantic City.

"Riverboat casinos are a lot different than going to Las Vegas," Goldstein said. "Riverboats are like any other night of entertainment. Instead of going to a movie, or bowling, you can go to the riverboat and have a good time and not spend a lot more.

"We're an alternative entertainment and you don't have to fly to Las Vegas or Atlantic City to be able to gamble. It's a laid-back, friendly experience where you know the dealers personally and they know the regulars."

The riverboat at Caesars Indiana is aptly named **The Glory of Rome.**

The neon-lit Bossier City Isle of Capri stands out at night.

Ilsle of Capri Casinos Inc.

Ameristar Council Bluffs provides gaming action in Iowa.

Goldstein said the key demographics of his company are that 80 percent of the riverboat patrons are repeat customers and most live within 150 miles of the casino. In some of the Isle's casinos, bettors spend an unremarkable $40 per visit.

The tragedy of Sept. 11, 2001 hit Las Vegas hard partly because some people were afraid to fly and they were pulling back financially as the economy slipped. That doesn't mean that gamblers suddenly quit gambling. The gamblers in the Midwest, Dakotas and deep South could stay home to play at tribal casinos or on riverboats.

"Instead of going to Las Vegas, a lot of people could stay closer to home by going to the riverboats. They could spend the night in a nice hotel, have a nice meal and a gambling experience without having to fly somewhere," Goldstein said.

Gaming continues expansion

Goldstein expects the expansion of gaming to continue. His own company, though, is likely to stay primarily with riverboat gaming. The company does own the Lady Luck Hotel and Casino in downtown Las Vegas and a limited-stakes, land-based casino in Black Hawk, Colo.

Black Hawk, Colo., got its name from the Black Hawk mining equipment company, a defunct company that was based in the Quad-Cities where the tribal chief Black Hawk was important to the development of the area.

In 1949, Goldstein married his wife, Irene, in the beautiful, old Blackhawk Hotel in downtown Davenport. Now he owns it. Isle of Capri purchased the hotel when it also purchased the President Casino, which had been Goldstein's original competition in the market.

It has been quite an adventure for the self-made entrepreneur. He isn't done.

Goldstein's "retirement" plan is to expand the Isle of Capri's business as additional states allow riverboat gaming.

"There is still a lot of room for growth in the industry," he said. "When the economy took a downturn in 2001 after Sept. 11, a lot of states started hurting for money. Instead of cutting back on programs and having to cut billions of dollars out of budgets, those states are going to look at riverboat gambling.

"Look at the entire Northeast ... big population states like Pennsylvania, Ohio, Michigan, New York ... that don't have riverboat gambling at this time."

Goldstein spends the winter in a condo community in Florida with a large population of retired businessmen.

"All of Florida is a retirement community, isn't it?" Goldstein joked. "I know a lot of retired guys who are bored because they aren't involved in anything. I'm bad at golf. I took golf lessons. They didn't work the first time so why would they work now?"

> *"Instead of going to Las Vegas, a lot of people could stay closer to home by going to the riverboats. They could spend the night in a nice hotel, have a nice meal and a gambling experience without having to fly somewhere."*
>
> *— Bernie Goldstein*

Midwest and Southern Riverboats

Illinois

Argosy Alton Belle, Alton
Casino Queen, East St. Louis
Empress, Joliet
Grand Victoria, Elgin
Harrah's, Joliet
Hollywood, Aurora
Jumer's Casino Rock Island, Rock Island
Par-A-Dice, East Peoria
Players, Metropolis

Indiana

Argosy, Lawrenceburg
Belterra, Belterra
Blue Chip, Michigan City
Caesars, Elizabeth
Casino Aztar, Evansville
Grand Victoria, Rising Sun
Harrah's, East Chicago
Horseshoe, Hammond
Majestic Star, Gary
Trump, Gary

Iowa

Ameristar, Council Bluffs
Argosy Belle, Sioux City
Catfish Bend, Fort Madison
Diamond Jo, Dubuque
Isle of Capri, Marquette
Isle of Capri, Bettendorf
Lakeside, Osceola
Mississippi Belle II, Clinton
Rhythm City, Davenport

Louisiana

Argosy, Baton Rouge
Bally's Belle of Orleans, New Orleans
Boomtown Westbank, Harvey
Casino Magic, Bossier City
Casino Rouge, Baton Rouge
Delta Queen Steamboat Co., New Orleans
Harrah's Lake Charles, Lake Charles
Harrah's Shreveport, Shreveport
Isle of Capri, Bossier City
Isle of Capri, Westlake
Treasure Chest, Kenner

Mississippi

Ameristar, Vicksburg
Bally's Saloon and Gambling Hall, Robinsonville
Bayou Caddy's Jubilee, Greenville
Boomtown, Biloxi
Casino Magic, Biloxi
Casino Magic, Bay St. Louis
Copa Casino, Gulfport
Fitzgeralds, Robinsonville
Gold Strike, Robinsonville
Grand, Biloxi
Grand, Robinsonville
Grand, Gulfport
Harrah's, Vicksburg
Harrah's Robinsonville
Hollywood, Robinsonville
Imperial Palace, Biloxi
Isle of Capri, Biloxi
Isle of Capri, Lula
Isle of Capri, Robinsonville
Isle of Capri, Vicksburg
Isle of Capri, Natchez
Lighthouse Point, Greenville
President Broadwater, Biloxi
Rainbow, Vicksburg
Sam's Town, Robinsonville
Sheraton, Robinsonville
Treasure Bay, Biloxi

Missouri

Isle of Capri, Boonville
Ameristar, St. Charles
Argosy, Kansas City
Aztar, Caruthersville
Harrah's, North Kansas City
Harrah's, Maryland Heights
Isle of Capri, Kansas City
President by the Arch, St. Louis
Frontier, St. Joseph

Slot machines are arranged in an ornate setting in the casino of the Ameristar Casino Hotel Kansas City.

One of the features of the casino at Ameristar Casino St. Charles is an enormous chandelier.

A spacious casino offers games of chance to customers at the Ameristar Casino Vicksburg.

Deadwood Lives Again

▌ *Gambling Brought South Dakota City Back to Life*

By Craig Cooper

A portrait shows Wild Bill Hickok, who was gunned down in Deadwood in 1876.

A modern-day Wild Bill Hickok meets his fate in a re-enactments of that fateful day when he was shot in the back while playing poker. Chad Coppess photo.

D eadwood wasn't dead, only on life support. The historic little town tucked into the Black Hills of South Dakota still had a faint pulse in the 1980s after years of decline and neglect.

The infrastructure of the former mining boom town, where James Butler Hickok — "Wild Bill" to his friends — was murdered and buried in the Mount Moriah Cemetery, was falling apart. Historic buildings that were an important attraction for tourists arriving in Deadwood were deteriorating.

"These historic buildings would burn down simply because it would take 30 to 45 minutes to get the water pressure up high enough to fight the fire," explained Rich Turbiville, a lifelong resident of the Rapid City area. "We were losing the Victorian architecture that was one of the reasons people came here at all.

"There was no money to fix the sewers, streets or anything like that and there wasn't money to replace the buildings that were falling apart."

Everyone agreed something had to be done.

"I think Deadwood would have been a ghost town by now if nothing had been done," said Victoria Johnson, a native of the area who works for the Deadwood Visitors Bureau. "It was falling apart pretty quickly."

Gold rush days revisited

Deadwood town leaders came up with an idea that probably sounded far-fetched at the time. The suggestion was made that gambling be reintroduced to

If you think the Main Street of Deadwood, S.D., looks like the set of a western, you'd be right. The city has gone to great lengths to preserve many of the buildings from the 1800s when Deadwood was a wild western town.

the town. Gambling had been a tradition in Deadwood from the gold rush in 1876 until 1947, when there was a crackdown that shut down gaming establishments that had actually been illegal since 1905.

Deadwood's leaders found political support for their plan as long as there were restrictions. The stipulation for legalizing gaming in Deadwood was that it had to be small-stakes gaming. Only certain games were allowed. The casinos also had to be limited to no more than 30 devices and tables per casino room.

If the state legislature was going to approve the deal, the other stipulation was that Deadwood had to preserve its historic landmarks.

When the Deadwood casinos opened in November 1989, South Dakota became only the third state to allow casino gaming within its borders. Only Nevada and New Jersey had casinos before South Dakota did.

Thirteen years later, the wheels of fun and fortune are still spinning with an estimated 1 million visitors per year and a gaming handle of $624 million in 2001. Deadwood is a travel destination for tourists who want to mix a little gaming with a history lesson or two.

Deadwood was a trendsetter in the expansion of gaming industry. Once the door was opened in Deadwood, the Indian-owned casinos and riverboat casinos followed throughout the Midwest in the next three years.

Faced with the growing competition from new casinos and their full range of games, Deadwood's $5 maximum bet was raised to $100 in November 2000. The range of games is still limited to live blackjack, live poker, and the various machines. Roulette and craps are not legal in Deadwood but are available electronically on the multi-game machines.

In late 2001, there were more than 80 casino rooms in Deadwood. Many are located in historic, renovated buildings.

Photos courtesy of South Dakota Tourism

Tourists enjoy T-shirt weather as they check out the casinos along Deadwood's historic Main Street.

Blackjack is the most popular game in Deadwood's 80 casinos.

Photos courtesy of South Dakota Tourism

Main Street lives on in Deadwood.

Carrying out the theme

Deadwood's unique place in the expanding gaming industry is its heritage combined with the architecture and the Wild West theme of the casinos. Visitors find low-key gaming in attractive old hotels and in national chain motels.

Visitors can flirt with Lady Luck at casinos with names like the Wild Bill Bar, the Bodega Bar (est. 1879); Hickok's Saloon, B.B. Cody's, Miss Kitty's, and the Lady Luck. The services vary between the establishments. Some are basically bars and the 30 games. Others offer entertainment, full-service restaurants, and attractive hotel rooms.

If you are in the right place at the right time, you may see actor Kevin Costner. He owns the Midnight Star hotel-casino with his brother, Dan, who runs the casino. Kevin Costner stops by once or twice a year to see how things are going.

The entire town is a National Historic Site. Gaming profits have allowed the town to rebuild its water, sewer and electrical systems. In the high tourist season, trolley cars bounce over brick streets. The street lamps will all eventually be electric-powered replicas of the old gaslights.

Last hand for Wild Bill

"Wild Bill" Hickok's story is important to Deadwood lore. Every day during the tourist seasons "Wild Bill" is killed again by the low-life, lily livered, yellow, scumbag Jack McCall. "The Trial of Jack McCall" show is a popular and worthwhile break for gamers. Part of the show is staged out on the street. There is an admission charge for the entire show, although portions of the show can be watched by hanging out on the street.

The legend is that Hickok was a womanizing dandy who historians say may have even had a fling with Libbie Custer, the wife of George Armstrong Custer. Hickok usually would position himself at the poker table with his back to the wall.

Photos courtesy of South Dakota Tourism

Wild Bill Hickok and friends play a hand of poker at the historic Saloon No. 10 in Deadwood. Where Hickok was actually shot is a matter of continuing debate.

Photos courtesy of South Dakota Tourism

Tourists take some time from sightseeing to play slot machines in Deadwood.

On the fateful Aug. 4, 1876, Hickok took the only seat available at the table in Saloon No. 10. Hickok's back was exposed when McCall slithered up like the snake he was. McCall had been hired to kill Hickok. He got the job done. When Hickok fell over his cards, he was holding two pair, aces and eights. The hand would become known as the "dead man's hand."

Turbiville, president of the Deadwood Gaming Association and general manager of the Gold Dust casinos, said the Wild West image is part of the lure of Deadwood.

"One of the questions we get a lot is 'where was Wild Bill shot?' We usually say, 'in the back of the head,'" Turbiville jokes.

There is no accurate answer other than the slightly sarcastic answer. There is still a gaming establishment named Saloon No. 10 in Deadwood, but it's not the same building where Hickok was whacked. It may not even be on the same land.

"Truth be known, at the time the Saloon No. 10 may have been a tent. No one knows for sure," Turbiville said.

Hickok is buried up on the hill at Mount Moriah. Tourists on the buses operated by three tour companies in the peak season still stop to pay their respects to Hickok and Calamity Jane, who was also buried at Mount Moriah.

A golden past

The gold rush that established Deadwood as a raucous boomtown was different than many other gold discoveries. There was enough gold in the hills to keep the mining industry profitable for more than 100 years. The Homestake gold mine was the largest in the Western Hemisphere and was still producing gold at the end of 2001 when the site was closed. Gold was still being found, but not enough to keep the large operation profitable.

Working the mine was considered to be a very good job for Deadwood's work force. Now it will be up to the casinos and tourism to carry the local economy.

A unique remnant of the gold rush is an underground tunnel system. Chinese mine workers were shunned in Deadwood and actually banned from streets at night. They used the tunnel system created when streets were raised to get around town.

The Chinese were entrepreneurs who ran the opium trade, prostitution and were involved in gambling in addition to their importance as mine workers. Out-of-sight tunnels may have been used for the opium business. Deadwood Underground (www.deadwoodunderground.com) conducts tours of the old tunnels.

The entire Black Hills area was a popular family destination decades before gambling was introduced. There are probably 100 or more major attractions and parks. The area is probably best-known for Mount Rushmore and the annual Sturgis motorcycle rally. Most of the attractions in the area are within an hour of Deadwood and are family oriented. It is a very touristy area. If you take the kids, take lots of cash.

Farther away, but worth the trip for history buffs, is the Little Bighorn Battlefield near Crow Agency, Mont. From Deadwood, the ill-fated battlefield where Custer met his end is a three- to four-hour drive.

For the adventurous and physically fit, George S. Mickelson Trail is a popular destination for cycling and hiking. The 114-mile trail on a former rail bed winds through the hills and through towns, giving cyclists plenty of opportunities for overnight stops.

Winter is the low tourist season in the area. Turbiville said casino owners would like to change that by attracting snowmobile enthusiasts. There are more than 350 miles of snow trails available in the vicinity of Deadwood.

Deadwood is not Las Vegas or Atlantic City. The glitz is missing, but that fact is also probably part of the attraction.

Photos courtesy of South Dakota Tourism

Bill Hickok's grave at Mount Moriah is one of Deadwood's tourist attractions.

A sign on Main Street puts in its claim as the site of Wild Bill Hickok's fatal shooting.

> *Deadwood is not Las Vegas or Atlantic City. The glitz is missing, but that fact is also probably part of the attraction.*

Atlantic City Is A Gaming Mecca

▌ *America's Favorite Playground Is A Shore Bet for Fun*

By Felicia Lowenstein

The names are as familiar as childhood if you grew up with Monopoly. Boardwalk, Park Place, Tennessee Avenue …these are the streets of America's Favorite Playground, Atlantic City, N.J. Perpetually memorialized in the popular game, Atlantic City seems the ideal place for gamers of all kinds. As a gambling destination, few rival this oceanside resort that melds rich history with some of the most exciting and innovative play around.

The casinos represent a $4 billion-plus industry to Atlantic City, which means many in the town specifically cater to the gaming traveler. Programs and promotions abound. Day trippers on casino buses from New York City and other nearby areas receive rolls of quarters that often more than compensate for the trip. Hotel packages incorporate coin bonuses, casino meals and amenities, and inland hotels also include shuttle transportation to the casinos. The casinos themselves offer gambler's cards, and reward frequent players with meal credits, shows, rooms, and more.

Atlantic City Convention & Visitors Authority

Atlantic City's Boardwalk and Beach.

Atlantic City Convention & Visitors Authority

The Absecon Lighthouse shines again after a $3 million facelift. Located on the corner of Pacific and Vermont Avenues, the lighthouse is the tallest of the 19 New Jersey lighthouses and is the only one to retain its original first-order fresnel lens.

It's a tradition that started in May 26, 1978, when the first Atlantic City casino, Resorts Casino Hotel, opened for business. A town known for tourism since the late 1800s, Atlantic City literally exploded with offerings as Resorts was followed by Caesars Casino Hotel Atlantic City and Bally's Park Place the following year. Today, visitors will find 12 luxurious casino properties, most stretched along the world-famous Atlantic City Boardwalk bordering the Atlantic Ocean, with a sprinkling of casinos along the bay.

Each one as different as the other, the casinos offer a full range of 24-hour gaming and entertainment for the gaming traveler, whether or not you choose to stay on property.

Looking for the best specialty drinks? Visit the Dizzy Dolphin bar at the Atlantic City Hilton. Its creations, like the Titanic and the Nautilus, have made it a favorite of the locals — respondents to *Atlantic City Magazine's* "Best of the Shore" poll. That same poll named the Temple Bar & Grill in Caesar's Atlantic City Hotel & Casino as "the place to be seen." Its dramatic four-story atrium is designed to resemble the Forum of Ancient Rome, complete with a star-studded sky.

In terms of gambling, Caesar's is said to have the best table games in *Atlantic City Magazine's* "Best of the Shore" reader's poll. But Harrah's Casino Hotel has the best slot machine payback, according to *Casino Player* magazine. Harrah's has earned the "Loosest Slots Award" three years in a row now.

For something different, Tropicana has a chicken that plays tic-tac-toe, a money machine, and life cycle slots where you can exercise as you play. It's also home to the Comedy Stop, celebrating its 17th anniversary, and Blanche the singing bartender, who will regale you with tunes as she serves your drinks.

The Tropicana also boasts the largest hotel to date, but it's the Trump Taj Mahal that has the largest smoke-free poker room. Trump can claim that honor not only in Atlantic City but on the East Coast. Its complex is among the largest in the world.

Bally's Park Place has earned the coveted Mobil Travel Guide Four-Star Award—an honor given to only 425 properties. Mobil said the casino is

The Towne of Historic Smithville is a quaint little town where the sounds of yesteryear are very much alive. Walk along the cobblestone paths passing rustic shoppes and fine restaurants and imagine yourself back in the 1700's.

With the bright liughts of 12 casinos, Atlantic City provides non-stop, 24-hour gaming action.

Atlantic City's entranceway features a laser lighthouse.

Mr. Peanut is one of the attractions at the Atlantic City Historical Museum on Garden Pier, which is free to the public and offers visitors a delightful trip through the decades in Atlantic City.

"worth a special trip," a sentiment echoed by locals who voted the property as having the best casino steak house, Bally's Prime Place, the best casino casual restaurant, Bally's Pickles, and the best health club.

And opening in the summer of 2003 will be the Borgata (Italian for "village"). This billion dollar bayside casino will feature 135,000 square feet of gaming in an atmosphere reminiscent of Tuscany, Italy, and southern Europe.

The Other Atlantic City

But Atlantic City is more than casinos, which enhances its appeal to many travelers. A town that catered to tourism for nearly a century before gambling was legalized, it showcases its rich heritage and culture in a variety of sites and activities.

From its pristine white beaches and fresh salt air, to its world-famous Boardwalk, Atlantic City is known for its "oceans of promotions"—a high-diving horse, a life-size peanut man, and a taffy created by a storm. See these and more at the **Atlantic City Historical Museum** on the Garden Pier at New Jersey Avenue and the Boardwalk. There you'll see the history of Miss America, *the* Atlantic City pageant, and receive a free Heinz pickle pin. If you have time, stay to see the video that provides an entertaining glimpse into this seaside resort. Or walk next door to see work by local artists at the **Atlantic City Art Center**. Admission to both museums is free. Hours are 10 a.m. to 4 p.m., Monday through Friday. For more information, call the museum at (609) 347-5839 or the art center at (609) 347-5837.

Shop at the only shopping mall located 900 feet over the Atlantic Ocean. This is **Ocean One Mall**, the former site of an amusement park known as Million Dollar Pier. It was also the original spot where proprietor of the pier, Captain John L. Young, lived in an ornate marble villa. The mall today is shaped like a cruise ship and is home to 120 specialty shops, 20 eateries, four full-service restaurants, and strolling entertainers.

If you're near the giant statue of King Neptune, you must be in **Gardner's Basin**, a waterfront park and marina. The Basin features Ocean

Described as Atlantic City's best kept secret, Historic Gardner's Basin offers marine education programs, fun-filled cruises, sailing adventures, fishing expeditions and annual festivals for the entire family.

The $87 million Sheraton Atlantic City Convention Center Hotel is home to the Miss America Organization. The 15-story hotel features street level display windows showcasing Miss America memorabilia and nostalgic pageant treasures.

Beautiful landscaping is part of the multi-billion dollar redevelopment renaissance taking place in Atlantic City and provides a scenic route for guests walking from the Convention Center to downtown Atlantic City.

Along the Intracoastal Waterway (ICW), Atlantic City offers a host of boating pleasures.

Life Center, a $4.5 million, 14,000 square foot, three-story marine life educational center. In good weather, the basin also offers charter boat cruises of Atlantic City's back bays as well as longer fishing excursions. With two restaurants and an antique shop, it's a beautiful place to spend the afternoon. For more information, call (609) 348-2880.

Browse through the exhibits at the **Noyes Museum of Art**, a collection of 19th and 20th century American fine, craft, and folk art with an emphasis on regional artists. The museum offers workshops and group tours, "Meet the Artist" gallery talks, concerts and more. Just 15 minutes from Atlantic City, the museum is open Wednesday through Sunday from 11 a.m. to 4 p.m. There is a small admission fee. For more information, call (609) 652-8848.

Stay and catch a game at the Sandcastle Stadium, home to the **Atlantic City Surf** minor league baseball team. The stadium plays a full schedule from May through September and offers fireworks for several Friday night games. For more information call (609) 344-SURF. And if you're in town during the winter months, stop by historic Boardwalk Hall to see a **Boardwalk Bullies** hockey game. The Bullies, who play from October to March, are Atlantic City's newest sports team. For more information, call (609) 348-PUCK.

Nearly 34 million people visit Atlantic City each year, making it one of the most popular destinations in the U.S. Atlantic City is 225 miles from Washington, D.C., 58 miles from Philadelphia and 120 miles from Manhattan. New Jersey Transit, Greyhound and Atlantic City-bound charter buses brought more than 10 million passengers to the city in 2000. The NJ Transit Rail Line carried more than a million. For more information, call the Atlantic City Convention & Visitors Authority at (609) 449-7100.

The $4 million, 14,300 square-foot Ocean Life Center is comprised of seven exhibit tanks ranging from 160 to 23,500 gallons, multimedia exhibits, meeting and lecture space and a gift shop.

How To Win At The Casino Comp Game

Knowing the Host, Joining Slot Club Will Pay Off

BY ANDREW N.S. GLAZER

The world of casino comps—those free rooms, meals, beverages, airfares, and sometimes more that are given to big players—has changed dramatically over the last 20 years or so.

In the "old days," casinos focused their marketing efforts primarily on The Big Player, who might come to down and drop a hundred grand or more in a weekend. The Big Player was treated like the biggest of big shots, and not only did he get an RFB (room, food and beverage) comp, he usually got his airfare returned (assuming the casino didn't send a private plane for him). And if he wanted something or someone who was, shall we say, "not on the menu," that thing or person was usually available, too. Even if you weren't a Big Player, rooms in Las Vegas were usually cheap, as casinos figured their hotel operations could lose money as long as their gambling operations made money.

Similarly, in the old days, casinos used to provide many comps up front, in the form of "junkets," where you posted a certain amount of cash up front and were given, before you had gambled a nickel, a free flight, free room and a VIP pass good for all the food and drink you wanted.

A couple finishes room service breakfast in their Reno Hilton hotel room and gets ready to head to the casino.

One of the amenities awaiting guests at Bally's Atlantic City is a sparkling spa and indoor pool.

Here is an example of the luxury available in Reno's Atlantis Casino Resort. The hotel's two new 4,000 square foot Grand Paradise Suites occupy the 27th floor and feature two huge bedrooms and this 2,000 square foot parlor, complete with fireplace, wet bar and high-definition TVs.

The old days are long gone.

Today's casinos are for the most part owned by corporations, not families, and they no longer focus on The Big Player. There just aren't enough of them. Instead of winning $100,000 from one guy in a weekend, they win $250 from 400 people, and the hotel side of the operation is expected to make money. Not only do they win $250 from 400 people, but those 400 people (as well as the few Big Players who still visit) are likely to spend considerable sums in hotel retail shops that are generally not selling their wares at bargain prices.

Junkets are also mostly long gone, because casinos realized that too many people were taking advantage of the junket to get a free trip and not gamble enough to justify what the casinos were giving away.

How to get freebies

In today's modern casino, the comps game has become both an art and a science, and here are some realities that will allow you to obtain the maximum in the way of freebies for the minimum in play. I'll discuss table games first, because the slot world works a little differently.

On the surface, the modern comps game is a purely mathematical equation. Most casinos will gladly tell you in advance exactly how much play you must give them in order to earn an RFB comp. At less expensive hotels, you might find that average bets of $25 for four hours a day might do it. At prime properties like the Bellagio, you're looking at more like 10 times that number. It doesn't have to be average bets of $250 for four hours. Average bets of $500 for two hours, or $125 for eight hours, will work just as well. If you want your airfare refunded too, crank up the bet size or the number of hours played daily accordingly.

If you don't want the full RFB comp—for example, you're just looking for free meals—you don't have to gamble anywhere nearly as high, or for anywhere nearly as long. Usually you can ask a floorman for a buffet comp after you've been sitting at a table for less than an hour, and if you want a free meal in the pricey restaurant, the casino's tracking system tells them if you've earned it.

Luxury, and a great lake view, await guests at the Hyatt Regency Lake Tahoe.

Joining a casino club is a good way to build up points for future "comps." One choice is the Players Club at Ameristar Casino Council Bluffs.

A pool table and dinette area are featured in the parlor of the Grand Paradise Suites in Reno's Atlantis Casino Resort.

Golfers complete a round at the scenic course at Hyatt Regency Las Vegas.

Casinos keep track

Tracking system? Things have changed! Yes, today's casinos employ a tracking system to keep an eye on your play. At most casinos, you get a card that identifies you in the casino's system (getting it takes a matter of moments and can usually be done right at the table while you're playing), and as soon as you sit down to play, you hand that rating card to the dealer or floorman, who keeps an eye on what sort of bets you are making, and how long you stay there. Every time you move on, the floorman makes a note in the computer system about what sort of action you've given the casino.

In some table games, the floorman doesn't get involved: you can insert your card right into a slot that reads your action precisely. A new breed of casino chip is on the way that will allow casinos to automatically track the precise size of every bet you make, and that's important, because people who try to "beat the comps game" will do little things like make $100 bets when they see the floorman is watching and switch to $25 bets when he isn't. If they are good enough at it, they get credit for being a $100 player, while in reality they are more like a $35 player.

A couple enjoys a gourmet meal at the Grand Victoria Casino & Resort in Indiana.

Host means the most

There are other ways to get around the mathematical system than the ethically questionable "fool the floorman" approach. Probably the most important is to develop a long-term relationship with a casino host—the person who will, ultimately, look at the numbers and decide if the casino should tear up your bill, or charge you like anyone staying at the hotel.

> **It's a very good idea to discuss your expected level of play with your casino host before you arrive.**

It's a very good idea to discuss your expected level of play with your casino host before you ever arrive, and if you come pretty close to the numbers you promised, the host probably isn't going to quibble about whether you played for three hours a day or four. This becomes especially true if you stick with the same casino host over time, and he comes to rely on you as one of his regulars. If you regularly visit one casino and use that one host, and the host moves to a similar quality property, it's a smart move to follow the host to that next property. That way, the host gets to show his new employers that he is bringing business to the hotel, and in return, the host becomes all the more flexible about how much play he needs from you to justify a comp.

Casino hosts usually are not allowed to accept cash tips—they look and feel too much like outright bribes—but often are allowed to accept gifts, and if you present your casino host with some sort of gift as a "thank you" for the way he treated you last time (maybe he just upgraded your room without an upgrade charge), your treatment will probably improve next time.

That's how the "comps game" works at the high end. On the low end, most casinos offer all sorts of little promotions that add up to $5 worth of equity here and $10 worth of free food there. Most of them hand you little books of coupons when you arrive, and as long as the coupon books don't suck you into playing a bad game for more than you'd intended, you're throwing away money if you don't take advantage of them.

A luxury suite with a Jacuzzi is one of the amenities in the Octagon Suite at the Ameristar Casino Council Bluffs.

Slot clubs pay dividends

Slots deserve a special discussion. Slots weren't considered to be all that important to a casino's bottom line, but today, they often represent 70 percent of a casino's revenue—not because slots are rip-offs, but rather that's where many of the casino's customers have migrated.

Almost every casino offers its customers membership in a "slot club," and if you are a frequent slot player, you are foolish not to join. For the price of standing in line once to fill out some paperwork, you get a card that you can and should insert into every slot machine you play. This lets the casino know *exactly* how much play you have given them, and at what kind of machine—none of this business of a floorman estimating your play.

As you play, you accumulate slot club points, and depending on the particular slot club, these points can be redeemed either for prizes, comps, or for straight cash. Most slot clubs let you accumulate points from one visit to the next (which is different from how things usually work at table games), and more and more national chain casinos are allowing you to accumulate points from one casino in their chain to another. This lets you play in more than one casino, and sometimes to play in more than one city.

The important thing to remember both about table game comps and about slot clubs is that to extract maximum comp benefit, you need to restrict your play to one hotel (the multi-hotel slot club card being an exception). If you move around a lot, you don't get a serious comp anywhere. If you want to play the comps game seriously, you need to stick to one property.

Finally, it is vital to remember that casinos aren't giving you comps because they think you're a swell guy. They give you comps because they know precisely how much your play should be worth to them, given the game you are playing and the kinds of bets you are making. Because comps seem like an attractive target, they entice many people into playing for far greater sums, or for far greater lengths of time, than they would otherwise play, and when that happens, your "free" room or lunch is probably going to cost you a fortune.

IF you are going to play anyway, it makes sense to work the casino for every dollar in comps they are willing to give you. The moment you start playing higher or longer than you want to, you're no longer taking smart advantage of the system. You're playing the casino's game, not yours.

Andrew N.S. ("Andy") Glazer is the author of "Casino Gambling the Smart Way" and writes a weekly gambling column for The Detroit Free Press. He is also a regular columnist for Poker Digest magazine, is the online poker guide for www.poker.casino.com and has had materials published in the British edition of Esquire magazine. Newsweek magazine called him "a poker scholar," and he has written for virtually every gambling magazine or Web site of note.

A couple enjoys their stay at Seven Feathers Hotel & Casino Resort in Oregon. Players can earn free hotel rooms at many casinos, depending on their level of play.

> *Most casinos offer all sorts of little promotions that add up to $5 worth of equity here and $10 worth of free food there.*

Chefs line up to proudly sport their dishes at the Sterling Brunch at Bally's Las Vegas, a Sunday tradition featuring caviar, lobster, and other delicacies.

Poker is a Good Deal

▌ *'Know When to Fold 'Em' Is A Classic Strategy for Players*

By Craig DeVrieze

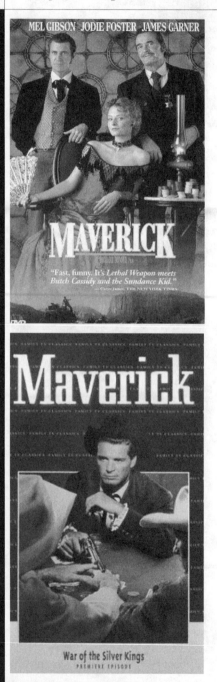

Brett and Bart Maverick enjoyed an occasional game of poker, and always seemed to win, on the 1960s TV series "Maverick," Mel Gibson played the starring role in the movie version of "Maverick," winning the big jackpot in a riverboat poker game.

"Who is the tall, dark stranger there? Maverick is the name … Riverboats ring your bell! Fare-thee-well Annabelle! Luck is the lady that I love the best. Natchez to New Orleans; living on Jacks and Queens, Maverick is a legend of the West."
— Maverick television theme

You can still sit down on a boat in New Orleans and dream that you are one of the notorious Maverick boys who get the ladies, along with an occasional royal flush. One you have virtually no chance of getting in your lifetime in a legitimate game, the other you have a slightly better chance at.

But you can dream.

The games Bart Maverick played on the 1960s TV series and the later movie are recreated every day on modern versions of the old riverboats the Maverick brothers patronized.

Hollywood loves poker, especially riverboat poker, but does not always play its cards particularly well.

Take, for instance, the climactic hand of five-card draw in the movie "Maverick."

Bret Maverick (aka Mel Gibson) wins with a royal flush, improbably besting a straight flush and a four-of-a-kind in the process.

This bit of dramatic license drew chuckles in card rooms across the country, where the real daily drama comes from three deuces besting two pair.

Two straight flushes and a four-of-a-kind in the same hand? You can play poker every day for three years and you almost certainly won't see that.

That is not to say that big hands don't happen in live poker or that great hands do not lose. But in many American casino poker parlors, that losing straight flush would have made "Maverick's" villain a big winner.

Finalists in the PartyPoker.com championship play for the first prize of $1 million.

That is because most casinos feature "Bad Beat" jackpots, which instantly reward a player holding a losing four-of-a-kind hand with riches typically hundreds or thousands of times larger than the pot in the middle of the table.

Like any money a player takes from a live poker game in a casino, the dollars that build these jackpots are not supplied by the house, but by the players themselves.

Typically, they are funded a dollar at a time from the pots that are *not* won by a royal flush beating four aces, which is to say virtually all of the thousands of hands that are dealt daily in poker rooms nationwide.

Meanwhile, remember, you don't have to be Maverick to win at live casino poker. Just know when to hold 'em and know when to fold 'em.

House has no edge, just a rake

If you are patient, attentive, and possess a sound understanding of the basic tenets of poker, your best odds of winning money in any casino can be found in the poker parlor.

There, the house edge does not exist.

It is you against the rest of the players at your table. And, if you play your cards right, you can leave with their money.

In live poker rooms in Las Vegas and across the country, the casino basically deals cards for a fee, or what is called a "rake." Typically, the house will take 10 percent of each and every pot, with a maximum "rake" of up to $3, $4, or $5.

Do the math. If a 15-table card room deals 30 hands per table per hour at $5 per hand, that is a house profit of $2,250 per hour.

So, yes. The casinos make money, but you are not gambling against a house that has stacked the rules of the game toward huge, guaranteed profits.

The take from a card-room rake is a fraction of the profit a casino stands to make from 15 blackjack tables, one craps table or a room stacked with one-armed bandits.

That is one reason why fewer and fewer casinos feature live poker. The space of the poker tables can be used for the more profitable electronic games.

It also is why, in those casinos where you find a poker parlor, you also will have found your best bet.

Watch for the sharpies

Don't be fooled, however. Casino poker moves faster than the kitchen games to which most players are accustomed. And, almost always, you will find your-

Poker flourishes in home games when players can't get to a casino. This poker table and equipment is available from Gamblers General Store in Las Vegas

> **The casinos make money, but you are not gambling against a house that has stacked the rules of the game toward huge, guaranteed profits.**

Kathy Liebert became the first woman to win a major poker championship, claiming the $1 million first prize in the finals of the PartyPoker.com tournament held aboard a cruise ship.

Kathy Liebert, went on to win the final round of the PartyPoker.com tournament.

Poker tables are ready for customers at Ameristar Casino Vicksburg.

An instructional video by Fifth Street Video tells poker players the fundamentals for winning at Texas Hold 'Em Poker.

self pitted against wise and wily card-room veterans waiting to separate you from your chips.

Taking the house odds out of the equation also removes much of the element of luck and, if you do not play your cards carefully, you will leave broke. And in a hurry.

Poker is a game of skill and most rooms are populated by skilled and practiced regulars who sit and wait for tourists and "rookies" to sit down and show their inexperience, and, thus, share their chips.

The two key words in parlor poker are "I fold." This is where patience comes in. Much more often than not, a player will get a weak starting hand, but the essential difference between poker and blackjack is that a player almost always can discard these bad hands without spending a thin dime. Few casinos allow blackjack players to "surrender" and save part of their bet.

Imagine how much cheaper and easier blackjack would be if you could just throw in your cards with every 15 or 16. It is that simple. All poker-room games have a forced first bet. If you aren't that forced bet and are holding a weak starting hand, you simply fold and have nothing invested in a hand you probably could not win.

A novice parlor player also is best advised to start with a low-stakes game. Many rooms offer games with a minimum bet of $1 and a maximum bet of $5, with a limit of three raises per betting round. Others offer $2 and $10.

Whatever the lowest limit, start there, because that is where you are likeliest to find an even match for your untested skills.

These low stakes still can build pots of $100 or more, but usually a winning hand will pull in between $25 and $50, depending on the game you are playing and the number of players who are seated at your table.

Be warned, though. You will run into stronger players and, if you are inattentive, they will have your chips before you know they are stronger players. They can be young, old, male or female and may act as dumb as a box of rocks. Avoid getting locked in too many hands with these vets.

Texas and Omaha hold the cards

Don't expect to play your standard kitchen games, either, where deuces and one-eyed jacks are wild and the players are even wilder.

Most casino parlors will offer a maximum of four types of poker, with varied stakes and limits: Texas Hold 'Em, Seven-Card Stud, Seven Card Stud High-Low, and Omaha. Some West Coast card rooms will offer draw poker as well.

Seven-Card Stud generally is the most familiar game played in card rooms and it is the game first-time parlor players are best advised to try.

Binion's Horseshoe Casino is the site of the famous annual World Series of Poker.

Like at home, players will receive three cards — two down, one up — to start a hand. This is followed by a round of betting. Most rooms will force the first bet by requiring the lowest up card to bet the minimum. Players then can either call or fold in turn.

After the first round of bets, each remaining player will receive another up card, followed by another round of betting. This time, the highest two cards showing will have the right to bet first. Only the very first bet of a hand is forced, which means that in subsequent betting rounds players can "check" until a bet is made. Then they must either call, raise, or fold.

With two cards showing, you are on what is called fourth street. This is followed, of course, by fifth street, with a round of betting. Then, sixth street and another round of betting.

Finally, the river card is dealt down to all remaining players. A final round of betting will ensue, followed by what is called the Showdown — when remaining players show their hands.

High-Low Seven-Card Stud is played the same way, with the significant difference being that the lowest hand — A-2-3-4-5 being the lowest possible — will split the pot evenly with the highest hand.

Here are two versions of an unbeatable, and unbelievable, straight flush with aces high.

Hold 'em or fold 'em

Texas Hold 'Em is far and away the most popular poker parlor game. This is largely because it is the fastest moving game, with dealers routinely dealing a hand every five minutes.

In Texas Hold 'Em, each player receives two down cards, followed by five cards that the dealer will turn up in the middle of the table. These are called community cards and are played by every player at the table.

The object is to make the best poker hand using those five cards and/or the two in your possession.

In Texas Hold 'Em, the forced opening bet is determined by a rotating marker, or button. The first two players behind this button are called the big and little blind and are required to bet a specified amount before all players are dealt their two down cards.

Once players receive their two down cards, players behind the blinds will be required to call, raise or fold.

After the opening betting round is completed, the dealer will place three cards in the middle of the table. This is called the flop. Another betting round will follow. Then the dealer places another card in the middle of the table. This is called the turn.

After another round of betting, the dealer will place the final card in the middle of the table. This is the river card and a final round of bets will follow.

Again, Texas Hold 'Em is fast-paced and sometimes free-wheeling and, even in a low stakes game, it generally will build bigger pots than low-stakes Stud. This is good when you win. Not so good when you don't.

Remember those two magic words — I fold.

In Omaha, watch for the flop

Omaha is a version of Hold 'Em.

In Omaha, each player receives four down cards, plus five community cards in the middle of the table. The object is to make the best poker hand, using two of your four down cards plus three community cards.

This differs from Hold 'Em, in that players cannot play just one of their own cards or "play the board," as in all five community cards. They must play two of their four down cards to make their hand.

Players will receive their four down cards followed by a betting round. The dealer then turns three community cards. As in Hold 'Em, this is called the flop, and it is followed by another round of betting.

The dealer then turns another community card — the turn — and players bet again. Then comes a final card — the river — and a final round of betting.

Omaha is a complicated game best suited to veteran poker-room players and novices are advised to avoid it.

> **Texas Hold 'Em is fast-paced and sometimes free-wheeling and, even in a low stakes game, it generally will build bigger pots than low-stakes Stud. This is good when you win. Not so good when you don't.**

You Can Conquer Craps

▌ *A Simple, Satisfying Strategy Is Your Best Bet*

By Frank Scoblete

Precision casino dice come in sets of five.

Gamblers General Store

Craps has some of the very best bets in the casino.

raps is a game that is equal parts allure and dread. Players see the intensity of the game, hear the cheers or moans, and think to themselves that there sure must be a lot of excitement at a craps table. So they wander over and take one look at the layout and all the bets and betting and they then think they'll never learn this game, it's way too complicated.

Even though craps has fallen from its perch as the number one table game in the casinos, a title held by blackjack since the mid-1960s, there are still more craps players and more craps tables nationwide than ever before in history. Once a player learns to play craps, it's hard to go back. Recall that great WWI song that went: "How you gonna keep them down on the farm after they've seen Paree?" The same applies to craps. Anyone who has spent any time in casinos knows that craps is the most exciting and compelling game. The highs are sky high, the lows are "dig-a-hole-and-bury-me" low, and the action is hot — win, lose or draw.

Craps has some of the very best bets in the casino, bets that come in with house edges of anywhere from a fraction of a percent to 1.52 percent. The good bets at craps are the *Pass Line, Don't Pass, Come, Don't Come, Place the Six, Place the Eight,* and *Buy the 4 or 10* — if the commission is extracted on winning bets only.

Craps also has bets with high house edges. These are the *proposition bets* such as the *Field,* the *Hardways, Any Seven, Any Craps,* and others with house edges ranging from 5.26 percent to more than 16 percent. People make these bets in the mistaken belief that, because most of them pay premium returns (for example 9 to 1 on the Hard 6 or Hard 8), they are getting a good deal. Not so.

Therefore, in the interests of making you a good craps player, if I don't discuss a bet in this chapter, then that bet isn't really worth making.

But, first, let's take a look at how craps is played.

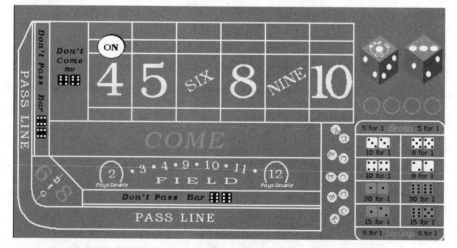

A typical craps table layout features the Pass Line, Come, and other bets.

How the Game is Played

The *Pass Line* goes around the whole table. Note that the *Don't Pass Line* tends to ride on top of it around most of the table as well. These are the two basic bets of craps.

The game starts with the shooter placing a bet on the *Pass Line* or the *Don't Pass Line*. Since 95 percent of the players are "right" bettors, that is, they bet with the dice, we'll look at the game from the point of view of the *Pass Line* bettor. He is given the dice, usually five or six, from which he selects two, and the game begins.

The shooter now rolls the dice. If he rolls a 7 or 11, the *Pass Line* bettors win even money — i.e., bet $10, win $10. The *Don't Pass* bettors lose. However, if the shooter rolls a 2, 3 or 12, the *Pass Line* bettors lose and, on the 2 or 3, the *Don't Pass* bettors win. On the 12, the *Don't Pass* bettors push, neither winning nor losing.

If the shooter rolls any one of the following numbers: 4, 5, 6, 8, 9, or 10; this number becomes the *point*. For the *Pass Line* bettor to win, the shooter must roll that number again before he rolls a 7. The reverse holds true for the *Don't Pass* bettor. If a 7 is rolled before the point, the *Don't Pass* bettor wins.

The game is as simple as that!

The Best Bets at Craps

Playing the *Pass* or *Don't Pass* gives the casino an approximately 1.4 percent edge. This means that for every $100 wagered, the player will lose approximately $1.40 in the long run. However, the player can reduce the casino edge still more by taking advantage of the "Free Odds" bet option. Here's how this option works:

The 7 can be made six different ways with two dice. The 4 can be made three different ways with two dice. Thus, the odds of a 7 appearing in relation to a 4 are six ways to three ways or two to one. Once the shooter has established his point number (let's keep it the 4), the player has the option of placing an amount equal to (single odds), twice as much (double or 2X odds), three times as much (triple or 3X odds), five times as much (5X Odds), ten times as much (10X Odds), 20 times as much (20X Odds), or 100 times (100X Odds) or more, as his *Pass Line* bet in "odds" immediately behind it. Let's analyze the bet based on double odds, the most common odds bet in the country.

The point is 4 and you have $10 on the *Pass Line*. You can now place $20 in odds behind it. If the shooter rolls a 4, you will be paid even money for your $10 *Pass Line* bet and the true odds for the Odds bet — thus, you would win $40 for your $20 Odds bet. The casino has no edge whatsoever on this bet in the long run. The Free Odds bet reduces the casino edge on the *Pass Line* as follows (the *Don't Pass* is fractionally less):

Two other low-percentage bets are the *Come* and *Don't Come* bets. These function in exactly the same way with exactly the same house edges as the *Pass* and

Smiling faces await the results of a roll of the dice at Atlantis Casino Resort in Reno, Nev.

Bettors cheer on the shooter at a craps table at Ameristar's Cactus Petes Resort Casino in Jackpot, Nev.

Best Bets

— Play Pass or Don't Pass.

— Use "Free Odds" option

Don't Pass bets, except they are made *after* the point is established. Once the shooter has a point, you can place a bet in the large *Come* area on the layout or on the smaller *Don't Come* area in the upper left and right hand corners of the layout. A 7 or 11 wins the *Come* bet at even money, loses the *Don't Come* bet. A 2, 3 or 12, loses the *Come* bet. While the 2 or 3 wins the *Don't Come* bet. Again the 12 is a push. However, should one of the point numbers be rolled (i.e., 4, 5, 6, 8, 9, or 10), that number now must be rolled before the 7 for the *Come* bettor to win. Should the seven appear before the number, the *Don't Come* bettor wins. The *Come-Don't Come* is merely a game within a game. As with the *Pass* and *Don't Pass*, the *Come* and *Don't Come* players are also offered the option of Free Odds.

The last of the low-percentage bets is the *placing* of the 6 and/or 8, which can be done at any time. Here you simply place a wager in multiples of $6 on the table and say: "Place the 6," or "Place the 8," and for what amount. The money goes right up on the number. The casino will pay off a winning bet at "casino odds" of $7 for every $6 wagered. The casino edge on this bet is 1.52 percent.

The only other bet worth considering is the *buying* of the 4 or 10 under certain circumstances. Essentially, buying these numbers means paying a 5 percent commission. Some casinos ask for this commission up front and on winning and losing bets. The best you can hope to do in these casinos is reduce the house edge on

BET	CASINO EDGE	EXPECTED LOSS
Pass Line with no odds	1.41%	$1.40 per $100 wagered
Pass Line with 1X odds	0.85%	85 cents per $100
Pass Line with 2X odds	0.61%	61 cents per $100
Pass Line with 3X odds	0.47%	47 cents per $100
Pass Line with 5X odds	0.33%	33 cents per $100
Pass Line with 10X odds	0.18%	18 cents per $100
Pass Line with 20X odds	0.10%	10 cents per $100
Pass Line with 100X odds	0.02%	2 cents per $100

The true odds for the point numbers are as follows:

Number:	Ways to Make	Ways to Make Seven	Odds
4	3	6	2 to 1
5	4	6	3 to 2
6	5	6	6 to 5
8	5	6	6 to 5
9	4	6	3 to 2
10	3	6	2 to 1

A dealer at Seven Feathers Hotel & Casino Resort in Oregon watches as bettors eagerly await the results of a roll.

The Best Strategies To Play Craps

The fastest and safest way to get into a craps game is to place a *Pass Line* bet and, when the point is established, back it with full odds — *if you can afford it*. The key to getting the best bang for your craps bucks is to have as much money in "odds" as possible and the least money on the *Pass Line* or *Come* bets. For example, if you want to bet a total of $15, you are much better off putting a $5 *Pass Line* bet and backing it with $10, then you are putting the entire $15 on the *Pass Line*. The casino cut of 1.4 percent comes only on the *Pass Line* bet. The odds bet has no casino edge whatsoever. Remember that for the 6 and 8 your odds bets must be made in multiples of $5 as the payoff is 6 to 5.

Many players like to have more than one number working for them. If you want more than one bet working, utilize the Pass Line and make two subsequent Come bets — backing each with whatever odds you can afford to make. An alternative is to make a Pass Line bet and then Place the Six and Eight if the point is one of the other numbers (or buy the 4 or 10 in the right

games). If the point is a 6 or 8, just place the alternative one — which means you will be on the two numbers that hit with the second greatest frequency. Either method of betting will give you two to three numbers and keep the house edge relatively low.

If you want to bet the Don't side, wait until the shooter has established his point and then place a Don't Come bet. If the bet gets past the initial roll without losing to the seven or eleven and gets onto a number, only bet one bet against any given shooter. If you win, chances are the shooter has sevened out and you'll then bet against the next shooter. If you lose, there's a fair to decent chance that the shooter may be having a good roll.

If you utilize any of the above methods of play, you will be able to get into the action immediately and experience the thrill of a craps game. However, once you've played craps, it is important to read further, as it's a game that can win players large sums and lose them large sums in short order.

the 4 or 10 from 6.67 percent to around 3 percent; not good enough. However, some casinos only extract the commission on winning bets. This can reduce the house edge to a low of approximately 1.3 percent — a good bet.

The Final Consideration

Craps is a game where money can be won or lost rather quickly. I recommend having ten times the amount of your total minimum bet for a given session. If you are playing cautiously and have only a *Pass Line* with odds, let us say a $5 *Pass Line* with $10 in odds, then you should have $150 for the session as that is ten times your minimum bet. If you are playing somewhat aggressively and have three numbers working most times then you'll need *ten times those three bets*. Thus, $5 on the Pass Line with $10 odds and — let us say — two come bets of $5 with odds of $10 on each, you'll need $450, as you are risking $45 when you have your maximum bet out.

Bettors enjoy the cameraderie of craps in the Saddle West Casino in Pahrump, Nev.

> *Craps is a game where money can be won or lost rather quickly. I recommend having ten times the amount of your total minimum bet for a given session.*

Other Bets at Craps

The following bets can be placed at any time, including during the come out roll. If you want the bets at risk during the come out, just say: "My bets are working." If you want the bets not to be at risk, just say: "My bets are off."

Place Bets

Place the 4 or 10: You place the 4 or 10 in multiples of $5. If it is rolled before the 7, the player wins $9. The house edge is 6.67 percent. Not recommended.

Place the 5 or 9: You place the 5 or 9 in multiples of $5. If the it rolls before a seven, the player wins $7. Casino edge is 4 percent. Not recommended.

Hardways

Hard 6 or 8: A bet that a 6 or 8 will be made as 3:3 or 4:4, respectively, before a 7 or before that number is rolled any other way. House edge: 9.09 percent. Not recommended.

Hard 4 or 10: A bet that the 4 or 10 will be made as 2:2 or 5:5, respectively, before a 7 or before that number is rolled any other way. House edge: 11.11 percent. Not recommended.

Place to Lose

You can also place the numbers to lose, sometimes this is called *laying* the numbers, as in: "Lay the 4!" In such a case, you are rooting for a 7 to be thrown before the number appears.

Place the 4 or 10 to Lose: Here you bet in multiples of $11 that the 7 will come up before the 4 or 10. If you win, you receive $5. The house edge is 3.03 percent. Not recommended.

Place the 5 or 9 to Lose: Here you bet in multiples of $8 that the 7 will come up before the 5 or 9. If you win, the bet is paid off at $5. The house edge is 2.5 percent. Not recommended.

Place the 6 or 8 to Lose: Here you are betting in multiples of $5 that the 7 will be rolled before the 6 or 8. If you win, the bet is paid off at $4. The house edge is 1.82 percent. Marginally recommended.

One-Roll Proposition Bets

The bets listed are one-roll wagers and the usual payoff for them. Some casinos will pay at a higher rate. The more the casino pays, the lower the house edge.

The Field: A one-roll wager that the next number will be one of the Field numbers: 2, 3, 4, 9, 10, 11, 12. Sometimes the 5 is substituted for the 9. If the 2 or 12 hits, it is paid off at 2 to 1. The other numbers are paid off at 1 to 1. The house edge is 5.26 percent. Not recommended.

The 2 or 12: A one-roll wager that the next number will be a 2 or 12. Pays off at 30 to 1. The house edge is 13.89 percent. Not recommended.

Hard 4 or 10 Hop: A one-roll wager that the next number will be a 4 made as 2:2 or a 10 made as 5:5. Pays off at 30 to 1. The house edge is 13.89 percent. Not recommended.

Hard 6 or 8 Hop: A one-roll wager that the next number will be a 6 or 8 made as 3:3 or 4:4, respectively. Pays off at 30 to 1. The house edge is 13.89 percent. Not recommended.

The 3 or 11: A one-roll wager that the next number will be a 3 or 11. Pays off at 15 to 1. The house edge is 11.11 percent. Not recommended.

Any Craps: A one-roll wager that the next number will be a craps: 2, 3, or 12. Pays off at 7 to 1. The house edge is 11.11 percent. Not recommended.

Any 7: A one-roll wager that the next number will be a seven. Pays off at 4 to 1. House edge is 16.67 percent. Not recommended.

Horn Bet: A one-roll wager that the next number will be either a 2, 3, 11 or 12. House pays off at the odds for the individual number as above. House edge is a combined 12.50 percent. Not recommended.

Frank Scoblete is the #1 best-selling gaming author in America and the author of the books "Forever Craps: The Five-Step Advantage-Play Method" and "Guerrilla Gambling: How to Beat the Casinos at Their Own Games." His books and tapes have sold over a million copies. For the best information on all casino games, order his free catalog: 1-800-944-0406 or write to: Paone Press, Box 610, Lynbrook, NY 1156

Craps: On A Roll

▌ *Casino classic is a friendly, team game*

BY Mike Hlas

Whenever you hear people whooping it up and having fun together in a casino, chances are good that it's happening at a craps table. Other casino games are lonelier pursuits. Slot machines pit a human being against an emotionless, money-draining gadget. There is no give-and-take. Mostly there is only giving.

Blackjack tables have a collection of players with the same objective, which is defeating the dealer. But each player is going one-on-one against the house. You will often find a white-hot player sitting next to someone who is ice-cold. Rarely do other players shout with glee when another has turned a 13 into a 21.

As for poker rooms, everyone is the enemy. The house is taking its rake off each pot, the dealer is the meanie who is giving you the deuce when you need the king, and every player at your table is trying to fleece you of your cash. There is little love being shown between players.

A craps table is where a person can stand alongside friends and share in their successes and failures. It is where players can become fast friends with total strangers. It is where people are committed to the same hopes and goals and dreams. Namely, that the numbers that turn up on the dice are numbers that take the money from the table instead of shoving it the casino's way.

And there is someone rolling those dice who is the engineer of each run at riches, who is responsible for the wins and the losses, the highs and the lows. That person is held to high standards. He or she must make the dice do magical things, like coming up with a pair of 3s for a "hard 6" when players have a hunch such a roll is imminent.

Shooter Can Be A Hero

The shooter who makes a lot of friends and attains hero's status is the one who artfully dodges 7s. Once a come-out number has been established — be it 4, 5, 6, 8, 9 or 10 — the fun begins. Bets of all sorts are made on all sorts of numbers and combinations. The only thing that can ruin the vast majority of such wagers is the number 7. Seven is sinister. Seven stinks.

Photo courtesy of Gamblers General Store

A typical craps table layout includes the croupier's stick, dice and chips.

> **A craps table is where a person can stand alongside friends and share in their successes and failures.**

Customers cheer for their number in a craps game at Grand Casino Biloxi.

> *Once you play a few times, chances are great it will become your favorite casino game.*

> *Few things are more delightful in craps than $5 bettors winning on the pass line while a $100 bettor is getting his brains beaten on the don't pass.*

> *In craps, you have to stay alert. Things change quickly.*

Seven also happens to be the number most likely to show up on any single roll. Funny how that works.

But the player who can "roll numbers" and "make points" while avoiding a 7 is a friend to all. Except for the small and pitiful group of players who bet on the "don't pass." They are wagering that the shooter will not make his number. They have just as good a chance of winning as any player, but they make no friends. They bring bad karma to the table, silently rooting for the shooter to fail. They don't share in the shooter's successes, they don't cheer him on, they don't want to be part of something bigger than themselves.

Few things are more delightful in craps than $5 bettors winning on the pass line while a $100 bettor is getting his brains beaten on the don't pass. You should never be the table's "don't pass" bettor unless it's clear that the table is colder than a casino parking lot in Siberia in January.

There are times — many, in fact — in which betting against the shooter is the smarter choice percentage-wise. Cold craps tables are as common in casinos as glassy-eyed slots players.

But playing craps is a noble calling. You aren't just trying to win money, you're trying to do it and have a memorable social experience, to share in a triumph with friends and strangers alike, to cheer for your fellow human being and receive their support along the way.

All right, you're mainly interested in winning money. But if you can have some fun in doing so, all the better.

Craps Is For The Adventurer

Craps isn't for everyone. It is a pocket of the casino reserved the more adventurous. A big reason the slot machines are so popular is that they require no thought, no strategy, no interaction with others. Many people prefer to just jam in their coins and hope for the best. They get their occasional rewards, sure.

In craps, you have to stay alert. Things change quickly. You need at least a working knowledge of mathematics to grasp the odds, to know the correct amount to place on certain bets. Too many times, players don't understand the math and let a lot of money go un-won by having placed the wrong amount of money on the odds bets. They are doomed.

There is nothing on a craps table that tells you how to play, and it probably wouldn't help if it did. You learn craps as you go. It takes some courage to step up to a craps table and admit to the dealers that you don't really know what you're doing and would appreciate helpful hints on how to play the game. Often, players and dealers alike are glad to help the admittedly uninformed. It is those who pretend they know what they're doing and bog things down for everyone who are held in contempt.

You can read all you want about craps, and watch the game being played for hours. But you won't fully understand it until you play it a few times. Once you do, chances are great that it will become your favorite casino game. The occasional hot craps table is one of life's great pleasures. You are winning, the people around you are winning, the vibes are wonderful, and it seems as if fate has chosen to bring you to a special moment in time.

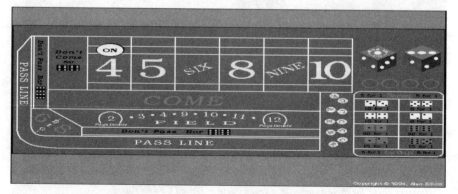

A home-style craps table layout is available from Gamblers General Store

This will not happen every time you visit a craps table. If it happens once in five trips, consider yourself fortunate. But it will happen. If you are with friends at the time, you will giddily talk about it all the way home and for a long time thereafter.

You will fondly remember the shooters who created the glorious streaks. They can physically remind you of the Elephant Man and may have the personality of a ballpeen hammer, but they will be lovely and charming in your eyes.

Alas, not all journeys to the craps table result in heartwarming memories. There is a reason why casinos offer craps, and that is because it is a game that systematically removes money from customers. Sometimes that money vanishes with amazing haste.

A cold craps table is no place for a happy personal interaction. A shooter who doesn't deliver is a bum, a pariah, a pox. Some people pass the dice on to the next player in line because they don't want the responsibility, or have no faith in themselves. A craps table is not a good place for someone with low self-esteem.

Leather dice cups are familiar to craps players.

Shooters Like Vituals

Shooters would be described by mental-health professionals as goofy. They think all kinds of things will make them roll the numbers they desire. They blow on the dice, they pound them on the felt, they fiddle with them like a cat playing with yarn.

All of which is perfectly tolerable and even endearing when the shooter is making numbers. That person is someone who knows exactly what he's doing, who has a method to every step of his madness. The player who goes through an extended routine of ticks and twitches only to seven-out is just a neurotic loser who drives everyone else nuts.

Hot shooters find a zone, the same kind of zone that a rock band hits on a night when everyone in the group is locked in, the audience is attentive and happy, and the venue is right. Hot shooters just know that if they consistently roll those bones their specific way, the next 7 is far in the distance. All other players at the table hitch themselves to a hot shooter's star.

On the other hand, cold shooters have sevens falling out of their hair. They are the world's most irritating people. They do not roll the dice correctly.

Former Chicago Bears coach Mike Ditka, a craps afficionado, reportedly once hollered angrily at someone at his table who sevened-out and cost Ditka a large chunk of coin. "Show some enthusiasm!" Ditka allegedly screamed at the culprit.

It's always good to bet on players who are throwing dice at a craps table for the first time in their lives. They seldom know what they're doing, which is a good thing. They are playing with fear, but it isn't the fear of losing. Rather, it's the frightening prospect of not rolling the dice correctly and getting chewed out by the stick men or fellow players.

Like all casino table games, there are rules to be followed. You can only hold the dice with one hand. New shooters invariably use both hands. You must keep the shooting hand held high. You are supposed to roll the dice all the way to the

A woman puts her enthusiasm and hope on the line as she rolls the dice at Rio Casino Resort in Las Vegas.

A craps table includes padded armrests and a bowl style.

Hot shooters find a zone, the same kind of zone that a rock band hits on a night when everyone in the group is locked in, the audience is attentive and happy, and the venue is right.

> *You don't have to be a high-roller to have fun playing craps.*

A craps table is set up for action at the Ameristar Casino in St. Charles, Mo.

> *Tip the dealers. If you can afford to play, you can afford to tip.*

backboard at the other end of the table. New shooters often fail to do one or all of these things right off the bat, are told to do so, and then obsess more over following protocol than making the point.

Which is all good. Instead of worrying about, say, hitting a 9 instead of a 7, their main concern is avoiding the dealers' criticism. When they do hit numbers and induce cheers, they often are stunned and confused. But they don't let thinking about the numbers get in the way of simply shooting and letting the dice do the rest of the work. To them, they're just firing away and watching chips go from the dealers to the players. Later, it will be explained to them what happened and they'll complain about not having wagered more, or more correctly.

New shooters are precious angels who rarely fail. Once they learn how craps works, they become mortal like the rest of us.

It is great fun to play craps with rookies. The constant action at a craps table is intoxicating for veterans, so imagine the jolt a newbie gets when a few bets work his way. Getting paid just because the dice showed eight spots and you had money on the 8? First-time players wonder how does anyone ever lose at this game?

Then they play again. And they find out.

You don't have to be a high-roller to have fun playing craps, and it probably helps if you aren't. If your bankroll is $50, all you can lose is $50. But if you nurse your money, limit your bets to the ones in which the house has a minimal advantage, and react properly when a table has heated up, you can end up with a tray full of chips. It isn't likely, of course. But it happens every day in casinos that offer the game.

When you don't have a lot at stake, you're more inclined to have fun. You also find yourself paying more attention to other players, some of whom can be as grim as the gravy at the casino's all-you-can-eat buffet.

Some players may not be Ditka-esque, but still mutter unpleasantries about shooters who stink up the joint. To them, rolling the right numbers is an opportunity other players either choose to make or frivolously squirt away. These same sullen players usually bomb out on their turns to roll. Dice don't react well to negativity. Any renowned scientist will tell you that.

Nicknames Add To Enjoyment

It can be great fun to give strangers at the table nicknames. Then you have something to call them as you're rooting for them when they have the dice. Some shooters find this annoying. Others are amused. Most are locked in their own dice-rolling orbit and pay no attention.

It is preferable, though, to call them something like "Brad Pitt" or "Paul Newman" instead of, say, "Hannibal Lecter" or "Goat Boy."

A final piece of advice for newcomers to the world of craps: Tip the dealers. If you can afford to play, you can afford to tip. Dealers are hard-working, fast-thinking people who deal with a lot of customers who don't fully know what they're doing. Surly, incompetent dealers should be stiffed, of course, but the majority are good folks doing an often-thankless job very well. Their straight salaries are usually nothing to gloat about, and they rely on tips for a decent wage.

If you place a bet for the dealers early in your playing session, you have a much better chance of being treated well by them. This matters. They will tend to be more forgiving when you inevitably commit a craps faux pas, like throwing the dice too sharply and sending them off the table two or three times in a row.

Actually, some of us believe an occasional dice-over-the-table is a good thing, feeling it knocks off the bad mojo that had been collecting on it. As incredible as it may seem, some gamblers are superstitious.

You may notice that I have referred to players as males. Craps is played predominantly by men. Craps is favored by more men than women because it features a lot of yelling, a lot of testosterone, and a lot of generally silly and strange behavior.

But it sure is fun.

Blackjack Winners

▌ *The Best Blackjack Strategies Can Beat the House*

By Frank Scoblete

B lackjack has been the most popular casino table game since the mid-1960s when Edward O. Thorp wrote his seminal book, *Beat the Dealer*, revealing that expert players could get a small edge over the casino by keeping a "count" of the cards and by playing a computer-derived basic strategy. Even without learning how to count cards, if you use the *Generic Basic Strategy* from this chapter, you will face a house edge of between .62 percent down to almost zero percent, depending on the games you play. In fact, you don't have to memorize anything, either, just make a copy of the page that has the *Generic Basic Strategy* and refer to it when you are at the table.

Blackjack is one of the best games in the casinos for players who play the proper strategies and one of the worst games for players who don't. Your decisions count heavily towards how much you'll win or lose. So the key to this game is — make the right decisions!

The Objective of the Game

The objective of blackjack is to beat the dealer. You can do this by having a hand that is 21 or less that is higher than the dealer's hand, or you can do this by having the dealer bust, which means going over 21. The player plays his hand first, then the dealer plays the house's hand according to set rules. If the player busts, and the dealer subsequently busts, the player still loses his hand. That one factor gives the house its edge.

Card Values

All cards have their face value with picture cards (jack, queen, king) counting as 10. All aces are worth either one or 11, depending on how they are used. Hands where the ace can be used as either a one or 11 are called soft hands. All other hands are called hard hands. Thus A:3, A:4, and A:5 are respectively a soft 14, 15, and 16 while 10:4, 10:5, 10:6 are respectively a hard 14, 15 and 16. If a player has an A:6 and receives a ten card, the player now has a hard hand of 17. There are certain hard hands that you never hit, no matter what the dealer is showing. These are 17, 18, 19, 20 and 21.

The perfect hand — 21.

Best Blackjack and Armada Strategies for Spanish 21 are two books by Frank Scoblete that will arm blackjack players for a winning performance.

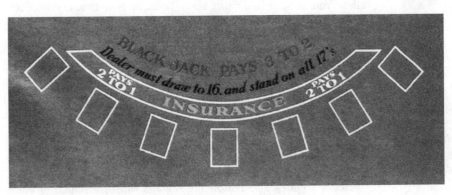

A typical blackjack table layout includes some of game's basic rules.

Players are thrilled when a winning hand beats the dealer in a
blackjack game at Reno Hilton.

A winning hand of 21 is shown in a Saddle West
Casino blackjack game.

Saddle West Casino

How the Game is Played

Most blackjack tables have spots for six or seven players. The dealer gives every player two cards and himself two cards. One of the dealer's cards is face up and the other is face down. In multiple-deck games, the players' cards are usually dealt face up; in single-deck and double-deck games, the players' cards are usually dealt face down. Once all players have their cards, they are faced with several strategy choices and options.

You Can Hit: The player can ask for another card. This is called taking a hit. In a multiple-deck game, the player points to the hand indicating a hit. In single-deck games where the cards are being held in the player's hands, the player scratches the cards along the felt to indicate a hit. A player may hit as many times as he desires — as long as he doesn't go over 21. The generic basic strategy chart will tell you when hitting is the best option for a given hand against a given dealer upcard. Proper hand hitting decreases the house edge.

Scobe's Quick Tip: Always hit your hands of 12, 13, 14, 15 and 16 when the dealer is showing a 7 or better.

You Can Stand: The player doesn't want to take a hit. To stand in a face-up game, simply wave your hands over your cards to indicate "no more." To stand in a facedown game, simply tuck your cards under your bet. The basic strategy chart will tell you when standing is the best option for a given hand against a given dealer upcard. Proper standing decreases the house edge.

Scobe's Quick Tip: Stand on all your hands of 17 or better.

You Can Double Down: The player can put up an extra bet equal to or lower than his original bet and double down. The player will then receive only one card on the hand. In face-up games, the player simply puts the bet next to his original bet. In facedown games, the player must turn over his first two cards and then put the new bet next to the original bet. Proper doubling decreases the house edge.

Scobe's Quick Tip: Always double down your 11 when the dealer is showing 10 or lower; always double your 10 when the dealer shows a 9 or lower.

You Can Split Pairs: If a player receives a pair, he can opt to *split* them by putting up a bet that is equal to his original bet. The dealer will then deal him a card on each hand and the player will play each hand separately. A pair of aces can only receive one card on each ace but all other pairs may be hit as many times as the player wishes. Proper pair splitting decreases the house edge.

Scobe's Quick Tip: Always split a pair of aces and a pair of 8s. Never split a pair of 5s or a pair of 10-valued cards.

You Can Resplit Pairs: Many casinos allow players to *resplit* pairs. Thus, if you have two 8s, split them and receive another 8 on the first hand, you may split this hand as well. Some casinos will allow you to split like cards up to three or four times. With each split, however, you must put up another bet equal to your original bet. Proper resplitting will decrease the house edge.

Scobe's Quick Tip: If it was the right move to split the pair originally, it is the right move to resplit.

You Can Double After Splitting: Many casinos will allow players to *double down after splitting* pairs. The procedure for this is the same as for doubling on the original two cards. Once you split your pair and receive a second card on one of the splits, you may place an additional bet that is equal to or smaller than your original bet and indicate that you want to double. The dealer will then give you only one card. Proper doubling after splits will decrease the house edge.

Scobe's Quick Tip: Follow the regular rules for doubling when doubling after splits.

You Can Take Insurance When the Dealer Has an Ace: If the dealer has an ace showing, players can take *insurance* by placing a bet up to one-half the size of the original bet in the playing area marked *insurance.* This bet is a side bet that the dealer has a blackjack and is paid off at two to one. Insurance bets increase the house edge over the player.

Scobe's Quick Tip: Never take insurance.

You Can Surrender: After you see your first two cards, some casinos allow you to *surrender* your hand without playing it by giving up half your bet. However, if the dealer subsequently has a blackjack, you lose the entire bet. Proper use of this rare option will decrease the house edge on the player.

Scobe's Quick Tip: Surrender all your 16s, except a pair of 8s, against a dealer's 9, 10 and ace.

The above options are common throughout the country. However, many casinos also offer other options to their players, or limit the exercise of certain options. Most casinos do not have surrender; many casinos will not let you split more than once, and some casinos restrict which hands you can double down on. The better the rules, the better the game. Here are two other considerations as well.

The Number of Decks: Given the same set of rules, the fewer the number of decks, the better the game for the basic strategy player. Even using the *Generic Basic Strategy,* which does not distinguish between single and multiple-deck games, a player will play essentially even with the casino at single-deck blackjack that allows doubling down on any first two cards, splitting and resplitting pairs, and doubling down after splits, while the player will face approximately a half percent disadvantage at an eight-deck game with those exact same rules.

Soft 17: All casinos have the dealer hit and stand according to a prescribed set of rules. The dealer will hit anything that is 16 or less and stand on anything that is 17 or more. The one exception is the hand of soft 17 (A:6). If the casino treats this hand like any other 17 and stands, it is favorable for the player. Hitting the hand is unfavorable for the player.

> ### Summation
>
> | **Favorable Player Options:** | **Unfavorable Player Options:** |
> | --- | --- |
> | doubling on any first two cards | restricted doubling |
> | splitting pairs | no doubling after splitting |
> | resplitting pairs | no resplitting |
> | doubling after splitting | insurance |
> | surrender | Over-Under 13 |
> | bonus hands requiring no side bet | multiple-action |
> | dealer stands on A:6 (soft 17) | dealer wins all ties |
> | blackjack pays three to two | blackjack pays even money |
> | specific blackjacks pay extra | bonuses requiring extra bet |

Money Management for Blackjack

Using whole numbers, by utilizing basic strategy in blackjack, the player wins about 44 percent of the time, the dealer wins about 48 percent of the time, and about eight percent of the hands are ties or pushes. However, by properly employing the *Generic Basic Strategy,* with the correct rules for doubling and splitting, the player can cut the house edge to almost nothing because proper doubling and splitting are to the player's advantage. Still, because you lose more hands than you win, you will find that blackjack is a rollercoaster. You will be down one moment and suddenly, with a few successful double-downs or splits in a row, you will come roaring back. Likewise, if you lose those hands, you fall into an even deeper hole.

Therefore, you must have enough money behind you to properly play the game and weather downturns. For a single session of blackjack, a stake of approximately 40 units or 40 times your minimum bet would be sufficient. If you are betting $10 minimum bets, then $400 should be your stake. If you are betting $25 then $1,000 would be the proper stake.

Blackjack is a fun game and the *Generic Basic Strategy* will stand you in good stead. Remember, you can cut it out or photocopy it and take it to the table. Just about every casino in the country now allows players to refer to strategy cards. So here's one game that you can play almost perfectly in the time it takes you to tear out a page!

> **Never take insurance.**

Under ornate chandeliers, players are dealt the cards in the casino of the Hyatt Regency Lake Tahoe.

> **Always split a pair of aces and a pair of 8s. Never split a pair of 5s or a pair of 10-valued cards.**

Sure Bets

Always hit your hands of 12, 13, 14, 15 and 16 when the dealer is showing a 7 or better.

Stand on all your hands of 17 or better.

Frank Scoblete's "Generic" Basic Strategy for Blackjack
S=Stand, H=Hit, D=Double, SP=Split

dealer upcard >	2	3	4	5	6	7	8	9	10	A
17-21	S	S	S	S	S	S	S	S	S	S
16	S	S	S	S	S	H	H	H	H	H
15	S	S	S	S	S	H	H	H	H	H
14	S	S	S	S	S	H	H	H	H	H
13	S	S	S	S	S	H	H	H	H	H
12	H	H	S	S	S	H	H	H	H	H
11	D	D	D	D	D	D	D	D	D	D
10	D	D	D	D	D	D	D	D	H	H
9	H	D	D	D	D	H	H	H	H	H
8 or less	H	H	H	H	H	H	H	H	H	H

dealer upcard >	2	3	4	5	6	7	8	9	10	A
A:9	S	S	S	S	S	S	S	S	S	S
A:8	S	S	S	S	S	S	S	S	S	S
A:7	S	D	D	D	D	S	S	H	H	H
A:6	H	D	D	D	D	H	H	H	H	H
A:5	H	H	D	D	D	H	H	H	H	H
A:4	H	H	D	D	D	H	H	H	H	H
A:3	H	H	H	D	D	H	H	H	H	H
A:2	H	H	H	D	D	H	H	H	H	H

dealer upcard >	2	3	4	5	6	7	8	9	10	A
A:A	SP	SP	SP	SP	SP	SP	SP	SP	SP	SP
10:10	S	S	S	S	S	S	S	S	S	S
9:9	SP	SP	SP	SP	SP	S	SP	SP	S	S
8:8	SP	SP	SP	SP	SP	SP	SP	SP	SP	SP
7:7	SP	SP	SP	SP	SP	SP	H	H	H	H
6:6	SP	SP	SP	SP	SP	H	H	H	H	H
5:5	D	D	D	D	D	D	D	D	H	H
4:4	H	H	H	SP	SP	H	H	H	H	H
3:3	SP	SP	SP	SP	SP	SP	H	H	H	H
2:2	SP	SP	SP	SP	SP	SP	H	H	H	H

Players at the Atlantis Casino Resort in Reno, Nev., compare their hands.

Frank Scoblete is the #1 best-selling gaming author in America and the author of the books "Best Blackjack" and "The Armada Strategy for Spanish 21." His books and tapes have sold over a million copies. For the best information on all casino games, order his free catalog: (800) 944-0406 or write to: Paone Press, Box 610, Lynbrook, NY 11563

Mementos Can Bring Rewards

▌ *Collectors Hit the Jackpot with Casino Collectibles*

By Howard W. Herz

America's rush to legalized gaming that began in the 1980s has been the source of an entire field of collectibles, from casino chips to slot machines.

Although legal gambling in America was once the exclusive monopoly of the state of Nevada, gaming expansion into first New Jersey and then other jurisdictions has brought casinos within miles of most Americans.

The gaming industry of today has evolved from years of both unlicensed and licensed operations that began in the early part of the 20th century. In the early 1900s, gambling was largely prosecuted by legal authorities as a vice. Most illegal operations did little to advertise their presence in a city, and those that did operated with caution.

Many American bars and "clubs" had a back room that catered to gamblers known to the operators. The "speakeasy" days of the 1920s brought gambling from individual operations to coordinated business ventures run by syndicates and organized groups. With this organization came standardized procedures that spawned companies who produced the paraphernalia of gaming.

Today sophisticated collectors find early gaming equipment that ranges from slot machines, Faro case keepers, tables, cheating devices, and other paraphernalia to be irresistible. The prices of these items reflect the demand and enthusiasm for early American gambling material and have driven prices well into the hundreds of dollars for fairly common items.

With the legalization of slot and table gaming in Nevada in 1931, gambling operations came out of the basements and back rooms. As gambling houses in the state began to compete for players in an open and legal environment, they resorted to advertising specialty items. The gambling chips (called checks) began to have the names and locations of casino operations and gaming could openly be depicted in advertisements and souvenirs.

The Toiyabe die are from Gabbs, Nev.

The first issue of Flamingo's $5 chip is now worth more than $5,000.

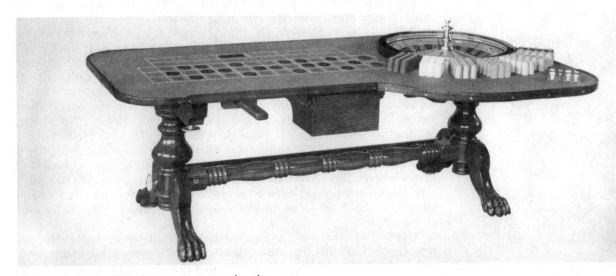

Your own roulette table makes a great conversation piece.

A Caesars 50-cent token is one of only a handful of the 1971 tokens that are undrilled and has a value of $250.

A historical souvenir hails from Harvey's Silver Strike.

This is the first token that Harrah's issued.

A match book from Harolds is a classic 1950s artifact from Reno.

By the mid-1930s, Nevada gambling houses boasted of their hospitality and range of games. Their advertising promotions began to include match books, ashtrays, key chains, postcards as well as their own gaming chips, dice, and table layouts. It was this expansion of casino advertising that serves today as the basis for most areas of serious casino collecting. Serious gaming collectors today are challenged by a number of areas in which they can collect, all of which are interrelated and seem to enhance one another.

Gaming Equipment: Perhaps the most popular item of gaming equipment collected today is the slot machine. There is also a wide range of other gambling paraphernalia that intrigues collectors. Faro equipment, from the game popular in the days of the wild west, has an exceptional following. The tables for games like roulette, poker and Faro are very collectible and hard to find. Cheating devices like hold-outs and card trimmers are sought after by sophisticated collectors and students of gaming history.

Gaming Chips and Checks: Although the organized hobby of collecting gaming chips and checks is less than 20 years old, casinos have been using them since the 1700s. (Note: "Chips" have no stated value while "checks" have a set value.) Checks and chips have evolved from rather plain looking clay chips to multi-colored checks that range in denominations from 1 cent to $10,000 and more. With the introduction of today's limited editions issued by casinos as commemoratives, the range of chip collecting has become almost unlimited, challenging the collector to define and limit the areas of interest. Until the spread of gaming throughout America, most of the gaming checks originated in Nevada. Today a collector can find checks and chips from Indian casinos across America, riverboat casinos in the Midwest and high roller operations in Atlantic City. The supply seems endless and the variety of colors and artistic expression continues to evolve. The value of chips and checks ranges from the multi-thousands for an original Bugsy Segal Flamingo $25 to just a few dollars for the latest limited edition from the local casino.

Gaming Tokens: With the demise of the silver dollar in the 1960s, casinos were forced to create a dollar size coin for their slot machines. Starting in 1965, Nevada casinos issued dollar gaming tokens. These tokens are very collectible and today come in denominations from 25 cents to $1,000. By exploiting minting techniques, gaming tokens have become a form of medallic art with intricate designs, multi-colored images and classic levels of artwork. Besides having the lure of coin collecting, they also are artifacts of gambling houses with histories that can be as intriguing as any story of fact or fiction.

Tokens range in rarity from the unique 1965 Harrah's $1 token struck in platinum (one struck) to the common issues of operations like Circus-Circus that order tokens in quantities of hundreds of thousands. Like coins, the quality of the token is a factor in its price with circulated items at face value or less and special frosted proof issues bringing high premiums.

Premium Silver Strikes: The introduction of special slot awards that can be redeemed for cash created an entire area of collecting in the 1990s. Called "Silver Strikes" for their appearance and silver content, award tokens could be won on special machines. Although they could be redeemed for cash, most of the pieces that players win are kept as a souvenir of play.

Dice: Although dice collecting has not expanded to the level of collecting seen by chips and tokens, dice are one of the collectible artifacts of gaming. Most casinos, including many illegal clubs from the 1920s and 1930s, monogrammed their dice as a security matter. Dedicated dice collectors recognize the historical significance that dice have played in gambling all the way back to the Roman empire. Today's dice are primarily used on crap games and canceled examples can usually be purchased at casino gift shops. Prices for rare dice can range upward of $200 for an extremely rare pair to only a few dollars for common examples.

Cards: Older decks of playing cards are collected by their brand name and type. Newer decks that are custom made for specific gaming houses are very collectible. Casino gift shops frequently offer canceled decks and a number of colors at a very reasonable price.

A Diamond Jim's ashtray is a find from Jackpot, Nev., valued at $20 to $30.

An ashtray from Harrah's is a Reno classic.

A Sahara ashtray is a true rarity from Las Vegas.

Matchbooks: Smoking, drinking, and gambling seem to have grown up together and were for years inseparable. Almost every gambling house issued its own matchbooks for advertising. Starting with the earliest matchbooks that might have hinted at a good time and going to the most blatant advertisement of gaming, these small advertisements are one of the most collectible and interesting casino items. Values range from several cents for common books to several hundred dollars for the rare and unique. Without a doubt, matchbooks are one of the best historical artifacts to collect, frequently providing locations and vivid graphics that make them a pleasure to own.

Ashtrays: Casinos have used ashtrays as an advertising medium for decades. With their logos prominently displayed, a stolen ashtray always reminds the owner of a good time and keeps the casino's name prominently in mind. Collectors of casino memorabilia have always found ashtrays interesting because they have all of the collectible attributes: name, style, and a link to history. Values range from a few dollars for the common to several hundred for a rare and classic item.

Gaming Memorabilia: Grand opening press kits, cocktail napkins, advertising flyers, free play coupons and tokens and a blizzard of other material are all collectible when the casino applies its logo to these otherwise rather common everyday items. Collectors find that the logo items make great background for shadow boxes or displays. Cocktail glasses and china emblazoned with a fancy casino name can bring several dollars at a garage sale to several hundred dollars in a collector's auction.

The bottom line for gaming collectors seems to be "how much romance and history" does an artifact have, whether it is a used matchbook or a spectacular gaming chip. The fun of collecting gaming items comes from the ability it affords to hold some American history in your hand and speculate if Bugsy Segal once held it. Some of the greatest collectibles from the 1940s and '50s exist today because someone took a trip to Reno or Las Vegas and kept what they thought was an insignificant souvenir of that trip. Today's casinos are flooded with souvenir items that range from free matchbooks to cards, dice, and logo merchandise that can be purchased at the gift shop.

So if you want to collect gaming items, start with anything that you find interesting. Define what you collect so that the range of items that you encounter does not overwhelm you. Be systematic in your collecting and soon you will have more than just an assortment of casino items. Most of all, have fun and enjoy your hobby. Someday, in 30 years, another collector will be thankful that you saved that matchbook, an artifact of American gaming history.

Howard Herz has collected chips, tokens and gaming history since 1965. He can be reached at P.O. Box 1000, Minden, NV 89423, or by e-mail at chipmaster@chipmaster.com

A Pioneer match book features Vegas Vic.

Collector's Club

The Casino Chip & Gaming Token Collectors Club
www.ccgtcc.com
membership@ccgtcc.com
Membership officer
Ralph Myers
P.O. Box 35769
Las Vegas, NV 89133-5769

Books for Collectors

Gamblers General Store
800 South Main St.
Las Vegas, NV 89101
800-322-2447
gamblersgeneralstore.com

Books & Auctions

Gaming Archæology
P.O. Box 1000
Minden, NV 89423
chipmaster.com

Sure Bets

The Pari-Mutuel Admiration Society

▌ *Bettors Find It's No Handicap to Try the Ponies.*

By Craig Cooper

War and Remembrance wins by a nose at Los Alamitos Race Course in California.

f it's 11:25 a.m., it's post time somewhere. The schedule says it's Beulah Park's last day with a first post of 11:25. The first thoroughbred race at Calder also goes off at 11:25. The first races at Tampa Bay Downs and Aqueduct are set for 11:30. Thoroughbred racing at Laurel Park starts at 11:35.

The where doesn't matter to the room full of bettors who are going through their routine before the action develops on the dozens of television screens. There is a giant screen in the middle of the room. Very few of the bettors waiting for action know, or care, where the heck Beulah Park is located.

The action is what matters at off-track betting sites.

Most bettors at off-track sites, just as they would at the track, start with the Daily Racing Forms for the tracks they are interested in. Tip sheets to help handicap the races from tracks all over the country are also available. Until a customer understands how to read the racing form, their "system" is probably going to be, "isn't that 1 horse pretty?" and "7 is my favorite number because you were born on that date," or "I'm betting a 2-3 quinella because that is

Spurred on by their jockeys, horses strain toward the finish line at Chicago's Arlington Park.

Benoit Photo

Michael Jordan's number." That last system works in roulette, too. We've played 23 with some success over the years.

But the people taking the time to show up to watch horse racing on television probably are not basing their bets on whims. They are typically educated horse and dog players who understand how to handicap a race by looking at past performances, breeding, jockeys and trainers.

They have their own language about "wheels" and "boxes," mudders and more colorful language about an offensive jockey who has burned them in the past.

Simulcasting saves live racing

Developing technology that allows players all over the country to wager on the race program at Santa Anita in California or Churchill Downs in Louisville has been a boost to what had become a stagnant horse racing industry. The effect has been that at the same time that the number of live races has continued to fall, the pari-mutuel handle fueled by off-track betting has risen consistently.

In 1995 the North American pari-mutuel handle was nearly $10.5 billion, according to Jockey Club statistics. By 2000, the handle had risen to $14.9 billion, although 83 percent of that handle came from off-track wagers.

Essentially, the handle has reversed. Not many years ago the entire racing handle came from live track wagering. Off-track wagering now accounts for nearly 85 percent of the nationwide handle.

A sports fan still is likely to prefer going to the track to sitting down at a table in a smoky, off-track betting parlor. Hanging out on the rail on a warm day watching the four-legged athletes rumble down the stretch in front of you is thrilling. No one is ever going to proudly tell his pals, "I had Secretariat across the board out at the OTB when he won the Preakness." The downside of the tracks is that there are long breaks between races.

Off-track wagering is convenient and the action is constant. You might be 1,500 miles away from the top tracks in Florida, but you can see the races of those tracks every day at the parlor only a few miles from your home.

A huge mural of racehorses decorates the space above a bank of TVs at Paris Las Vegas' Race Book.

Rows and rows of personal monitors at Bally's Las Vegas Race Book complement the giant TV screens overhead.

The Arlington Park grandstand.

The SuperBook in the Reno Hilton is one of the world's largest, featuring 27 projection TVs.

A bank of TVs marks the entrance to the sports and race book at MGM Grand in Las Vegas.

Off-track parlors allow the bettor to skip around between tracks, or between dog racing and horse racing. As one race finishes, there is another race hitting post time on another screen. There are so many tracks and so many races available that a bettor often has his choice of several races in the same time period. The constant action explains how the betting handle from off-track sites has risen so rapidly.

Slots, off-track bets foot the bill

Prairie Meadows in Des Moines, Iowa, may be the wave of the future in the racing industry. The track features a concept that is fairly new in the gaming industry. Built as a horse racing facility in the 1980s, it became apparent within a few years that horse racing alone was not going to support the facility. Polk County taxpayers were on the hook for the bonds to build the place and had to consider the possibility, maybe even the probability, that they would have to pay off the place with higher taxes.

When Iowa passed riverboat gambling, Prairie Meadows wasn't allowed to have all of the games the riverboats are allowed, but the track did get the concession of electronic games and slot machines. The introduction of the slots didn't just save taxpayers the burden of having to foot the bill for the failing track: The slots also saved live horse racing at the track.

Prairie Meadows does more than hold its own with the 10 riverboat casinos in the state. The track, even without table games, is the highest grossing casino in the state.

During the live racing seasons at Prairie Meadows, players can divide their time and gaming dollars between the 1,400 slot machines on the lower level, live pari-mutuel wagering, and off-track betting from more than a dozen horse and dog tracks scattered around the country.

Gamblers deposited more than $2.3 billion into those machines in fiscal year 2001. Nickels, quarters and dollars, one at a time. The casino kept 5.9 percent ($137.4 million) before taxes. Horsemen, local government, state government, and county residents have all benefited from the action on the slots.

Only Delaware, West Virginia, Rhode Island, New Mexico, Iowa, and Louisiana allow race tracks to also have gaming machines. There is some movement in Florida, a major racing state, to allow gaming machines.

The effect of the mixing of live racing, off-track betting, and the gaming machines has been dramatic at Prairie Meadows and may end up being a model

Spectators enjoy a day in the sun between races at Arlington Park.

Benoit Photo

for racing's future.

In 1993 for a 60-day live racing meet at Prairie Meadows, the total purse for the horsemen was $1.25 million. In 2001, with 118 racing dates, the purse was $17 million.

Dog tracks that were struggling in Dubuque and Council Bluffs are also back on sound financial ground because they also have gaming machines.

"There is no question that introducing the slot machines has saved racing in Iowa," said Jack Ketterer, executive director of the Iowa Racing and Gaming Commission. "The tracks are also putting a lot back into the economy through taxes."

Churchill Downs a force in the industry

On a recent Saturday at Prairie Meadow we bet only the simulcasted races from Hollywood Park in California. The attraction of Hollywood Park was jockeys we'd heard of —Kent Desormeaux, Laffit Pincay Jr., Eddie Delahoussaye — and horses with racing legends like Secretariat and Seattle Slew in their genetics.

Hollywood Park is part of the Churchill Downs Inc. (CDI) conglomerate that is one of the forces in the racing industry. In addition to Churchill Downs, the traditional home of the Kentucky Derby, Churchill Downs Inc., also owns the gorgeous Arlington Park in suburban Chicago, Calder Race Course in Miami, Ellis Park in Kentucky, and a network of nine off-track betting facilities.

Arlington Park hosts the prestigious Breeder's Cup races in October 2002.

There are obvious differences between live racing and the off-track betting experience, but there are also similarities. Like the live tracks, the off-track parlors are comfortable, with amenities like bars and restaurants. They are similar to sports bars with the added attraction of live wagering.

Hundreds of spectators line the rail and cheer from the grandstand at Arlington Park.

> **"There is no question that introducing the slot machines has saved racing in Iowa."**
> **— Jack Ketterer**

Benoit Photo

Horses burst from the starting gate at Arlington Park.

America's Day at the Races
ARLINGTON PARK
12 11 10 9 8 7 6 5 4 3 2 1

Benoit photos

They're off. Thoroughbreds leave the starting gate at Arlington Park in Illinois.

Slot machines may be the savior for some race tracks, such as Prairie Meadows in Iowa.

If you're not hitting your bets, there is always the diversion of sports on the televisions scattered around the off-track parlors.

Education helps the odds

One of the important similarities between the live racing and simulcasted racing is the importance of the Daily Racing Form. The forms are textbooks for horse and dog players. What you'll find in the form is a race-by-race preview with pertinent information on each animal in a particular race.

Important bits of information include recent past performances, career earnings records, breeding, jockeys or drivers, and in dog racing, weights. All of the bits of information become jigsaw puzzle pieces that a bettor puts together to form a personal picture of what is going to happen in the race.

Or you can close your eyes and let the pencil be guided by the racing gods to the right spot on the program. Don't laugh too much. Many Daily Doubles and lucrative exactas have been hit that way. The squeals of laughter at a track or in an off-track parlor may be coming from someone who just picked a winner that way.

It's too early to say positively that off-track betting can help reverse several negative trends in the racing industry — fewer tracks, fewer live races, smaller fields, fewer thoroughbreds being foaled — but on a temporary basis the racing industry is showing signs of rebounding.

Morning Snow wins in a tight finish at Los Alamitos Race Course in California.

> *You can close your eyes and let the pencil be guided by the racing gods to the right spot on the program. Many Daily Doubles and lucrative exactas have been hit that way.*

Sports wagering dictionary

Cover – When a favorite wins by more than the spread.

Daily double – Picking the winners of two straight races.

Dime -- $1,000.

Exacta – Picking two horses or dogs to finish 1-2 in exact order.

Exotic – The gimmick bets or propositions. For example, "which team will win the coin flip in the Super Bowl?"

Futures – A wager on the outcome of a future event.

Handle – The money taken in by a track or sports book.

Line – The point spread.

Money line – Odds based on $1. A minus sign (-) before the number means the team is the favorite. A plus sign (+) before the number means the team is an underdog. If an underdog that is +150 wins, it means that for a bet of $100, you will get back $250.

Nickel -- $500.

Off-the-board – A bet is taken off because of unusual circumstances. Weather or injuries to key players are possible reasons a bet is postponed.

Over-under – A proposition bet on whether the two teams involved will score more or fewer points than a designated number. Also used in boxing as in the number of rounds a fight will last before a conclusion.

Pick 'em – Neither team is favored.

Place bet – Betting that a horse will finish second or first.

Pressing – Increasing the money involved in your bets to catch up with losses.

Quinella – Picking two horses or dogs to finish 1-2 or 2-1 in a race.

Show bet – Betting that a horse will finish third, second or first.

Spread – The "line" or point spread.

Straight bet – A bet on a single game or race.

Teaser – A bet that requires picking more than one team. Not favored by serious bettors.

Tout sheet – A sheet of picks from a "tout," who is considered to be an "expert" on sports bets.

Trifecta – Picking the first three finishers of a race in order.

Vigorish – The cut the sports book keeps for handling the bets. Also referred to as "vig" or "juice."

Win bet – Picking a horse or dog to win.

The plush Vessels Club on the top level of the grandstand at Los Alamitos Race Course in California is typical of clubhouse amenities available at horse tracks.

Scoring on Sports

Betting the Spread's the Ultimate Game

By Craig Cooper

Whether the ball goes through the net or bounces off the rim can make all the difference to sports bettors

The joint is jumping on one of the great weekends in sports, which also makes it one of the great weekends for Las Vegas sportsbooks. The first games of the NCAA basketball tournament are being televised on two dozen screens. Every seat is taken.

Every basket sets off another round of wild cheers and agonized groans as Game One of 16 for the day is drawing to a still uncertain conclusion. Only a few people in the luxurious sports betting parlor (they are called sportsbooks) are emotionally attached to the teams on the screen. The players may not recognize a single player on either team. By the end of the game they have figured out what the mascots are and which team the mascots represent.

What the viewers do know about the game is that the team that is losing isn't losing by enough. The point spread is 17, but the underdog, State College of Sociopaths (+17 on the board), is gamely hanging around. That can be good or bad, depending on which way your money went. If you bet the favorite, you are groaning every time the despicable little point guard from State College makes another three-point goal. The kid couldn't defend a traffic cone, but he is killing you with those 3-pointers. If you have bet with the Sociopaths, you are loving Las Vegas and can't believe how easy this stuff is.

Five seconds left and the point guard has somehow hit another 3-pointer from 24 feet with two guys in his face. Two seconds. Buzzer! What an upset! The Sociopaths have "covered" the spread and it's a wonderful accomplishment.

College and pro basketball share the winter spotlight for sports fanatics, and sportsbooks.

Their coach, whoever the heck the guy is, is your new best friend and you would like to introduce the point guard to your daughter.

The hapless folks in the room who bet the favorite are cursing the coach, the mascot, the university president and all three celebrity alums of the school — the TV announcers mentioned them — even though the team won by 14.

But the losers will get another chance quickly. From early in the morning until early the next morning there are more games and more opportunities for action.

That's life in a Las Vegas sportsbook. The play at the end of a game that looks so insignificant on television in your living room may be one of the most exciting moments of the day at the Las Vegas sportsbooks. That insignificant play may have made the difference between winning and losing to thousands of bettors.

Every sports player has his favorite stories about fantastic days when they hit every game right. Our personal story is winning bets on seven straight NCAA tournament games, betting only the over-under lines (betting on the points scored in a game), in between periods of extreme winning at the $2 blackjack tables. That is the kind of day that accounts for the remarkable figure that nearly 75 percent of Vegas visitors have been there before. Win or lose, you are probably going to return. At least the statistics say so.

Best odds in the casino

At first glance, a sportsbook can be overpowering. The place is so wired, figuratively and literally, that it takes a while to get acclimated. On one wall are the omnipresent horse races. On another wall are the games in progress, depending upon the season. The rest of the walls in the large room are covered with the cryptic numbers. In the seats are the gamers who may or may not realize that statistically, they are in the best gaming seats, and most would tell you the most comfortable seats, in the entire casino.

"The sportsbooks quite often are the least profitable parts of the casino. In some cases the sportsbooks are there only because they are a service the gamblers want," explained Rich Moss, president and founder of Off-Shore Gaming Association, an organization that oversees the burgeoning on-line gaming industry.

Nowhere are the odds better for the gambler than they are in the sportsbooks.

The advent of online sportsbooks has given an opportunity for more fans to bet on basketball games

The excitement mounts for bettors as football season proceeds toward the college bowl games and NFL playoffs.

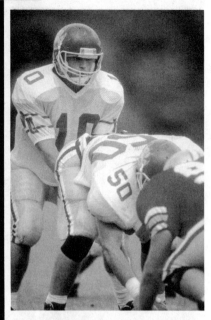

A good quarterback's the key to a good team, and could mean a shift of odds in Las Vegas sportsbooks.

A bank of giant TV screens and personal monitors help sports fans keep track of all the action at Bally's las Vegas sports book.

Racing flags and TVs set the theme at the sports book in Harrah's las Vegas.

One advantage is that some of the luck has been taken out of the equation. Cards at the blackjack can go hot and cold and can stay cold for an individual player for hours at a time while the person in the next seat is winning and howling with laughter. You hope that he passes out face down in a $1 chili dog so you can steal his seat.

Slot machines are even more capricious. There is no reliable strategy that works consistently. If there were such a strategy, the casinos wouldn't exist.

Roulette wheels have so many numbers that the chances of hitting "your numbers" often enough to win are not great. When the hot streak comes though, it is a heart-pounding experience.

Another reason the odds are better for the sports bettor is that most bets give the player a 50-50 chance of winning. If you have bet on a basketball game, you win or lose with your team. Those are very good odds in a casino.

Most importantly for the sports bettor, knowledge matters. The fact that you follow a particular sport closely can help when you go to the window to place the wager. If you have information about a team that might not be common knowledge, you have a better chance to win.

Las Vegas books offer a variety of bets on nearly every major sport. The sport doesn't even have to be in season because of something called futures betting. You may have read about professional golfer Phil Mickelson hitting two long-shot futures bets when he picked the Baltimore Ravens in the 2001 Super Bowl (2000 season) and the Arizona Diamondbacks in the 2001 World Series. Not that he needed the money, but Mickelson reportedly pocketed hundreds of thousands of dollars with the two bets.

Futures allow the gambler to bet on his favorite team, the Chicago Bears for example, to win the Super Bowl. The odds of the Bears actually winning may be 100-1 or even higher. A 100-1 bet means you will get back $100 for each $1 wagered. The two teams Mickelson picked to win both had high odds.

No off-season here

The basic menu of sportsbooks is the seasonal sports. Sports betting doesn't really have an off-season because there is always a sport being played or a race being run. Baseball, basketball, boxing, football, hockey and horse racing all are staples of sports books. Two of the growth sports for sports betting are auto racing and golf. That makes sense because both sports take only a few weeks off from competition every year.

In a sportsbook, you can bet on a team, individual or horse to win the event or lose a competition, or you can take advantage of the proposition bets. Proposition bets include picking one NASCAR driver over another to finish higher in a race, Tiger Woods against a group of other golfers, or the over-under lines.

The over-under bet allows players to project how many points will be scored in a game. The "over" is the bet that the teams will combine to score more points than the number the sports book oddsmakers have set. The "under" is a bet that the teams will combine to score under the designated number. For example, the number for a basketball game might by 172. If you bet the "under" and the final score is 73-70, you win.

A money line bet indicates how much you must bet to win $100, minus what the casino keeps as its cut (aka, Vigorish, Vig, Juice). If a team is –140, that team is the favorite and you must bet $140 to get your investment back plus $100 of the house's money back. The money line is the standard for boxing wagers.

Parlays are bets featuring multiple numbers of teams. On a Sunday in September, you might pick your three favorite teams all to win. The odds will vary from those for a straight bet.

The spread's the secret

Sports betting is based on numbers, or odds, set by professional oddsmakers. For example, you may be getting three points (+3) for your bet on the Washington Wizards against the Chicago Bulls. If the Wizards win outright or lose by less than three points, you win. The number is called the spread.

What the oddsmakers attempt to do is set the spread at a number that will attract action to both sides of the bet.

"They are nothing short of amazing the way they can pick the odds," Moss said of the oddsmakers. "What the oddsmakers always hope to do is load up on both sides of the bets. They want the line to result in balanced betting.

"If you had the answer to how they do it, you would be a millionaire."

Odds are set using extensive research on the teams involved. Information on statistics, trends, weather, injuries and other variables are all considered. A team's fans can also sway the betting line. A team with loyal fans who bet can be a factor in the line.

Occasionally the oddsmakers do miss badly on a game. It doesn't happen often, but if you can find those particular games, maybe because one of the teams is a team you follow closely, you can take advantage at the window.

"But they don't miss by much very often," said Moss, a veteran of the Las Vegas sports books. "You can look at a game and think, 'wow, that line looks way off.' Then the game is played and the oddsmakers have gotten very close."

There are hundreds of "experts" offering their personal picks for a price. They are often called "tout sheets," but go by various names and can be reached by telephone or on the Internet. Moss and many others believe that a bettor who follows a certain sport or certain college conference may be just as successful at picking winners as the "experts."

Little things like comfortable seating, a snack bar and restrooms close by mean a lot when you are planning on spending an entire night in a sports book. Those wide, leather seats at Bellagio are inviting. Other popular Las Vegas sports books are those at the Las Vegas Hilton, MGM Grand and the ESPNZone at New York New York.

With a computer and a major credit card, it is possible to remain in the comfort of your home and get plenty of sports action. Only Nevada presently allows sports betting in casinos, but there are dozens of sports book sites floating out there in cyberspace.

Moss' Off-Shore Gaming Association can direct home bettors to the reputable sites. Try www.gamblersworld.com for further information about the cyber sports books.

Seasonal sports, such as football and basketball provide the bulk of business for sportsbooks, but individual sports such as golf also draw bets.

Doing your homework and knowing the odds will improve your chances of winning a sports bet.

Sports players can improve their chances of winning by following a few tips.

Shop for the best odds — Odds will vary slightly from casino to casino. You may be able to get a better number down the street.

Don't be a sucker — Moss and others consider the multiple-team parlays to be "sucker" bets and suggest staying with single teams or straight bets.

Do your homework — Don't just play because you want to watch the game while your wife is shopping. Bet on events you know. The exception to that, of course, is during the NCAA basketball tournament when lots of people will be clueless about the teams playing.

Know the Racing Form — Figure out how to read the Racing Form and you'll be on your way to handicapping races. If one game doesn't interest you, try a few races if you still want the action. The Racing Form is the textbook for horse and dog players.

Watch for cute "dogs" — Just because the game is a mismatch of traditions doesn't mean it will be a mismatch on the field. Traditional football powers like Nebraska and Notre Dame have thousands of loyal fans whose bets can sway the line to a number higher than it should be against underdog opponents.

"Any Given Sunday" — Be wary of NFL favorites giving more than a touchdown to an opponent. Even poor NFL teams can come up with a big game. There is a great deal of parity in the NFL. College point spreads will typically be higher.

The excitement mounts for bettors as football season proceeds toward the college bowl games and NFL playoffs.

Bet on the Net

▪ *Online Casinos Give Gamblers Easy Access to Games*

By Andrew N.S. Glazer

The Off Shore Gaming Association is an independent "watchdog" agency that monitors the Internet gaming industry in an effort to provide the public an avenue to find reputable companies to wager with. The graphics that accompany this article are of OSGA members and are provided by the association.

A little more than a quarter century ago, a gambling "revolution" of sorts occurred. You no longer had to go to Las Vegas to gamble legally. You could now go to Atlantic City.

In the time since, the Las Vegas-Atlantic City oligopoly has been shattered by a combination of Indian and riverboat gambling, and new state laws that add up to "Hey, we don't want all that gambling tax revenue going across the state line, so we're going to legalize gambling here too, and of course use the money for a noble purpose like education."

As a result, you can now find some form of casino gambling in 30 states, and the total will probably be higher by the time you read this.

Then, about 10 years ago, the Internet started getting used a lot by members of the general public. Originally its prime public use was the distribution of pornography to folks who didn't want to be seen buying those magazines that so many stores keep wrapped up behind the cash register.

The Internet also had the advantage of being cheaper and much easier to access by a minor.

Pretty soon, folks who couldn't afford expensive gaming licenses or ultra-expensive hotels starting getting the idea that the Internet could make the breakdown of the Las Vegas-Atlantic City oligopoly seem, by comparison, like a minor footnote in gambling history.

A potpourri of sports images greets visitors to the World Wide Tele Sports site.

Before we knew it, everyone who was anyone had his own Internet casino or sports book. While it was clear enough that it wasn't legal to place the server in the United States, because the Founding Fathers had no idea back in 1776 that something like the Internet would ever come along, we were left with an extraordinarily confusing set of state-by-state rules about whether Internet gambling was legal.

As a consumer (player) of these Internet gambling services, you don't have to worry much about the legality issues. As of this writing, you can count on the fingers of one hand the number of cases where someone gambling on the Internet has been prosecuted for doing so, and in those few cases, the prosecutors wanted the defendant for other reasons. Only casino and sports book operators need to worry about the legal issues.

As a consumer, all you have to worry about are these three tiny little points: Will easy access to Internet gambling increase your chances of a dangerous gambling addiction, are the games honest, and will you get paid if you win?

Hmm, maybe those points aren't so minor after all. Let's examine them in increasing order of importance:

Will Internet gambling increase your chances of becoming a gambling addict?

The precise answer: Of course, silly, how could it not? The more important answer: Probably not enough to make Internet gambling one of those Societal Dangers against which the public must be protected at all costs, like cigarette smoking (oops, I forgot that a Societal Danger is OK if it pays enough tax revenue to the government).

The reality is that it is so easy to gamble these days in legal casinos (let alone the huge numbers of illegal games that exist) that merely adding the Internet to the list of gambling options an addict (or potential addict) has isn't going to make a lot of difference. Yes, being able to gamble right from your desk in the comfort of your own home is going to make access easier (or quitting tougher), much as having cigarettes lying around the house will make smoking easier. Without the Internet, you have to at least GO somewhere to gamble (if you don't count the ability to call your illegal bookmaker).

The Internet does make access to minors, like college students who want to bet on sports, much easier, and that is a problem.

Nonetheless, if your gambling problem is that severe, you can always take the modem out of the house, and there are usually limits on how much you can

Colorful graphics and offers advertising discounts attract gaming enthusiasts to wager on Off Shore Gaming Association casinos and sports books.

Hundreds of Internet gaming sites compete for business from online gamblers.

gamble away in a short period on the Internet, limits that don't exist in brick and mortar casinos. While the addiction problem shouldn't be ignored, issues two and three are much more important to most gamblers.

Are the games honest?

The answer: Probably, and for the same reason that most brick and mortar casino games are honest: The built-in casino edge is more than enough to beat you long term, without the need to resort to cheating.

However, just because a smart Internet casino operator doesn't need to cheat you doesn't mean you won't get cheated. Major brick and mortar casinos can handle big fluctuations in luck because they are well capitalized. Many Internet casinos are undercapitalized operations that don't have the money to pay up if customers have a lucky few weeks. Their response to this problem is more likely to affect whether you get paid than whether they "cook" the software, though.

Why? The majority of Internet casinos buy their software in turnkey packages from software developers who (like the folks who made a lot more money selling blue jeans and oats to 49ers during the gold rush days than most prospectors made) are just making money by writing good software. Most Internet casino owners wouldn't know how to cook their software if they wanted to.

Will you get paid if you win?

The answer: A definite "maybe," depending entirely on whom you have chosen to do business with.

Small, undercapitalized casinos or sports books may go into business with good intentions, but sometimes things don't go well, and these small shops can just close their virtual doors and reopen under a new name a few days later. Your chances of getting paid increase dramatically if you go with a virtual casino that has been around for years (hint: don't take their word for how long they've been around), and increase yet again if that Internet casino is associated with a known, respected land-based operation, as some of the British operations are.

It's important to draw a distinction between sports books and casinos here. Casinos have to get VERY unlucky for their customers to hammer them for several months. A sports book has to get only mildly unlucky, especially if it takes bets that are too big. You'll probably run into more problems with Internet sports books than with Internet casinos, and it becomes doubly important to deal with reliable, long-lasting businesses when betting sports.

Many sports books are perfectly reliable as long as you are losing or breaking even. If you start to win, though, they get paranoid that you might be part of some "syndicate" that knows too much. If that happens, they will cut you off from playing, and if you're very lucky, pay you before closing your account. They "justify" this with fine print in the agreement you click on when you start playing, where you promise that you aren't part of an information syndicate.

In other words, with a few stable, honest, long-lasting exceptions, you are probably playing a "heads I win, tails you lose" game with most smaller sports books. They might as well hang out a sign that says "Suckers Only" on their doors. Like casinos that welcome basic strategy blackjack players but who bar card counters, if you're good enough to win consistently, many Internet sports books will cut you off. They'll pay the occasional winning wager, but someone who hits them week after week is likely to find himself on the sidelines. Why bother to play if the only action they'll take is losing action?

If you have a complaint about how such and such sports book or casino is operating, good luck getting the third world country where the site is "licensed and regulated" to do anything about it.

In order to give the consumer some information to work with, a number of alleged Consumer Reports-type sites have sprung up, promising to publish complaints about the bad guys. The "only" problem with these sites is that they are, almost without exception, funded entirely by Internet sports books, so you go figure whether they are going to ding a major advertiser. Some of these alleged "consumer reporting" sites are actually involved in secret partnerships with the casinos or sports books they are recommending. The absence of ads on a site doesn't mean the site isn't receiving support from the casino it is evaluating.

There are also a number of very official-sounding associations that award their very official looking "seals of approval" to supposedly sound sites. Ask these associations where their operating capital comes from, and then draw your own conclusions about how much that seal of approval is worth.

The bottom line:

Right now, Internet gambling is at much the same stage as gambling was in America's wild, wild West days: You pays your money, you takes your chances. Be paranoid and skeptical about any claim any Internet casino or sports book makes, and you might be safe. If you MUST gamble on the Internet, make sure you do it with a casino or sports book that has been around for a while, is regulated by a country that cares about something other than the licensing fees it collects, and build your way up to large bets very, very gradually.

The day will come when Internet gambling is as reliable as the brick and mortar variety, but that day won't come in 2002, and it probably won't come in any year whose last two digits start with "0." Check back in 2010, and if you're lucky, you'll have just as good a chance to win in any random Internet casino as you do any random brick and mortar casino.

Andrew N.S. ("Andy") Glazer is the author of "Casino Gambling the Smart Way" and writes a weekly gambling column for *The Detroit Free Press*. He is also a regular columnist for *Poker Digest* magazine, is the online poker guide for www.poker.casino.com and has had materials published in the British edition of *Esquire* magazine. *Newsweek* magazine called him "a poker scholar," and he has written for virtually every gambling magazine or Web site of note

Keeping Your Head Pays Off

▮ *Proper Etiquette in a Casino Can Improve Your Odds*

By Tony Boylan

Camaraderie is one of the joys of playing casino games, as these players at the Hilton Atlantic City found.

A cheerful attitude goes a long way to contributing to the atmosphere of a casino. This player at Rio Casino Resort in Las Vegas celebrates her good fortune at a slot machine.

After a night of savage luck at a high-stakes blackjack table, I'd finally gotten on a small run.

I had $600 in the betting circle, one $500 chip on the bottom and a $100 on top.

Slap, slap, slap, went the cards. I was looking good with two tens.

The dealer began turning what seemed to be an endless series of small numbers until she dropped the last one. She looked at me with remorse in her eyes, as if she had just run over my dog.

She mumbled a few sympathetic words about her 21 as she leaned over the table to begin picking up chips. I was contemplating a gambler's recovery program as I caught a glimpse of my green $500 chip scooting back into the disorganized pile in front of me.

The dealer had actually used one of her long, painted fingernails to deftly flick more than 80 percent of my bet back to me.

Now I could fool myself and say it's because she was flirting with me, but a large difference in our ages and a rock worthy of a casino chandelier on her hand made that unlikely. She could have pitied me, but there were others at the table who were far more pathetic souls on longer losing streaks.

And, of course, you can argue about her unethical and illegal act.

But I could only come to one conclusion: The dealer wanted to help me because I stood out at that table due to my casino etiquette. Yes, despite evidence to the contrary, casino etiquette is not an oxymoron.

On other occasions I have had dealers pay me when we pushed, or leave my bet in place on a loss, as if we had pushed.

Players enjoy the action at a roulette table at the Atlantic City Hilton.

Great expectations for behavior

Etiquette may seem like a foreign concept to a place where gambling and drinking are encouraged while the world's oldest profession is tolerated with a wink. But there is an appropriate behavior during the practice of any vice. There are expectations of how you will behave in a bar, so why wouldn't there be in a casino?

And the good news is that it's not hard to stand out when the competition consists of drunken tourists, chronic gamblers with nervous disorders and lots of people who believe a $5 wager makes them a member of the Rat Pack.

Be polite. Say thanks when you score a nice win. And don't act like the chips are made of plutonium when it comes time to toss a few back to the dealer.

Dealers of blackjack, craps, or any other game, deal thousands of hands in an eight-hour shift. During that time they are on their feet more than five hours and have to concentrate every single moment, often while ignoring angry fits from tourists who seem to believe they are owed a win.

Well you are not owed a winning experience in any casino. If you ever are in doubt of this, take a look around at the beautiful waitresses, the glittering lights, and ornate fixtures. Who do you think pays for them?

What are you owed? A fair cut of the cards, dice that roll true, a wish of good luck when you buy in to a game, and an edible prime rib for $5.99. That's all.

While most of what you can do to improve your odds of winning involves your playing strategy, knowledge of the game and self-discipline for wagering, the way you behave can get you an important ally in the dealers, croupiers, and other employees who run the games. Here are a few tips:

Small talk:

Read the dealer. Most will enjoy the fact you are friendly and engaging them in conversation. I find it helpful to chat about where they are from. Those home towns are printed on their name tags for a reason.

Many of them have interesting stories about what brought them to Vegas, what it's like living there and areas of personal interest. And few and far between are the people of any occupation who don't enjoy talking about themselves.

Once in awhile I get a dealer who runs the other direction. They seem tired of answering the same questions from small-talking rubes all day long. When this happens I simply try to ask a few open-ended questions to see where they want to take some conversation, if they want one at all. Those who don't want some friendly conversation are the exception, however.

A slot machine at the Claridge casino in Atlantic City produces a jackpot and some thrilled customers. Politeness, and a show of appreciation after a big win, go a long way in a casino

The dealer at the Claridge casino in ATlantic City deals blackjack cards to appreciative patrons. Gaming experts say don't forget to tip the dealers, especially after a win.

A group of smiling bettors crowd around a table at the Tropicana in Las Vegas. A good attitude is important to enjoying the gaming experience.

Good service always deserves a tip. A waiter brings a bottle of wine to diners at the Oaks Steakhouse at the Hilton Atlantic City.

A good dealer earns a tip from your earnings. This blackjack dealer works at Ameristar's Cactus Petes Resort Casino in Jackpot, Nev.

Tipping:

You will read different schools of thought on tipping. Some experts claim you should only tip at the end of a session, and then only if you won.

Let's say you were having a business lunch and trying to close a deal with a client. If you had a good meal and excellent service, but couldn't make your sale, should the waiter or waitress get stiffed?

Tipping is in large part designed to ensure good service in the future. If you tip on your first round at a crowded bar, you'll get the rest of your drinks with a lot less hassle for the rest of the night.

My practice in cards is to tip every time I'm dealt a blackjack, or if I win on a complex hand that involved multiple splits and doubles. You can assume how this would translate to baccarat, Pai Gow poker, and any of the myriad other games in the casino.

At the craps table, I throw a $1 "Yo" bet (a 15-1 play in the middle of the table that pays if an 11 hits on that roll) for the dealers at least once during every point. It doesn't cost much and it is always appreciated. Besides, yelling out "give me a Yo for the boys," once in awhile will make you more memorable to the dealers, and it's darn fun to say, too.

Now, you won't find dealers at a heavily scrutinized craps table tossing any undeserved chips your way. And that's good. But they will make sure you have the correct dollar amounts on each bet to collect the best odds.

Mistakes are not uncommon at a crowded craps table because of all the commotion. But, if you are one of the few people at your end of the table tipping consistently, the dealer will be particular about making sure your bets are paid, and that you get down all the bets you want in between rolls.

> **Tipping is in large part designed to ensure good service in the future.**

Don't get mad:

Remember that the dealer is not much more than a robot. The house plays are established in the rules. And a run of luck, good or bad, is not the dealer's doing.

Besides, they didn't force you to play. In fact, dealers often politely suggest to agitated players they quit for awhile because things aren't working out for them.

I have seen many a gambler sit down and foul the mood with his histrionics over losing a large bet, or a long cold streak. Harassing the dealer about your luck with the cards or dice, raising your voice, slamming the table or any other tantrums only will hurt your cause.

Southern hospitality shows through at a blackjack table in the Grand Casino Tunica.

Blackjack players interact with a dealer aboard the Caesars Indiana Glory of Rome riverboat, maintaining good casino etiquette.

Granted, the dealer can't work against you. And instances of them bending the rules in your favor are so rare that you never should count on them.

But they can affect your game in other ways. They might deal more quickly, increasing the likelihood of you making a math error or failing to put your strategy into play. They won't be helpful if you make a wrong gesture, an incorrect wager or ask for their opinion on a play.

In fact, they will begin to want you to lose, just so you leave their table.

And if your behavior goes beyond just being discourteous, the pit boss might have you escorted from the casino altogether. While that no longer carries the threat of a beating it might have had on the old Vegas Strip, it still is a good way to ruin your night and embarrass yourself and your friends.

Keep your head and use appropriate language. If you are getting frustrated by a streak of bad luck, go do something else for awhile. Catch the house band's cover of "Proud Mary." Walk to the sports book and see what the championship odds are on your favorite team. Or just call it a night.

Know the game:

A dealer will be most likely to help those who help themselves.

Most dealers know the best strategies of the game they are working and are happy to share their experience with you. But they are not babysitters, nor are they interested in teaching you their game from the ground up.

Take blackjack, for example. A big part of winning is based on doubling down and splitting; basically getting more money on the table when the odds are in your favor.

You may find a dealer who will help you if you are about to take a stupid hit against a six showing. But they are not going to start explaining soft doubles or when to split nines to an obvious beginner.

At a crowded craps table, a dealer will remind you what denominations you need for each bet and what odds they pay. But don't expect them to explain the basic elements of the game. You should already know all of that before you are putting your money at risk, anyway.

And making stupid plays is a sure way to drive other players from your table. Fewer players at a table mean fewer tips for a dealer. Think that dealer is going to go out of his way to keep you around?

So behave in a casino the way you'd want your friends to behave if you had them over for a poker night. Even if it doesn't make you any extra money, it will help everyone involved have a better time.

Good spirits, and good vibes, are a win-- win situation for bettors at a craps table in Bally's Atlantic City.

> **Keep your head and use appropriate language.**

South Dakota Tourism photo by Chad Coppess

A dealer in Deadwood, S.D., draws cards for a table of bettors.

Another table game, baccarat, puts players in a good mood at Harveys Lake Tahoe.

Vacation in Vegas

▌ *Gambling Isn't the Only Game in This Desert Delight*

By Craig Cooper

dvertisements for Las Vegas usually don't show Hoover Dam, roller coasters, arcades and museums. They show glitz, neon, slots, blackjack tables and winners. They never show the folks headed home with only a few bucks left for airport snacks. And rarely do they show families.

The pitch works. Las Vegas welcomes 35 million or more tourists each year and the numbers are rising. Visitors fill up about 130,000 hotel and motel rooms and fill up slot machines 24, 7, 365. The visitors spend more than $5.5 billion just on wagers in Las Vegas.

It's not that kids aren't welcome in Las Vegas. There are dozens of attractions they would be interested in. The numbers, though, indicate that Vegas is still very much an adult destination.

Despite the occasional pitches that Las Vegas is becoming a family destination, the number of visitors with children has stayed stable at 10 to 12 percent, according to figures from the Las Vegas Convention and Visitors Authority.

The same statistical surveys indicate that 85 percent of the visitors make a bet at some point in their stay. Add in the underage kids and the percentage of

The famous Las Vegas Strip is a "National Scenic Byway," and it is one of the most recognizable streets in the world.

Las Vegas News Bureau

adult visitors who don't make even one pull of a nickel machine drops to 3 percent or less.

One other tidbit from the convention authority is that visitors gamble about four hours per day. That leaves a lot of hours for other attractions.

Those other attractions include everything from natural beauty, to the glamorous shows, water parks and great restaurants.

Natural and man-made wonders

Stunning natural beauty and stunning human achievement are within easy drives of Las Vegas. Only 35 miles from Las Vegas you'll find both in the Hoover Dam and the Colorado River corridor that is one of the great recreational areas of the West.

Historians do not regard Herbert Hoover as one of the great presidents. In a ranking, the only president born in Iowa might not even be ranked in the top 35. He gave the country the Great Depression — more because of bad timing than mismanagement, according to some historians — and was in office when construction began on Boulder Dam in 1931.

The dam is generally considered to be one of the great engineering and construction marvels in the United States. The impact of the dam has been dramatic in the development of the desert around Las Vegas.

Hoover Dam and the lakes area can be turned into a fun and educational day trip away from Las Vegas.

Start with the Hoover Dam experience. The Discovery Tour is the highlight. Ticket sales begin at 9 a.m., but you might want to consider lining up a few minutes early. The tours do fill up in the peak season and the heat can be stifling later in the day.

For $10 for adults and $4 for kids 7-16 (under 6 free) you'll get the whole dam experience. Ask how many people died in the construction of the dam. The dam tour guides only hear that one several times a day. The best answer is 96, not counting workers who died from heat stroke, heart attack and other physical maladies. The claim is that no dead workers were buried in the 3.25 million cubic yards of concrete used to build the dam.

When you've had the entire dam experience, head to the Lake Mead Cruises

The Lake Mead Marina is a jumping off point for water sports enthusiasts who sail, fish, water ski and scuba dive. Lake Mead, with its shoreline of more than 550 miles, is the reservoir created by the construction of Hoover Dam, which spans the Colorado River.

The desert surrounding Las Vegas is barren yet alive with plants and animals. Red Rock Canyon located west of las Vegas, anmed for its brilliant colors, is a favorite destination for hikers and riding enthusiasts.

A couple combines a cool dip in the pool at the Tropicana Resort & Casino with a game of blackjack.

A chef at the Tropicana prepares a flaming dessert at tableside for appreciative diners.

Landing. It's only a few minutes away in Boulder City, which was built to house construction workers at the dam.

Lake Mead Cruises (www.lakemeadcruises.com) offer mid-day sightseeing cruises departing at 10 a.m., noon, 2 p.m. and 4 p.m. There are also dinner cruises and dinner-dance cruises. All of the cruises are on 300-passenger, three-level paddlewheel boats. You'll see Hoover Dam again, plus some of the spectacular scenery of Lake Mead.

If you've caught an early boat, you can still head for Chloride, Ariz., which is located south of Hoover Dam. Chloride was a boomtown of the 1860s when silver, gold, lead, zinc and turquoise were all found. When the boom ended and the mines shut down, Chloride seemed destined to become one of the ghost towns scattered around the area.

Attracted by the climate and the history, Chloride is populated and trendy again. The Las Vegas Leisure Guide suggests stopping at the Tennessee Saloon for a hamburger.

Visitors who are more adventurous might want to design their own boat tour by renting one of the watercraft available from the marinas on or near Lake Mead. The available craft include houseboats, fishing and skiing boats and personal watercraft.

Other day trip recommendations are Red Rock National Park (20 miles west of Las Vegas), the historic Pioneer Saloon in Goodsprings, Nev., and Goldfield, Nev.

Recreate

Gambling usually means a lot of sitting. Too much gambling or too many of those wonderful Vegas buffets and you are going to need to work off a few pounds. That's easy to accomplish in Vegas. You go in July and walk down the street a block or two. That should about do it. But it's a dry heat. Remember that.

Las Vegas has great recreational opportunities that have nothing to do with sitting in a sports book for five hours.

Casino hopping is a suggestion for first-time visitors or visitors who haven't been to Las Vegas for several years. You can put miles of walking on your new shoes just checking out the lavish casinos on the strip. Stop every once in a while at the shops inside the resorts for drinks or snacks. The variety is amazing.

Resort managers frown on "pool hopping." Some tourists still do more than just check out the pools at the different hotels. There are usually ways to sneak in, talk your way in, tip your way in, or simply walk in if you look like you

Las Vegas offers challenging and intriguing golf courses designed by world-renowned golfers and designers.

belong by the pool. Our "expert" sources suggest The Mirage (tough to crash), Tropicana, Flamingo, Monte Carlo and Mandalay Bay, which has a wave pool, lazy river and sand beach.

If you want to golf, understand first that you are in a large resort city. If you are escaping winter to play golf and have some fun in Vegas, you are going to pay a premium just as you would in Phoenix, Florida or Palm Springs. You may be able to play several rounds at home for what you will pay to play one winter round on a quality Las Vegas course.

One of the most exclusive and enjoyable golf experiences, according to those who have done it, is available at Shadow Creek. You need two things to play a course that is generally regarded as one of the top 10 in the United States: You need to be a guest of The Mirage and you need at least $500 if you aren't being comped.

And it would be useful to have some game. You'll need it.

New in 2002 is Bear's Best Golf Club. Legendary golfer Jack Nicklaus took 18 of the favorite holes from courses he has designed and put them together as a single course not far from the strip. Again, bring your "A game" and about $200 depending on the day and time of the year.

The two Angel Park Golf Club courses are testers, but a little less pricey.

Locals know Black Mountain Golf & Country Club in nearby Henderson. The challenge is still there at a more affordable ($50-$100) green fee.

The fees go down in the summer. People do still golf. They just go out early before the worst heat.

Spectate

In one sense Las Vegas isn't a pro sports town. There are no major league professional sports franchises, although the rapidly growing area seems destined to land at least one NFL, NBA or NHL team eventually.

In one pro sport though, Las Vegas is the center of the universe. You aren't a contender unless you've boxed in Las Vegas. All the great ones have.

Since the "fight 'til you drop" championship fights in makeshift, outdoor arenas decades ago, "Sin City" and Nevada have lured the best fighters and the best fight fans.

You don't have to be a fan to enjoy a big Vegas fight. Vegas fights are a spectacle, a raw competition, and an emotional rush. Buy a ticket and watch the celebrities arrive at ringside. Listen to the crowd noise rise just before the main event fighters are introduced. Stand up and cheer or boo the fighters who enter with cockiness and flamboyance.

Las Vegas News Bureau

Showgirls show off the sign welcoming visitors to Las Vegas

Tropicanna Resort & Casino

The Folies Bergere is the long-running show at the Tropicana, one of many forms of entertainment available in Las Vegas.

Las Vegas News Bureau

From roller coasters to white tigers to wax museums and gondola rides, Las Vegas has attractions for all ages and interests.

The fountains of the Bellagio, above, are one of Las Vegas' free shows. Bally's hotel tower is below.

There is a palpable sensation of impending danger. Somebody could get knocked out. Somebody could get carried out. Somebody is going down. Somebody is going to leave the ring stripped of all dignity.

Vegas' other big-league professional sports attractions are auto racing, golf and rodeo.

The Las Vegas Speedway is a complete motorsports complex that hosts its big NASCAR week in March. There are other racing events throughout the year.

Depending on the time of the year, you can make a trip to Vegas and possibly see the best golfers in the world. The PGA Tour visits in October. The Three Tour Challenge featuring players from the PGA, Senior PGA and LPGA Tour also plays Las Vegas in December.

Even if you haven't worn a cowboy hat and boots since you were five years old, you can wear both during the National Finals Rodeo in December and fit in perfectly. And belt buckles the size of dinner plates are chic. There are real cowboys all over the city and other "cowboys" who are cowboys only because they have seen Gene Autry, George "Gabby" Hayes and Jimmy Durante, Jimmy Durante? in "Melody Ranch." Get tickets if you can.

There are major college sports events at the University of Nevada-Las Vegas throughout the school year.

From April through September the Los Angeles Dodgers' Triple A baseball affiliate plays Vegas.

At New York New York, you can get your fill of Sports Center at the new ESPN Zone, which doubles as the casino's sports book and triples as a restaurant.

Just for the thrill of it

To attract families to Las Vegas, there has to be something for the kids to do.

Shake them up at the "Stratosphere High Roller" at the Stratosphere, "Grand Slam Canyon" at the Adventuredome at Circus Circus, "Speed

Downtown Las Vegas has been transformed into the glittering Fremont Street Experience. The nightly sound and light show features 2.1 million lights and 540,000 watts of sound and music.

The Ride" at the Sahara, and the 203-foot tall "Manhattan Express" coaster at New York New York. The coaster billed as the tallest and fastest in the United States is "The Desperado" at Buffalo Bill's Resort and Casino in Primm, south of Las Vegas.

Circus Circus has been one of the favored family resorts in Las Vegas since its opening in 1968. Circus acts still perform daily at Circus Circus and the "Big Top" is surrounded by a midway and numerous snack and fast-food stops.

In 1993 Circus Circus took the theme a step further by opening the Adventuredome, the world's largest indoor theme park. The five-acre Adventuredome ranked 19th in North American theme park attendance in 2000. There is never a bad weather day at the park, which helps keep attendance consistent throughout the year.

For less thrills but as much fun, check out the free Ethel M Chocolate Factory self-guided tour, Dophin Habitat at The Mirage, the wildlife exhibit at the Flamingo Hilton, Lion Habitat at the MGM Grand, Star Trek, The Experience at the Las Vegas Hilton and Shark Reef at the Mandalay Bay.

The best free shows are the fountains at Bellagio, the Buccaneer Bay battle at Treasure Island, The Mirage volcano eruption and the Fremont Street Experience downtown.

Gameworks is a game palace that features everything from old-time pinball machines to the newest interactive games that you may not find anywhere else. Gameworks is next to the MGM Grand.

Wet 'N Wild is a water theme park next to the Sahara.

The gondola ride at The Venetian and the Eiffel Tower at Paris will give the families an

One of the newest attractions. Paris Las Vegas, brings the Eiffel Tower and Arch of Triumph to the Strip. New York, Egypt, Venice, and Rio are among other "worlds" depicted in Las Vegas resorts.

From Elvis-look-a-like attendants to "drive thru" wedding chapels, marriage Las Vegas style makes fantasies come true.

Las Vegas News Bureau

internationally flavored experience without leaving the desert.

Museums to check out are Elvis-A-Rama behind the Fashion Show Mall, the Imperial Palace car museum (ask around the casino for free tickets), the Guinness World of Records Museum on Las Vegas Boulevard, the Lied Children's Museum and Liberace Museum.

It does not exist

Forget Area 51. There is no such thing. Do not even try to find it. Why waste your time when the government says it doesn't even exist?

Because it is really out there and everyone can tell you how to at least get close to the secret air base where stealth aircraft were designed and tested. There are tours to the site near Rachel, Nev.

Area 51 is supposedly where the UFOs and creatures from outer space were taken when they landed near Roswell, N.M. The Little A Le Inn (Little Alien, get it?) is a suggested stop.

Love is in the hot, breathless air

Few marriage counselors would suggest spending $200 of your winnings on a quickie wedding, but if you are so inclined, go for it at any of the dozens of chapels. Even the casinos have chapels.

At the Candlelight Wedding Chapel, couples can walk down the same aisle that Whoopi Goldberg and Bette Midler did. Wedding packages start at $179 with add-ons for limo service and cakes.

Other chapels offer extravagances like first-class dining for guests and a helicopter trip over the Grand Canyon.

Many couples also remarry at the chapels.

Finally, eat, drink, and be merry

Las Vegas has always been known for the $3.99 steak and eggs specials after 11 p.m., inexpensive buffets and free adult beverages. In recent years it has become known as a destination where visitors can have food prepared by some of the top chefs and their protégés.

The variety is endless. You can eat your way around the world — France, Italy, the Orient, American — without leaving one of the big casino resorts.

At the Forum Shops at Caesars Palace, you can choose from Wolfgang Puck, Planet Hollywood and the Cheesecake Factory to name only a few.

As Emeril would say, "Bam!" His restaurant is the Delmonico Steakhouse at The Venetian.

Entertainment and excitement are Las Vegas' 24-hour businesses.

A dining mecca in the desert, Las Vegas offers Mobil five-star restaurants, outdoor and theme cafes, quaint eateries and classic buffets.

Las Vegas News Bureau

Highly rated Las Vegas restaurants:

By Dennis Thornton

Picasso (Bellagio)

Winner of Mobil Travel Guide's 5 Star Award for three straight years, Picasso is a Mediterranean-style restaurant featuring fine cuisine by Chef Julian Serrano. Adding to the atmosphere is a priceless collection of original Picasso artwork.

Renoir (The Mirage)

This is Las Vegas' other Mobil 5 Star Award winner, with another priceless art collection from French impressionist Renoir. Chef Alessandro Stratta features contemporary French cuisine, including seasonal products available in signature dishes.

Delmonico Steakhouse (The Venetian)

Celebrity TV chef Emeril Lagasse owns and operates Delmonico, creating a New Orleans-style cuisine. The restaurant's décor includes 12-foot oak doors, vaulted ceilings and a grand piano.

Postrio (The Venetian)

One of several Wolfgang Puck restaurants in Las Vegas, Postrio features contemporary American cuisine, from steak to lobster. The elegant dining room also showcases its wine list.

808 (Caesars Palace)

Hawaiian and Euro-Pacific cuisine is on the menu at Caesar Palace's 808 Restaurant. Chef Wesley Coffel also features luscious desserts, combining tropical fruits, ice cream, and sweets.

Emeril's (MGM Grand)

Another award-winning restaurant from celebrity chef Emeril Lagasse, Emeril's serves modern Creole/Cajun cuisine that includes fresh meat and produce from around the country. A seafood bar is featured.

Eiffel Tower Restaurant (Paris Las Vegas)

A panoramic view from far above the Strip is the drawing card for Paris Las Vegas' signature restaurant. The menu is, of course, classic French cuisine.

Gallagher's Steakhouse (New York New York)

One of New York's finest steakhouses, in business since 1927, is recreated at Las Vegas' version of New York City. The menu at Gallagher's featured prime beef as well as seafood.

Bamboleo (Rio)

Exotic flavors of Mexico, Brazil and Argentina are in the spotlight at Rio's Bamboleo. And don't miss the Wine Cellar & Tasting Room, which has 45,000 bottles of wine to choose from.

Top of the World (Stratosphere)

Taking the top prize in the romantic restaurant category is the Top of the World restaurant. Seafood, steaks and pasta are served while the restaurant revolves high atop the Stratosphere, 800 feet above the Strip.

Park Place Entertainment

Films Capture Vegas' Flavor And Flair

1. "Ocean's Eleven" (1960), Frank Sinatra, Dean Martin, Sammy Davis Jr., Angie Dickinson, Peter Lawford. The "Rat Pack" classic about a gang of friends who plan a heist of five Las Vegas casinos on the same night. Watch for other stars in minor roles. The pack worked on the movie during the day and entertained at night. Remade in 2001 with George Clooney, Julia Roberts, et al. The remake may be better but it's fun seeing some of the people who made Vegas Vegas.

2. "Bugsy" (1991), Warren Beatty, Annette Bening, Harvey Keitel. The story of gangster Benjamin "Bugsy" Siegel and his 1940s dream of building a casino in the desert of Las Vegas.

3. "Casino" (1995), Robert De Niro, Joe Pesci, Sharon Stone, James Woods, Don Rickles, Alan King. The story of the rise and fall of the mob's influence in Las Vegas. De Niro is casino boss Sam Rothstein and Stone is Ginger, his money-grubbing wife.

4. "Viva Las Vegas" (1963), Elvis Presley, Ann-Margret, William Demarest. What would Vegas be without "The King"? Elvis is a race car driver in this one who needs money to drive in the upcoming Las Vegas Grand Prix. Ann-Margret is the love interest.

5. "Leaving Las Vegas" (1995), Nicolas Cage, Elisabeth Shue, Julian Sands. Not the best Vegas settings, but possibly the best Vegas movie. Cage cannot cure his drinking and goes to Las Vegas to drink himself to death. Shue is a hooker who befriends Cage's character.

6. "Honeymoon in Vegas" (1992),

James Caan, Nicolas Cage, Sarah Jessica Parker. The unsuspecting Cage loses his fiancé (Parker) in a high-stakes poker game with Caan, who cheats to win. Cage manages to get his fiancé back after escapades that include jumping from a plane with a group called "The Flying Elvises."

7. "Vegas Vacation" (1996), Chevy

Chase, Beverly D'Angelo, Randy Quaid, Wayne Newton. The hapless Clark Griswold (Chase) blows the family's vacation money while his family members are off on various misadventures. Ellen Griswold (D'Angelo) is infatuated with "Mr. Vegas" Wayne Newton.

8. "Indecent Proposal" (1993), Robert

Redford, Demi Moore, Woody Harrelson. Rich playboy (Redford) makes an incredible offer to a couple that is down on its luck. He will pay the couple (Moore and Harrelson) $1 million if he can spend a night with Moore.

9. "Mars Attacks" (1996), Jack Nicholson,

Glenn Close, Martin Short, Pierce Brosnan, Jim Brown, Sarah Jessica Parker. Critics pretty much hated this one, but you're headed to Vegas not a film festival. Nicholson plays President Dale and also Art Land, a colorful Vegas developer. Martians are attacking Vegas and everywhere else. A funny twist kills them off.

10. "Honey, I Blew Up the Kid"

(1992), Rick Moranis, Marcia Strassman, Lloyd Bridges. Disney sequel to "Honey, I Shrunk the Kids." Inventor Moranis reverses his shrinking process and blows up a 2-year-old to more than 100-feet tall. The giant toddler proceeds to create chaos in Vegas.

— Craig Cooper

Indian Gaming Hits Jackpot

❚ *Pioneer Casino Continues to Pay Off for Oneida Tribe*

By Sean Schultz

A 200-seat bingo hall opened in Oneida, Wis., in 1976 by some women from the Oneida Tribe of Indians launching the tribe on its path to becoming the first Indian casino gaming center in Wisconsin and a model among Native American tribes engaged in gaming in the United States.

Today, the Oneida casino operation is the fourth largest in the nation and still a model for others. And that 200-seat bingo hall? It has given way to three casino locations that in 2001 drew more than 7.6 million people to try their hands at bingo, slot machines, and blackjack.

An average of 22,000 people a day travel to the Oneida casino centers, arriving by car or in the capable hands of the tour operators who show up each day with as many as 25 busloads of people, all with gambling on their minds.

Each of the three casinos has its own appeal, according to Eric McLester, interim gaming general manager for the tribe. The Oneida Casino adjacent to the ever-expanding, 300-plus room Radisson Hotel is the tribe's showcase with its 1,300 slot machines and 115,000 square feet. This is where the high rollers meet to make top bets of $200 in blackjack and where one lucky farm couple from Wisconsin hit the jackpot, taking $4 million from the Totem Pole progressive slot machine game a couple years back. This casino is the glittering star among the Oneidas' tourist attractions.

Oneida Casino

Players hit it big at one of 1,300 slot machines at the Oneida casino.

The Pavilion Nights series brings top-flight entertainment to the Oneida casino.

Players mark their cards at the Oneida bingo hall, the tribe's original game that opened in 1976 near Green Bay and has been the foundation of the tribe's success.

A half-block away on this Oneida Reservation property on the outskirts of Green Bay sits the original home of Indian gaming in Wisconsin, The Irene Moore Activity Center. It boasts 1,000 slot machines, plus blackjack and bingo games that seem to run continuously. It attracts "an older crowd because of the bingo," McLester said. "It's not as fast-paced as the main casino or the one on Mason Street."

A few miles away, on a more urban parcel of reservation property, the newest casino keeps perking all night long on one of Green Bay's main streets, just a block from the local Wal-Mart and Sam's Club stores and a quarter-mile from the technical college. Bright lights inside lead the way to 750 slot machines. Here, in 30,000 square feet, McLester said, "we cater to our local and loyal customers."

Gamblers are drawn by favorable odds and the chance to experience the thrill of Las Vegas in their own backyards.

The Oneidas are on to a good thing for themselves, the reservation and the surrounding communities that benefit from the surge in tourism and employment. But they haven't become a big draw by accident. The tribe and its management teams and staff work hard to ensure they keep customers satisfied at the casinos and keep them coming back for more.

And they do come back. Casino management knows it, because they track their customers — whether they come by bus or by car, stay an hour or all weekend, play bingo, blackjack or everything the house has to offer.

Oneida Casino

Players at the Oneida bingo hall enjoy the thrill of victory.

Oneida Casino

A dealer "hits" blackjack players with more cards in their effort to total 21 and beat the house.

> **Gamblers are drawn by favorable odds and the chance to experience the thrill of Las Vegas in their own backyards.**

Oneida Numbers:

Number of gaming employees: 1,482 (12/01)
Number of Oneida-enrolled gaming employees: 592 (39.9 percent)
Number of visitors to Oneida casinos in 2001: 7,665,470
Number of slot machines at Oneida casinos: 3,360
Average number of blackjack players per day: 450
Bingo hours: 10 a.m. and 6 p.m. Monday-Friday; 10 a.m. and 5 p.m. Saturday and Sunday; 10 p.m.
    Nite Owls Fridays; 9 p.m. Nite Owls Saturday and Sunday
Slot and video hours: 24 hours daily, seven days a week
Blackjack hours: 10 a.m. to 4 a.m. daily

Sources: National Indian Gaming Association Resource Library and Oneida Bingo & Casino

> *"We'll make it airy with plants and bright colors. We're responding to what our customers said."*
> *— Eric McLester*

Keeping pace despite tough economic times

McLester has worked for the casino for six years, more than two of them as assistant gaming manager before landing the top spot. He noted that all management positions must be held by a tribal member. Before that, he served on the other side of the tribe's gaming interest, the Oneida Gaming Commission. "It was from a regulatory perspective with the gaming commission," he said. "Now I'm looking at profitability and efficiencies throughout the operation, along with staying in compliance with audits and regulations."

Like the rest of the nation, Indian gaming was hit with the recession in 2001 that dragged on into 2002. "In the last 18 months the economy has certainly impacted our revenues," McLester said. "We had a major shortfall in revenues in 2001 ... We had to hold off on purchasing new machines and equipment and renovating."

Still, the casinos began Phase I of renovation efforts in the spring of 2002. "We're getting an overall facelift on the gaming floor at the main casino," he said. "We do it to stay competitive."

The casinos "have a glitzy Las Vegas look now," McLester added. That's on its way out. "There will be no midnight blue ceiling. This will brighten it up. We'll make it airy with plants and bright colors. We're responding to what our customers said. They don't like darkness. They want more lighting on the floor." He said Las Vegas casinos are heading in the same direction.

The renovation will be completed to coincide with the grand opening of the Radisson with its additions of rooms and an Expo Hall, a permanent venue for live entertainment that has boosted attendance at the hotel/casinos. The third season of Pavilion Nights entertainment was announced in the spring, with events scheduled May through September. Live music inside the main casino is part of the renovation plan, McLester said.

Get them in the door, and they'll come back

It is Carol Smith's task as in-house marketing manager to get Oneida customers in the door. She travels to state and national trade shows, as a member of the National Tour Association and Circle Wisconsin, to meet with hundreds of tour operators and interest them in making Oneida one of their stops.

"I tell them it's the classiest casino in Wisconsin," Smith said. "I build 'er up real good."

Those tour operators she doesn't meet in person solicit her by phone, mail, or fax. She sends out dozens of information packets a month, plus video tapes. Operators must apply and show proof of insurance to get the nod from Smith.

Green Bay, with its casinos, NFL football team, and other attractions, has become a mini-vacation destination, Smith added. "With Keshena and Bowler (casinos) being close, sometimes they do all three casinos in three days. And sometimes they go to the local attractions and Door County (a nearby Wisconsin resort area)."

A total of 3,360 slot machines are provided at three locations in the Green Bay area for Oneida customers.

Smith sees tour buses coming from Illinois, Minnesota, and northern Michigan, but they primarily come from within Wisconsin, plenty of them from Milwaukee just 110 miles away. "Seventy-five percent of the bus passengers return," she said. "Some tour operators come every day out of Milwaukee."

Offering discounts leads to data collection

She makes it worth their while before they even get off the buses, offering them discounted packages and membership in the tribe's Fun Club. The Fun Club not only gives casino visitors points to redeem for cash, food discounts, and Radisson stays, it also tracks them as they move through the casino system, from bus to casino and from game to game.

"It tells us how long they're here, how much they spend, and how much they use their cards," Smith said. "We can figure out the busiest times of the day and which tour operators give us the best customers."

Tribal dancing at the Oneida Nation Museum continues the proud traditions of the Oneidas.

But Oneida tracks more than that. Casino operators know that the majority of their patrons play the slot machines, but 35 to 45 percent try their hands at blackjack, too. Bingo games draw the middle-aged to elderly set, while blackjack has special allure for the men by a 70/30 split. "It's a man who has a competitive nature," said Frank Cornelius, table games director.

As casino traffic has grown, Smith said Oneida has become a model for other Indian gaming setups. "I meet all the time with other business managers from Native American casinos. We discuss the bad tours, the good tours. They're always interested in our program. They look to me for answers on things, on how we get so many buses."

On the job since 1986, she remembers when all she had to offer was bingo to seven or eight busloads of people a day, and still the gamblers came. Today, the tour operators apply to her for permission to bring their passengers, and the operators pay per person for the privilege.

Patrons are pleasantly surprised at the payback

It's probably not surprising that the tribe keeps adding new slot machines and varying promotions, McLester explained. With new technology comes video and reel slots so "there's that freshness," despite the fact that Indian gaming in Wisconsin is restricted to slots, bingo and blackjack, with no options to offer roulette or poker.

A spacious entryway to the Oneida Casino is just off the corridor to the tribe's Radisson Hotel.

But what may be surprising is the level of payout, the gamblers' favorite part of the action at Oneida casinos. "We have to stay competitive with others, and most casinos keep just 6 to 8 percent" of what customers slide into the slots, McLester said. "We're holding about 7 percent of the coin that goes into our machines."

Blackjack pays even higher dividends, according to Cornelius. "The payback of blackjack is 99.7 percent," he said. "It's a very marginal game for the house. Blackjack is the only game in the casino that can be mathematically beaten by the players. The machines are all set. That's why blackjack is the No. 1 game out there. If there's hope, people are going to play it. And believe me, we pay out."

Gamblers in the know prefer the odds at the Oneida casinos to playing the state lottery, which Cornelius said pays back just 45 to 55 percent.

Gaming compacts hammered out between the tribe and the state of Wisconsin a decade ago have hamstrung Indian gaming in many respects. Poker and roulette are not allowed in state casinos, and there are limits on the games that are allowed. At his blackjack tables, for instance, Cornelius' team of dealers can accept minimum bids of $3 and maximum bids of $200. The blackjack tables are only allowed to be open 16 hours a day. His 150 dealers shut down between 4 a.m. and 10 a.m. each day, "not because it's slow, but because we have to. We open the pits again at 10 a.m. and there will be 20 or 30 people waiting."

> *"The payback of blackjack is 99.7 percent. That's why blackjack is the No. 1 game out there."*
> *— Frank Cornelius*

Players take a chance at hitting 21 in a game of blackjack at the Oneida Casino, one of the nation's earliest Indian casinos.

A towering entryway greets visitors to the Oneida Casino, right across the street from the Green Bay airport.

The tribe's Radisson Hotel offers an inviting setting among tall trees in the Green Bay area.

Oneida works hard to keep customers happy

It's not just the payouts that keep gamblers coming to Oneida. It's the customer service, maintains Lucy Neville, customer relations director. "We're not a large department, but we're open 24 hours a day," she said. Her staff sees to valet parking and shuttle busing outside the casino. Shuttles not only go between the three casinos, but to other attractions in the area. During the football season, the casino offers fans a park and ride option, shuttling them to Lambeau Field to help them avoid the parking crush there.

Hospitality hosts serve the regular customers while executive hosts "cater to the high spenders," she said. Her goal is to "take customer service to a higher level," Neville said. "This area is fairly saturated with quite a few casinos you could go to if you're a real player. But we have regular crowds. We have the opportunity to build better relationships with our regular people."

Her staff has to be knowledgeable about what's available in the casinos, from timing of bingo games to what the different promotions are each week. "When customers want to know how to play the different games, people on the floor need to be knowledgeable about gaming."

Cornelius' area, for instance, offers tables for the novice at blackjack, a place to learn the game and the dealer-player etiquette that's involved. With the Phase I renovations will come a new player lounge for high stakes customers, "so they can get out of the casino action for awhile," Cornelius said.

Hospitality hosts circulate with soda carts, and see to coat check and special services for high stakes gamblers and the overall friendly atmosphere inside the casinos. No alcohol is served in the casinos, although Neville said offering near-beer products is under consideration and the hotel has restaurants and bars. Wardrobe services for her staff is another area Neville oversees. "We support the areas that generate income," Neville said. "We are truly the frontline for internal and external customers."

Just as they are in Las Vegas, "comps" are part of the game at Oneida. They may come in the form of the Fun Club free money options, the beverages that are distributed to players, or such things as meal discounts, free meals, or lodging at the Radisson.

For all phases of the casino operation, customers are surveyed. The Oneidas' operation routinely gets high marks from the gamblers who play money games there. "The biggest thing for customer satisfaction is a friendly dealer who genuinely cares if someone has a good time or not," Cornelius said.

'Mega-opportunity' for Native Americans

I *National Indian Gaming Association Unites U.S. Tribes*

By Sean Schultz

O ver the past decade, as Indian tribes turned to gaming as a solution to their members' economic problems, two Wisconsin men have led the way.

Of the 561 federally-recognized Indian tribes in the nation, 196 tribal governments are engaged in gaming. Two men, both from the Oneida Tribe of Indians in Green Bay, Wis., have taken their turn at the helm of the National Indian Gaming Association since 1992.

Ernie Stevens Jr. was elected chairman of NIGA, based in Washington, D.C., in April 2001. He took over where Rick Hill, immediate past president of NIGA, left off.

Hill, now 49, got involved in tribal government when he was just 23 years old. He served for 13 years on the Oneida Tribal Council. His father, Norbert Hill, "was in tribal government his whole life," Hill said. Hill was vice chairman of NIGA in 1992, then chairman from 1993 to April 2001.

Stevens, 42, said he and Hill have been longtime friends, as were their fathers. "Both Rick and I are the product of a long line of great leaders of the Oneida Nation," Stevens said. "We both had great role models growing up and I can only hope to be as strong and as effective as those leaders were. Those leaders helped to usher in Indian gaming and have helped make Oneida the success it is today."

NIGA

CASINO OF THE SUN
PASCUA YAQUI TRIBE

Rick Hill, left, and Ernie Stevens Jr., both of the Green Bay, Wis., area, are the past and current chairmen of the National Indian Gaming Association, which includes the 196 tribal governments involved in U.S. gambling operations.

"With the amount of money we have put into the state and local economy, we should be recognized as someone helping build tribal futures and small communities' futures."
— Ernie Stevens Jr.

National Indian Gaming Association

A Legislative and Public Policy Resource on Indian Gaming Issues and Tribal Community Development

He calls his father, Ernest Stevens Sr., "one of the many heroes of my life. My father was always an advocate for tribal sovereignty and economic development in Indian Country."

In interviews, Hill and Stevens offered their unique perspective on Indian gaming, the NIGA and the outlook for Native Americans in the United States:

Q. What is involved in chairing the NIGA?

RH: "Lots of fights, lots of meetings coast to coast. I have testified before Congress and other forums in local, state, and national disputes."

ES: "As chairman, my primary goal is to protect and preserve the general welfare of tribes striving for self-sufficiency through gaming enterprises in Indian Country. At NIGA, we work hard to protect tribal sovereignty, and to ensure that every tribal government has the opportunity to generate governmental revenue through gaming."

Q. In many cases the gaming compacts between states and tribes are short-term agreements. Is that a problem?

ES: "There are some compacts with longevity. There are some good ones out there. Wisconsin is not very good. It's hard to build our economy with that limited timeframe. You really can't build the future with that short window. With the amount of money we have put into the state and local economy, we should be recognized as someone helping build tribal futures and small communities' futures."

Q. How has Indian gaming helped the tribes?

RH: In Green Bay 15 years ago, he noted, "there was no major business doing business with the Indians. But lending institutions and the rest decided this is really viable. Now the Oneidas' industrial park has been able to attract Sam's Club, Wal-Mart, Festival Foods." Gaming "turned into a mega-opportunity. Of 557 recognized tribes, one-third of the Indian nations do gaming. But there is still a lot of poverty in Indian Country."

Hill was elected to the Gaming Hall of Fame in October 2001, "an acknowledgement of the work the tribes did," he said. "We created over 300,000 jobs, brought benefits for surrounding communities and got compacts in 24 states."

Q. During your tenure at NIGA, have you had to deal with organized crime's efforts to infiltrate Indian gaming?

RH: The Mob is not a factor in Indian gaming. "It's been reported several times in Congress: there is no infiltration of organized crime. If there are isolated instances, the tribe finds out about it and ends it."

And, he added, "Any business with cash flowing through it is going to be heavily regulated. Gaming operations are regulated by Indian gaming organizations, tribal, and state compact negotiation, the federal government, NIGA and the BIA (Bureau of Indian Affairs), the FBI and all the entities doing background checks."

ES: "An NIGA survey shows the tribes spend $150 million annually on regulating gaming. We give $30 million to the states and $8 million to the federal government for the National Indian Gaming Commission as well."

Q. Do the wealthy tribes help their struggling tribes' members?

RH: "If there's a need somewhere, other tribes help the struggling tribes quietly. These are the most giving people, probably the best neighbors. There are consortiums of tribes that put a bank together and do business opportunities."

Q. How does the Oneida Tribe's gaming operation in Green Bay compare to other Indian gaming in the nation?

RH: Oneida holds its own among the tribes, especially when you consider the state allows only slots, blackjack, and bingo. Some tribes are situated in more heavily populated areas, like San Diego and Arizona, where they have more traffic and different levels of income. Negotiating a full casino with roulette and poker rooms, high stakes rooms, compared to Oneida with pot lim-

Indian Gaming By the Numbers

Tribal governments in the U.S. engaged in gaming:	196
Number of tribal government gaming operations:	309
Number of states with tribal government gaming:	29
Number of tribal-state gaming compacts:	255
Total gaming revenue in 1999:	$9.6 billion
Total number of jobs:	200,000
National percentage of Indian to non-Indian employees:	75 percent non-Indian, 25 percent Indian

Source: National Indian Gaming Association Resource Library

its, Class 2 machines, not a full-blown Vegas casino. . . I'd still say in the mix with a number of tribes, we got out of the blocks earlier than a lot of people. We were a model and still are a model in a lot of ways with our projects and building infrastructure."

Q. Can Oneida remain competitive in Indian gaming with its compact limitations?

RH: "To remain competitive, we should offer more. It just makes economic sense to expand our scope and stay ahead of the market curve. Look at it from the business view to the political view. In California, the tribes are building strong relationships with local and state governments. It's beneficial to all concerned."

In Wisconsin, he added, "We would need a whole state referendum to get out of this box. It's a necessary thing to be considered."

ES: "It's about the ability to offer quality resources for people to utilize their recreational dollars," he said. With the limited gaming opportunities for Wisconsin Indian gaming, "it gets a little bit 'same old thing.' With more diversity in the games, we might be able to keep more people in our area. If Wisconsin or any of the states want to keep the dollars coming into our communities, they really have to look at that. I hope upcoming negotiations will look at that."

Q. What has the success of Indian gaming brought to the Oneida tribal members and to northeastern Wisconsin?

RH: "We're near a metropolitan community where the economy is stable and there are not a lot of entertainment opportunities. The tribe is growing. We're hoping for a golf course. . .we're developing all the amenities to be a full-service entertainment destination. That's complementary to everybody. The tax base is going up. Without the Indian nation, there would be unemployment. Now we offer competitive wages for people trained or at entry level.

"My parents had the federal relocation program. They moved to Detroit, dismantled the family. Now people are able to come home and work. The tribe has initiated a big sewer project and that works to protect the environment. We did a creative housing program, Dream, where a down payment on a house is not a must. We have the majority share of Bay Bank. We put a lot of money into the local banks and borrowed our own money back. We should take a page from the Jewish book in handling finances. Money stays in the community seven times before it leaves.

"The tribe needs a better land base and housing, a health center, expanded recreation, private sector and retail. Gaming proceeds help stimulate that. We couldn't leverage these things without gaming."

ES: "All throughout Indian Country there are tremendous leaders. Rick's Dad and my Dad were buddies, they worked together. . .We've been blessed to be able to be so entrusted. It's not an Oneida thing. It's good leaders, good elders, and determination."

Q. How does Indian gaming affect a state's tourism options?

RH: "When Wisconsin government is looking at a business plan, the biggest thing is tourism. The Indian community is a natural place for tourism from the top of the state down. It's a billion dollar industry and states should build strong relationships with the Indian nations. It's marketable around the world. Treat the nations as a strong asset."

Q. How does Indian gaming differ from Las Vegas gaming?

ES: "The major difference between Indian gaming and commercial gaming is how gaming revenues are spent. Federal law outlines very specific uses for Indian gaming revenues. Tribes must re-invest all gaming profits back into their communities for basic government functions. Tribal gaming revenues are being used to build and renovate communities that have been historically impoverished.

"On the other hand, profits from commercial gaming go right into the pockets of a few individual businesses."

Q. Do you believe the states where Indian gaming is not allowed should let their tribes bring in gaming?

RH: "The federal compact process hasn't been resolved yet for Oklahoma, Massachusetts, Texas, and Rhode Island. They're like the wild, wild West. They don't want to treat the Indian nations as governments and treat them in good faith.

"But they are sound-minded business people. They are now supporting the charities that used to help them. The tribes now have the opportunity to buy businesses, build industrial parks, do joint projects, do bonding for schools, and like middle America, have a fire department, police, schools, health care centers."

Gaming for the Oneidas, he said, "was God-sent. It brings all different walks of life together, we can educate and teach the real American history in a comfortable, safe environment.

"We built all the regulation processes before the government did. It's not perfect, but it gave a lot of hope to Indian communities across the land.

"In the past, tribes didn't have portfolios or opportunities to make investments themselves. Now we have meaningful employment and competitive wages. We made our own welfare to work program — took tribal men and other people in locations where people couldn't or didn't have jobs."

ES: "Indian gaming is opportunity. Native Americans have historically suffered from high levels of poverty and unemployment, poor health status and premature death, loss of language and culture, and lack of economic opportunities on Indian homelands. Indian gaming is helping Indian people to overcome many of these obstacles. The benefits of Indian gaming come in the form of improved infrastructure — roads, water, communication systems, public safety, schools, hospitals — and added governmental programs for Indian people. It provides tribes with capital which empowers them to diversify their economies. "Most tribes are still impoverished and still struggling to get back on their feet. . .It is my goal to see that every tribe in the nation has the opportunity to raise revenue for their communities either through gaming or some other enterprise. While Indian Country is making great strides, there is still plenty of work that needs to be done."

Q. What do you see for the future of Indian gaming and tribal/state relationships?

RH: "The future is bright. The Oneidas in New York are doing business there, and some are doing trade missions overseas. The states should include tribes as part of their trade missions. We bring culture and resources and tourism. We will see the tribes anywhere and everywhere because we have opportunities now. They're building an Indian museum in Washington, D.C., with a worldwide marketing theme to it.

"I hope for a stronger working relationship with governments and tribes. We can eliminate a lot of controversy. We all have the same goals — improving the quality of life for our members."

ES: "What the future entails is to continue to promote the integrity, continue to build and maintain the professionalism in Indian gaming. We have to help tribes who have limited or no gaming with their futures.

"We work very hard to educate the U.S. Congress, state legislators and the public, but we still face many challenges. . .We continue to assert that by law, tribes are the primary regulators of Indian gaming. . . . And, as always, we must be vigilant in our work to stop any attacks on tribal sovereignty by the U.S. Congress.

"We're starting to get there and we don't want anyone to impede the progress."

Part 2: Gambling Directory

How to use the Gambler's Digest Directory

Listings for gaming establishments include pertinent information for visitors, including address; phone numbers for local, toll-free, reservations and fax; games played and number of machines or tables where available; names of restaurants; size of casino; hotel rooms and rates; Web site and e-mail address; type of entertainment; and amenities, as current at press time.

State laws vary widely on the number and type of casino games and hours of play.

Hotel room rates are subject to change without notice; listings include the range of rates but it's best to check on special rates and room availability before arrival.

Entertainment listings include entertainers and shows that are currently appearing or have recently appeared at showrooms. Check with the establishment for a current entertainment schedule and for any changes in the schedule.

Information provided to Gambler's Digest about amenities such as buffets, 24-hour operation, and shopping at the site. Many casinos also have a players club or casino club that gives discounts or credits to customers who join the club. Details on club rules are available from the casinos.

ARIZONA

Apache Gold Casino Resort

U.S. Highway 70
P.O. Box 1210
San Carlos, AZ 85550
90 miles east of Phoenix
(800) APACHE-8
Fax: (928) 475-7692
CASINO@cybertrails.com
www.apachegoldcasinoresort.com
■ **Hotel:** 146 rooms
■ **Restaurant(s):** Wickiup Buffet, Apache Grill
Resort features 60-space RV park, 18-hole golf course, pool, convenience store, gift shop, convention center.
Live entertainment in the Cabaret Showroom.
■ **Games Available:** Keno, Race book, Poker, Slots - 500

BlueWater Resort and Casino

11300 Resort Drive
Parker, AZ 85344
On the Colorado River
(520) 669-7000
(888) 243-3360
www.bluewaterfun.com
■ **Hotel:** 200 rooms, $39-$119
■ **Restaurant(s):** Three restaurants: The River Willow, The Feast Buffet, River's Edge Cantina.
164-slip marina, beach, video arcade, miniature golf, indoor water slide, fitness center, 8,000 square foot conference center.
Variety of live concerts including Roy Clark and Hal Ketchum.
■ **Games Available:** Bingo, Poker - 6, Keno, Slots - 460

Bucky's Casino

1500 E. Highway 69
Prescott, AZ 86301
90 miles northwest of Phoenix

(800) SLOTS-44
info@buckyscasino.com
www.buckyscasino.com
Connected to Prescott Resort
■ **Restaurant(s):** Thumb Butte Room
■ **Games Available:** Keno, Slots - 300, Poker

Casino Arizona

101 and Indian Bend
101 and McKellips
Scottsdale, AZ 85256
Two locations in Scottsdale.
(480) 850-7734
www.casinoaz.com
■ **Restaurant(s):** Cholla Restaurant, The Eagle's Nest, The Blue Coyote Grill, Sopol Café, Salt River Café, Wandering Horse Café.
Showroom features entertainment six nights a week. Showstoppers Live, Arizona Room Piano Lounge.
■ **Games Available:** Bingo, Slots - 500, Keno - 40, Table games, Poker - 50

Casino of the Sun

7406 S. Casmino De Oreste Rd.
Tucson, AZ 85746
(520) 883-1700
(800) 344-9435
www.casinosun.com
■ **Games Available:** Bingo, Slots - 500

Cliff Castle Casino

555 Middle Verde Road
Camp Verde, AZ 86322
(800) 381-SLOT
www.cliffcastle.com
■ **Hotel:** 82 rooms

■ **Reservations:** (800) 524-6343
■ **Restaurant(s):** Storytellers, The Gallery, Bountiful Basket, Johnny Rockets.
Entertainers in the Stargazer Pavilion and Dragonfly Lounge.
■ **Games Available:** Bingo, Poker, Keno, Slots - 475

Cocopah Casino

Highway 95
Somerton, AZ 85350
(928) 627-2102
(800) 23SLOTS
www.wincocopah.com
■ **Games Available:** Bingo, Slots - 475

Desert Diamond Casino

I-19
Tucson, AZ 85734
(520) 294-7777
(866) DDC-WINS
www.desertdiamondcasino.com
■ **Restaurant(s):** Agave Restaurant
■ **Games Available:** Poker - 30, Slots - 500

Desert Diamond Casino Nogales

Nogales Highway
Tucson, AZ 85734
(520) 294-7777
(866) DDC-WINS
www.desertdiamondcasino.com
■ **Games Available:** Bingo, Slots - 500

Fort McDowell Casino

Fort McDowell Road
Fountain Hills, AZ 85269
(800) THE-FORT
www.fortmcdowellcasino.com

■ **Restaurant(s):** Red Rock Café, China Bistro, Casino Deli, Baja Food Court.
Live entertainment on weekends.
■ **Games Available:** ,Bingo, Poker, Keno, Race book, Slots - 475

Gila River Casino Vee Quiva

6443 N. Komatke Lane
Laveen, AZ 85339
(800) WIN-GILA
www.wingilariver.com
■ **Games Available:** Bingo, Slots - 500, Poker

Golden Hasan Casino

Highway 86
Why, AZ 85321
(520) 362-2746
www.desertdiamondcasino.com
■ **Games Available:** Slots

Harrah's Ak-Chin Casino Resort

15406 Maricopa Rd.
Maricopa, AZ 85239
Phoenix area
(480) 802-5000
www.harrahs.com/our_casinos/akc/index.html
■ **Hotel:** 146 rooms
40,000 square feet

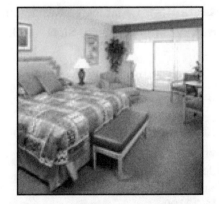

Harrah's Phoenix Ak-Chin Casino Resort features 142 premium rooms and four luxury suites, plus a courtyard and pool.

- **Reservations:** (800) HARRAHS
- **Restaurant(s):** Harvest Buffet, The Range Steakhouse, Agave's Southwestern Restaurant, Munchies Snack Bar.

Gift shop, health club, outdoor pool, business services.

Live entertainment in Oasis Lounge. Concerts held frequently.
- **Games Available:** Bingo, Poker, Keno, Slots - 475

Hon-Dah Casino Resort

777 Highway 260
Pinetop, AZ 85935
(928) 369-0299
(800) WAY-UP-HI
www.hon-dah.com
- **Hotel:** 128 rooms, $79-$99
- **Restaurant(s):** Indian Pines Restaurant.

Resort includes a 200-space RV park and a convenience store.

Entertainment Tuesdays through Sundays.
- **Games Available:** Poker, Slots - 500

Mazatzal Casino

P.O. Box 1820
Payson, AZ 85547
(800) 777-PLAY
www.777play.com
38,000 square feet
- **Restaurant(s):** Cedar Ridge Restaurant
- **Games Available:** Bingo, Slots - 400, Keno

Barona Casino

1000 Wildcat Canyon Rd.
Lakeside, CA 92040
Near San Diego
(619) 443-2300
www.barona.com

- **Restaurant(s):** Buffet, 'Iipay Corner Café, food court.

Barona was completing work in 2002 on a $225 million expansion including a new casino, resort hotel, wedding chapel, and 18-hole golf course, the Barona Creek Golf Club. Casino has 32 table games.
- **Games Available:** 3-card poker, Let It Ride, Blackjack, Pai Gow, Slots - 2000

Paradise Casino

450 Quechan Drive
Yuma, AZ 85366
(888) 777-4946
www.paradisecasinoyuma.com
- **Restaurant(s):** Seahorse Restaurant

Entertainers include Leann Rimes, Kenny Rogers, B.B. King, Little Richard, Willie Nelson.
- **Games Available:** Bingo, Poker, Keno, Slots - 500

Wild Horse Pass Casino

5550 Wild Horse Road
P.O. Box 6790
Chandler, AZ 85246
800-WIN-GILA
www.wingilariver.com
- **Games Available:** Bingo, Poker, Keno, Slots - 500

Yavapai Casino

P.O. Box 10190
Prescott, AZ 86301
(800) SLOTS-44
www.buckyscasino.com
- **Games Available:** Bingo, Slots - 175, Poker

CALIFORNIA

Cache Creek Indian Bingo and Casino

14455 Highway 16
Brooks, CA 95606
Near Sacramento
(530) 796-3118
(800) 452-8181
www.cachecreek.com
■ **Restaurant(s):** Creekside, China Camp, Wintun Lounge.
■ **Games Available:** Bingo, Pai Gow, Blackjack, Poker, Slots

Cahuilla Creek Casino

52702 Highway 371
Anza, CA 92539
(909) 763-1200
Live bands and karaoke
www.cahuilla.com
■ **Games Available:** Blackjack, Slots

California Grand Casino

5867 Pacheco Blvd.
Pacheco, CA 94553
(925) 685-8397
Fax: (925) 686-6596
www.calgrandcasino.com
■ **Games Available:** Blackjack, Poker, Pai Gow

Casino Morongo

49750 Seminole Drive
Cabazon, CA 92230
20 miles west of Palm Springs
(800) 252-4499
www.casinomorongo.com
■ **Restaurant(s):** Café Serrano, West End Café.
■ **Games Available:** Blackjack, Let It Ride, Mini-baccarat, Poker, Slots - 2000, Bingo

Casino Pauma

777 Pauma Reservation Road
Pauma Valley, CA 92061
North of San Diego
(760) 742-2177
Fax: (760) 742-2438
www.casinopauma.com
35,000 square feet
■ **Restaurant(s):** Pauma Bay Café
Casino opened in May 2001 and has 24 table games.
■ **Games Available:** 3-card poker, Blackjack, Let It Ride, Pai Gow, Poker, Slots - 850

Outdoor seating on the patio is available at the Pauma Bay Café at the Casino Pauma.

Cher-Ae Heights Casino

27 Cher-Ae Lane
Trinidad, CA 95570
(707) 677-3611
(800) 684-2464
www.cher-ae-heights-casino.com
■ **Games Available:** Bingo, Poker, Slots

Chicken Ranch Casino

16929 Chicken Ranch Road
Jamestown, CA 95327
(209) 984-3000
■ **Games Available:** Bingo, Slots - 270

Chumash Casino

3400 East Highway 246
Santa Ynez, CA 93460
35 minutes from Santa Barbara
(800) 728-9997
www.chumashcasino.com
73,000 square feet
■ **Restaurant(s):** Chumash Café
■ **Games Available:** 3-card poker - 1, Bingo, Blackjack - 24, Let It Ride - 1, Poker - 8, Slots - 2000

Club One Casino

1033 Van Ness Ave.
Fresno, CA 93721
Downtown Fresno
(559) 497-3000
clubone@gnis.net
■ **Hotel:** 300 rooms, $25
■ **Restaurant(s):** Asian-American menu, open 24 hours a day.
Daily and weekly poker tournaments. Horse racing book.
Showroom events.
■ **Games Available:** Blackjack $5, Poker - 35

Colusa Casino

3770 Highway 45
Colusa, CA 95932
(530) 458-8844
www.colusacasino.com
50,000 square feet
■ **Restaurant(s):** Jack's Bar & Grille
■ **Games Available:** Bingo, Blackjack, Pai Gow, Poker, Slots - 500

Commerce Casino

6131 East Telegraph Rd.
Commerce, CA 90040
Five minutes from downtown Los Angeles
(323) 721-2100
Fax: (323) 838-3472
cust-service@commercecasino.net
www.commercecasino.com

■ 200 rooms
■ **Restaurant(s):** California Grill, Las Vegas Buffet, New York Deli, Tropical Snack Bar, Sushi Bar.
Crowne Plaza Hotel, which opened in the fall of 2001, has health and fitness facility, retail stores and restaurants, more than 20,000 square feet of meeting space. Casino has 250 table games and features poker tournaments.
Players Lounge features live entertainment.
■ **Games Available:** Blackjack, Pai Gow, Poker

Crystal Park Casino Hotel

123 E. Artesia Blvd.
Compton, CA 90220
Five miles from Los Angeles; five miles from Long Beach
(310) 631-3838
(800) 717-1000
admin@crystalparkcasino.com
www.crystalparkcasino.com
■ **Hotel:** 236 rooms, $49-$299
Banquet rooms, gift shop, workout room, pool tables, arcade games.
Variety, including comedy clubs, night clubs, karaoke, concerts, special events.
■ **Games Available:** Blackjack - 13, Pai Gow, Poker - 12

Crystal Park Casino Hotel in Los Angeles sports a modern look.

Fantasy Springs Casino

84-245 Indio Springs Parkway
Indio, CA 92203
(760) 342-5000
(800) 827-2WIN
www.fantasyspringsresort.com

■ **Restaurant(s):** Players Fine Dining, Fantasy Bar & Grille.

Bowling center available. Off-track betting available.

■ **Games Available:** 3-card poker, Bingo, Blackjack, Let It Ride, Poker - 9, Race book, Slots - 1150

Feather Falls Casino

3 Alverda Drive
Oroville, CA 95966
(530) 533-3885
(877) 652-4646
www.featherfallscasino.com

■ **Restaurant(s):** Village Restaurant

Showroom entertainment includes Willie Nelson, Glen Miller Orchestra, boxing. Live entertainment on weekends.

■ **Games Available:** Blackjack - 8, Slots - 1000

Gold Country Casino

4020 Olive Highway
Oroville, CA 95966
(530) 538-4560
(800) 334-9400
www.gold-country-casino.com

■ **Restaurant(s):** Hungry Bear Restaurant

A bowling center is available.

Showroom features entertainers including Sawyer Brown, Alan Jackson, the Temptations.

■ **Games Available:** Bingo, Blackjack - 8, Let It Ride - 1, Pai Gow - 1, Poker - 4, Slots

Havasu Landing Resort and Casino

P.O. Box 1707
Havasu Lake, CA 92363
(800) 307-3610

Resort includes a marina, RV Park and Campground, air strip, hunting and fishing guides.
www.havasulanding.com

■ **Games Available:** Slots

Hollywood Park Casino

3883 W. Century Blvd.
Inglewood, CA 90303
Five miles from Los Angeles
(310) 330-2800
(800) 888-4972
casinoinfo@playhpc.com
www.playhpc.com

■ **Restaurant(s):** Citation Restaurant, Deli Derby.

Banquet rooms, gift shop, 24-hour health club and massage center, pool tables, arcade games. Bingo hall has 1,000 seats.

Weekly entertainment includes jazz, comedy, karaoke, and special events.

■ **Games Available:** Bingo, Blackjack - 40, Pai Gow, Poker - 80

Hopland Sho-Ka-Wah Casino

13101 Nakonas Rd.
Hopland, CA 95449
(707) 744-1395

■ **Restaurant(s):** Iris Steakhouse, Deli

Plans are in the works to build a new 200-room hotel and a new casino. Casino has 15 table games.
Comedy Café.

■ **Games Available:** Blackjack, Pai Gow, Slots - 800

Jackson Rancheria

12222 New York Ranch Road
Jackson, CA 95642
East of Sacramento
(209) 223-1677
(800) 822-WINN
www.jacksoncasino.com

■ **Hotel:** 102 rooms, $59-up

n Restaurant(s): Raging River Restaurant, Indian Star Café, Gary's Grand Buffets.

Hotel includes pool, two spas, salon, exercise room and a conference center. Casino has 33 table games.

Dalton Town Hall hosts entertainers including Bill Cosby, Huey Lewis, Merle Haggard, Tim Conway.

■ **Games Available:** 3-card poker, Blackjack, Let It Ride, Pai Gow, Slots - 900

Kelly's

408 O St.
Antioch, CA 94500
35 miles east of San Francisco
(925) 757-7120

■ **Restaurant(s):** Continental menu
■ **Games Available:** Blackjack $2 - 2, Pai Gow, Poker - 3

Konocti Vista Casino

2755 Mission Rancheria
Lakeport, CA 95453
(800) FUN-1950
www.kvcasino.com

■ **Restaurant(s):** Checkers Diner
■ **Games Available:** Blackjack, Let It Ride, Pai Gow, Slots

Lucky 7 Casino

350 North Indian Road
Smith River, CA 95567
(866) 777-7170
Fax: (707) 487-5007
www.lucky7casino.com

■ **Restaurant(s):** House of Howonquet
■ **Games Available:** Bingo, Blackjack, Slots - 250

Mono Wind Casino

37302 Rancheria Lane
Auberry, CA 93602
(559) 855-4350

www.monowind.com
■ **Restaurant(s):** Broken Arrow, Trails End Steakhouse
Casino has 10 table games.
■ **Games Available:** Blackjack, Let It Ride, Pai Gow, Slots - 315, Spanish 21

Old Cayucos Tavern and Card Room

130 N. Ocean Ave.
Cayucos, CA 93430
16 miles to San Luis Obispo
(805) 995-3209
(805) 995-2297
Pool tables, video games, golf course.
Live bands
■ **Games Available:** Poker - 2

Pala Casino

12194 Pala Mission
Pala, CA 92059
(877) WIN-PALA
guestservices@palacasino.com
www.palacasino.com

■ **Restaurant(s):** Oak Room, Terrace Buffet, Pala Café, The Deli.
Casino has 50 table games.
Concerts in the Events Center and entertainment in the lounges.
■ **Games Available:** Blackjack, Let It Ride, Mini-baccarat, Pai Gow, Poker, Slots - 2000

A drawing shows the casino at Pala Casino.

Palace Indian Gaming Center

17225 Jersey Ave.
Lemoore, CA 93245
South of Fresno
(559) 924-7751
www.thepalace.net
■ **Restaurant(s):** Sierra Grille
Casino has 26 table games.
■ **Games Available:** Bingo, Blackjack, Let It Ride, Pai Gow, Poker, Slots

Pechanga Entertainment Center

45000 Pala Road
Temecula, CA 92592
45 minutes from San Diego
(888) PECHANGA
info@pechanga.com
www.pechanga.com
100,000 square feet
■ **Restaurant(s):** Pechanga Café, Kelsey's Steakhouse.
A new 522-room hotel opened in mid-2002, featuring seven restaurants, a new showroom and more casino space.
Showroom concerts include Chubby Checker and The Temptations. Live entertainment is featured in the Monte Carlo Lounge.
■ **Games Available:** Bingo, Blackjack - 37   , Poker - 13, Slots - 2000

Rincon Casino

P.O. Box 217
Pauma Valley, CA 92061
(760) 751-3100
www.harrahs.com
The Rincon Band and its partner, Harrah's, began construction in 2001 on a new $125 million casino and hotel, which was expected to open in the fourth quarter of 2002.
■ **Games Available:** Slots - 750

Robinson Rancheria Casino

1545 E. Highway 20
Nice, CA 95464
(707) 275-9000
(800) 809-3636
www.robinsonrancheria.biz
■ **Games Available:** Bingo, Poker, Slots - 380, Blackjack

San Manuel Indian Bingo and Casino

5797 N. Victoria Ave.
Highland, CA 92346
(800) 359-2464
www.sanmanuel.com
Shows include Bad Company, Julio Iglesias, Willie Nelson.
■ **Games Available:** Bingo, Blackjack, Poker, Slots - 2000

Soboba Casino

23333 Soboba Road
San Jacinto, CA 92583
(909) 654-2883
(888) 772-7626
Fax: (909) 654-5844
soboba@soboba.net
www.soboba.net
Casino has added 26,000 square feet and hundreds of slot machines.
Concerts at outdoor venue, boxing and wrestling are featured.
■ **Games Available:** Bingo, Blackjack, Poker, Slots - 2000

Spa Resort Casino

100 N. Indian Canyon Drive
Palm Springs, CA 92262
(800) 258-2946
■ **Hotel:** 230 rooms
■ **Reservations:** (800) 854-1279
222.sparesortcasino.com
■ **Restaurant(s):** The Steakhouse at The Spa, Agua Bar and Grill.

Resort has a spa, outdoor pool, solarium, fitness center. There is access to two local golf courses. Outdoor arena features Styx, Joan Jett, Pat Benatar, boxing matches.

■ **Games Available:** Blackjack, Pai Gow, Poker, Slots - 1000

Sycuan Casino & Resort

5469 Casino Way
El Cajon, CA 92019
San Diego area
(619) 445-6002
(800) 2-SYCUAN
www.sycuancasino.com
305,000 square feet

■ **Restaurant(s):** Paipa's Oasis Buffet, Wachena Falls Café, Pearls of the Sea, Turf Club, Sunset Deli.

Singing Hills Resort has two 18-hole courses, 11 tennis courts. Casino has 60 table games.

Showcase Theater opened in 2002.

■ **Games Available:** Baccarat, Bingo, Blackjack, Pai Gow, Poker, Race book, Slots

Table Mountain Casino

P.O. Box 445
Friant, CA 93626
(559) 822-2485
(800) 541-3637
www.tmcasino.com

■ **Restaurant(s):** Eagles Landing Restaurant

■ **Games Available:** Bingo, Pai Gow, Blackjack, Poker - 9, Slots - 2000, Let It Ride

Trump 29 Casino

46-200 Harrison Place
Coachella, CA 92236
(760) 775-5566
www.spotlight29casino.com

■ **Restaurant(s):** 29 Palms Café

A $60 million expansion was under way in 2002 to include a 200-room hotel, a showroom, and a casino addition.

Live bands in the Casablanca Lounge.

■ **Games Available:** 3-card poker, Blackjack $2, Let It Ride, Pai Gow, Slots - 1400

The Trump 29 Casino, formerly Spotlight 29, opened in 2002 in Coachella, Calif., offering new gaming, dining, and entertainment opportunities

Twin Pine Casino

22223 Hwy. 29
Middletown, CA 95461
(707) 987-0197
(800) 564-4872
Fax: (707) 987-0375
info@twinpine.com
www.twinpine.com

■ **Games Available:** Blackjack, Pai Gow, Slots

Valley View Casino

16300 Nyemii Pass Rd.
Valley Center, CA 92082
(866) 726-7277
info@valleyviewcasino.com
valleyviewcasino.com

■ **Restaurant(s):** Market Square Buffet, Café De View.

■ **Games Available:** 3-card poker, Blackjack, Slots - 750

Viejas Casino

5000 Willows Road
Alpine, CA 91901
30 miles from downtown San Diego
(619) 445-5400
(800) 84-POKER
www.viejas.com
255,000 square feet

■ **Restaurant(s):** Five restaurants: Harvest Buffet; Grove Steakhouse; Sunrise Diner; Mezz Deli and Lounge; China Camp Express.

There are 57 stores and eateries; discounts available at nearby Country Inn Hotel.

National acts including Hootie and the Blowfish, Gregg Allman, Dwight Yoakum.

■ **Games Available:** Bingo - 1500, Blackjack $3-$3,000 - 35, Off-track Horse Book, Pai Gow - 16, Poker, Slots $1 - 330, Slots $100 - 2, Slots $25 - 2, Slots $5 - 23, Slots Multiple Denom - 140, Slots Nickel - 701, Slots Quarter - 802

Win-River Casino Bingo

2100 Redding Rancheria Rd.
Redding, CA 96001
(800) 280-UWIN
info@win-river.com
www.win-river.com
25,000 square feet

Hilton Garden Inn, with 96 rooms, was scheduled to open in September 2002, along with 50,000 square feet of additional gaming area.

■ **Games Available:** 3-card poker, Bingo, Blackjack, Let It Ride, Slots - 700

A 96-room Hilton Garden Inn and an additional 50,000 square feet of casino and restaurant space comprised the addition at Win-River Casino in California.

COLORADO

Black Diamond Casino

425 E. Bennett Ave.
Cripple Creek, CO 80813
45 miles from Colorado Springs
(719) 689-2898
Fax: (719) 689-3988
■ **Restaurant(s):** Snack Bar
■ **Games Available:** Slots $1 - 13, Slots Nickel - 36, Slots Quarter - 51

Black Hawk Casino by Hyatt

111 Richman St.
Black Hawk, CO 80422
(303) 567-1234
www.blackhawkcasinobyhyatt.com
55,000 square feet
■ **Restaurant(s):** Kitchens of the World Action Buffet, Hickory Grill Restaurant, Starbucks.
The largest casino in Colorado opened in December 2001 and a hotel is planned. Casino has 22 table games.
Wild Fire Entertainment Lounge.
■ **Games Available:** Blackjack - 16, Poker - 6, Slots - 1332, Video poker

The new Black Hawk Casino By Hyatt is stocked with 1,332 slots, 16 blackjack tables and six poker tables.

Black Hawk Station

141 Gregory St.
Black Hawk, CO 80422
(303) 582-5582
■ **Games Available:** Blackjack, Slots

Brass Ass Casino

264. E. Bennett Ave.
Cripple Creek, CO 80813
(719) 689-2104
Fax: (719) 689-3399
www.midnightrose.com
■ **Games Available:** Slots

Bronco Billy's Casino

233 Bennett Ave.
Cripple Creek, CO 80813
(719) 689-2142
Fax: (719) 689-2869
■ **Restaurant(s):** Home Café, The Steakhouse.
■ **Games Available:** Blackjack, Slots - 600

Bull Durham Casino

P.O. Box 486
Black Hawk, CO 80422
(303) 582-0810
■ **Games Available:** Blackjack - 6, Poker - 1, Slots - 144

Colorado Central Station

340 Main St.
Black Hawk, CO 80422
(303) 279-3000
www.coloradocentralstation.com

Restaurant(s): Whistle Stop Buffet, Fire Box Grille.

Games Available: 3-card poker, Blackjack, Slots - 750

Colorado Grande Casino

300 E. Bennett Ave.
Cripple Creek, CO 80813
(719) 689-3517

Restaurant(s): Maggie's Restaurant

Games Available: Slots

Creeker's Casino

274 Bennett Ave.
Cripple Creek, CO 80813
(719) 689-3239

Games Available: Slots - 204

Doc Holliday Casino

101 Main St.
Central City, CO 80427
35 miles west of Denver
(303) 582-1400

Hotel: 4 rooms, $80-$120
14,000 square feet

Restaurant(s): Snack Bar open 10 a.m.-10 p.m.
Overall Payout: 94%

Games Available: Slots - 120

Double Eagle Casino

442 E. Bennett Ave.
Cripple Creek, CO 80813
One hour from Colorado Springs
(800) 711-7234
www.decasino.com

Hotel: 170 rooms

Restaurant(s): Lombard's Restaurant, Jackpot Deli.

Games Available: Blackjack, Let It Ride, Poker,   Slots - 600

Famous Bonanza Casino

107 Main St.
Central City, CO 80427
(303) 582-5914
Fax: (303) 582-0447
info@Famousbonanza.com
www.famousbonanza.com

Restaurant(s): Ponderosa Restaurant

Games Available: Blackjack, Slots

Fitzgeralds Casino Black Hawk

101 Main St.
Black Hawk, CO 80422
(800) 538-LUCK
www.fitzgeralds.com
27,000 square feet

Restaurant(s): Shamrock Café

Games Available: Blackjack - 6, Slots - 597

Gilpin Casino

111 Main St.
Black Hawk, CO 80422
(303) 582-1133
Fax: (303) 582-1154

Restaurant(s): Lucille Malone's, Jonathan's Restaurant.

Games Available: Slots - 470, Table games - 4

Gold Rush Hotel & Casino

209 E. Bennett Ave.
Cripple Creek, CO 80813
(719) 689-2646
(800) 235-8239

Hotel: 13 rooms, $59-$79

Restaurant(s): Grapevine Restaurant

Games Available: Blackjack, Poker, Slots - 284

Golden Gates Casino

261 Main St.
Black Hawk, CO 80422
20 miles west of Denver
(303) 277-1650
Bands
■ **Games Available:** Blackjack - 4, Slots - 264

Imperial Casino Hotel

123 N. 3rd St.
Cripple Creek, CO 80813
(719) 689-7777
(800) 235-2922
info@imperialcasinohotel.com
www.imperialcasinohotel.com
■ **Hotel:** 29 rooms, $55-up
■ **Restaurant(s):** Stratton's Grill, 3rd Street Deli.
■ **Games Available:** Slots

Isle of Capri Black Hawk

401 Main St.
Black Hawk, CO 80422
(800) THE-ISLE
www.isleofcapricasino.com/Black_Hawk/
■ **Hotel:** 236 rooms
■ **Restaurant(s):** Farraddays' Restaurant, Calypso's Buffet, Tradewinds Grill.
Casino has 12 table games.
Entertainers in Flamingo Bay Ballroom and Caribbean Cove.
■ **Games Available:** 3-card poker, Blackjack, Let It Ride, Slots - 1100

J.P. McGill's Hotel Casino

232 East Bennett Ave.
Cripple Creek, CO 80813
(719) 689-3955
(888) 461-7529
Fax: (719) 689-2911
www.midnightrose.com
■ **Hotel:** 37 rooms, $39-$110
■ **Restaurant(s):** JP's Grill
■ **Games Available:** Slots - 290

Johnny Nolon's Saloon

301 E. Bennett Ave.
Cripple Creek, CO 80813
(719) 689-2080
■ **Games Available:** Blackjack, Slots

Mardi Gras Casino

300 Main St.
Black Hawk, CO 80422
(303) 582-5600
www.mardigrasbh.com
68,000 square feet
■ **Restaurant(s):** Café Orleans
■ **Games Available:** Blackjack - 8, Slots - 700

Midnight Rose Hotel and Casino

256 East Bennett Ave.
Cripple Creek, CO 80813
(800) 635-5825
www.midnightrose.com
■ **Hotel:** 19 rooms, $39-$110
■ **Restaurant(s):** Midnight Rose Restaurant, Down Under Steakhouse.
■ **Games Available:** Blackjack, Poker , Slots - 400

Palace Hotel & Casino

Second and Bennett
Cripple Creek, CO 80813
(719) 689-2992
(800) 585-9329
www.palacehotelcasino.com
■ **Hotel:** 15 rooms, $49-$69
■ **Restaurant(s):** Guilded Cage Deli
■ **Games Available:** Slots - 74

Richman Casino

101 Richman St.
Black Hawk, CO 80422
(303) 271-0400
■ **Games Available:** Blackjack, Slots

Riviera Black Hawk

P.O. Box 9
Black Hawk, CO 80422
(303) 582-1000
www.theriviera.com/blackhawk
Restaurant(s): World's Fare Buffet, Pizza Hut.
Casino has 12 table games.
■ **Games Available:** Blackjack, Slots - 1000

Sky Ute Casino

P.O. Box 340
Ignacio, CO 81137
25 minutes from Durango
(970) 563-3000
(888) 842-4180
www.skyutecasino.com
■ **Reservations:** (800) 876-7017
■ **Restaurant(s):** Pino Nuche Restaurant,
Rolling Thunder Café.
Hotel available.
Concerts, boxing are offered.
■ **Games Available:** 3-card poker, Bingo,
Blackjack, Slots - 400

The Lodge Casino at Black Hawk

240 Main St.
Black Hawk, CO 80422
(303) 582-1771
Fax: (303) 582-0237
www.thelodgecasino.com
Hotel: 50 rooms
■ **Restaurant(s):** White Buffalo Grille, Seasons
Buffet, Jake's Deli.
Casino has 27 table games.
■ **Games Available:** Blackjack, Poker - 12,
Slots - 870

Ute Mountain Casino

3 Weeminuche Drive
Towaoc, CO 81334
(970) 565-8800
(800) 258-8007
Fax: (970) 565-6553

www.utemountaincasino.com
■ **Restaurant(s):** Kuchu's Restaurant
RV Park and Campground available.
■ **Games Available:** 3-card poker, Bingo,
Blackjack, Keno, Let It Ride, Poker, Slots - 500

Virgin Mule

269 E. Bennett Ave.
Cripple Creek, CO 80813
(719) 689-0930
■ **Games Available:** Slots

Womack's Saloon

210 E. Bennett Ave.
Cripple Creek, CO 80813
(719) 689-0333
■ **Games Available:** Blackjack, Poker , Slots

A couple is thrilled with their winnings from a slot machine at Womack's Saloon in historic Cripple Creek, Col.

Womacks Casino & Hotel in Cripple Creek maintains its old-time Main Street look.

CONNECTICUT

Foxwoods Resort

39 Norwich Westerly Rd.
Mashantucket, CT 06339
Between Hartford and Providence
(800) FOXWOODS
information@foxwoods.com
www.foxwoods.com
Hotel: 1400 rooms
315,000 square feet in six casinos

■ **Restaurant(s):** 24 restaurants: Paragon, Al Dente, Cedars Steak House, Fox Harbour, Han Garden, The Bistro, Festival Buffet, The Veranda, Branches at the Two Trees Inn, Intermezzo Lounge, Golden Dragon Café, Sports Bar, Rainmaker Café, Sidewalk Café, Garden Food Court

Hotels include the Grand Pequot Tower, Great Cedar Hotel, Two Trees Inn. More than a dozen stores are in 12,000 square foot shopping area. Salon, spa and pool are available and the Boulder Hill golf course has 18 holes. Casino has 350 table games.

The 4,000 seat Foxwoods Arena hosts entertainers including Luciano Pavarotti as well as boxing events and basketball. The Fox Theatre has hosted Frank Sinatra, Bill Cosby, Carrot Top, and Barry Manilow.

■ **Games Available:** Baccarat, Bingo, Blackjack Craps, Keno, Let It Ride, Pai Gow, Poker - 55, Race book, Roulette, Slots - 6400

Mohegan Sun

1 Mohegan Sun Blvd.
Uncasville, CT 06382
(860) 862-7163
(888) 226-7711
www.mohegansun.com
Hotel: 1200 rooms
300,000 square feet

■ **Restaurant(s):** Bamboo Forest, The Cove, The Longhouse, Michael Jordan's Steakhouse, Pompeii and Caesar, Rain, Todd English's Tuscany, Chief's Deli, Mohegan Territory, Seasons, Sunburst Buffet, Big Bubba's BBQ, Fidelia's, Jasper White's Summer Shack, Johnny Rockets,

A 1,200-room hotel opened in April 2002, along with a 10,000-seat arena, 300-seat Cabaret and a second 115,000 square foot casino. The resort also added 12 restaurants, 30 shops, the Body and Soul spa and fitness center, and 100,000 square feet of co

Entertainment in the new arena has included Janet Jackson, as well as basketball, Arena Football and boxing, while Phyllis Diller and Shirley Jones starred in the Cabaret.

■ **Games Available:** Blackjack, Craps , Keno Pai Gow, Poker , Race book, Roulette, Slots - 6100, Spanish 21

The plush Mohegan Sun offers more than 50 fine shops and boutiques, as well as a selection of restaurants, entertainment, and games.

FLORIDA

Brighton Seminole Bingo and Gaming

Route 6, Box 611
Okeechobee, FL 34974
(800) 360-9875
www.seminoletribe.com
■ **Games Available:** Bingo, Poker, Slots

Coconut Creek Casino

5550 NW 40th St.
Coconut Creek, FL 33073
(866) 2-CASINO
www.seminoletribe.com
■ **Games Available:** Bingo, Poker, Pull-tab games - 800

Miccosukee Indian Casino

500 SW 177th St.
Miami, FL 33194
(305) 925-2555
(877) 242-6464
www.miccosukee.com
■ **Hotel:** 302 rooms
■ **Restaurant(s):** Empeeke Aaweeke Buffet, Empeeke Aya Deli, Empeeke-Cheke.
Hotel includes indoor pool, spa, fitness center
■ **Games Available:** Bingo, Poker, Pull-tab games

Seminole Casino Hollywood

4150 North State Road 7
Hollywood, FL 33024
(866) 2-Casino
■ **Games Available:** Bingo, Poker - 48

Seminole Gaming Palace

5223 N. Orient Road
Tampa, FL 33610
(800) 282-7016
www.seminoletribe.com
■ **Games Available:** Bingo, Poker

Seminole Gaming Palace & Casino

506 S. First St.
Immokalee, FL 34142
(941) 658-1313
■ **Games Available:** Bingo, Poker, Pull-tab games

IDAHO

Clearwater River Casino

17500 Nez Perce Road
Lewiston, ID 83540
(208) 746-0723
(877) NP-TRIBE
info@crcasino.com
www.crcasino.com
RV Park with 33 spaces and 15 tent spaces, pool.
■ **Games Available:** Bingo, Slots - 400

Coeur D'Alene Casino

Highway 95
P.O. Box 236
Worley, ID 83876
(800) 523-2464
info@cdacasino.com
www.cdacasino.com
■ **Hotel:** 96 rooms
■ **Restaurant(s):** High Mountain Steakhouse,
High Mountain Grill, High Mountain Express.
Concerts and boxing are scheduled. Off-track betting is available.
■ **Games Available:** Bingo, Race book

It'Se Ye-Ye Casino

Highway 12
Kamiah, ID 83536
(208) 935-1638
www.crcasino.com
■**Games Available:** Bingo, Slots

Kootenai River Inn & Casino

Kootenai River Plaza, Hwy 95
Bonners Ferry, ID 83805
(208) 267-8511
(800) 346-5668
Fax: (208) 267-3744
www.kootenairiverinn.com
■ **Hotel:** 65 rooms, $75-up
■ **Games Available:** Slots

Shoshone Bannock Casino

I-15
P.O. Box 868
Fort Hall, ID 83203
(208) 237-8774
(800) 497-4231
www.sho-ban.com
■ **Games Available:** Bingo, Blackjack, Slots

Illinois, Indiana, Iowa just have riverboats

IOWA

Bluffs Run Casino

2701 23rd Ave.
Council Bluffs, IA 51501
(800) BET-2WIN
www.harrahs.com/our_casinos/hbr/index.html
■ **Restaurant(s):** Fireside Steakhouse, Grand Buffet, Winners Grill.
Free Show Lounge has live entertainment. Casino is connected to a greyhound track.
■ **Games Available:** Slots - 1500

Casino Omaha

1 Blackbird Bend
P.O. Box 89
Onawa, IA 51040
(712) 423-3700
(800) 858-8238
Overall Payout: 96%
■ **Games Available:** Blackjack $2 - 8 , Craps - 1, Poker - 3, Roulette - 1, Slots - 404

Meskwaki Bingo Casino Hotel

1504 305th St.
Tama, IA 52339
50 miles NE of Des Moines
(800) 728-GAME
(800) 728-GAME
www.Meskwaki.com
■ **Hotel:** 210 rooms, $59-$99
■ **Restaurant(s):** Three restaurants: Water's Edge Buffet; Dreamcatcher's Café; Garden Park Deli
Indoor pool, exercise area and whirlpool at hotel. Two Rivers Gift Shop.
Various entertainers, including Bill Cosby, Dwight Yokum, Brenda Lee, rodeos.
■ **Games Available:** Bingo, Blackjack $3-$1,000 - 12, Craps, Keno, Pai Gow, Poker - 10 Roulette, Slots 1 cent-$100 - 1400

Winnavegas Casino

1500 330th St.
Sloan, IA 51055
20 miles south of Sioux City
(712) 428-9466
(800) 468-WINN
■ **Hotel:** 53 rooms
www.winnavegas-casino.com
■ **Restaurant(s):** Flowers Island Restaurant & Buffet.
Lee Greenwood, Ray Price are among entertainers.
■**Games Available:** Bingo, Blackjack, Craps, Poker, Roulette, Slots - 600, Spanish 21

KANSAS

Golden Eagle Casino

1121 Goldfinch Road
Horton, KS 66439
(888) GO 4-LUC
www.goldeneaglecasino.com

Golden Eagle Showroom has entertainers including Mickey Gilley, Gary Puckett.

■ **Games Available:** Bingo, Blackjack, Craps, Let It Ride, Poker, Roulette, Slots

Harrah's Prairie Band

12305 150th Road
Mayetta, KS 66509
15 miles north of Topeka
(785) 966-7777
(800) 427-7247
www.harrahs.com/our_casinos/top/index.html

Hotel: 100 rooms

Restaurant(s): Fresh Market Square Buffet, Fresh Market Express.

Live entertainment in Prairie Pub Club.

■ **Games Available:** 3-card poker, Blackjack Craps, Let It Ride, Roulette, Slots - 900

Sac and Fox Casino

P.O. Box 105A
Powhattan, KS 66527
(913) 742-7438

Restaurant(s): Lodge Buffet, Chop House, Deli.

Casino has 10 table games.

■ **Games Available:** Blackjack, Craps, Let It Ride, Roulette, Slots - 448

LOUISIANA

Cypress Bayou Casino

832 Martin Luther King Road
Charenton, LA 70523
45 miles south of Lafayette
(318) 923-7284
(800) 284-4386
Fax: (318) 923-7882
www.cypressbayou.com
■ **Restaurant(s):** Mr. Lester's Steakhouse, Café Bayou.
■ **Games Available:** 3-card poker, Blackjack, Craps, Let It Ride, Poker, Roulette, Slots - 1200

Grand Casino Coushatta

777 Coushatta Drive
Kinder, LA 70648
Three hours from New Orleans, 2 1/2 hours from
  Houston
(337) 738-1370
(800) 58-GRAND
info@gccoushatta.com
www.gccoushatta.com
Hotel: 223 rooms
107,000 square feet
■ **Restaurant(s):** Six restaurants: Seven Clans Seafood and Steaks, Market Place Buffet, Big Sky Steakhouse, The Grill, Café Grande, Grand Circus of Slots Food Court.
Second hotel, the Coushatta Grand Inn, opened in 2002. RV Resort has 158 spaces and 50 chalets. Casino has 80 table games.
Concerts and performances in the Grand Pavilion
■ **Games Available:** Blackjack, Craps, Mini-baccarat, Poker - 12, Roulette, Slots - 3200

The 195-room Coushatta Grand Inn opened in 2002.

Harrah's New Orleans

512 S. Peters St.
New Orleans, LA 70130
(800) VIP-JAZZ
www.harrahs.com/our_casinos/nor/index.html
■ **Restaurant(s):** Magnolia Buffet, The Manor Room, Barataria Cove, Club Cappuccino.
Casino offers 125 table games.
Jazz Court features live music.
■ **Games Available:** Baccarat, Blackjack, Craps Poker - 20, Slots - 2900

Horseshoe Casino Hotel Bossier City

711 Horseshoe Blvd.
Bossier City, LA 71111
(318) 742-0711
(800) 895-0711
www.horseshoe.com
■ **Hotel:** 606 rooms
■ **Restaurant(s):** Jack Binion's Steak House, Four Winds Asian Restaurant, Village Square Buffet, Oak Creek Café & Grille.
Casino has 50 table games.
Entertainers include B.B. King, Loretta Lynn, Clint Black, Chicago.
■ **Games Available:** 3-card poker, Blackjack, Craps   Let It Ride, Mini-baccarat, Roulette, Slots - 1500

The 26-story Horseshoe Hotel has 606 suites.

Paragon Casino Resort

711 Paragon Place
Marksville, LA 71351
(800) 946-1946
www.grandcasinoavoyelles.com
Hotel: 270 rooms
74,000 square feet
Reservations: (800) 642-7777

Restaurant(s): Marceline's, Big Daddy E's, Roxy's Diner, Marketplace Buffet.

Resort, formerly called the Grand Casino Avoyelles, includes hotel, RV Park with 166 spaces and cabins and chalets as well as a conference center. Casino has 46 table games.

Entertainers in the Mari Center include Waylon Jennings, Sawyer Brown, Jeff Foxworthy.

■ **Games Available:** Blackjack, Craps, Let It Ride, Mini-baccarat, Pai Gow, Poker - 7, Roulette Slots - 2100

Check for more in Riverboats section.

MICHIGAN

Bay Mills Resort & Casinos

11386 West Lakeshore Drive
Brimley, MI 49715
Upper Peninsula of Michigan
(877) 229-6455
(888) 422-9645
www.4baymills.com
■ **Hotel:** 144 rooms, $45-up
Two casinos: Bay Mills and Kings Club
■ **Restaurant(s):** Back Bay Grill and Games, Chums Café, Sasy's Restaurant.
Hotel features a convention center and the Wild Bluff 18-hole golf course.
■ **Games Available:** Blackjack, Craps, Let It Ride, Roulette, Slots

Chip-In's Island Resort & Casino

W399 US2&41
Harris, MI 49845
(906) 466-2941
(800) 682-6040
info@chipincasino.com
www.chipincasino.com
■ **Hotel:** 113 rooms, $75-up
■ **Restaurant(s):** Firekeeper's Restaurant, Coral Reef Buffet, Snack Bar.
Hotel has a pool, salon, convention center, gift shop.
Headliners include Sawyer Brown, Cheap Trick, Gordon Lightfoot, Carrot Top.
■ **Games Available:** 3-card poker, Blackjack - 20, Craps - 2, Keno, Let It Ride - 2, Poker, Roulette, Slots - 970, Spanish 21

Greektown Casino

555 E. Lafayette Blvd.
Detroit, MI 48226
(866) 473-3581
greektowncasino.net

■ **Restaurant(s):** The Alley Grille
Entertainment in Trapper's and Apollo Lounge.
■ **Games Available:** Blackjack, Craps, Let It Ride, Mini-baccarat, Roulette, Slots

Greektown Casino is in the heart of downtown Detroit.

Kewadin Casino Christmas

N7761 Candy Cane Lane
Christmas, MI 49862
(800) 539-2346
(800) KEWADIN
www.kewadin.com
■ **Restaurant(s):** Frosty's Bar and Grill.
■ **Games Available:** Blackjack, Let It Ride, Slots

Kewadin Casino Hessel

P.O. Box 189
Hessel, MI 49745
(906) 484-2903
(800) KEWADIN
www.kewadin.com
■ **Games Available:** Blackjack, Slots

Kewadin Casino Manistique

U.S. 2 East
Manistique, MI 49854
(906) 341-5510
(800) KEWADIN
www.kewadin.com

■ **Hotel:** 40 rooms, $55-up
■ **Restaurant(s):** Mariner's Cove.
■ **Games Available:** Blackjack, Craps, Roulette, Slots

_____

Kewadin Casino Sault Ste. Marie

2186 Shunk Rd.
Sault Ste. Marie, MI 49783
(906) 632-0530
(800) KEWADIN
www.kewadin.com

■ **Hotel:** 320 rooms, $50-$79
■ **Restaurant(s):** Dreamcatchers Restaurant. Headliners appear in Dreammaker Theater.
■ **Games Available:** 3-card poker, Bingo, Blackjack, Craps, Let It Ride, Roulette, Slots - 2500

_____

Kewadin Casino St. Ignace

3039 Mackinac Trail
St. Ignace, MI 49781
(906) 643-7071
(800) KEWADIN
www.kewadin.com

■ **Restaurant(s):** Market Square Buffet
Outdoor entertainment in the summer.
■ **Games Available:** 3-card poker, Blackjack, Craps, Let It Ride, Poker, Roulette, Slots - 1700

_____

Lac Vieux Desert Casino

N5384 Highway 45
P.O. Box 249
Watersmeet, MI 49969
(800) 634-3444

■ **Hotel:** 76 rooms, $60-up

■ **Restaurant(s):** Katekitegoning Restaurant
The AmericInn was adding 59 rooms to open in fall 2002. A 9-hole golf course is available.
■ **Games Available:** Bingo, Blackjack Craps, Let It Ride, Roulette, Slots $1 - 70, Slots $5 - 4, Slots 1 cent - 14, Slots 50 cents - 27, Slots Nickel - 205, Slots Quarter - 301

_____

Leelanau Sands Casino

2521 NW Bayshore Drive
Peshawbestown, MI 49682
20 miles north of Traverse City, Mich.
(231) 271-4104
(800) 922-2WIN
www.casino2win.com

■ **Games Available:** 3-card poker, Blackjack Craps, Let It Ride, Poker, Roulette, Slots

_____

Leelanau Super Gaming

2649 NW Bayshore Drive
Suttons Bay, MI 49682
(231) 271-6852
(800) 922-2946

■ **Games Available:** Slots, Table games

_____

Little River Casino

U.S. 31 and M22
Manistee, MI 49660
(888) 568-2244
www.littlerivercasinos.com

■ **Restaurant(s):** Little River Café
■ **Games Available:** Blackjack, Craps, Let It Ride, Roulette, Slots - 800

_____

MGM Grand Detroit

1300 John C. Lodge
Detroit, MI 48226
(313) 393-7777
(877) 888-2121
detroit.mgmgrand.com
75,000 square feet

■ **Restaurant(s):** Hollywood Brown Derby, MGM Grand Buffet, Venti Uno, Java Coast Grill
Casino has 86 tables.

■ **Games Available:** Baccarat, Blackjack, Craps Mini-baccarat, Pai Gow, Poker, Roulette, Slots - 2500

Motor City Casino

2901 Grand River Ave.
Detroit, MI 48201
(877) 777-0711
www.motorcitycasino.com
70,000 square feet

■ **Restaurant(s):** Iridescence, La Shish, Classics Buffet, Deli Unique, High Octane Coffee Bar.
Casino has 100 table games.
Entertainment in Chromatics Lounge and Overdrive Lounge.

■ **Games Available:** 3-card poker, Blackjack, Craps, Let It Ride, Mini-baccarat, Pai Gow, Roulette, Slots - 2500

Ojibwa Casino & Resort I

797 Michigan Ave.
Baraga, MI 49908
Upper Michigan
(800) 323-8045
www.ojibwacasino.com

■ **Hotel:** 40 rooms, $60-$90

■ **Restaurant(s):** Bear's Den
Overall Payout: 98%

■ **Games Available:** Bingo, Blackjack - 13, Craps - 1, Poker - 2, Roulette - 1, Slots - 350

Ojibwa Casino & Resort II

113 Acre Trail
Marquette, MI 49855
13 miles west of Marquette, Mich.
(906) 249-4200
(888) 560-9905
www.ojibwacasino.com
Overall Payout: 98%

■ **Games Available:** Bingo, Blackjack - 13, Craps - 1, Poker - 2, Roulette - 1, Slots - 350

Soaring Eagle Casino & Resort

6800 Soaring Eagle Blvd.
Mt. Pleasant, MI 48858
(800) 7EAGLE7
hotel-info@sagchip.org
www.soaringeaglecasino.com

■ **Hotel:** 512 rooms, $119-up
205,000 square feet

■ **Reservations:** (877) 2EAGLE2

■ **Restaurant(s):** Water Lily Restaurant, Sinii Kaung Steak and Chop House, Firefly Buffet
Recipient of 4 Diamond Award, 26,000 square feet of meeting space, spa and health club, indoor pool, Ziibiwing Cultural Society's Naanooshke Art Gallery.
Comedy, music and sports entertainment.

■ **Games Available:** Blackjack - 44, Slots - 4305

Turtle Creek Casino

7741 M-72 E.
Williamsburg, MI 49690
Near Traverse Bay, Mich.
(231) 267-9546
(888) 777-UWIN
www.casino2win.com

■ **Restaurant(s):** Turtle Creek Food Court

■ **Games Available:** Blackjack, Craps , Poker Roulette, Slots

Victories Casino

1966 U.S. 131 South
Petoskey, MI 49770
40 miles from Mackinaw City
(231) 439-6100
(877) 4GAMING
www.victories-casino.com
33,000 square feet

■ **Restaurant(s):** Mukwa Café, Players Sports Lounge
Bands every weekend.

■ **Games Available:** Blackjack $5, Craps - 2, Poker - 1, Roulette - 1, Slots - 700

MINNESOTA

7 Clans Casino

1012 E. Lake St.
Warroad, MN 56763
120 miles from Winnipeg
(218) 386-3381
(800) 815-8293
■ **Hotel:** 40 rooms, $48-up
■ **Restaurant(s):** Lake View Restaurant
18-hole golf course.
Regional bands on weekends
Overall Payout: 92%
■ **Games Available:** Blackjack $2 - 3 ,
Blackjack $25 - 1, Blackjack $5 - 3, Slots $1 - 21,
Slots 1 cent - 38, Slots 2 cents - 27, Slots Nickel -
364, Slots Quarter - 75

Black Bear Casino

1785 Highway 210
Carlton, MN 55718
(218) 878-BEAR
(888) 771-0777
www.blackbearcasinohotel.com
■ **Hotel:** 218 rooms, $49-up
■ **Reservations:** (800) 553-0022
■ **Restaurant(s):** Black Bear Grill, Skywalk
Café.
Resort has indoor pool, arcade, gift shop, and con-
ference center.
■ **Games Available**
Bingo   Blackjack - 18   Slots - 1250

Firefly Creek Casino

Highway 67 East
Granite Falls, MN 56241
(320) 564-2121
■ **Restaurant(s):** Flying Eagle Restaurant
■ **Games Available:** Blackjack - 8, Slots - 400

Fond-du-Luth Casino

129 E. Super St.
Duluth, MN 55802
(218) 722-0280
(800) 873-0280
fdlinfo@fdlrez.com
www.fondduluthcasino.com
■ **Games Available:** Bingo, Blackjack - 12,
Slots - 510

Fortune Bay Resort Casino

1430 Bois Forte Road
Tower, MN 57790
On Lake Vermilion near Boundary Waters wilder-
ness area
(800) 555-1714
www.fortunebay.com
■ **Hotel:** 115 rooms, $66-up
■ **Restaurant(s):** Tamarack Dining Room, Bay
Street Deli.
Hotel has indoor pool, fitness area. RV Park has
34 sites.
■ **Games Available:** Bingo, Blackjack,
Slots - 500

Grand Casino Hinckley

777 Lady Luck Drive
Hinckley, MN 55037
Duluth/Superior area of Minnesota
(800) 472-6321
commentsgch@grcasinos.com
www.grandcasinosmn.com
■ **Hotel:** 281 rooms
■ **Reservations:** (800) 468-3517
■ **Restaurant(s):** The Winds Steakhouse, Grand
Casino Buffet, Grand Grill Americana, Cherry's
Snack Bar.
Hotel has indoor pool and exercise room, retail
shops, 10,000 square feet of convention space.

Entertainers include Phyllis Diller, Oak Ridge Boys, the Monkees.

■ **Games Available:** Bingo, Blackjack $3 - 28, Pull-tab games, Slots - 1500

Grand Casino Mille Lacs

777 Grand Ave.
Highway 169 West Shore
Lake Mille Lacs Onamia, MN 56359
North of Twin Cities
(800) 626-5825
milwebmail@grcasinos.com
www.grandcasinosmn.com
■ **Hotel:** 284 rooms
■ **Restaurant(s):** The Woodlands, Grand Casino Buffet, Grand Northern Grill, Plums Deli
Hotel has indoor pool, exercise room. Lakes, golf courses, snowmobile trails available.
■ **Games Available:** Bingo, Blackjack - 35, Pull-tab games, Slots - 1500

Grand Portage Lodge & Casino

P.O. Box 233
Grand Portage, MN 55605
(218) 475-2401
(800) 543-1384
www.grandportagemn.com
■ **Hotel:** 100 rooms
15,000 square feet
Indoor pool and sauna.
■ **Games Available:** Bingo, Blackjack, Slots - 400

Jackpot Junction Casino Hotel

P.O. Box 420
Morton, MN 56270
(507) 644-4000
(800) WIN CASH
www.jackpotjunction.com
■ **Hotel:** 276 rooms, $30-up
■ **Restaurant(s):** Cafe Dacotah, Carousel Buffet, Full Deck.

Hotel has 38,000 square feet of convention space and the Dakotah Ridge Golf Course is available. Gallagher, Ronnie Milsap, others appear in the Dacotah Exposition Center.

■ **Games Available:** Bingo, Blackjack - 36, Slots - 1650

Little Six Casino

County Road 83
Prior Lake, MN 55372
(612) 445-8982
■ **Games Available:** Blackjack, Slots

Mystic Lake Casino Hotel

2400 Mystic Lake Blvd.
Prior Lake, MN 55372
(952) 445-9000
marketing@mysticlake.com
www.mysticlake.com
■ **Hotel:** 416 rooms, $59-up
■ **Reservations:** (800) 262-7799
■ **Restaurant(s):** Ribbons, The Buffet, Gambler's Grille, Minnehaha Café.
Neil Sadaka, Jeff Foxworthy and Bill Cosby are some of the stars to appear.
■ **Games Available:** Bingo, Blackjack - 100, Slots - 3300

Northern Lights Casino

6800 Y Frontage Road NW
Walker, MN 56484
(218) 547-2744
(800) 252-PLAY
www.northernlightcasino.com
■ **Restaurant(s):** Northstar Restaurant
■ **Games Available:** Blackjack - 8, Slots - 550

Palace Bingo & Casino

6280 Upper Cass Frontage NW
Cass Lake, MN 56633
(800) 228-6676
palace@paulbunyan.net
www.palacecasinohotel.com
■ **Hotel:** 80 rooms
■ **Reservations:** (800) 442-3910
■ **Restaurant(s):** Palace Garden Restaurant
Hotel has indoor pool, hot tubs.
■ **Games Available:** Bingo, Blackjack - 8,
Pull-tab games, Slots - 500

Seven Clans Red Lake

P.O. Box 574
Red Lake, MN 56671
30 miles north of Bemidji, Minn.
(218) 679-2111
(800) 568-6649
www.redlakegaming.com
■ **Games Available:** Bingo, Slots

Seven Clans Thief River Falls

Route 3, Box 168A
Thief River Falls, MN 56701
Renamed from River Road Casino.
(800) 881-0712
www.redlakegaming.com
13,000 square feet
■ **Games Available:** Bingo, Blackjack, Pull-tab
games

Seven Clans Warroad Casino

1012 Lake St. NE
Warroad, MN 56763
(800) 815-8293
www.redlakegaming.com
Reservations: (800) 881-0712
■ **Games Available:** Bingo, Blackjack,
Pull-tab games, Slots - 300

Shooting Star Casino

777 SE Casino Rd.
Mahnomen, MN 56557
(800) 453-STAR
www.starcasino.com
■ **Hotel:** 390 rooms, $60-$100
■ **Restaurant(s):** Reflections, Biindiggan Buffet,
Delights Deli.
A $26 million expansion has added 110 more
hotel rooms, a new poker room, restaurant, gaming area and Event Center. Riverside RV Park has
58 spaces for RVs and tents.
Entertainers in the Event Center.
■ **Games Available:** Bingo, Blackjack - 18,
Poker, Pull-tab games, Slots - 1300

Treasure Island Casino

P.O. Box 75
Red Wing, MN 55066
(800) 222-7077
info@treasureislandcasino.com
www.treasureislandcasino.com
■ **Hotel:** 250 rooms
■ **Reservations:** (888) 867-STAY
■ **Restaurant(s):** Tradewinds Buffet, Mongo
Bay Snack Bar, Java's Restaurant.
The recently expanded resort includes a 137-slip
marina, 95-space RV Park, Spirit of the Water
cruise ship. It added 58,000 square feet of gaming
space. The hotel includes an indoor pool and spa.
Headliner entertainment events appear in the
1,000-seat Indigo Bay Showroom.
■ **Games Available:** Bingo, Blackjack - 64,
Slots - 2400

White Oak Casino

45830 U.S. Hwy. 2
Deer River, MN 56636
(218) 246-9600
(800) 653-2412
www.whiteoakcasino.com
■ **Games Available:** Blackjack - 2, Slots - 200

MISSISSIPPI

Beau Rivage Resort & Casino

875 Beach Blvd.
Biloxi, MS 39530
(228) 386-7111
(888) 567-6667
www.beaurivage.com

■ **Hotel:** 1710 rooms, $59-up

■ **Restaurant(s):** Coral, Spuntino Deli, The Roasted Bean.

Resort has an outdoor pool, spa and salon, 31-slip marina, charter fishing packages, Southern Links golf packages and a Shopping Promenade.

Headliners appearing include Julio Iglesias and Earth, Wind and Fire.

■ **Games Available:** Baccarat, Blackjack, Craps Poker, Roulette, Slots

Horseshoe Casino Tunica

1021 Casino Center Drive
Robinsonville, MS 38664
(800) 303-7463
www.horseshoe.com

■ **Hotel:** 505 rooms

■ **Restaurant(s):** Jack Binion's Steak House, Yasmin's Asian Restaurant, Café Sonoma, Village Square Buffet.

Hotel has pool, sauna, exercise room. Casino has 70 table games.

Entertainers include Alan Jackson, Brooks & Dunn, the New Shanghai Circus.

■ **Games Available:** Blackjack, Craps, Poker Roulette, Slots - 2000

Isle of Capri Lula

777 Isle of Capri Parkway
Lula, MS 38644
On the Mississippi-Arkansas border.
(888) 782-9582
www.isleofcapricasino.com/Lula/

■ **Restaurant(s):** Farraddays' Restaurant, Calypso Seafood Buffet, Tradewinds Marketplace.

Palm Terrace and Coral Reef hotels available at the resort. Casino has 40 table games.

Live entertainment in the 1300 seat Flamingo Bay Ballroom.

■ **Games Available:** Blackjack, Let It Ride Roulette, Slots - 1500

MISSOURI

Ameristar Casino Hotel Kansas City

3200 North Ameristar Drive
Kansas City, MO 64161
(816) 414-7000
(800) 499-4961
www.ameristarcasinos.com/corporate/kcfacts/
■ **Hotel:** 184 rooms
140,000 square feet
■ **Reservations:** (888) 289-0303
■ **Restaurant(s):** Bugatti's, Orleans Seafood, Pancho Villa's Cantina, Hofbrauhaus, The Buffet, Viva Salsa, Orleans Oyster, Pizza Presto, Arthur Bryant's.
Extras include Kid's Quest center, Royal Chieftain Cigar Bar. Casino has 126 table games.
The 1,332-seat Grand Pavilion has entertainers including George Carlin, Oak Ridge Boys, Carrot Top, George Jones, as well as boxing. New Phoenix Jazz Club opened in early 2002.
■ **Games Available:** Blackjack, Craps, Let It Ride, Pai Gow, Poker - 17, Roulette, Slots - 3200

Harrah's St. Louis

777 Casino Center Drive
Maryland Heights, MO 63043
20 minutes from downtown St. Louis
(314) 770-8100
(800) HARRAHS
www.harrahs.com/our_casinos/stl/index.html
■ **Hotel:** 291 rooms
120,000 square feet in two casinos
■ **Restaurant(s):** The Range Steakhouse, Town Square Buffet, Club Aroma, The Jester's Deli & The Island Deli, Antonio's Italian Ristorante, Stage Left Lounge.
Casinos have 75 table games.
Entertainment includes Y98 Saturday Night

Fever Dance Party at Stage Left every Saturday.
■ **Games Available** 3-card poker, Blackjack, Craps, Let It Ride, Mini-baccarat Roulette, Slots - 3200, Spanish 21

Palace Casino Resort

158 Howard Ave.
Biloxi, MS 39533
60 miles east of New Orleans
(800) PALACE9
www.palacecasinoresort.com
■ **Hotel:** 234 rooms
33,000 square feet
■ **Restaurant(s):** Four restaurants: Palace Buffet; Café and Bakery; Point Cadet Grill; Jazzmins fine dining.
Pool, spa, salon, gift shop, beach volleyball and golf putting range are available at the hotel, which opened in 2000. Guest rooms feature Internet phone jacks, WebTV and Nintendo 64. Hotel features 12,000 square feet of meeting and banquet space plu
Various headliners in 500-seat theater include the Oak Ridge Boys, Drifters, Commodores, Chubby Checker.
■ **Games Available:** Blackjack - 27, Craps - 3, Roulette - 2, Slots $1 - 154, Slots $10 - 4, Slots $100 - 2, Slots $25 - 2, Slots $5 - 41, Slots 1 cent - 2, Slots 2 cents - 4, Slots Nickel - 363, Slots Quarter - 355

Silver Star Hotel & Casino

Highway 16 West
P. O. Box 6048
Choctaw, MS 39350
35 miles northwest of Meridian
(800) 557-0711

publicrelations@silverstarresort.com
www.silverstarresort.com

■ **Hotel:** 500 rooms
90,000 square feet

■ **Restaurant(s):** Phillip M's, Villa 16 West, Terrace Café, Chef's Pavilion, Dolce, Rally Alley Deli.

Hotel has spa, fitness center, shops, 30,000 square feet of convention space. Two 18-hole golf courses available at Dancing Rabbit Golf Club.

Entertainers including The O'Jays, Travis Tritt, Wayne Newton.

■ **Games Available:** Blackjack, Let It Ride, Poker, Slots - 3100

Look for more Mississippi casinos under riverboats.

MONTANA

4 C's Café & Casino

P.O. Box 544
Box Elder, MT 59521
(406) 395-4863

■ **Games Available:** Slots - 59

Gran Tree Inn

1325 North 7th Ave.
Bozeman, MT 59715
(406) 587-5261
(800) 624-5865
grantree@grantreeinn.com
www.bestwestern.com/grantreeinn

■ **Hotel:** 120 rooms

Hotel has pool and fitness center.

■ **Games Available:** Slots

KwaTaqNuk Resort & Casino

303 U.S. Hwy. 93 East
Polson, MT 59860
(406) 883-3636

■ **Hotel:** 112 rooms

Hotel has indoor, outdoor pools and a marina.

■ **Games Available:** Slots

Little Big Horn Casino

P.O. Box 580
Crow Agency, MT 59022
(406) 638-4444

■ **Games Available:** Bingo, Slots

Press Box

835 E. Broadway
Missoula, MT 59802
(406) 721-1212

■ **Games Available:** Slots

Silver Wolf Casino

P.O. Box 726
Wolf Point, MT 59201
(406) 653-3476

■ **Games Available:** Bingo, Slots

NEBRASKA

Rosebud Casino

HC 14 Box 135
Valentine, NE 69201
(605) 378-3800
(800) 768-ROSE
Fax: (605) 378-3870
mktg@rosebudcasino.com
www.rosebudcasino.com

■ **Hotel:** 60 rooms

■ **Restaurant(s):** Rosebud Room, Rose Garden Café.

Concerts indoors. Outdoor events include pow-wows, rodeos, concerts.

■ **Games Available:** Bingo, Blackjack, Poker, Slots

NEVADA - Las Vegas

49er Saloon & Casino

1556 N. Eastern Ave.
Las Vegas, NV 89101
(702) 649-2421

■ **Games Available:** Slots - 22

Aladdin Resort

3667 Las Vegas Blvd S.
Las Vegas, NV 89109
(702) 785-5555
reservations@aladdincasino.com
www.aladdincasino.com

■ **Hotel:** 2600 rooms
100,000 square feet

■ **Reservations:** (877) 333-WISH

■ **Restaurant(s):** Six restaurants: Elements, Tremezzo, Spice Market Buffet, Zanzibar Café, P.F. Chang's China Bistro, Commander's Palace.

The 475,000 square foot Desert Passage includes 130 shops and 14 restaurants. Elemis Spa offers salons and fitness center. Hotel has 75,000 square feet of convention facilities.

The 7,000 seat Theatre for the Performing Arts features performers including Alicia Keys, Prince, Dennis Miller, Sting. Blue Note Jazz Club has live music.

■ **Games Available:** Baccarat, Blackjack, Pai Gow, Roulette, Slots

Alibi Casino

1690 N. Decatur
Las Vegas, NV 89108
(702) 648-1961

■ **Games Available:** Slots - 35

Arizona Charlie's

740 S. Decatur Blvd.
Las Vegas, NV 89107
(702) 258-5111
(800) 342-2695
Fax: (702) 258-5192
Hotel@azcharlies.com
www.arizonacharlies.com/west

■ **Hotel:** 258 rooms, $40-up
56,000 square feet

■ **Restaurant(s):** Yukon Grill, China Charlie's, Wild West Buffet, Sourdough Café.

■ **Games Available:** Bingo, Blackjack, Craps, Keno, Pai Gow, Roulette, Slots - 1600, Sport Book

Arizona Charlie's East

4575 Boulder Highway
Las Vegas, NV 89121
(877) 951-0002
(800) 362-4040
Fax: (702) 951-5334
Hotel@arizonacharlies.net
www.arizonacharlies.com/east

■ **Hotel:** 303 rooms, $40-up

■ **Reservations:** (702) 951-5900

■ **Restaurant(s):** Yukon Grill, Panda Express, Wild West Buffet, Deli.

Resort features 207-space RV park, pool, spa.

■ **Games Available:** Blackjack, Craps , Pai Gow, Roulette, Slots - 800, Sport Book

Aztec Inn Casino

2200 Las Vegas Blvd. South
Las Vegas, NV 89104
(702) 385-4566
Hotel: 400 rooms, $38-up
Bands nightly

■ **Games Available:** Slots - 40

Bally's Las Vegas

3645 Las Vegas Blvd. South
Las Vegas, NV 89109-4307
Las Vegas Strip
(702) 739-4111
(800) 7BALLYS
www.ballyslv.com
Hotel: 2814 rooms
67,000 square feet

■ **Restaurant(s):** Six restaurants: Seasons, al
Dente, Bally's Steakhouse, Chang's, The Sidewalk
Café, Big Kitchen Buffet; also two snack bars and
three restaurants in the mall area.

Completely renovated hotel and casino, pool and
spa, Avenue Shoppes with 20 stores, monorail
connecting with MGM Grand, eight tennis courts,
Celebration Wedding Chapel.

Donn Arden's Jubilee! appears twice daily.

■ **Games Available:** Blackjack, Craps,
Keno, Let It Ride, Pai Gow, Poker, Roulette, Slots
- 1800, Sport Book

Bally's Las Vegas is a veteran of the Strip and has been completely renovated.

Barbary Coast Hotel

3595 S. Las Vegas Blvd.
Las Vegas, NV 89109
(800) 844-9593

■ **Hotel:** 200 rooms, $49-up
30,000 square feet

■ **Restaurant(s):** Drai's, Michael's, Victorian
Room, Seattle's Best Coffee House.

Entertainers and karaoke in the lounge.

■ **Games Available:** Blackjack, Craps, Keno,
Pai Gow, Poker, Roulette, Slots - 900

Barcelona Hotel and Casino

5011 E. Craig Rd.
Las Vegas, NV 89115
(800) 223-6330
www.barcelonalasvegas.com

■ **Hotel:** 168 rooms, $35-up

■ **Games Available:** Blackjack, Roulette,
Slots - 200, Sport Book

Beano's Casino

7200 W. Lake Mead Blvd.
Las Vegas, NV 89128
(702) 255-9150

■ **Games Available:** Slots - 35

Bellagio

3600 S. Las Vegas Blvd.
Las Vegas, NV 89109
(702) 693-7111
(888) 987-6667
guestservices@bellagiolasvegas.com
www.bellagio.com

■ **Hotel:** 2688 rooms, $179-up

■ **Restaurant(s):** Le Cirque, Palio, Pool Café,
Café Bellagio, The Buffet, Café Gelato.

Bellagio is known for its fountains and its Gallery
of Fine Art as well as the Botanical Garden. There
are six pool courtyard settings. Shops include
Giorgio Armani and two wedding chapels are
available.

Featured attraction is "O" Cirque du Soleil. The Light Nightclub is another highlight.

■ **Games Available:** Baccarat, Blackjack, Craps, Roulette, Slots, Sport Book

Best Western Mardi Gras Inn

3500 Paradise Road
Las Vegas, NV 89109
(702) 731-2020
(800) 634-6501
Fax: (702) 733-6994
www.bestwestern.com

■ **Hotel:** 314 rooms

Hotel has pool and spa. Free parking.

■ **Games Available:** Slots

Big Dog's Bar and Grill

1511 N. Nellis Blvd.
Las Vegas, NV 89110
(702) 459-1099
Fax: (702) 459-7730

■ **Games Available:** Slots - 35

Big Dog's Cafe and Casino

6390 W. Sahara Blvd.
Las Vegas, NV 89146
(702) 876-DOGS
Fax: (702) 876-4453

■ **Games Available:** Slots - 35

Binion's Horseshoe

128 E. Fremont St.
Las Vegas, NV 89101
Downtown Las Vegas
(702) 382-1600
(800) 937-6537
Fax: (702) 384-1574
reservations@lvcm.com
www.binions.com

■ **Hotel:** 366 rooms, $35-$75

■ **Restaurant(s):** Six restaurants: Binion's Ranch Steakhouse, Gee Joons, Buffet, coffee shop, two snack bars.

Home of The World Series of Poker.

■ **Games Available:** Blackjack $3 - 50, Craps - 10, Keno, Mini-baccarat - 3, Pai Gow - 1, Poker - 13, Roulette - 4 , Slots - 35, Slots $1 - 126, Slots $5 - 20, Slots Nickel - 428, Slots Quarter - 749, Sport Book

Boardwalk Hotel & Casino

3750 S. Las Vegas Blvd.
Las Vegas, NV 89109
(800) 635-4581
www.hiboardwalk.com

■ **Hotel:** 654 rooms, $39-up

33,000 square feet

■ **Restaurant(s):** Caffe Boardwalk, Surf Buffet, The Deli, Catch a Cup of Coffee.

Hotel features a Coney Island midway façade. Hotel has a pool and a wedding chapel.

A musical tribute to Elvis and Purple Reign, the Prince tribute band, are featured in the Lighthouse Showroom.

■ **Games Available:** Blackjack, Craps, Keno, Poker, Roulette, Slots - 600, Sport Book

Boulder Station Casino

4111 Boulder Highway
Las Vegas, NV 89121
(800) 683-7777
www.boulderstation.com

■ **Hotel:** 300 rooms, $49-up

■ **Restaurant(s):** Iron Horse Café, Pasta Palace, Guadalajara Bar and Grille, The Feast Buffet, The Broiler.

Casino has 48 table games.

Live music in The Railhead. Movie theater with 11 screens.

■ **Games Available:** 3-card poker, Bingo, Blackjack, Craps, Keno, Let It Ride, Mini-baccarat, Poker, Roulette, Slots - 3000, Sport Book

Bourbon Street Hotel

120 East Flamingo Rd.
Las Vegas, NV 89109
(800) 844-9593
Hotel: 166 rooms, $49-up
■ **Restaurant(s):** French Market Restaurant.
Comedy Theater
■ **Games Available:** Slots, Table games

Caesars Palace

3570 Las Vegas Blvd. South
Las Vegas, NV 89109
Las Vegas Strip
(702) 731-7331
www.caesars.com

The glory of Rome is carried out in the columns of Caesars Palace's casino.

■ **Hotel:** 2456 rooms, $89-$500
■ **Reservations:** (800) 634-6661
■ **Restaurant(s):** Eighteen restaurants: 808, Cafe Lago, La Piazza, The Palatium, Neros, Empress Court, Terrazza, Cafe Caesars, Hyakumi, Caesars Magical Empire, Bertolini's, Chinois, Forum Cafe, Caviarteria, The Cheesecake Factory, Forum Cafe, La Salsa, The Palm.

Forum Shops has 105 different shops and restaurants and Appian Way has 20 shops. Three swimming pools, two outdoor whirlpool spas, The Spa fitness facility, 28 salons, Caesars Palace Chapel, Palace Tower convention area.

Singer Celine Dion starts a three-year, 600 show engagement in 2003. The Terrazza Lounge features the Live Jazz Trio Tuesday -Saturday;

Galleria Bar: Pianist Billy Stevenson; Cafe Lago Restaurant: Pianist and Bass Player; Cleopatra's Barge Nightclub
■ **Games Available:** Blackjack - 45, Craps - 12, Keno, Pai Gow - 2, Poker - 8, Roulette - 12, Slots - 2059, Sport Book

California Hotel Casino

12 Ogden Ave.
Las Vegas, NV 89101
(702) 385-1222
(800) 634-6255
www.thecal.com
■ **Hotel:** 781 rooms
■ **Restaurant(s):** Market Street Café, Redwood Bar & Grill, Pasta Pirate, Cal Club Snack Bar. Bridge Avenue Retail Area offers shopping.
■ **Games Available:** Blackjack - 20, Craps, Keno, Let It Ride, Pai Gow, Roulette, Slots - 1000, Sport Book

Casino Royale & Hotel

3411 Las Vegas Blvd. S.
Las Vegas, NV 89109
(800) 854-7666
www.casinoroyalehotel.com
■ **Hotel:** 152 rooms, $49-up
■ **Restaurant(s):** Café Trilussa, Denny's, Subway.
■ **Games Available:** Blackjack, Craps , Roulette Slots - 500, Spanish 21

Castaways Hotel Casino

2800 Fremont St.
Las Vegas, NV 89104
(800) 826-2800
Fax: (702) 383-9238
www.showboat-lv.com
■ **Hotel:** 447 rooms, $40-up
80,000 square feet

■ **Restaurant(s):** Blue Marlin, Prime Cuts Steakhouse, San Brisas Buffet, Pelican Rock Café.

The former Showboat Hotel includes an 84-space RV Park and a 106-lane bowling center. Windjammer Lounge offers a variety of entertainment.

■ **Games Available:** Bingo, Blackjack, Craps, Keno, Roulette, Slots - 1400, Sport Book

Circus Circus

2880 Las Vegas Blvd. S.
Las Vegas, NV 89109
(702) 734-0410
(877) 2CIRCUS
www.circuscircus.com

■ **Hotel:** 3700 rooms, $29-up

Three casinos available.

■ **Restaurant(s):** Circus Buffet, The Steak House, Stivali Italian Ristorante, Blue Iguana, Pink Pony, Pizzeria, West Side Deli.

Circusland RV Park has 384 spaces. Five-acre Adventuredome Theme Park has games, theaters. New 40,000 square foot Promenade has 20 shops. Chapel of the Fountain hosts weddings.

World's largest permanent circus is featured.

■ **Games Available:** Blackjack, Craps, Keno, Pai Gow, Poker - 10, Roulette, Slots - 2700, Sport Book

Days Inn Town Hall Casino

4155 Koval Lane
Las Vegas, NV 89109
(702) 731-2111
(800) 634-6541
www.daysinntownhall.com

■ **Hotel:** 360 rooms, $35-up

■ **Games Available:** Slots

El Cortez Hotel & Casino

600 Fremont St.
Las Vegas, NV 89101
(800) 844-9593
Hotel: 308 rooms, $20-$40
80,000 square feet

■ **Restaurant(s):** Roberta's Cafe, Emerald Room Coffee Shop.

Casino has 20 table games.

■ **Games Available:** Blackjack, Craps, Let It Ride, Pai Gow, Poker, Roulette, Slots - 1180, Sport Book

Ellis Island Casino & Brewery

4178 Koval Lane
Las Vegas, NV 89109
(702) 733-8901
Karaoke is featured nightly.

■ **Games Available:** Bingo, Blackjack, Slots

Excalibur Hotel and Casino

3850 Las Vegas Blvd. S.
Las Vegas, NV 89109
(702) 597-7777
(877 750-5464
info@excaliburcasino.com
www.excaliburlasvegas.com

■ **Hotel:** 4008 rooms, $59-up

■ **Restaurant(s):** Six restaurants: Roundtable Buffet, The Steakhouse at Camelot, Sir Galahad's Pub & Prime Rib House, Regale Italian Eatery, Sherwood Forest, Village Food Court.

Hotel has two pools, salon, 24-hour room service, 18 retail shops, Canterbury Wedding Chapels.

Entertainment includes the Tournament of Kings jousting dinner theater, Catch a Rising Star comedy club and the Court Jester's Stage as well as bands in the Minstrel's Lounge.

■ **Games Available:** Blackjack, Craps, Pai Gow, Poker, Roulette, Slots, Sport Book

Fiesta

2400 N. Rancho Drive
Las Vegas, NV 89130
(800) 844-9593
Hotel: 100 rooms, $49-up
50,000 square feet
■ **Restaurant(s):** Old San Francisco Steakhouse, Festival Buffet, Garduno's.
Hotel has a pool.
■ **Games Available:** Bingo, Blackjack, Craps, Keno, Poker, Roulette, Slots - 1200, Sport Book

Fitzgeralds Casino Las Vegas

301 Fremont St.
Las Vegas, NV 89101
(800) 274-LUCK
www.fitzgeralds.com
■ **Hotel:** 638 rooms, $23-up
42,000 square feet
■ **Restaurant(s):** Limericks Steakhouse, Molly's Buffet, Shamrock Café.
Casino has 23 table games.
■ **Games Available:** 3-card poker, Blackjack, Craps, Keno, Let It Ride, Roulette, Slots - 1000

Flamingo Las Vegas

3555 Las Vegas Blvd. South
Las Vegas, NV 89109
Las Vegas Strip
(702) 733-3111
(888) 308-8899
Fax: (702) 733-3353
www.flamingolasvegas.com
Hotel: 3626 rooms
77,000 square feet
■ **Reservations:** (800) 732-2111
■ **Restaurant(s):** Nine restaurants: Alta Villa, Conrad's Steakhouse, Bugsy's Deli, Flamingo Room, Hamada's, Lindy's, Paradise Garden Buffet, Peking Market, Pool Bar & Grille.
Four tennis courts, health spa, beauty salon, two swimming pools, Shopping Arcade, Garden

Wedding Chapel, 50,000 square feet of banquet and meeting space, free parking. Casino has 71 table games.
Entertainment includes the Second City in Bugsy's Theatre, "Bottoms Up" show twice daily.
■ **Games Available:** Blackjack, Craps, Keno, Poker, Slots - 2100, Let It Ride

Four Queens

202 Fremont St.
Las Vegas, NV 89101
(800) 844-9593
■ **Hotel:** 700 rooms, $20-up
50,000 square feet
■ **Restaurant(s):** Magnolia's Veranda, Hugo's Cellar.
■ **Games Available:** Blackjack, Craps, Keno, Let It Ride, Poker, Roulette, Slots, Sport Book

Fremont Hotel & Casino

200 E. Fremont St.
Las Vegas, NV 89101
(702) 385-3232
(800) 634-6460
www.fremontcasino.com
■ **Hotel:** 447 rooms
32,000 square feet
■ **Reservations:** (800) 634-6182
■ **Restaurant(s):** Paradise Buffet, Paradise Café, Tony Roma's, Lanai Express, Second Street Grill.
Guest rooms are newly remodeled.
■ **Games Availablef:** Blackjack, Craps - 4, Keno, Poker, Roulette - 3, Slots - 1000, Sport Book

New Frontier Hotel and Gambling Hall

3120 S. Las Vegas Blvd.
Las Vegas, NV 89109
(800) 844-9593
www.frontierhotelcasino.com

■ **Hotel:** 986 rooms, $50-up
100,000 square feet
■ **Restaurant(s):** Daily Buffet, Frontier Deli, Gilley's Saloon, Dance Hall and Barbeque, Margarita's Cantina, Phil's Angus Steakhouse, The Orchard.
Hotel has pool, tennis courts.
Country music is featured in Gilley's Dancehall and Saloon.
■ **Games Available:** Blackjack, Craps , Let It Ride, Keno, Pai Gow, Poker, Roulette, Slots

Gold Coast

4000 W. Flamingo Rd.
Las Vegas, NV 89103
(888) 402-6278
www.goldcoastcasino.com
Hotel: 750 rooms, $29-up
100,000 square feet
■ **Restaurant(s):** Monterey Room, Arriva, Ping Pang Pong, Cortez Room, Terrible Mike's, Kate's Korner, Ports O' Call Buffet, Seattle's Best Coffee House.
Hotel has a pool, health club, salon
Entertainment in the Showroom and the Gold Coast Lounge. A 72-lane bowling center is available.
■ **Games Available:** Baccara, Blackjack, Craps, Keno, Pai Gow, Poker, Roulette, Slots, Sport Book

Gold Spike Hotel & Casino

400 E. Ogden
Las Vegas, NV 89101
(702) 384-8444
(800) 634-6703
reservations@goldspikehotelcasino.com
www.goldspikehotelcasino.com
■ **Hotel:** 110 rooms, $25-up
■ **Games Available:** Bingo, Blackjack $1, Keno, Slots - 410

Golden Gate Hotel

1 Fremont St.
Las Vegas, NV 89101
Downtown Las Vegas
(702) 385-1906
(800) 426-1906
www.goldengatecasino.net
■ **Hotel:** 106 rooms, $29-$49
■ **Restaurant(s):** Bay City Diner, Shrimp Bar & Deli
Live piano music is available from noon to midnight.
■ **Games Available:** Blackjack $3, Craps, Roulette, Slots

Golden Nugget Hotel

129 E. Fremont St.
Las Vegas, NV 89101
(702) 385-7111
(800) 846-5336
guestservices@goldennugget.com
www.goldennugget.com
■ **Hotel:** 1907 rooms, $49-up
36,000 square feet
■ **Restaurant(s):** The Buffet, The Lounge, Starbucks.
Hotel has outdoor pool, spa and salon, and access to Fremont Street Experience.
Tony Orlando is among headliners to appear.
■ **Games Available:** Baccarat, Blackjack, Craps, Let It Ride, Pai Gow, Roulette, Slots

Golden Palm Casino

3111 W. Tropicana Ave.
Las Vegas, NV 89103
(702) 798-1111
(702) 798-7138
www.hojo.com/lasvegas01140
■ **Hotel:** 150 rooms, $39-$49
■ **Restaurant(s):** International House of Pancakes Karaoke
■ **Games Available** Slots - 28, Slots $1 - 7, Slots Nickel - 15, Slots Quarter - 7, Sport Book

Greek Isles Hotel & Casino

305 Convention Center Dr.
Las Vegas, NV 89109
(702) 734-0711
(800) 633-1777

■ **Hotel:** 207 rooms

■ **Restaurant(s):** Yanni's Restaurant & Bar.
Former Debbie Reynolds Hotel
"Country Heroes and Divas" perform in the show-room.

■ **Games Available:** Slots

Green Valley Ranch Resort

P.O. Box 230160
Las Vegas, NV 89123
(702) 221-6560
(888) 319-4661
www.greenvalleyranchresort.com

■ **Hotel:** 247 rooms

■ **Restaurant(s):** Seven restaurants: Il Fornaio,
Border Grill, Bullshrimp Steak and Seafood, Fado,
Trophy's Restaurant, Original Pancake House,
Feast Around the World.

Green Valley Ranch opened in December 2001. It
features an 8,300 square foot spa with pool and 13
treatment rooms.

Whiskey Sky offers entertainment. Resort has 10
movie theaters.

■ **Games Available:** Blackjack, Craps , Poker,
Roulette, Slots, Sport Book

Hard Rock Hotel Casino

4455 Paradise Road
Las Vegas, NV 89109
(702) 693-5000
(800) HRDROCK
info@hrhvegas.com
www.hardrockhotel.com

■ **Hotel:** 657 rooms, $70-up

■ **Reservations:** (702) 693-5544

■ **Restaurant(s):** A.J.'s Steakhouse, Mortoni's,
Mr. Lucky's, Nobu, Pink Taco.

Rock memorabilia is featured. Hotel includes
beach club, spa, salon.

Entertainment by stars including Guns 'N Roses,
Limp Bizkit, Stone Temple Pilots. Baby's
Nightclub is also available.

■ **Games Available:** Baccarat, Blackjack,
Craps, Roulette, Slots, Sport Book

Harrah's Las Vegas

3475 Las Vegas Blvd. South
Las Vegas, NV 89109
(702) 369-5000
(800) 392-9002
www.harrahs.com/our_casinos/las/index.html

■ **Hotel:** 2500 rooms, $29-up
89,000 square feet

■ **Reservations:** (800) HARRAHS

■ **Restaurant(s):** Eight restaurants: Asia, Café
Andreotti, Carnaval Court Bar & Grill, Fresh
Market Square Buffet, Garden Café, Range
Steakhouse, Winning Streaks, Club Cappuccino.

Hotel has 15 stores, health club, spa and salon.
Casino has 70 table games.

Entertainment includes The Improv comedy, Clint
Holmes show, Skintight revue, Mac King comedy/
magic show.

■ **Games Available:** Baccarat, Blackjack,
Craps, Keno, Slots - 1500, Sport Book

*Harrah's Las Vegas has 2,500 hotel rooms and eight
restaurants.*

Hotel San Remo Casino & Resort

115 E. Tropicana
Las Vegas, NV 89109
(702) 739-9000
(800) 522-7366
roomres@sanremolv.com
www.sanremolasvegas.com
■ **Hotel:** 711 rooms
■ **Restaurant(s):** Paparazzi Grille, Saizen,
Ristorante dei Fiori, Luigi's Place.
Hotel has a heated pool, wedding chapel and convention facilities.
Showgirls of Magic perform nightly.
■ **Games Available:** Blackjack, Craps , Keno,
Let It Ride, Poker, Roulette, Slots - 570

Imperial Palace

3535 Las Vegas Blvd. South
Las Vegas, NV 89109
(702) 731-3311
(800) 634-6441
Fax: (702) 735-8578
ip@imperialpalace.com
www.imperialpalace.com
■ **Hotel:** 2700 rooms, $25-up
75,000 square feet
■ **Restaurant(s):** Ming Terrace, The Seahouse,
The Embers, Rib House, Pizza Palace, Teahouse
& Imperial Buffet, Emperor's Buffet, Burger
Palace, Betty's Diner.
The Auto Collections features antique and vintage
cars. The hotel features a pool, spa, salon and
wedding chapel. Casino has 42 table games.
Legends in Concert is the featured stage show. A
poolside Luau is held twice weekly.
■ **Games Available** 3-card poker, Blackjack,
Craps, Let It Ride, Mini-baccarat, Pai Gow,
Roulette, Slots, Sport Book

JW Marriott

221 N. Rampart Blvd.
Las Vegas, NV 89128
(877) 869-8777
(800) 844-9593

www.gowestmarriott.com/lasvegas
■ **Hotel:** 541 rooms
50,000 square feet
■ **Restaurant(s):** Ceres, Hamada of Japan,
Spiedini Ristorante, Oxo, Cafe Concerto,
Waterside Cafe, The Palms Patio.
Hotel has two pools, spa, health club, shops and a
wedding chapel as well as access to golf courses.
Casino has 40 table games.
Entertainment in J. C. Woolloughan pub, Addison's
Lounge and the Round Bar.
■ **Games Available:** Blackjack, Craps, Poker,
Roulette, Slots - 1139, Sport Book

Key Largo Casino

377 East Flamingo Rd.
Las Vegas, NV 89014
(702) 733-7777
(800) 634-6617
Fax: (702) 369-6911
www.keylargocasino.com
■ **Hotel:** 300 rooms, $40-up
■ **Restaurant(s):** The Coral Café
Hotel has a pool and spa.
■ **Games Available:** Blackjack, Craps, Roulette,
Slots - 250

Klondike Inn

5191 Las Vegas Blvd. South
Las Vegas, NV 89119
(702) 739-9351
■ **Hotel:** 150 rooms, $30-up
■ **Games Available:** Blackjack, Roulette, Slots

Lady Luck Casino Hotel

206 N. Third St.
Las Vegas, NV 89101
(800) LADY LUCK
ladyluck@islecorp.com
www.ladyluck.com
■ **Hotel:** 792 rooms, $29-up

■ **Restaurant(s):** Burgundy Room, 3rd Street Grill, Lady Luck Express, Tower Bar.

Hotel has pool, lounge, showroom, gift shop. Casino has 28 table games.

Stars of the Strip afternoon show is featured.

■ **Games Available** Blackjack, Craps, Let It Ride, Mini-baccarat, Roulette, Slots - 800

Las Vegas Club Casino Hotel

18 E. Fremont St.
Las Vegas, NV 89101
(702) 385-1664
(800) 634-6532
www.playatlvc.com

■ **Hotel:** 410 rooms

■ **Reservations:** (877) 621-ROOM

■ **Restaurant(s):** Great Moments Room, Upper Deck, Seventh Inning Scoop.

Sports Hall of Fame features sports memorabilia.

■ **Games Available:** Blackjack, Craps, Keno, Let It Ride, Roulette, Slots, Sport Book

Las Vegas Hilton

3000 Paradise Road
Las Vegas, NV 89109
(888) 732-7117
www.lv-hilton.com

■ **Hotel:** 3000 rooms, $39-up

■ **Restaurant(s):** Ten restaurants: Benihana, Robata, Hilton Steakhouse, Garden of the Dragon, Margarita Grille, Andiamo, Paradise Café, The Buffet, Quark's, Food on the Go.

Hotel has spa, outdoor heated pool, tennis courts, jogging track, Regis Salon, Sports Zone Video Arcade, seven shops. The Hilton has 200,000 square feet of convention facilities and is next to the Las Vegas Convention Center.

Live entertainment in The NightClub, concerts in the Hilton Theatre including Johnny Mathis, the Commodores, the Righteous Brothers. Star Trek: The Experience attraction is open daily.

■ **Games Available:** Baccarat, Blackjack, Keno Roulette, Slots, Sport Book

Longhorn Hotel/Casino

5288 Boulder Strip
Las Vegas, NV 89122
(702) 435-9170

■ **Hotel:** 150 rooms, $40-$45

6,500 square feet

■ **Restaurant(s):** Chuck Wagon specials around the clock.

Dyamite local singles' and duos' acts.

■ **Games Available:** Blackjack $1 - 4, Slots - 240

Luxor Las Vegas

3900 Las Vegas Blvd. S.
Las Vegas, NV 89119
(888) 777-0188
www.luxor.com

■ **Hotel:** 4408 rooms, $79-up

120,000 square feet

■ **Restaurant(s):** Nine restaurants: Isis, Sacred Sea, Luxor Steakhouse, Papyrus, Pharaoh's Pheast Buffet, Pyramid Café, Nile Deli, International Grounds, Luxor Food Court.

Attractions include IMAX Theatre, King Tut's Museum, Oasis Spa, five swimming pools, Giza Galleria of retail shops, 20,000 square feet of convention facilities. Casino has 106 table games.

Blue Man Group performs in the Luxor Theater and Midnight Fantasy in Pharaoh's Theater. More entertainment in RA Nightclub and Nefertiti's Lounge.

■ **Games Available:** Baccarat - 1, Blackjack - 66, Craps - 8, Let It Ride - 2, Mini-baccarat - 4 Pai Gow - 6, Roulette - 11, Slots - 2000, Sport Book

Main Street Station

200 N. Main St.
Las Vegas, NV 89101
(702) 387-1896
(800) 713-8933
www.mainstreetcasino.com

■ **Hotel:** 406 rooms
28,000 square feet
■ **Reservations:** (800) 465-0711
■ **Restaurant(s):** Pullman Grill, Garden Court Buffet, Triple 7 Restaurant and Brewery.
Shopping available at Bridge Avenue Retail Area. Collection of antiques and artifacts displayed in hotel.
■ **Games Available:** Blackjack, Craps - 4, Keno, Let It Ride, Pai Gow, Roulette - 2 Slots - 900

Mandalay Bay Resort & Casino

3950 Las Vegas Blvd. S.
Las Vegas, NV 89119
(877) 632-7800
www.mandalaybay.com
■ **Hotel:** 3220 rooms, $99-up
135,000 square feet
■ **Restaurant(s):** 13 restaurants: Aureole, 3950, Bayside Buffet, Border Grill, China Grill, Rock Lobster, House of Blues Restaurant, Raffles Café, Red Square, Rumjungle, Shanghai Lilly, Noodle Shop, Trattoria del Lupo.
Shark Reef has 100 species of animals and fish. The 11- acre Beach has cabanas, restaurants and entertainment. The 30,000 square foot Spa has 21 salons. There are also a dozen retail shops and two wedding chapels. Casino has 122 table games.
Storm Theatre six nights a week. Mandalay Bay Events Center, seating 12,000, hosts entertainers including Placido Domingo, The Eagles, Ricky Martin plus boxing. House of Blues has hosted Bob Dylan and B.B. King.
■ **Games Available:** Baccarat, Blackjack, Craps, Poker, Roulette, Slots - 2400, Sport Book

MGM Grand

3799 Las Vegas Blvd. South
Las Vegas, NV 89109
(702) 891-7777
(877) 880-0880
www.mgmgrand.com
■ **Hotel:** 5034 rooms, $70-up
171,500 square feet

■ **Reservations:** (800) 929-1111
■ **Restaurant(s):** 15 restaurants: Hollywood Brown Derby, Olio, Nob Hill, Pearl, Emeril's, Neyla, Mark Miller's Grill Room, Coyote Café, Wolfgang Puck Café, MGM Grand Buffet, Ricardo's Mexican Restaurant, Rainforest Café, Grand Wok, Studio Café, Cabana Grill.
Lion Habitat, CBS Television City research center, 380,000 square foot Conference Center, five pools, Studio Walk shopping, Grand Spa, Wedding Chapel, MGM Grand/Bally's Monorail.
EFX Theatre has $45 million musical production EFX Alive starring Rick Springfield. Entertainment Dome includes Showbar Lounge with bands. Grand Garden Arena, with 17,157 seats, features concerts, boxing matches and special events. Hollywood Theatre
■ **Games Available:** Baccarat, Blackjack, Craps, Keno, Mini-baccarat, Pai Gow, Roulette Slots - 3700, Sport Book

Mirage

3400 S. Las Vegas Blvd.
Las Vegas, NV 89109
(702) 791-7111
(800) 374-9000
www.mirage.com
■ **Hotel:** 3313 rooms, $79-up
■ **Restaurant(s):** Kokomo's, Caribe Café, The Roasted Bean.
Mirage is known for its volcano eruptions, white tiger habitat and dolphin habitat, its tropical rainforest and 20,000 gallon aquarium. The hotel offers a spa and salon, and a Street of Shops.
Siegfried & Roy perform twice nightly in the 1,504-seat Siegfried & Roy Theatre. Danny Gans is featured in his own 1,265-seat theater.
■ **Games Available:** Baccarat, Blackjack, Craps, Keno, Roulette, Slots, Sport Book

Monte Carlo Resort & Casino

3770 Las Vegas Blvd. S.
Las Vegas, NV 89109
(702) 730-7777
(888) 529-4828

www.monte-carlo.com

■ **Hotel:** 3002 rooms, $79-up

■ **Restaurant(s):** Blackstone's Restaurant, Buffet, Café, Monte Carlo Pub & Brewery, Andre's French Restaurant, Dragon Noodle, Market City Café.

Hotel has spa, fitness center, 11,000 square foot pool area, three tennis courts, salon. Shopping is available at Street of Dreams. A wedding chapel is available. Casino has 95 table games.

Headliners are featured along with magician Lance Burton.

■ **Games Available:** Baccarat, Blackjack, Craps, Keno, Pai Gow, Roulette, Slots - 2100, Sport Book

Nevada Palace Hotel and Casino

5255 Boulder Highway
Las Vegas, NV 89122
(702) 458-8810
(800) 634-6283
www.nvpalace.com

■ **Hotel:** 210 rooms, $25-$100

15,000 square feet

■ **Restaurant(s):** Three restaurants: Boulder Café, LaBella Restaurant, Hermann's Deli

Jimmy Limo, guitarist, performs.

■ **Games Available:** Blackjack - 4, Craps - 1, Keno, Poker, Roulette - 1, Slots $1 - 5, Slots $5 - 2, Slots 1 cent - 6, Slots Nickel - 197, Slots Quarter - 237, Sport Book

New York New York Hotel & Casino

3790 Las Vegas Blvd. South
Las Vegas, NV 89109
(702) 740-6969
(800) 693-6763
www.nynyhotelcasino.com

■ **Hotel:** 2023 rooms, $69-up

84,000 square feet

■ **Restaurant(s):** 10 restaurants: America, Chin Chin Café, Coney Island Pavillion, ESPN Zone, Gallagher's Steakhouse, Gonzalez Y Gonzalez, Il Fornaio, Il Fornaio Panetteria, Schrafft's Ice

Cream, Village Eateries.

The 12 hotel towers recreate New York's famous sites, including Statue of Liberty, Brooklyn Bridge, Empire State Building and Manhattan Roller Coaster. Shopping available at a dozen specialty stores. Casino has 80 table games.

Broadway Theater, seating 1,000, hosts Michael Flatley's Lord of the Dance. Cabaret Theater features comic Rita Rudner.

■ **Games Available:** Blackjack, Craps, Mini-baccarat, Pai Gow, Roulette, Slots - 2000

O'Shea's Casino

3555 Las Vegas Blvd. South
Las Vegas, NV 89109
(702) 697-2711
O'Shea's Magic & Movie Hall of Fame is available.

■ **Games Available:** Blackjack, Craps, Let It Ride, Poker, Roulette, Slots - 500

Orleans Hotel Casino

4500 W. Tropicana Ave.
Las Vegas, NV 89103
(800) ORLEANS
www.orleanscasino.com

■ **Hotel:** 840 rooms, $39-up

112,000 square feet

■ **Restaurant(s):** Canal Street Grille, Don Miguel's, La Louisiane, Courtyard Cafe, Terrible Mike's, Big Al's Oyster Bar, Kate's Korner, French Market Buffet, Seattle's Best Coffee House, Sazio, Brendan's Irish Pub and Koto.

Hotel has two outdoor pools, salon, video arcade.

Orleans Showroom, with 827 seats, features Jerry Lewis, Willie Nelson, Smothers Brothers. A 70-lane bowling center and 18 movie theaters are available.

■ **Games Available:** Blackjack, Craps, Keno, Let It Ride, Pai Gow, Poker - 20, Roulette Slots - 2200, Sport Book

Palace Station

2411 West Sahara Ave.
Las Vegas, NV 89102
(800) 544-2411
www.palacestation.com

■ **Hotel:** 1022 rooms, $70-up

■ **Reservations:** (702) 367-2411

■ **Restaurant(s):** The Broiler, Pasta Palace, The Feast Buffet, Iron Horse Café, Guadalajara Bar & Grille.

The casino's remodeled Pit reopened in November 2001 with a Victorian theme. The casino offers 55 table games, a 600-seat bingo hall and two keno lounges.

Variety of entertainment includes new Laugh Trax comedy club.

■ **Games Available:** Baccarat - 1, Bingo, Blackjack - 23, Craps - 6, Keno - 2, Let It Ride - 1, Pai Gow - 4, Poker - 9, Roulette - 3, Slots - 2200, Sport Book

Palms Resort Casino

4321 W. Flamingo Rd.
Las Vegas, NV 89103
(702) 942-7777
(866) 942-7777
Fax: (702) 942-7001
www.palms.com

■ **Hotel:** 447 rooms, $59-up
95,000 square feet

■ **Reservations:** (866) 942-7770

■ **Restaurant(s):** Little Buddha, Garduno's of Mexico, 9 Steak House, Sunrise Café, Festival Market Buffet, Blue Agave Oyster Bar.

The $265 million, 42-story hotel and casino opened in late 2001. Hotel has 18,000 square foot spa and fitness center and pool.

Goo Goo Dolls, Bad Company are among entertainment in the showroom. Entertainment in the Ghost Bar and Island Bar. Also available are 14 movie theaters.

■ **Games Available:** Blackjack, Craps, Keno, Poker, Roulette, Slots - 2200, Sport Book

Paris Las Vegas

3655 Las Vegas Blvd. South
Las Vegas, NV 89109
Las Vegas Strip
(702) 946-7000
Fax: (702) 946-4405
www.parislasvegas.com

■ **Hotel:** 2916 rooms
85,000 square feet

■ **Reservations:** (877) 796-2096

■ **Restaurant(s):** Eight restaurants: Eiffel Tower Restaurant, Les Artistes Steakhouse, Mon Ami Gabi, La Chine, Le Provencal, Le Village Buffet, Le Café Ile St. Louis, Ortanique, Jean Jaques' Boulangerie, du Parc. Also five lounges.

Resort features replicas of Paris landmarks the Eiffel Tower, Arc de Triomphe, Paris Opera House and the Louvre. Rooftop swimming pool, health spa, two wedding chapels, salon, 140,000 square feet of ballroom space. Le Boulevard has French-style bouti

Paris Le Theatre des Arts has headliners including Natalie Cole, Dennis Miller, Whoppi Goldberg and Tony Bennett. Le Cabaret Show Lounge features live entertainment.

■ **Games Available:** Slots - 2000, Sport Book, Table games - 100

A 50-story replica of the Eiffel Tower marks the Paris Las Vegas resort.

Plaza Hotel and Casino

1 Main St.
P.O. Box 760
Las Vegas, NV 89125
Downtown Las Vegas
(702) 386-2110
(800) 634-6575
reservations@plazahotelcasino.com
www.plazahotelcasino.com
■ **Hotel:** 1034 rooms, $35-$75
■ **Restaurant(s):** Center Stage Restaurant, Chop Chop Chinese Buffet, food court with McDonald's and Subway.

Kid's game room, workout room, tennis courts, pool, covered parking, valet parking, Greyhound bus terminal.

Revues in Omaha Lounge
■ **Games Available:** Bingo, Blackjack $2, Craps - 4, Keno - 1, Pai Gow - 2, Poker - 10, Roulette - 4, Slots $1 - 150, Slots $5 - 10, Slots Nickel - 493, Slots Quarter - 600, Sport Book

Ramada Inn Speedway

3227 Civic Center Dr.
Las Vegas, NV 89130
(800) 844-9593
■ **Hotel:** 95 rooms, $50-$70
■ **Restaurant(s):** 24-Hour Speedway Café
Hotel has outdoor pool.
■ **Games Available:** Slots, Sport Book, Table games

Rio All-Suite Hotel and Casino

3700 West Flamingo Road
Las Vegas, NV 89103
(702) 777-7777
(888) 746-7153
www.playrio.com
■ **Hotel:** 2500 rooms
120,000 square feet
■ **Reservations:** (888) 396-2483
■ **Restaurant(s):** 13 restaurants: Antonio's Italian Ristorante, Buzios Seafood Restaurant,

Fiore Steakhouse, Wine Cellar & Tasting Room, All- American Bar and Grill, Bamboleo, Carnival World Buffet, Mamma Maria's Cucina, Mask, Sao Paulo Café, Toscano's Deli and Market

Ipanema Beach, four pools, spa, largest public collection of wines in the world, Rio Secco Golf Club, three wedding chapels. Casino has 100 table games.

Masquerade Show in the Sky, Samba Theater with headliners including Louie Anderson and Penn and Teller, the Ronn Lewis afternoon show, The Scintas, Earl Turner, interactive comedy dinner show.
■ **Games Available:** Blackjack, Craps, Let It Ride, Mini-baccarat, Roulette, Slots - 2500

Riviera Hotel Casino

2901 S. Las Vegas Blvd.
Las Vegas, NV 89109
(800) 634-3420
www.theriviera.com
■ **Hotel:** 2100 rooms, $49-up
100,000 square feet
■ **Restaurant(s):** Kristofer's Steak House, Ristorante Italiano, Kady's Coffee Shop, World's Fare Buffet, Mardi Gras Food Court.

The hotel features a spa, convention center, wedding chapel and more than a dozen retail shops.

Splash, An Evening at La Cage, Crazy Girls Fantasy Review and the Riviera Comedy Club are featured entertainment.
■ **Games Available:** Baccarat, Blackjack, Craps, Let It Ride, Pai Gow, Roulette, Slots - 1400, Sport Book

Royal Hotel Casino

99 Convention Center Drive
Las Vegas, NV 89109
(702) 735-6117
(800) 634-6118
■ **Hotel:** 160 rooms
■ **Games Available:** Slots - 125

Sahara Hotel and Casino

2535 Las Vegas Blvd. South
Las Vegas, NV 89109
(702) 737-2111
(888) 696-2121
www.saharavegas.com

■ **Hotel:** 1720 rooms, $29-$375

85,000 square feet

■ **Restaurant(s):** Six restaurants: Caravan Coffee Shop, Paco's Bar & Grill, Sahara Steak House, Sahara Buffet, NASCAR Café, Jitters Gourmet Coffee

Six stores, pool and spa are in the hotel, along with a business center. Speed The Ride and CyberSpeedway are hotel features.

Steve Wyrick's magic show and "The Rat Pack is Back" variety show are featured.

■ **Games Available:** Blackjack $1 - 34, Craps - 3, Keno, Pai Gow - 2, Poker - 5, Roulette - 4, Slots $1 - 185, Slots $5 - 14, Slots 50 cents - 21 Slots Nickel - 456, Slots Quarter - 497, Sport Book

Sam's Town Hotel & Gambling Hall

5111 Boulder Highway
Las Vegas, NV 89122
(702) 456-7777
(800) 897-8696
www.samstownlv.com

■ **Hotel:** 648 rooms

■ **Restaurant(s):** Firelight Buffet, Billy Bob's Steak House and Saloon, Willy and Jose's Cantina, Fresh Harvest Café, Fellini's.

New this year is a 1,100 seat multi-use event center, an 18-screen movie theatre complex, bowling center, a rotisserie buffet, a new coffee shop, new casino area, and a 1,000-space valet parking garage. Two RV parks have 500 spaces.

Headliners appear in Sam's Town Live. A 56-lane bowling center and 18-screen movie theater have opened. Sunset Stampede is a free laser light and water show in Mystic Falls Park.

■ **Games Available:** Bingo, Blackjack, Craps, Keno, Let It Ride, Poker, Roulette, Slots - 3300, Sport Book

Santa Fe Station

US 95 At North Rancho
Las Vegas, NV 89108
(702) 658-4900
(800) 6-STATIO
www.stationsantafe.com

■ **Hotel:** 200 rooms, $20-up

■ **Restaurant(s):** Taos Steakhouse, Santa Fe Café, Capri, Food Court.

Casino has 27 table games.

Live entertainment in Lizard Lounge and Iguana Bar.

■ **Games Available:** 3-card poker, Bingo, Blackjack - 16, Craps - 3, Let It Ride, Pai Gow, Roulette - 2, Slots - 2000, Sport Book

Silverton Hotel, Casino, RV Park

3333 Blue Diamond Road
Las Vegas, NV 89139
(866) 668-6688
www.silvertoncasino.com

■ **Hotel:** 300 rooms

30,000 square feet

■ **Restaurant(s):** Buffet, Fireside Café.

Hotel has a pool. RV Park is available. Casino has 18 table games.

Entertainers include Ricky Van Shelton, Chubby Checker, Sha Na Na.

■ **Games Available:** 3-card poker, Blackjack, Craps, Let It Ride, Pai Gow, Roulette, Slots - 1100

Slots-A-Fun Casino

2890 Las Vegas Blvd. South
Las Vegas, NV 89109
North Strip, Las Vegas
(702) 734-0410
(800) 354-1232

17,700 square feet

■ **Restaurant(s):** Subway sandwich shop; Nobel Romans Pizza.

■ **Games Available:** Blackjack $1, Craps, Roulette, Slots $1 - 63, Slots 1 cent - 10, Slots 2 cents - 4, Slots Nickel - 205, Slots Quarter - 264

Stage Door Casino

4000 Audrie St.
Las Vegas, NV 89109
(702) 733-0124
■ **Games Available:** Slots

Stardust Resort & Casino

3000 Las Vegas Blvd. S.
Las Vegas, NV 89109
(702) 732-6111
(800) 824-6033
www.stardustlv.com
■ **Hotel:** 1500 rooms, $39-up
85,000 square feet
■ **Restaurant(s):** Five restaurants: William B's, Coco Palms, Sushi King, Island Paradise Café, Tony Roma's.

Outdoor complex includes two pools. Hotel has spa and fitness center.

Wayne Newton appears for 40 weeks a year. Big bands and other entertainment available.
■ **Games Available:** Baccarat - 1, Blackjack - 42, Craps - 6, Keno, Let It Ride - 2, Mini-baccarat - 1, Pai Gow - 4, Poker - 10, Roulette - 5, Slots - 1590, Sport Book

Stratosphere Casino Hotel & Tower

2000 Las Vegas Boulevard South
Las Vegas, NV 89104
(800) 998-6937
Reservations@stratospherehotel.com
www.stratospherehotel.com
■ **Hotel:** 2444 rooms, $30-up
80,000 square feet
Restaurant(s): Top of the World, Crazy Armadillo, Lucky's Café, Courtyard Buffet, Roxy's Diner, Triple Crown Deli, Hamada Asian Village, Fellini's Tower of Pasta.

The Stratosphere Tower, at 1,149 feet, is the tallest structure west of the Mississippi River and hosts the Big Shot thrill ride and the High Roller roller coaster. A new 24-story, 1,000-room addition opened in 2001. The hotel has a wedding chapel.

Viva Las Vegas and American Superstars are featured shows.
■ **Games Available:** Blackjack, Craps, Pai Gow, Roulette, Slots - 1551, Sport Book

Suncoast Hotel & Casino

9090 Alta Drive
Las Vegas, NV 89145
www.suncoastcasino.com
(877) 677-7111
■ **Hotel:** 440 rooms, $55-up
80,000 square feet
■ **Restaurant(s):** Via Veneto, Senor Miguel's, Primo's, The Oyster Bar, Cafe Sienna, St. Tropez Buffet, Terrible Mike's, Kate's Korner, Seattle's Best Coffee House.

Hotel has pool and fitness center.

A 500-seat Showroom features acts from Air Supply to Debbie Reynolds. A 64-lane bowling center and 16 movie theaters are available.
■ **Games Available:** Bingo, Blackjack, Craps, Let It Ride, Pai Gow, Poker, Roulette, Slots, Sport Book

Super 8 Motel and Casino

4250 Koval Lane
Las Vegas, NV 89109
(800) 844-9593
■ **Hotel:** 290 rooms, $48-up
■ **Restaurant(s):** Ellis Island Restaurant
Motel has an outdoor pool.
■ **Games Available:** Slots, Sport Book

Terribles Hotel & Casino

4100 Paradise Road
Las Vegas, NV 89156
(702) 733-7000
(800) 640-9777
■ **Hotel:** 373 rooms
■ **Restaurant(s):** Bougainvillea Cafe, Terrible's Buffet.

■ **Games Available:** Blackjack, Craps, Pai Gow, Roulette, Slots - 750, Sport Book

Treasure Island at the Mirage

3300 S. Las Vegas Blvd.
Las Vegas, NV 89109
(702) 894-7111
(800) 288-7206
Fax: (702) 894-7414
www.treasureisland.com

■ **Hotel:** 2900 rooms, $59-up

70,000 square feet

■ **Restaurant(s):** Buccaneer Bay Restaurant, Treasure Island Buffet, Terrace Café, The Delicatessen.

Buccaneer Bay battle of the pirate ships rages every 90 minutes. Hotel has pool, salon and spa, and Shadow Creek Golf Course. A variety of boutiques are available for shopping and hotel has two wedding chapels.

Mystere Cirque du Soleil is the featured production.

■ **Games Available:** Baccarat, Blackjack, Craps, Keno, Pai Gow, Poker, Roulette, Slots Sport Book

Tropicana Resort & Casino

3801 Las Vegas Blvd., South
Las Vegas, NV 89109
(702) 739-2222
(888) 826-TROP
hotelres@tropicanalv.com
www.tropicanalv.com

■ **Hotel:** 1878 rooms, $30-$130

61,000 square feet

■ **Restaurant(s):** Eight restaurants: Pietro's, Savanna, Mizuno's Japanese Steak House, The Golden Dynasty, Calypsos, Island Buffet, Legend's Deli, Java Java.

Five acres of landscaped grounds, pools, lagoons and waterfalls are between the twin towers. Casino Legends Hall of Fame features casino and entertainment memorabilia. Hotel has 106,000 square feet of convention space, Health Spa, Wedding Chapel.

■ **Entertainment:** Best of the Folies Bergere, Illusionary Magic of Rick Thomas are performed daily. Other acts include The Birdman of Las Vegas, T. Fox & The Fox City Show and Comedy Stop at the Trop.

■ **Games Available:** Baccarat, Blackjack, Craps, Roulette, Slots

The Folies Bergere is the featured entertainment at Tropicana in Las Vegas.

Tuscany Hotel Casino

255 E. Flamingo Road
Las Vegas, NV 89109
(877) TUSCAN1
www.tuscanylasvegas.com

■ **Hotel:** 1000 rooms, $85-up

60,000 square feet

■ **Restaurant(s):** Palazzo Ristorante, Cabana Bar & Grill.

In 2002, Tuscany opened a 60,000-square-foot casino, a sports book, a buffet, a coffee shop, Sports Deli and more meeting space.

■ **Games Available:** Slots - 1000, Sport Book, Table games

Vacation Village

6711 Las Vegas Blvd. South
Las Vegas, NV 89119
(702) 897-1700
(702) 897-1700
■ **Hotel:** 315 rooms
■ **Games Available:** Blackjack, Roulette, Slots,
Sport Book

Venetian Resort-Hotel-Casino

3355 Las Vegas Blvd. S.
Las Vegas, NV 89109
(702) 414-1000
(877) 2-VENICE
www.venetian.com
■ **Hotel:** 3036 rooms
■ **Restaurant(s):** Canaletto, Lutece, Pinot
Brasserie, Postrio, Star Canyon, Valentino,
Tsunami Asian Grill, Zefferino Ristorante.
Guggeheim Las Vegas offers art exhibits. Gondola
rides are available on the Grand Canal. The casino
has 122 table games.
Melinda First Lady of Magic is featured in the
Showroom. Other attraction is Madame Tussaud's
Wax Museum.
■ **Games Available:** Baccarat, Blackjack, Craps,
Keno, Let It Ride, Pai Gow, Roulette, Slots, Sport
Book

Western Hotel Casino

889 Fremont St.
Las Vegas, NV 89101
(702) 384-4620
(800) 634-6703
Hotel: 116 rooms, $22-up
■ **Games Available:** Bingo, Blackjack, Keno,
Slots

Westward Ho Casino

2900 Las Vegas Blvd. S.
Las Vegas, NV 89109
(702) 731-2900
(800) 634-6803
reservations@westwardho.com
www.westwardho.com
■ **Hotel:** 777 rooms, $25-up
■ **Restaurant(s):** The Ca-Fae
The hotel has seven pools and Jacuzzis.
Entertainment in the Crown Room.
■ **Games Available:** 3-card poker, Blackjack,
Craps, Let It Ride, Roulette, Slots - 1000

Wild Wild West Casino

3330 W. Tropicana Ave.
Las Vegas, NV 89103
(800) 634-3488
■ **Hotel:** 300 rooms, $20-up
■ **Games Available:** Blackjack, Craps, Roulette,
Slots, Sport Book

Wildfire Casino

1901 N. Rancho
Las Vegas, NV 89106
(702) 648-3801
20,000 square feet
Restaurant(s): Dante's
* **Games Available:** Blackjack $1 - 5, Slots $1 -
21, Slots Nickel - 115, Slots Quarter - 83, Sport
Book

NEVADA

Airport Plaza Hotel & Casino

1981 Terminal Way
Reno, NV 89502
(775) 348-6370
■ **Hotel:** 270 rooms, $70-$100
■ **Games Available:** Slots - 47

Alamo Travel Center

1950 Greg St.
Sparks, NV 89431
(702) 355-8888
Fax: (702) 359-8245
info@thealamo.com
www.thealamo.com
Truck drivers area, Super 8 Motel, barber shop, gas and diesel pumps, convenience store.
■ **Games Available:** Blackjack, Keno, Slots - 225

Atlantis Casino Resort

3800 S. Virginia St.
Reno, NV 89502
(775) 825-4700
(800) 723-6500
www.atlantiscasino.com
■ **Hotel:** 1000 rooms, $49-$249
■ **Restaurant(s):** Toucan Charlie's Buffet & Grille, Purple Parrot, Café Alfresco, Atlantis Seafood Steakhouse, Oyster Bar, MonteVigna
New 27-story hotel tower has been added, along with expanded pool deck area and 16,000 square foot casino addition. Golf course nearby.
Musical Cabaret and Atlantis Nightclub offer live entertainment.
■ **Games Available:** Blackjack, Craps, Keno, Pai Gow, Poker, Roulette, Slots - 1400, Sport Book

Avi Resort and Casino

10000 Aha Macau Parkway
Laughlin, NV 89029
(800) AVI-2-WIN
info@avicasino.com
www.avicasino.com
■ **Hotel:** 300 rooms, $19-up
25,000 square feet
■ **Restaurant(s):** Native Harvest Buffet, Moon Shadow Grill, Feathers Café, Beach Club.
Hotel has a pool, spa and fitness center, beach and marina, as well as access to the Mojave Resort Golf Club. An RV Park has 260 spaces. Casino has 23 table games.
River Garden Pavilion hosts entertainers including Marshall Tucker, Edgar Tucker, Keanu Reeves. ArrowWeed Lounge also has live entertainment.
■ **Games Available:** Bingo, Blackjack, Craps, Keno, Let It Ride, Pai Gow, Roulette, Slots - 777, Sport Book

Baldini's Sports Casino

865 S. Rock Blvd.
Sparks, NV 89431
(775) 358-0116
www.baldinissportscasino.com
Sports Store sells sports memorabilia.
■ **Games Available:** Blackjack, Keno, Slots - 700, Sport Book

Barley's Casino & Brewing Company

4500 E. Sunset Rd.
Henderson, NV 89014
(702) 458-2739
19,000 square feet
Restaurant(s): Brewer's Café
Micro-brewery in the casino brews 3,000 barrels of beer a year.
■ **Games Available:** Slots - 199, Sport Book, Table games - 6

Barton's Club 93

P.O. Box 523
Jackpot, NV 89825
(775) 755-2341
(800) 258-2937
■ **Hotel:** 100 rooms
■ **Games Available:** Blackjack, Craps, Let It Ride, Roulette, Slots - 600

Bighorn Casino

3016 E. Lake Mead Blvd.
North Las Vegas, NV 89030
(702) 642-1940
■ **Games Available:** Blackjack, Slots - 150

Bill's Lake Tahoe

U.S. Highway 50
Lake Tahoe, NV 89449
(775) 588-2455
■ **Restaurant(s):** Bill's Roadhouse
■ **Games Available:** Blackjack $3, Craps, Roulette, Slots

Bonanza Casino

4720 N. Virginia St.
Reno, NV 89506
(775) 323-2724
■ **Games Available:** Blackjack, Craps,Slots, Sport Book

Bonanza Inn & Casino

855 W. Williams Ave.
Fallon, NV 89406
(775) 423-6031
■ **Hotel:** 75 rooms, $45-up
■ **Games Available:** Blackjack, Slots

Bonanza Saloon

P.O. Box 95
Virginia City, NV 89440
(775) 847-0789
■ **Games Available:** Slots

Boomtown Hotel Casino

I-80, exit 4
Verdi, NV 89431
Reno area
(877) 726-6686
www.boomtowncasinos.com
■ **Hotel:** 318 rooms, $50-up
■ **Restaurant(s):** Cassidy's, Sundance Cantina, Silver Screen Buffet.
Resort includes an RV Park.
Nightly entertainment in the Cabaret.
■ **Games Available:** Blackjack, Craps, Keno, Poker, Roulette, Slots - 1100, Sport Book

Border Inn & Casino

P.O. Box 30
Baker, NV 89311
(775) 234-7300
■ **Hotel:** 29 rooms, $29-up
■ **Games Available:** Slots - 20

Bordertown Casino

19575 Hwy 395 N.
Reno, NV 89506
(775) 972-1309
(800) 443-4383
www.statelinecasinos.com
■ **Restaurant(s):** Kafana
RV Resort has 50 spaces.
■ **Games Available:** Blackjack, Slots - 175

Bruno's Country Club

300 Main St.
Gerlach, NV 89412
(775) 557-2220

■ **Hotel:** 42 rooms
■ **Games Available:** Slots - 11

Bucket of Blood Saloon

P.O. Box E
Virginia City, NV 89440
(775) 847-0322

■ **Games Available:** Slots - 50

Buffalo Bill's Resort & Casino

I-15
P.O. Box 19119
Primm, NV 89019
35 miles south of Las Vegas
(702) 386-7867
(800) FUN-STOP
www.primadonna.com

■ **Hotel:** 1242 rooms
46,000 square feet
■ **Restaurant(s):** Batelli's Italiano Resaurante, Wagonmaster, Baja Bar & Grille, Miss Ashley's Boarding House Buffet.

The resort features the Desperado roller coaster, Turbo Drop ride, Ghost Town Motion Simulator Theater and the Adventure Canyon Log Flume Ride. Casino features 43 table games.

Star of the Desert Arena, seating 6,000, features stars such as Melissa Etheridge, Brooks and Dunn, Reba McEntire, and B.B. King.

■ **Games Available:** Blackjack, Craps , Pai Gow, Poker, Roulette, Slots - 1723, Sport Book

Burro Inn

P.O. Box 7
Beatty, NV 89003
(775) 553-2445
(800) 843-2078

Fax: (775) 553-2892
burroinn @beattynv.com
www.burroinn.com
Motel and RV park available.

■ **Games Available:** Blackjack. Slots

Cactus Petes Resort Casino

1385 Highway 93
Jackpot, NV 89825
Idaho/Nevada border
(775) 755-2321
(800) 821-1103
www.ameristarcasinos.com

■ **Hotel:** 300 rooms
26,000 square feet
■ **Restaurant(s):** Plateau Restaurant, Gala Showroom, Desert Room, Coyote Café, Canyon Cove

Pool, tennis courts, golf course, RV park with 90 spaces, meeting facilities, Bristlecone Emporium shop, general store, styling salon.

Dinner showroom offers entertainers including Crystal Gayle, Louise Mandrell and the Smothers Brothers.

■ **Games Available:** 3-card poker - 1, Blackjack - 11, Craps - 2, Keno, Let It Ride - 1, Poker - 6, Roulette - 2, Slots - 907, Sport Book

Caesars Tahoe

55 Highway 50
Tahoe, NV 89449
60 miles from Reno
(800) 648-3353
www.caesars.com/tahoe

■ **Hotel:** 440 rooms, $99-$250
40,000 square feet
■ **Restaurant(s):** Seven restaurants: The Broiler Room, Primavera, Empress Court, Roman Feast Buffet, Aroma Café, Planet Hollywood, Subway.

Galleria of Shops, full service business center, 16,000 square feet of convention space, health spa, indoor pool, tennis courts, The Odyssey 58-foot luxury yacht, multiple outdoor recreation opportunities.

Variety of entertainment, including comedy, country, pop, production. Entertainers include David Copperfield, Wynonna, the Beach Boys, Carrot Top, Moody Blues.

■ **Games Available:** Blackjack - 40, Craps - 6, Keno - 2, Pai Gow - 3, Poker - 3, Roulette - 5, Slots - 237, Slots $1 - 214, Slots $10 - 12, Slots $5 - 2, Slots Nickel - 227, Slots Quarter - 401, Sport Book

Caesars Tahoe is nestled in a scenic location on Lake Tahoe, with the Sierras towering in the distance.

Cal-Nev-Ari Casino

1 Piute Valley Drive
Cal-Nev-Ari, NV 89039
(702) 297-9289
■ **Hotel:** 10 rooms, $35
■ **Games Available:** Slots - 33

Cal-Neva Resort

P.O. Box 368
Crystal Bay, NV 89402
Lake Tahoe
(800) 225-6382
www.calnevaresort.com

■ **Hotel:** 220 rooms
Cal-Neva is known for its European Health Spa and its wedding facilities. It has an outdoor pool, fitness center, arcade and gift shop. It was once owned by Frank Sinatra.
Entertainment in the Frank Sinatra Celebrity Showroom
■ **Games Available:** Blackjack, Craps, Roulette, Slots

Carson City Nugget

507 N. Carson St.
Carson City, NV 89701
(775) 882-1626
(800) 426-5239
www.ccmotel.com
Hotel: 82 rooms
■ **Restaurant(s):** Steakhouse, Garden Coffee Shop, buffet, Oyster Bar.
■ **Games Available:** Bingo, Blackjack, Craps, Keno, Roulette, Slots - 700

Carson Horseshoe Club

402 N. Carson St.
Carson City, NV 89701
(775) 883-2211
■ **Games Available:** Slots

Carson Station Hotel and Casino

900 South Carson St.
Carson City, NV 89701
(877) 519-5567
carsonstation@pyramid.net
www.carsonstation.com

■ **Hotel:** 92 rooms
■ **Restaurant(s):** The Station Grill & Rotisserie, Station Restaurant.
Casino has eight table games.
Cabaret Lounge has live entertainment.
■ **Games Available:** Blackjack, Craps, Keno, Roulette, Slots - 300

CasaBlanca Resort

950 W. Mesquite Blvd.
Mesquite, NV 89027
(800) 459-PLAY
www.casablancaresort.com
■ **Hotel:** 500 rooms, $39-up
40,000 square feet
■ **Restaurant(s):** Katherine's, Purple Fez Café, Buffet.
Hotel has pool, spa, salon and arcade as well as wedding planning. An RV Park with 45 sites is available. CasaBlanca Golf Course is 18 holes.
Entertainers include Rita Rudner, Juice Newton, Charlie Daniels, as well as free comedy shows.
■ **Games Available:** 3-card poker, Blackjack, Craps, Let It Ride, Pai Gow, Roulette, Slots - 750

Casino West

11 N. Main
Yerington, NV 89447
(775) 463-2481
(800) 227-4661
■ **Hotel:** 79 rooms
Movie theater, bowling center
■ **Games Available:** Slots, Table games

Circus Circus Reno

500 North Sierra St.
Reno, NV 89503
(775) 329-0711
(800) 648-5010
ccrmktg@mrgmail.com
www.circusreno.com

■ **Hotel:** 1572 rooms
■ **Restaurant(s):** Amici's Pasta & Steaks, Art Gecko's Southwest Grill, Courtyard Buffet, Kokopelli's Sushi, Main Street Deli & Ice Cream Shoppe, Three Ring Coffee Shop.
New Mandalay Convention Center opened early in 2002 with 18,000 square feet of additional space. Five retail shops available. Casino has 83 table games.
Circus Stage provides circus acts free of charge.
■ **Games Available:** Blackjack, Craps, Keno, Pai Gow, Poker, Roulette, Slots - 1600, Sport Book

Club Cal-Neva Casino

140 North Virginia St.
Reno, NV 89501
(877) 777-7303
info@clubcalneva.com
www.clubcalneva.com
■ **Hotel:** 125 rooms
■ **Restaurant(s):** Virginian Steak House, Top Deck Restaurant, Copper Ledge Restaurant, Hofbrau Buffet, Gridiron Grill.
Rooms and lobby of hotel were recently remodeled. Wedding packages are available.
Riverfront Theatre offers live entertainment.
■ **Games Available:** Blackjack, Craps, Let It Ride, Pai Gow, Poker, Roulette, Slots - 1600, Sport Book

Club Fortune

725 S. Racetrack Rd.
Henderson, NV 89015
(702) 566-5555
■ **Games Available:** Bingo, Slots

Colorado Belle Hotel & Casino

2100 S. Casino Drive
Laughlin, NV 89028
90 miles south of Las Vegas
(702) 298-4000
(866) 35-BELLE

www.coloradobelle.com

Hotel: 1201 rooms

65,000 square feet casino is a paddlewheel replica

Restaurant(s): Captain's Food Fare, Orleans Room, Mississippi Lounge, Paddlewheel Restaurant.

Four stores, Boiler Room Brew Pub. Hotel has two pools and a spa.

■ **Games Available:** Blackjack, Craps, Keno, Poker, Roulette, Slots, Sport Book

Commercial Casino

345 Fourth St.
Elko, NV 89801
(800) 648-2345
www.fh-inc.com

Casino features gunfighters artwork and a huge stuffed polar bear.

■ **Games Available:** Slots

Crystal Bay Club Casino

P.O. Box 37
Crystal Bay, NV 89402
(775) 831-0512

■ **Games Available:** Blackjack, Craps, Roulette, Slots

Delta Saloon

18 S. C St.
Virginia City, NV 89440
(775) 847-0789

■ **Games Available:** Slots

Diamond's Casino

1010 E. Sixth St.
Reno, NV 89512
(800) 648-4877

■ **Hotel:** 277 rooms, $60-up

■ **Games Available:** Blackjack, Craps, Slots

Edgewater Hotel & Casino

2020 S. Casino Drive
Laughlin, NV 89029
90 miles south of Las Vegas
(702) 298-2453
(800) 677-4837
www.edgewater-casino.com

■ **Hotel:** 1421 rooms, $22-up

60,000 square feet

■ **Restaurant(s):** Hickory Pit Steakhouse, Garden Room, Grand Buffet, Edgewater Deli, McDonald's.

Edgewater Belle paddlewheeler gives tours of Colorado River. Hotel has sundeck, spa, riverwalk.

Variety of entertainment includes the Coasters, Wild at Heart, Hotel California.

■ **Games Available:** Bingo, Blackjack $2 - 25, Craps - 3, Ken, Pai Gow - 1, Roulette - 4, Slots $1 - 186, Slots $5 - 15, Slots 1 cent - 12, Slots 50 cents - 22, Slots Nickel - 402, Slots Quarter - 568, Sport Book

Eldorado Casino

140 Water St.
Henderson, NV 89015
(702) 564-1811
Fax: (702) 564-5369
www.eldoradocasino.com

■ **Restaurant(s):** Mariana's Cantina, The Café, Snack Bar.

Casino has 11 table games.

■ **Games Available:** Bingo, Blackjack, Craps, Keno, Pai Gow, Roulette, Slots - 600, Sport Book

Eldorado Casino Reno

345 N. Virginia St.
Reno, NV 89501
(775) 786-5700
(800) 648-5966
Fax: (775) 348-7513
www.eldoradoreno.com

■ **Hotel:** 817 rooms

■ **Restaurant(s):** La Strada, Chef's Buffet, Golden Fortune, Tivoli Gardens, Seafood Buffet. Entertainment in Eldorado Showroom, BuBinga Lounge.

■ **Games Available:** Blackjack, Craps, Keno, Pai Gow, Poker, Roulette, Slots - 2000, Sport Book

Eureka Casino Hotel

275 Mesa Blvd.
Mesquite, NV 89027
(702) 346-4600
(800) 346-4611
Fax: (702) 346-8526
hotel@eurekamesquite.com
www.eurekamesquite.com

■ **Hotel:** 210 rooms

■ **Restaurant(s):** Tumbleweed Café

Live bands, karaoke.

■ **Games Available:** Bingo, Blackjack, Craps, Poker, Roulette, Slots, Sport Boo

Fernley Truck Inn Casino

485 Truck Inn Way
Fernley, NV 89408
(775) 351-1000
www.truckinn.com

■ **Hotel:** 46 rooms, $30-$45

■ **Games Available:** Slots

Fiesta Henderson

777 West Lake Mead Dr.
Henderson, NV 89015
(800) 844-9593

■ **Hotel:** 224 rooms, $39-up

37,000 square feet

■ **Restaurant(s):** Baja Beach Cafe, Fuego, Festival Buffet, MacKenzie River Pizza Co.

Recently changed its name from the Reserve Hotel.

Free entertainment in Lava Lounge.

■ **Games Available:** Bingo, Blackjack, Craps, Keno, Roulette, Slots - 1000

Fitzgeralds Casino Reno

255 N. Virginia St.
Reno, NV 89504
(800) 535-LUCK
www.fitzgeraldsreno.com

■ **Hotel:** 351 rooms, $24-up

■ **Restaurant(s):** Lord Fitzgeralds Feast and Merriment, Molly's Garden Restaurant, Limericks Pub & Grille.

■ **Games Available:** Blackjack, Craps, Keno, Let It Ride, Roulette, Slots

Flamingo Laughlin

1900 S. Casino Drive
Laughlin, NV 89029
(888) 662-LUCK
(800) FLAMINGO
www.laughlinflamingo.com

■ **Hotel:** 1900 rooms, $22-$270

60,000 square feet

■ **Restaurant(s):** Alta Villa, Beef Barron, Flamingo Diner, Fruit Basket Buffet.

Tours of the Colorado River, 30,000 feet of meeting space in Convention Center, Wedding Chapel, hotel has 90 suites, 60 table games.

Reflections of the Rat Pack at the Club Flamingo Showroom, concerts at the Flamingo Outdoor Amphitheatre including Tom Jones, Engelbert Humperdinck, Wynonna, Chicago.

■ **Games Available:** Blackjack, Craps, Pai Gow, Roulette, Slots - 1500

Gold Dust West

444 Vine St.
Reno, NV 89503
(800) 438-9378

■ **Hotel:** 100 rooms, $70-up

■ **Games Available:** Slots, Sport Book

Gold Strike Hotel

No. 1 Main St.
Jean, NV 89019
25 miles south of Las Vegas
(702) 477-5000
(800) 634-1359
www.nevadalanding.com
■ **Hotel:** 812 rooms, $19-up
37,000 square feet
■ **Restaurant(s):** Gold Rush Café, Gold Strike Steak House, Gold Strike Bonanza Buffet, Sutter's Snacks.
Casino has 22 table games.
■ **Games Available:** Blackjack, Craps, Keno, Roulette, Slots - 1000

Golden Nugget Laughlin

2300 S. Casino Drive
Laughlin, NV 89028
(702) 298-7111
(800) 955-7278
guestservices@gnlaughlin.com
www.gnlaughlin.com
■ **Hotel:** 300 rooms
■ **Restaurant(s):** The Lobster Bar, Jane's Grill, River Café, The Buffet, The Deli.
Hotel has a pool and spa.
Entertainment in Tarzan's Nightclub.
■ **Games Available:** Blackjack, Craps, Keno, Roulette, Slots, Sport Book

Hacienda Hotel & Casino

Highway 93
Boulder City, NV 89005
(702) 293-5000
(800) 245-6380
www.haciendaonline.com
Hotel: 378 rooms, $39-up
Restaurant(s): Tango Buffet, Hacienda Steak House, Food Court.
Helicopter flights available over Lake Mead, Hoover Dam and the Grand Canyon.

BC Cinemas.
■ **Games Available:** Bingo, Slots, Sport Book, Table game

Harrah's Lake Tahoe

15 Highway 50
Stateline, NV 89449
(800) HARRAHS
www.harrahs.com
Hotel: 525 rooms
88,000 square feet
Restaurant(s): The Summit, American River Café, Ice Creamery, Forest Buffet, Friday's Station Steak & Seafood Grill, North Beach Deli, Club Cappucchino.
Tahoe Star yacht has daily cruises with dinner available.
Harrah's Legendary South Shore offers headliners including Jim Belushi, George Carlin, Willie Nelson, George Thorogood.
■ **Games Available:** Baccarat, Blackjack, Craps, Let It Ride, Pai Gow, Roulette, Slots - 2300, Sport Book

Harrah's Laughlin

2900 South Casino Drive
Laughlin, NV 89109
(702) 298-4600
(800) 221-1306
www.harrahs.com
■ **Hotel:** 1600 rooms
■ **Restaurant(s):** Five restaurants: William Fisk's Steakhouse, Cabo Café, The Grill, Fresh Market Square Buffet, Club Cappuccino.
Gift shop, boutique, salon, Del Rio Beach Club.
The 3,156 seat Rio Vista Outdoor Amphitheater has Smokey Robinson, Sinbad, Lee Greenwood. Fiesta Showroom hosts Jerry Van Dyke, others.
■ **Games Available:** Blackjack - 21, Craps - 3, Let It Ride, Pai Gow - 2, Roulette - 4, Slots - 1200, Sport Book

Harrah's Reno

219 N. Center St.
Reno, NV 89501
(775) 786-3232
(800) HARRAHS
www.harrahs.com

■ **Hotel:** 950 rooms

Restaurant(s): Cafe Andreotti, Café Napa, Harrah's Steakhouse, North Beach Deli, Fresh Market Square Buffet, Club Cappuccino.

Hotel has health club and spa, two gift shops, business center.

Gordie Brown performs in Sammy's Showroom, Whisper adult revue.

■ **Games Available:** Baccarat, Blackjack, Craps, Let It Ride, Roulette, Slots - 1600

Harveys Lake Tahoe

Highway 50 at Stateline Avenue
Lake Tahoe, NV 89449
(775) 588-2411
(800) HARRAHS
Fax: (775) 588-4732
www.harrahs.com

■ **Hotel:** 740 rooms

88,000 square feet

■ **Restaurant(s):** Llewellyn's, Sage Room Steakhouse, Seafood Grotto, El Vaquero, Garden Buffet, Carriage House, Hard Rock Café.

Health club, spa and salon. Wedding chapel.

The Improv has comedy acts.

■ **Games Available:** Baccarat, Blackjack, Craps, Let It Ride, Pai Gow, Roulette, Slots - 2300, Sport Book

Horizon Casino Resort

50 Highway 50
Lake Tahoe, NV 89449
(800) 648-3322
www.horizoncasino.com

■ **Hotel:** 539 rooms, $99-up

42,000 square feet

■ **Restaurant(s):** Josh's, Four Seasons, Le Grande Buffet.

The resort has an outdoor pool, hot tubs, as well as a wedding chapel.

Three showrooms offer live entertainment and the resort has eight movie theaters.

■ **Games Available:** 3-card poker, Blackjack, Craps, Keno, Pai Gow, Roulette, Slots, Sport Book

Horseshu Hotel and Casino

Highway 93
Jackpot, NV 89825
Idaho/Nevada border
(775) 755-7777
(800) 432-0051
www.ameristarcasinos.com/corporate/hsfacts

■ **Hotel:** 120 rooms, $27-$85

■ **Restaurant(s):** Frontier Kitchen

Pool, tennis courts, golf course, general store. Casino has seven table games.

■ **Games Available:** Blackjack, Craps, Keno, Slots - 120

Hotel Nevada and Gambling Hall

501 Aultman St.
Ely, NV 89301
(888) 406-3055
www.hotelnevada.com

■ **Hotel:** 62 rooms, $20-$85

■ **Restaurant(s):** Frontier Room Restaurant

■ **Games Available:** Bingo, Blackjack, Poker, Roulette, Slots - 203

Hyatt Regency Lake Las Vegas

101 MonteLago Blvd.
Henderson, NV 89011
17 miles to downtown Las Vegas
(702) 567-1234
Fax: (702) 567-6067
sbingham@lasrlpo.hyatt.com
www.lakelasvegas.hyatt.com

■ **Hotel:** 493 rooms, $75-$1,500

■ **Restaurant(s):** Six restaurants: Japengo, Café Tajine, Sandsabar Pool Bar and Grill, Marrakesh Express Coffee Bar, Salon Maroc, Arabesque.

18-hole golf course, private 320-acre lake, two swimming pools, Spa and Fitness Center.

■ **Overall Payout:** 94.6%

■ **Games Available:** Blackjack $5, Craps, Roulette, Slots

Hyatt Regency Lake Tahoe Resort & Casino

P.O. Box 3239
Incline Village, NV 89450
(888) 899-5019

■ **Hotel:** 450 rooms

■ **Restaurant(s):** Sierra Café, Lone Eagle Grille, Ciao Mein, Cutthroat's Saloon.

Resort also has 24 lakeside cottages as well as wedding facilities.

■ **Games Available:** Blackjack, Craps, Roulette Slots, Sport Book

Jailhouse Motel Casino

211 5th St.
Ely, NV 89301
(702) 289-3033
(800) 841-5430
www.elyjailhouse.com

■ **Restaurant(s):** Cell Block Steak House, Coffee Shop

■ **Games Available:** Slots, Table games

Jerry's Nugget

1821 Las Vegas Blvd. N.
North Las Vegas, NV 89030
(702) 399-3000
information@jerrysnugget.com
www.jerrysnugget.com

■ **Restaurant(s):** Magnolia Room, Canal Street Café, Cornucopia Snack Bar, European Bakery.

Entertainment on weekends in Royal Street Theater.

■ **Games Available:** Bingo, Blackjack, Craps, Keno, Roulette, Slots, Sport Book

Jim Kelley's Nugget

20 Highway 28
Crystal Bay, NV 89402
(775) 831-0455

■ **Games Available:** Slots

John Ascuaga's Nugget Casino Resort

1100 Nugget Ave.
Sparks, NV 89431
(800) 648-1177
www.janugget.com

■ **Hotel:** 1600 rooms, $39-up

75,000 square feet

■ **Restaurant(s):** John's Oyster Bar, Orozko, Rotisserie, Steakhouse Grill, Trader Dick's, General Store, Gabe's Pub and Deli, Farm House Coffee Shop.

Hotel features atrium-enclosed pool and spa.

Celebrity Showroom entertainers include Glen Campbell, Don Rickles, Mickey Gilley, Eddie Money.

■ **Games Available:** Blackjack, Craps, Keno Let It Ride, Poker, Roulette, Slots - 1500, Sport Book

Jokers Wild Casino

920 N. Boulder Highway
Henderson, NV 89015
(702) 564-8100
Fax: (702) 564-7550

■ **Restaurant(s):** Wild Card Buffet, Court Café, Pigskin Snack & Sports Bar.

Casino has 11 table games.

Live entertainment in Troubadour Lounge.

■ **Games Available:** Blackjack, Craps, Keno, Roulette, Slots - 640, Sport Book

Lakeside Inn and Casino

P.O. Box 5640
Stateline, NV 89449
(775) 588-7777
(800) 624-7980
mail@lakesideinn.com
www.lakesideinn.com
■ **Hotel:** 123 rooms, $79-up
■ **Restaurant(s):** Timber House Restaurant and Bar
■ **Games Available:** Blackjack, Craps , Keno, Roulette, Slots, Sport Book

Mahoney's Silver Nugget

2140 North Las Vegas Blvd.
North Las Vegas, NV 89030
Two miles north of downtown Las Vegas
(702) 399-1111
Fax: (702) 657-8354
www.mahoneyscasino.com
■ **Restaurant(s):** Mahoney's Café.
RV Park has 152 spaces, pool and spa. A 24-lane bowling center is available.
■ **Games Available:** Bingo, Blackjack, Craps, Keno, Slots - 400

Mint Casino

1130 B St.
Sparks, NV 89431
(775) 359-4944
■ **Games Available:** Slots

Model T Casino

1130 W. Winnemucca Blvd.
Winnemucca, NV 89446
(775) 623-2588
(800) 645-5658
info@modelt.com
www.modelt.com

■ **Hotel:** 75 rooms
RV Park has 58 spaces, outdoor pool.
■ **Games Available:** 3-card poker, Blackjack, Keno, Let It Ride, Slots, Sport Book

Nevada Landing

No. 2 Goodspring Rd.
Jean, NV 89109
(702) 387-5000
(800) 628-6682
www.nevadalanding.com
Hotel: 300 rooms, $19-up
35,000 square feet
Restaurant(s): Captain's Café, Jade Room, Bayou Belle Buffet, Dockside Grill.
■ **Games Available:** Blackjack, Craps , Keno, Pai Gow, Roulette, Slots - 1000

Nugget

233 N. Virginia St.
Reno, NV 89501
(775) 323-3454
■ **Games Available:** Slots

Oasis Resort Casino

P.O. Box 360
Mesquite, NV 89024
(800) 21-Oasis
Fax: (702) 346-5722
www.oasisresort.com
■ **Hotel:** 1000 rooms
The resort offers The Palms Golf Course, the Oasis Gun Club, a spa, convention facilities and a Family Fun Center. An RV Park is available.
■ **Games Available:** Blackjack, Craps, Let It Ride, Pai Gow, Poker, Roulette, Slots - 800

Owl Club Bar and Restaurant

Highway 50
Eureka, NV 89316
(775) 237-5280
Fax: (775) 237-5285
eurekaowlhoot@eurekanv.org
www.eurekaowlclub.com

■ **Games Available:** Slots

Peppermill Reno

2707 South Virginia St.
Reno, NV 89502
(775) 826-2121
(800) 648-6992
www.peppermillreno.com
Hotel: 1255 rooms
Reservations: (800) 282-2444
Restaurant(s): Seven restaurants: White Orchid, Romanza, Island Buffet, Coffee Shop, Reno's Premier Steak House, International Food Court, Café Espresso.

Hotel has waterfall pool and spa, health club, salon.

Headliners include Merle Haggard, The Marshall Tucker Band, Freddy Fender, Jefferson Starship. There's also free entertainment on the Cabaret Stage.

■ **Games Available:** Blackjack, Craps, Keno, Pai Gow, Poker, Roulette, Slots - 2100, Sport Book

Peppermill Wendover

680 Wendover Blvd.
West Wendover, NV 89883
(800) 648-9660
pepperm@peppermillwendover.com
www.peppermillwendover.com

■ **Hotel:** 224 rooms, $25-up
■ **Restaurant(s):** Grand Buffet
Daily entertainment available.

■ **Games Available:** Blackjack - 16, Craps, Keno, Roulette, Slots - 900, Sport Book

Pinion Plaza

2171 Hwy 50 East
Carson City, NV 89701
(877) 519-5567
carsonstation@pyramid.net
www.pinonplaza.com

■ **Restaurant(s):** Branding Iron Café, Steakhouse.

Best Western Hotel and RV Park available.

■ **Games Available:** Blackjack, Craps, Roulette, Slots, Sport Book

Pioneer Hotel & Gambling Hall

2200 S. Casino Drive
Laughlin, NV 89028
(702) 298-2442
(800) 634-3469
www.pioneerlaughlin.com

■ **Hotel:** 416 rooms, $25-up
■ **Restaurant(s):** Granny's Gourmet, Boarding House, Fast Draw.

■ **Games Available:** 3-card poker, Blackjack, Keno, Let It Ride, Roulette, Slots

Pioneer Inn Casino

221 S. Virginia St.
Reno, NV 89501
(888) 794-7913
Hotel: 252 rooms

■ **Restaurant(s):** Iron Sword Restaurant, Prime Rib Company, Coffee Shop.
■ **Games Available:** Slots, Table games

Poker Palace Casino

2757 Las Vegas Blvd. North
North Las Vegas, NV 89030
(702) 649-3799

■ **Games Available:** Blackjack, Craps, Let It Ride, Poker, Roulette, Slots, Sport Book

Pot O'Gold Casino

120 Market St.
Henderson, NV 89015
(702) 564-8488

■ **Restaurant(s):** Island Grille, Gold Mine Café.

■ **Games Available:** Bingo, Blackjack, Let It Ride, Slots

Primm Valley Resort and Casino

I-15
P.O. Box 19119
Primm, NV 89019
(702) 386-7867
(800) 386-7867
www.primmvalleyresorts.com

Hotel: 624 rooms

46,100 square feet

Restaurant(s): GP's, Greens Buffet, Gallery Café.

Adjoining the hotel is the Fashion Outlets of Las Vegas mall. The Bonnie & Clyde/Dutch Shultz-Al Capone display features historic cars. An RV Village features 199 spaces. Free parking is available. Casino has 33 table games.

Entertainment in the Primm Valley Piano Bar.

* **Games Available:** Blackjack, Craps, Keno, Roulette, Slots - 1510, Sport Book

---

Rail City Casino

2121 Victorian Ave.
Sparks, NV 89431
(775) 359-9440

■ **Games Available:** Blackjack, Craps, Roulette, Slots, Sport Book

---

Railroad Pass Hotel & Casino

2800 S. Boulder Highway
Henderson, NV 89015
(702) 294-5000
(800) 654-0877
www.railroadpass.com

■ **Hotel:** 120 rooms

21,000 square feet

■ **Restaurant(s):** Boxcar Buffet, Conductor's Room, Iron Rail Café.

Casino has seven table games.

■ **Games Available:** Bingo, Blackjack, Craps, Roulette, Slots - 368

Rainbow Club Casino

122 S. Water St.
Henderson, NV 89015
(702) 565-9776

■ **Games Available:** Slots

Ramada Express Hotel Casino

2121 S. Casino Drive
Laughlin, NV 89029
(800) 243-6846
www.ramadaexpress.com

■ **Hotel:** 1501 rooms

53,000 square feet

■ **Restaurant(s):** Passaggio Italian Gardens, The Steakhouse, Carnegie's 24-Hour Dining Car, Roundhouse Buffet.

Free rides on Gambling Train of Laughlin. American Heroes Museum of Memories has free admission. Hotel has pool, spa, free RV parking.

Live entertainment nightly in the Caboose Lounge.

■ **Games Available:** Blackjack, Craps, Keno, Roulette, Slots, Sport Book

---

Red Garter Hotel & Casino

P.O. Box 2399
Wendover, NV 84083
(800) 982-2111
www.fh-inc.com/RedGarter/

■ **Hotel:** 106 rooms

■ **Games Available:** Blackjack, Craps, Roulette, Slots - 430, Sport Book

Red Lion Casino

2065 Idaho St.
Elko, NV 89801
(775) 738-2111
(800) 545-0044
www.redlioncasino.com

■ **Hotel:** 223 rooms

■ **Restaurant(s):** Misty's, Coffee Garden Restaurant, Sports Bar.

Outdoor pool, arcade, salon, gift shop.

■ **Games Available:** Blackjack - 9, Craps, Keno, Let It Ride, Poker, Roulette, Slots - 400, Sport Book

Regency Casino

1950 Casino Way
Laughlin, NV 89029
(702) 298-2439

■ **Games Available:** Slots, Table games

Renata's Casino

4451 E. Sunset Road
Henderson, NV 89014
(702) 435-4000

■ **Games Available:** Slots - 200

Reno Hilton

2500 E. Second St.
Reno, NV 89595
132 miles east of Sacramento, Calif.
(775) 789-2000
(800) 648-3568
www.renohilton.com

■ **Hotel:** 2003 rooms, $69-$249

148 acres

■ **Restaurant(s):** Ten restaurants: The Steak House, Andiamo, Asiana, Lindy's 24-Hour Coffee Shop, The Grand Canyon Buffet, Chevy's Fresh Mex, Johnny Rockets, Café Espresso, Round Table Pizza, Subway Sandwich Shop.

Shopping arcade with more than 10 stores, 50-lane Bowling Centre, Fun Quest Family Fun Center, swimming pool, health club and spa, tennis courts, free parking, minigolf and go-karts, Ultimate Rush Thrill Ride, KOA Kampground, wedding chapel.

Production shows on the world's largest stage and headline entertainment in five venues including an outdoor amphitheater. Recent shows include Wynonna, John Mellencamp, The Temptations, James Taylor and Sinbad.

■ **Games Available:** 3-card poker - 2, Baccarat - 1, Blackjack - 33, Craps - 4, Keno, Let It Ride - 2, Mini-baccarat - 1, Pai Gow - 5, Roulette - 4, Slots - 1500, Sport Book

Reno Hilton offers gamblers a wide variety of games in its 100,000 square foot casino.

River Palms Resort

2700 S. Casino Rd.
Laughlin, NV 89029
(877) RVR-PALM
info@rvrpalm.com
www.rvrpalm.com

■ **Hotel:** 1000 rooms

65,000 square feet

■ **Restaurant(s):** Madeleine's Lodge, River Palms Café, D'Angelo's Italian Bistro, the No Ka Oi Buffet, Cast-A-Ways Snack Bar, Subway Sandwiches.

Live entertainment

■ **Games Available:** Bingo, Keno, Poker, Slots, Table games

Riverside Resort

1650 S. Casino Drive
Laughlin, NV 89029
(800) 227-3849
www.riversideresort.com

■ **Hotel:** 1404 rooms, $44-up

Restaurant(s): Gourmet Room, Prime Rib Room, Riverside Buffet, Riverview Restaurant, China River Wok, Sidewalk Café.

Don Laughlin's Classic Car Exhibit, a 34-lane bowling center, six movie theaters and cruises on the U.S.S. Riverside are featured.

Entertainers include Bellamy Brothers, Roy Clark, Mel Tillis.

■ **Games Available:** Bingo, Blackjack, Craps, Poker, Roulette, Slots - 1700, Sport Book

———————

Saddle West Hotel, Casino and RV Resort

1220 S. Highway 160
Pahrump, NV 89048
58 miles west of Las Vegas
(775) 727-1111
(800) 433-3987
swsam@saddlewest.com

A stagecoach contributes the western setting at Saddle West Hotel and Casino in Pahrump, Nev.

www.saddlewest.com

■ **Hotel:** 158 rooms, $30-$145

12,000 square feet

■ **Restaurant(s):** Silver Spur Restaurant and Buffet, Li'l Spur Snack Bar

Also features 80-space RV Resort, Saddle West Gift Shop, golf course

Club West Night Club with live DJ Friday nights.

■ **Games Available:** Bingo, Blackjack $1 - 2, Craps - 1, Keno, Poker - 2, Roulette - 1, Slots $1 - 60, Slots 2 cents - 4, Slots Nickel - 237, Slots Quarter - 111, Sport Book

———————

Sands Regency Casino Hotel

345 N. Arlington
Reno, NV 89501
(800) 648-3553

■ **Hotel:** 800 rooms, $19-up

■ **Restaurant(s):** Mel's the Original Diner, Tony Roma's, Antonia's, Cabana Café, Pizza Hut.

Hotel has a pool and health club.

Entertainment in the Empress Lounge and the Just For Laughs Comedy Club.

■ **Games Available:** Bingo, Blackjack, Craps, Keno, Roulette, Slots, Sport Book

———————

Searchlight Nugget Casino

100 N. Highway 95
Searchlight, NV 89046
(702) 297-1201

■ **Games Available:** Blackjack - 2, Poker, Slots - 100

———————

Si Redd's Oasis Resort

894 W. Mesquite Blvd.
Mesquite, NV 89027
(800) 806-0225
info@playandstay.com
www.playandstay.com

■ **Hotel:** 2050 rooms

50,000 square feet

■ **Restaurant(s):** Redd Room Steakhouse, Buffet, Coffee Shop.

The 2,000-acre resort features seven pools, health club, tennis courts, gun club, three golf courses, RV park.

■ **Games Available:** Blackjack, Craps , Let It Ride, Pai Gow, Poker, Roulette, Slots - 800, Sport Book

Siena Spa Casino

1 S. Lake St.
Reno, NV 89505
(775) 337-6260
(877) 743-6233
Fax: (775) 337-6608
www.sienareno.com

■ **Hotel:** 214 rooms

23,000 square feet

■ **Restaurant(s):** The Tuscan Table at Enoteca, Lexie's, Contrada Café.

Siena Hotel, which opened in July 2001, features its Spa. It also has an outdoor pool, conference center and golf and ski packages. Casino has 26 table games.

■ **Games Available:** 3-card poker, Baccarat, Blackjack, Craps, Keno, Let It Ride, Pai Gow, Roulette, Slots - 800, Sport Book

Silver Club

1040 Victorian Ave.
Sparks, NV 89431
(775) 358-4771
(800) 905-7774
silverclub@attglobal.net
www.silverclub.com

■ **Hotel:** 206 rooms, $30-up

■ **Restaurant(s):** Victoria's Steak House, Town Square Restaurant, Port of Subs

Casino has 12 table games.

Entertainment in the Gazebo Lounge.

■ **Games Available:** 3-card poker, Blackjack, Craps, Keno, Let It Ride, Roulette, Slots, Sport Book

Silver Legacy Resort

407 N. Virginia St.
Reno, NV 89501
(775) 329-4777
(800) 687-7733
www.silverlegacyreno.com

■ **Hotel:** 1720 rooms, $59-up

85,000 square feet

Restaurant(s): Sterling's, Sweetwater Café, Victorian Buffet, Fairchild's Oyster Bar, Fresh Express Food Court, Sips Coffee and Tea.

Hotel offers pool and spa, three shops and 90,000 square feet of convention space. Casino has 80 table games.

Catch a Rising Star comedy club, headliners including D.L. Hughley, Dennis Miller and the Righteous Brothers in the Grande Exposition Hall.

■ **Games Available:** Blackjack, Craps, Keno, Roulette, Slots - 2500, Sport Book

Silver Smith Casino

101 Wendover Blvd.
Wendover, NV 89883
Two hours from Salt Lake City
(775) 664-2221
(800) 648-9668

■ **Hotel:** 740 rooms

■ **Reservations:** (800) 848-7300

■ **Restaurant(s):** White Swan Buffet, The Pantry, Senor Jones

Casino has 80 table games.

Showroom features entertainers including Creedence Clearwater Revisited, Three Dog Night, Steppenwolf.

■ **Games Available:** Baccarat, Blackjack, Craps, Keno, Let It Ride, Pai Gow, Poker, Roulette, Slots - 1600, Sport Book

Skyline Restaurant and Casino

1741 N. Boulder Highway
Henderson, NV 89015
Five miles from Las Vegas

(702) 565-9116
30,000 square feet
■ **Games Available:** Blackjack $2, Keno, Slots $5, Slots 1 cent, Slots Nickel, Slots Quarter, Sport Book

Stagecoach Hotel & Casino

Highway 95
P.O. Box 836
Beatty, NV 89003
Six miles from California border near Death
  Valley
(775) 553-2419
(800) 424-4946
www.stagecoachhotel.com
■ **Hotel:** 48 rooms
■ **Restaurant(s):** Alexander's Steakhouse, Rita's Café.
Casino has 21 table games. An RV Park is also available. Hotel has a heated pool.
■ **Games Available:** Blackjack, Craps , Roulette, Slots

Stateline Casino

490 W. Mesquite Blvd.
Mesquite, NV 89027
(702) 346-5752
■ **Hotel:** 12 rooms
■ **Games Available:** Blackjack, Slots - 50

Stockman's Casino

1560 W Williams Ave.
Fallon, NV 89406
(702) 423-4648
www.nvohwy.com/h/holinexp.htm
■ **Hotel:** 59 rooms
■ **Games Available:** Blackjack, Craps, Keno, Slots

Stockmen's Hotel and Casino

340 Commercial St.
Elko, NV 89801
(800) 648-2345
www.fh-inc.com
■ **Hotel:** 141 rooms, $30-up
■ **Games Available:** Blackjack, Craps, Keno, Roulette, Slots, Sport Book

Sturgeon's Log Cabin

1420 Cornell Ave.
Lovelock, NV 89419
(775) 273-2971
(800) 528-1234
■ **Hotel:** 76 rooms
■ **Games Available:** Keno, Poker, Slots

Sundowner Hotel Casino

450 N. Arlington Avenue
Reno, NV 89503
(775) 786-7050
(800) 648-5490
info@sundowner-casino.com
www.sundowner-casino.com
■ **Hotel:** 600 rooms, $35-up
■ **Restaurant(s):** GK's Steakhouse, Garden Gazebo Buffet, Coffee Shop.
■ **Games Available:** Blackjack, Craps, Keno, Roulette, Slots

Sunset Station

1301 W. Sunset Rd.
Henderson, NV 89014
(702) 221-6789
(888) 786-7389
www.sunsetstation.com
■ **Hotel:** 457 rooms, $60-up
■ **Restaurant(s):** Capri Italian Ristorante, Costa Del Sol, Sunset Café, Sonoma Cellar Steakhouse, Feast Around the World Buffet, Guadalajara Bar

and Grille, Viva Salsa, Panda Express, Sbarro.
Hotel includes 110,000 square feet of convention
space. Casino has 55 table games.

Live entertainment in Club Madrid or 5,000 seat
outdoor amphitheater, including Paula
Poundstone, Gary Puckett, Taylor Dayne.

■ **Games Available:** Bingo, Blackjack, Craps,
Keno, Mini-baccarat, Pai Gow, Poker - 15,
Roulette, Slots - 3000, Sport Book

Tahoe Biltmore Lodge and Casino

5 Highway 28
Crystal Bay, NV 89402
(775) 831-0660
(800) BILTMOR
fun@tahoebiltmore.com
www.tahoebiltmore.com
■ **Hotel:** 92 rooms, $49-up
■ **Restaurant(s):** Café Biltmore, Pub and Grill.
■ **Games Available:** Blackjack, Craps , Keno,
Roulette, Slots, Sport Book

Texas Station

2101 Texas Star Lane
North Las Vegas, NV 89030
(800) 654-8888
www.texasstation.com
■ **Hotel:** 200 rooms, $50-up
91,000 square feet
■ **Restaurant(s):** Texas Star Oyster Bar, Texas
Café, Feast Around the World Buffet, Baja Fresh,
Sbarro.
Three wedding chapels are available.
A variety of acts appears at the Armadillo
LoungeX. The hotel also has a 60-lane bowling
center and 18 movie theaters.
■ **Games Available:** 3-card poker, Bingo,
Blackjack - 34, Craps, Keno, Let It Ride, Poker -
10, Roulette, Slots, Sport Book

The Gambler

211 N. Virginia St.
Reno, NV 89501
(775) 322-7620
■ **Games Available:** Slots

Topaz Lodge and Casino

P.O. Box 187
Gardnerville, NV 89410
Nevada-California border
(775) 266-3338
Fax: (775) 266-3046
www.enterit.com/topaz3338
■ **Hotel:** 102 rooms
RV Park, general store, fuel station are included.
■ **Games Available:** Slots - 250, Table games

Virgin River Hotel & Casino

100 Pioneer Blvd.
Mesquite, NV 89027
(702) 346-7777
(800) 346-7721
■ **Hotel:** 723 rooms
■ **Restaurant(s):** Chuckwagon Restaurant,
Branding Iron Buffet
A 24-lane bowling center and a 47-spot RV park
are available.
Live entertainment. Four movie theaters.
■ **Games Available:** Bingo, Slots, Table games

Walker River Resort

Box 90
Smith, NV 89430
60 miles from Carson City
(775) 465-2573
■ **Hotel:** 135 rooms
Overall Payout: 92%
■ **Games Available:** Slots Nickel, Slots Quarter

Western Village Hotel and Casino

815 Nichols Blvd.
Sparks, NV 89434
(800) 648-1170

■ **Hotel:** 285 rooms, $30-up

■ **Games Available:** Blackjack: Craps, Roulette, Slots, Sport Book

Whiskey Pete's Hotel Casino

I-15
P.O. Box 19119
Primm, NV 89019
(800) 844-9593
www.primadonna.com

■ **Hotel:** 777 rooms, $19-up

36,400 square feet

■ **Restaurant(s):** Silver Spur Steakhouse, Trail's End Coffee Shop, Wagon Wheel Buffet.

Hotel features a pool and a monorail to other Primm attractions. Casino has 30 table games.

The 700-seat Showroom features entertainers such as Crystal Gayle, Mickey Gilley, America, Captain & Tennille, Gallagher.

■ **Games Available:** Blackjack, Craps, Keno, Roulette, Slots - 1314, Sport Book

Winners Casino

185 West Winnemucca Blvd.
Winnemucca, NV 89445
(800) 648-4770
winners@winnerscasino.com
www.winnerscasino.com

■ **Hotel:** 123 rooms, $37-up

■ **Restaurant(s):** Grandma's Dinner House, Pete's Coffee Shop.

Live music, comedy, karaoke in Winners Lounge.

■ **Games Available:** Bingo, Blackjack, Craps, Let It Ride, Roulette, Slots

NEW JERSEY

Atlantic City Hilton Casino Resort

Boston and Boardwalk
Atlantic City, NJ 08401
(609) 347-7111
Fax: (609) 340-4858
www.hiltonac.com

■ **Hotel:** 802 rooms, $95-$300

60,000 square feet

■ **Reservations:** (877) 432-7139

■ **Restaurant(s):** Seven restaurants: Peregrines', The Oaks, Caruso's, Sterling Brunch, Cornucopia Buffet, Horizons, Empress Garden, Cappuccino's.

A Gift Shop and three other shops are available. The hotel has 23,000 square feet of convention facilities, a health spa, indoor pool and sauna. Atlantic City Country Club is available to guests. Casino has 83 table games.

The 1,200 seat theater has hosted Kenny Rogers, Susan Anton, Fabian, Lou Rawls, David Spade, and Joy Behar.

■ **Games Available:** Baccarat - 2, Blackjack - 39, Craps - 10, Let It Ride - 4, Pai Gow - 7, Roulette - 10, Slots - 1800

Slot machines provide some of the entertainment in Atlantic City's 12 casino-resorts.

Photo courtesy of Atlantic City Convention & Visitors Authority

Bally's Atlantic City

Park Place and Boardwalk
Atlantic City, NJ 08401
One hour from Philadelphia, 2 1/2 hours from New York City
(609) 340-2000
(888) 537-0007
www.ballysac.com

■ **Hotel:** 1246 rooms, $95-$300

80,000 square feet

■ **Restaurant(s):** Ten restaurants: Arturo's, Prime Place, Mr. Ming's, Animations, Pickles Deli, Gatsby's, Noodles & Zen Sum, Sbarro, Sunday Brunch at Prime Place, Sidewalk Buffet.

Bally's features eight shops and 50,000 square feet of convention facilities. The Spa at Bally's is 40,000 square feet and includes an indoor pool, sauna, courts and sun deck. Main casino and Wild West Casino offer a total of 154 table games.

Legends in Concert is Atlantic City's longest running revue show. Headliners such as Barbara Mandrell, the Righteous Brothers and Anne Murray, and championship boxing are also featured.

■ **Games Available:** Blackjack - 71, Craps - 14, Let It Ride - 8, Mini-baccarat - 3, Pai Gow - 15, Poker - 11, Roulette - 20, Slots - 1835, Spanish 21 - 5, Table games - 2

Caesars Atlantic City

2100 Pacific Ave.
Atlantic City, NJ 08401
(609) 348-4411
(800) CAESARS
www.caesarsac.com

Hotel: 1144 rooms, $95-$300

125,000 square feet

Restaurant(s): 11 restaurants: The Bacchanal, Nero's Grill, Primavera, Hyakumi, Imperial Garden, Tuscany Grille, Pompeii Pasta Pavilion, La Piazza Buffet, Café Roma, Temple Bar & Grill, Planet Hollywood.

Hotel includes Health Spa and Fitness Center, outdoor pool, two tennis courts, salon. The Shops on Appian Way include eight stores, and Oceans One Mall is across from Caesars. Casino has 123 table games and 3,856 slot machines.

Headliners at the 1,100 seat Circus Maximus Theater include Celine Dion, Cher, Whitney Houston, Hootie and the Blowfish, Johnny Mathis and Patti LaBelle.

■ **Games Available:** 3-card poker - 4, Baccarat - 2, Blackjack - 57, Craps - 13 , Let It Ride - 8, Mini-baccarat - 4, Pai Gow - 6, Poker - 5, Roulette - 15, Slots - 3856, Spanish 21 - 5

The fountain draws attention at Caesars Atlantic City.

Claridge Casino Hotel

Park Place and Boardwalk
Atlantic City, NJ 08401
(609) 340-3400
800-847-LUCK
Fax: (609) 340-3165
www.claridge.com

Hotel: 500 rooms, $95-$300

59,000 square feet

Reservations: 800-847-LUCK

Restaurant(s): Four restaurants: Luna, Twenties Steakhouse, Garden Café, Wok & Roll.

Hotel features indoor pool, spa and exercise room. Casino has 63 table games.

Palace Theater offer stars and shows such as Diahann Carroll, Peabo Bryson, Forever Plaid, Marshall Tucker Band, Leann Womack.

* **Games Available:** 3-card poker - 4, Baccarat - 1, Blackjack - 26, Craps - 6, Let It Ride - 3, Mini-baccarat - 5, Pai Gow - 4, Roulette - 4, Slots $1 - 197, Slots $25 - 4, Slots $5 - 33 , Slots 50 cents - 108, Slots Nickel - 214, Slots Quarter - 1221, Spanish 21 - 2, Video poker - 271

Harrah's Atlantic City

777 Harrah's Blvd.
Atlantic City, NJ 08401
(609) 441-5000
www.harrahs.com

■ **Hotel:** 1174 rooms

94,000 square feet

■ **Reservations:** (800) 2HARRAH

■ **Restaurant(s):** Six restaurants: Florentino's, The Steakhouse, FantaSea Reef Buffet, Reflections Café, The Deli, Club Cappuccino.

Another $113 million, 452-room hotel tower opened in April 2002 and a 50,000 square foot expansion of the casino will add 950 slot machines in 2002 and 2003. Hotel has health club, spa, salon, gift shop and business services.

Atrium Lounge has live entertainment.

■ **Games Available:** Poker - 7, Slots, Table games - 64

Resorts Atlantic City

1133 Boardwalk
Atlantic City, NJ 08401
(609) 340-6000
(800) 336-6378
Fax: (609) 340-6349
www.resortsac.com

■ **Hotel:** 668 rooms, $79-up

■ **Restaurant(s):** Asian Spice, Beachball Deli, Beverly Hills Buffet, Breadsteaks Café & Grill, Camelot, Capriccio, Le Palais.

Hotel has indoor and outdoor pools, health club, spa. Casino has 70 table games.

Superstar Theatre hosts entertainers including Tom Jones, Wayne Newton, Tony Bennett.

■ **Games Available:** Baccarat, Blackjack, Craps, Let It Ride, Mini-baccarat, Pai Gow, Race book, Roulette, Slots - 2000, Spanish 21

Sands Casino Hotel

Indiana Avenue & Brighton Park
Atlantic City, NJ 08401
(609) 441-4000
(800) AC-SANDS
Fax: (609) 441-4630
www.acsands.com

■ **Hotel:** 500 rooms

■ **Reservations:** (800) 257-8580

■ **Restaurant(s):** Beach Party Buffet, Bokoo Grill, Brighton Steak House, Cooney's Corner, Food Factory, Medici, Rossi's Gourmet Italian Buffet.

Hotel features Hollywood Spa and Salon.

Copa Room hosts entertainers including Liza Minelli, Robin Williams, Billy Crystal, George Carlin.

■ **Games Available:** Baccarat , Blackjack, Craps, Pai Gow, Poker, Roulette, Slots

The Atlantic City Sands features unique architecture.

Showboat Atlantic City

801 Boardwalk
Atlantic City, NJ 08401
(800) 621-0200
www.harrahs.com

■ **Hotel:** 755 rooms

■ **Restaurant(s):** Casa di Napoli, Champagne Charlie's, Courtyard Buffet, Crescent City Café, Sun Deck Café, Snack Bar & Pizzeria.

Showboat was undergoing a $34 million renovation in 2002. Hotel has spa, outdoor pool.

Bands perform in Showboat's New Orleans Square and Front Lobby.

■ **Games Available:** Baccarat, Blackjack, Craps, Poker, Roulette, Slots

Tropicana Casino and Resort-Atlantic City

Brighton and Boardwalk
Atlantic City, NJ 08401
(609) 340-4000
(800) THE-TROP
www.tropicana.net

■ **Hotel:** 1600 rooms, $60-$200

■ **Reservations:** (800) 345-8767

■ **Restaurant(s):** Six restaurants: Wellington & Chan's, II Verdi, Pier 7, Golden Dynasty, Seaside Café, Beachfront Buffet.

Hotel has indoor and outdoor pools, gift shop and variety of other stores.

Headliners in the Showroom, The Comedy Stop.

■ **Games Available:** Baccarat, Blackjack, Craps, Let It Ride, Pai Gow, Poker, Roulette, Slots

Trump Marina Hotel Casino

Huron Avenue & Brigantine Boulevard
Atlantic City, NJ 08401
(609) 441-2000
(800) 777-1177
Fax: (609) 441-8668
www.trumpmarina.com

■ **Hotel:** 728 rooms
70,000 square feet

■ **Reservations:** (800) 777-8477

■ **Restaurant(s):** Bayside Buffet, The Catamaran Café, The Deck, Harbor View Fine Seafood, High's Steaks, Imperial Court, Portofino, Upstairs Grille.

Hotel has recreation deck with a health spa, outdoor pool, tennis and shuffleboard courts, basketball courts, jogging track; 50,922 square feet of meeting and function space. The 640-slip marina is adjacent. Eight shops available.

Entertainment in Grand Cayman Ballroom, Viva's Nightclub, Shell Showroom by entertainers including Sting, Prince, Alice Cooper, Chris Rock, The Goo Goo Dolls.

■ **Games Available:** 3-card poker, Baccarat, Blackjack, Craps, Let It Ride, Mini-baccarat, Pai Gow, Roulette, Slots - 2000

Trump Plaza

Boardwalk at Mississippi Avenue
Atlantic City, NJ 08401
(609) 441-6000
(800) 677-RESV
www.trumpplaza.com

■ **Hotel:** 904 rooms, $125-up

■ **Restaurant(s):** The New Yorker, Harvey's Deli, Broadway Buffet, Atrium Café, Roberto's Ristorante, Fortunes, Max's Steakhouse.

Hotel has pool, spa, salon, tennis and shuffleboard courts as well as 55,000 square feet of convention space.

Headliners appear in Trump Plaza Theater.

■ **Games Available:** Baccarat, Blackjack, Craps, Mini-baccarat, Pai Gow, Roulette, Slots

Trump Taj Mahal

1000 Boardwalk at Virginia Avenue
Atlantic City, NJ 08401
(609) 449-1000
(800) 825-8888
www.trumptaj.com

Hotel: 1250 rooms

Restaurant(s): Nine restaurants: Dynasty, Mark Anthony's, Safari Steakhouse, Hard Rock Café, Sbarro, Stage Deli of New York, Sultan's Feast, Bombay Café.

More than a dozen shops are available. Hotel features spa and fitness center, 140,000 feet of conference space. Casino has 210 table games.

The 5,000 seat Arena and 1,400 seat Xanadu Showroom have hosted Britney Spears, Janet Jackson, Andrea Bocelli, Destiny's Child, Don Henley, Stevie Nicks.

* Games Available: 3-card poker, Baccarat, Blackjack, Craps, Keno, Let It Ride, Pai Gow, Race book, Roulette, Slots - 5000

NEW MEXICO

Apache Nugget Casino

Narrow Gauge Road
P.O. Box 650
Dulce, NM 87528
(505) 759-3777
(800) 294-2234
■ **Restaurant(s):** Apache Grill
■ **Games Available:** Bingo, Blackjack, Craps,
Slots - 90

Camel Rock Casino

17486A -Hwy 84/285
Santa Fe, NM 87504
(800) GO-CAMEL
www.camelrockcasino.com
■ **Restaurant(s):** Pueblo Artist Café
Camel Rock Suites nearby.
■ **Games Available:** 3-card poker, Bingo,
Blackjack - 8, Craps, Roulette, Slots - 700

Casino Apache

P.O. Box 205
Mescalero, NM 88340
(505) 630-4100
■ **Games Available:** Blackjack, Craps, Poker,
Roulette, Slots

Cities of Gold Casino

Highway 84-285
Santa Fe, NM 87506
(505) 455-3313
info@citiesofgold.com
www.citiesofgold.com
■ **Hotel:** 124 rooms
■ **Restaurant(s):** Golden Buffet and Cantina,
Gold Dust Restaurant
■ **Games Available:** Bingo, Blackjack, Craps,
Poker, Race book, Roulette, Slots

Dancing Eagle Casino

I-40
P.O. Box 520
Casa Blanca, NM 87007
(505) 552-1111
(877) 440-9969
Fax: (505) 552-0944
www.dancingeaglecasino.com
Casino has 10 table games.
Live music on weekends.
■ **Games Available:** Blackjack - 8, Craps - 1,
Roulette - 1, Slots - 319

Isleta Gaming Palace

11000 Broadway SE
Albuquerque, NM 87105
(505) 869-2614
(800) 460-5686
■ **Games Available:** Bingo, Poker, Slots

Ohkay Casino Resort

P.O. Box 1270
San Juan Pueblo, NM 87566
30 minutes from Santa Fe
(505) 747-1668
Fax: (505) 747-5695
www.ohkay.com
■ **Hotel:** 125 rooms, $65-$125
Reservations: 87-STAY-AT-OK
Arena is used for rodeos, bull-riding, boxing and
concerts.
■ **Games Available:** Blackjack, Craps ,
Roulette, Slots - 770

San Felipe's Casino Hollywood

25 Hagan Rd.
San Felipe, NM 87001
Between Albuquerque and Santa Fe
(505) 867-6700
(877) 529-2946
www.sanfelipecasino.com
Hollywood Hills Speedway, which opened in March 2002, is next door and the casino has been expanded. Casino has 15 table games.
The 1,250-seat Celebrity Showroom opened in 2001.
■ **Games Available:** Blackjack, Craps, Pai Gow, Roulette, Slots - 800

Sandia Casino

I-25 and Tramway
Albuquerque, NM 87184
(800) 526-9366
marketing@sandiacasino.com
www.sandiacasino.com
Summer concert series
■ **Games Available:** 3-card poker, Bingo, Blackjack, Craps, Keno, Let It Ride, Poker, Roulette, Slots - 1370

Santa Ana Star

54 Jemez Canyon Dam Road
Bernalillo, NM 87004
(505) 867-0000
sastar@rt66.com
www.santaanastar.com
■ **Restaurant(s):** The Feast Buffet
Santa Ana Star Casino is in its first phase of expansion including a 288-room hotel, three new restaurants, 3,000-seat special events center, 36-lane bowling center and conference rooms.
■ **Games Available:** Blackjack, Craps, Let It Ride, Poker, Roulette, Slots

Sky City Casino

P.O Box 519
San Fidel, NM 87049
(505) 552-6017
(888) SKY-CITY
skycity1@skycitycasino.com
www.skycitycasino.com
■ **Hotel:** 150 rooms
■ **Restaurant(s):** Huwaka Restaurant
Hotel has pool.
■ **Games Available:** Bingo, Blackjack, Craps, Keno, Poker - 6, Roulette, Slots - 600

Taos Mountain Casino

P.O. Box 1154
Taos, NM 87571
(505) 737-0777
(888) WIN-TAOS
www.taosmountaincasino.com
■ **Restaurant(s):** Lucky 7's Café
■ **Games Available:** Blackjack, Roulette, Slots

NEW YORK

Akwesasne Mohawk Casino

Route 37 P.O. Box 670
Akwesasne, NY 13655
Eight miles from Canadian border
(877) 99CASINO
Fax: (518) 358-4015
win@mohawkcasino.com
www.mohawkcasino.com

■ **Restaurant(s):** Native Harvest, Steel Deck Deli

■ **Games Available:** Blackjack, Craps , Mini-baccarat, Pai Gow, Poker, Roulette, Slots

Turning Stone Casino

5218 Patrick Rd.
Verona, NY 13478
East of Syracuse
(800) 771-7711
www.turning-stone.com

■ **Hotel:** 285 rooms, $79-up

■ **Restaurant(s):** Emerald Restaurant, Forest Grill Steakhouse, Peach Blossom, Pino Bianco Trattoria, Garden Buffet, Delta Café.

Resort includes RV park, golf packages, spa, salon, pool.

Showroom features entertainers including Wayne Brady. Boxing matches featured.

■ **Games Available:** Baccarat, Bingo, Blackjack, Craps, Keno, Let It Ride, Poker, Roulette, Slots

NORTH CAROLINA

Harrah's Cherokee Casino

777 Casino Drive
Cherokee, NC 28719
One hour west of Ashville
(828) 497-8882
(800) HARRAHS
www.harrahs.com/our_casinos/che/index.html

■ **Hotel:** 250 rooms

■ **Restaurant(s):** Fresh Market Square Buffet, Seven Sisters, Winning Streak Deli.

A new 15-story hotel and convention center opened in spring of 2002, including a 24-hour restaurant and Club Cappuccino, indoor pool, workout room. Gaming includes video poker, video blackjack, video craps.

Cherokee Pavilion, with 1,400 seats, features entertainers including Loretta Lynn, Charlie Daniels, Sinbad, Wynonna, Bill Cosby, Wayne Newton.

■ **Games Available:** Slots

A 15-story hotel and conference center is the centerpiece of Harrah's Cherokee in North Carolina. The 250-room hotel opened in 2002.

NORTH DAKOTA

Blue Wolf Casino

I-94 & S. University Drive
Fargo, ND 58103
(701) 232-2019
■ **Games Available:** Blackjack - 8, Pull-tab games

Dakota Magic Casino

16849 102nd St. SE
Hankinson, ND 58041
(800) 325-6825
www.dakotamagic.com
Live entertainment on weekends.
■ **Games Available:** Blackjack, Craps, Keno, Poker, Roulette, Slots - 600

Four Bears Casino

Highway 23
HC3, Box 2A
New Town, ND 58763
(800) 294-5454
Fax: (701) 627-3714
4bears@newtown.ndak.net
www.4bearscasino.com
■ **Hotel:** 97 rooms, $35-$99
The resort includes 85-space RV Park, marina.
Entertainers at 4 Bears Events Center include Chubby Checker, Mel Tillis, rodeo.
■ **Games Available:** Bingo, Blackjack - 8, Craps, Poker - 4, Slots - 500, Roulette

Prairie Knights Casino & Resort

Highway 1806
Fort Yates, ND 53538
(701) 854-7777
(800) 425-8277
www.prairieknights.com
■ **Hotel:** 96 rooms, $60-$120
■ **Restaurant(s):** Feast of the Rock, Hunters Club
Entertainers in the Pavilion include Bobby Vee and Roy Clark.
■ **Games Available:** Blackjack, Craps, Roulette, Slots - 500

Sky Dancer Hotel & Casino

P.O. Box 1449
Belcourt, ND 58316
(866) BIG-WINS
bigwins@hotmail.com
www.skydancercasino.com
■ **Hotel:** 97 rooms
■ **Restaurant(s):** Chippewa Trails Restaurant.
Entertainers include Ronnie Milsap and Gary Stewart.
■ **Games Available:** Bingo, Blackjack - 8, Poker, Race book, Slots - 397

Spirit Lake Casino & Resort

7889 Hwy. 57 South
St. Michael, ND 58370
90 miles west of Grand Forks, N.D.

(800) 946-8238
(800) WIN-UBET
Fax: (701) 766-4900
harlan@spiritlakecasino.com
www.spiritlakecasino.com

Hotel: 124 rooms, $70-$130

Reservations: (701) 766-4888

Restaurant(s): Three restaurants: Dakotan Buffet, The View (fine dining); Snack Bar.

Auditorium for up to 500 and other meeting rooms available. Resort's marina on Devils Lake features boat rentals, slip rentals and fishing guide service.

Big-name entertainers appear monthly.

■ **Games Available:** Bingo, Blackjack $1-$250, Craps, Poker, Roulette, Slots - 600

Turtle Mountain Casino

Highway 5 West
Belcourt, ND 58316
(701) 477-6438

■ **Games Available:** Slots

OKLAHOMA

Cherokee Casino

I-44 and 193rd
Catoosa, OK 74015
(918) 266-6700
(800) 760-6700
www.cherokeecasino.com
Other Cherokee Casinos in Roland and Siloam
Spring
■ **Games Available:** Bingo, Blackjack

Cimmaron Bingo Casino

West Freeman Avenue
Perkins, OK 74059
(405) 547-5352
■ **Games Available:** Bingo, Slots - 7

Fort Sill Apache Casino

2315 E. Gore Blvd.
Lawton, OK 73501
(580) 248-5905
■ **Games Available:** Bingo, Slots

Lucky Star Casino

Highway 81
Concho, OK 73022
(405) 262-7612
luckystarcasino.org
25,000 square feet
■ **Restaurant(s):** Concho Café
■ **Games Available:** Bingo, Blackjack, Slots

OREGON

Chinook Winds Casino

1777 NW 44th St.
Lincoln City, OR 97367
(888) CHINOOK
www.chinookwindscasino.com

■ **Restaurant(s):** Rouge River Restaurant and Lounge, Buffet, Deli.

Showroom hosts entertainers including Sha Na Na, Chuck Berry, Charley Pride, Brenda Lee.

■ **Games Available:** Bingo, Blackjack, Keno, Poker, Slots - 1200

Indian Head Casino

P.O. Box 1240
Warm Springs, OR 97661
(541) 553-6122
(800) 238-6946
www.kah-nee-taresort.com

■ **Hotel:** 139 rooms

25,000 square feet

■ **Restaurant(s):** Juniper Dining Room, Pinto Grill.

Kah-Nee-Ta Resort has pool, spa, 20 tee-pees, RV Park.

■ **Games Available:** Blackjack, Poker, Slots - 300

Kla-Mo-Ya Casino

34333 Highway 97N
P.O. Box 490
Chiloquin, OR 97624
22 miles north of Klamath Falls
(541) 783-7529
(888) 552-6692
Fax: (541) 783-7543
www.klamoya.com

Restaurant(s): Rapids Deli, Stillwater Buffet
Special events include prize giveaways. Bonus Club available.
Occasional bands

■ **Games Available:** Bingo, Blackjack $1, Blackjack $2, Blackjack $5, Poker, Slots - 300

Old Camp Casino

Old Camp Monroe Street
Burns, OR 97720
(541) 573-1500

■ **Games Available:** Bingo, Blackjack, Poker, Slots

Seven Feathers Hotel & Casino Resort

146 Chief Miwaleta Lane
Canyonville, OR 97417
Between Eugene and Medford
(800) 548-8461
info@sevenfeathers.com
7feathers.com

■ **Hotel:** 147 rooms

■ **Reservations:** (888) 677-7771

■ **Restaurant(s):** Camas Room, Cow Creek Restaurant.

Hotel has pool, spa and sauna. A 32-space RV Park is available. Golf available at 18-hole Myrtle Creek. Convention center includes 21,000 square foot ballroom.

Live entertainment in Cabaret Lounge.

■ **Games Available:** Bingo, Blackjack, Craps, Keno, Let It Ride, Poker, Roulette, Slots - 650

Seven Feathers Hotel and Casino in Canyonville, Ore., features a huge bald eagle sculpture.

Spirit Mountain Casino

P.O. Box 39
Grand Ronde, OR 97347
65 miles southwest of Portland
(800) 760-7977
Fax: (503) 879-2486
www.spiritmountain.com
Hotel: 100 rooms, $59-up
90,000 square feet
■ **Restaurant(s):** Legends, Summit View, Coyote's Buffet, Spirit Mountain Café, Rock Creek Court.

RV Park available.
■ **Games Available:** Bingo, Blackjack - 29, Craps - 3, Keno, Let It Ride - 3, Pai Gow - 3, Poker - 16, Roulette - 4, Slots - 1500

The Mill Casino

3201 Tremont St.
North Bend, OR 97459
(541) 756-8800
(800) 953-4800
themillcasino@themillcasino.com
www.themillcasino.com
■ **Hotel:** 115 rooms
■ **Restaurant(s):** Cook Shack Buffet, Plank House Restaurant, Timbers Café.
Live music nightly.
■ **Games Available:** Blackjack, Poker , Slots - 400

Wildhorse Resort and Casino

72777 Hwy. 331
Pendleton, OR 97801
4 miles east of Pendleton, Ore.
(541) 278-2274
info@wildhorseresort.com
www.wildhorseresort.com
■ **Hotel:** 100 rooms, $65-$110
85,000 square feet
■ **Restaurant(s):** Wildhorse Restaurant, Snack Bar

Indoor pool, whirlpool and spa available at hotel. Meeting rooms are available. Resort has 18-hole golf course and 100-space RV park. Also available is the Tamastslikt Cultural Center and Museum. Free parking, shuttle bus and valet service 24 hours.

Concerts and Celebrity Meet and Greet are offered.
■ **Games Available:** Bingo, Blackjack - 8, Craps - 1, Keno - 4, Pai Gow - 1, Poker - 3, Slots - 600, Sport Book - 4

SOUTH DAKOTA

B.B. Cody's

681 Main St.
Deadwood, SD 57732
(605) 578-3430
■ **Games Available:** Blackjack, Slots - 50

Best Western Hickok House

137 Charles St.
Deadwood, SD 57732
(605) 578-1611
(800) 837-8174
Fax: (605) 578-1855
www.bestwestern.com
■ **Hotel:** 45 rooms
Hotel has hot tub and spa. Free parking.
■ **Games Available:** Blackjack, Slots

Bodega Bar

664 Main St.
Deadwood, SD 57732
(605) 578-1996
■ **Games Available:** Blackjack, Slots

Buffalo Saloon

658 Main St.
Deadwood, SD 57732
(605) 578-9993
■ **Games Available:** Blackjack, Slots

Bullock Express

68 Main St.
Deadwood, SD 57732
(605) 578-3476
Restaurant(s): 76 Restaurant
■ **Games Available:** Slots

Tourists enjoy the sights along historic Main Street in Deadwood.

South Dakota Tourism photo

Bullock Hotel

633 Main St.
Deadwood, SD 57732
(605) 578-1745
(800) 336-1876
www.heartofdeadwood.com/Bullock/

■ **Hotel:** 28 rooms
■ **Restaurant(s):** Bully's Restaurant and Lounge
Hotel has been restored to 1895 look.
Seth's Cellar Theater features musical and variety
acts.
■ **Games Available:** Slots

Cadillac Jacks Gaming Resort

360 Main St.
Deadwood, SD 57732
(605) 578-1500

■ **Games Available:** Blackjack, Slots

Dakota Connection

I-29 and Highway 10
Sisseton, SD 57262
(800) 542-2876
www.dakotaconnection.net

■ **Restaurant(s):** Crossroads Restaurant
Casino has convenience store and gift shop.
■ **Games Available:** Bingo, Blackjack, Slots

Dakota Sioux Casino

16415 Sioux Conifer Road
Watertown, SD 57201
(800) 658-4717
www.dakotasioux.com

■ **Restaurant(s):** Rose Restaurant
■ **Games Available:** Bingo, Blackjack, Poker,
Race book, Slots - 200

Deadwood Dick's Saloon

51 Sherman St.
Deadwood, SD 57732
(605) 578-3224
(877) 882-4990
dwddicks@deadwood.net
www.deadwooddicks.com

■ **Hotel:** 11 rooms
■ **Games Available:** Slots

Deadwood Gulch Gaming

560 Main St.
Deadwood, SD 57732
(605) 578-1207

■ **Games Available:** Slots

Deadwood Gulch Resort

Highway 85 South
P.O. Box 643
Deadwood, SD 57732
(605) 578-1294
(800) 695-1876
www.deadwoodgulch.com

■ **Hotel:** 98 rooms, $62-up
■ **Restaurant(s):** Creekside Restaurant
Outdoor pool.
■ **Games Available:** Blackjack, Slots

Decker's Food Center & Gaming

124 Sherman St.
Deadwood, SD 57732
(605) 578-2722
Grocery store has slot machines.
■ **Games Available:** Slots

Fairmont Hotel

628 Main St.
Deadwood, SD 57732
(605) 578-2205
Hotel: 16 rooms

- **Restaurant(s):** Oyster Bay
- **Games Available:** Slots

First Gold Hotel & Gaming

270 Main St.
Deadwood, SD 57732
(605) 578-9777
(800) 274-1876
Fax: (605) 578-3979
www.firstgold.com

- **Hotel:** 98 rooms, $55-up
- **Restaurant(s):** Horseshoe Restaurant

Facilties include a hotel and two motels, five casinos, banquet rooms.

- **Games Available:** 3-card poker, Blackjack, Slots

Fort Randall Casino

P.O. Box 229
Pickstown, SD 57367
(605) 487-7871
(800) 362-6333
Hotel adjacent to casino.

- **Games Available:** Bingo, Poker, Slots

Four Aces Casino/Hampton Inn

531 Main St.
Deadwood, SD 57732
(605) 578-3232
(866) 578-2237
www.fouracescasino.org

- **Hotel:** 59 rooms, $69-up
25,000 square feet
- **Reservations:** (800) 529-0105

Meeting accommodations in newly expanded hotel.
Overall Payout: 89%

- **Games Available:** Blackjack $2, Slots

Franklin Hotel and Casino

700 Main St.
Deadwood, SD 57732
(605) 578-2241
(800) 688-1876

- **Restaurant(s):** 1903 Dining Room.

Historic hotel was built in 1903 and features rooms dedicated to guests including Babe Ruth, Theodore Roosevelt, Jack Dempsey, President William Taft and John Wayne.

- **Games Available:** Blackjack - 2, Poker - 1, Slots - 87

Gold Country Inn Casino

801 Main St.
Deadwood, SD 57732
(605) 578-2393
(800) 287-1251

- **Hotel:** 53 rooms, $55-up
- **Games Available:** Blackjack, Slots

Gold Dust Gaming

688 Main St.
Deadwood, SD 57732
(605) 578-2100
(800) 456-0533
www.golddustgaming.com

- **Games Available:** Blackjack, Poker, Slots

Golden Buffalo Casino

321 Sitting Bull Lane
Lower Brule, SD 57548
(605) 473-5577

- **Hotel:** 38 rooms, $39-up
- **Restaurant(s):** Golden Buffalo Restaurant
- **Games Available:** Blackjack, Poker , Slots

Grand River Casino

P.O. Box 639
Mobridge, SD 57601
(605) 845-7104
(800) 475-3321
www.grandrivercasino.com

■ **Restaurant(s):** Sage Restaurant

■ **Games Available:** Blackjack, Poker , Slots - 250

Gulches of Fun

Highway 85 South
Deadwood, SD 57732
(605) 578-7550
(800) 961-3096
www.gulchesoffun.com

■ **Hotel:** 71 rooms

Hotel has indoor pool, exercise room. Fun Park includes miniature golf, go carts, kiddie train, bumper boats.

■ **Games Available:** Blackjack, Slots

Hickok's Saloon

685 Main St.
Deadwood, SD 57732
(605) 578-2222

■ **Games Available:** Blackjack, Slots

Lady Luck Deadwood

660 Main St.
Deadwood, SD 57732
(605) 578-1162

■ **Games Available:** Slots

Lucky 8 Gaming

196 Cliff St.
Deadwood, SD 57732
(605) 578-2535

■ **Games Available:** Slots

McKenna's Gold Casino

470 Main St.
Deadwood, SD 57732
(605) 578-3207
www.deadwood.com/attractions/McKennas.html

■ **Games Available:** Slots

Midnight Star

677 Main St.
Deadwood, SD 57732
(605) 578-1555
(800) 999-6482
www.themidnightstar.com

■ **Restaurant(s):** Jakes, Diamond Lil's

■ **Games Available:** 3-card poker, Blackjack, Let It Ride, Slots

Mineral Palace Hotel

601 Main St.
Deadwood, SD 57732
(605) 578-2036
(800) 847-2522
www.mineralpalace.com

■ **Hotel:** 63 rooms, $79-up

■ **Games Available:** Blackjack, Slots

Miss Kitty's

649 Main St.
Deadwood, SD 57732
(605) 578-1811
(800) 668-8189
www.heartofdeadwood.com/MissKittys/

■ **Restaurant(s):** Chinatown Café, Consuela's Cantina.

■ **Games Available:** Blackjack, Poker , Slots

Mustang Sally's

634 Main St.
Deadwood, SD 57732
(605) 578-2035

■ **Games Available:** Slots

Nugget Bar

604 Main St.
Deadwood, SD 57732
(605) 578-1100
■ **Games Available:** Slots

Old Style Saloon # 10

657 Main St.
Deadwood, SD 57732
(605) 578-3346
(800) 952-9398
www.saloon10.com
Re-enactment of the shooting of Wild Bill Hickok
is featured.
Live music
■ **Games Available:** Blackjack, Poker , Slots

Royal River Casino

607 S. Veterans St.
Flandreau, SD 57028
(800) 833-8666
Fax: (605) 997-9998
www.royalrivercasino.com
■ **Hotel:** 60 rooms
Hotel has indoor pool, spa.
■ **Games Available:** Bingo, Blackjack, Poker,
Slots

Shedds

674 Main St.
Deadwood, SD 57732
(605) 578-2494
■ **Games Available:** Poker, Slots

Silverado Gaming Establishment & Restaurant

709 Main St.
Deadwood, SD 57732
(605) 578-3670

(800) 584-7005
info@silveradocasino.com
www.silveradocasino.com
■ **Restaurant(s):** Grand Buffet
■ **Games Available:** Blackjack, Slots - 223

Star of the West Casino

700 Main St.
Deadwood, SD 57732
(605) 578-2241
(800) 688-1876
■ **Games Available:** Blackjack, Poker , Slots

A woman looks for a jackpot while playing a slot machine in Deadwood, S.D.

South Dakota Tourism photo

Super 8 Lodge

196 Cliff St.
Deadwood, SD 57732
50 miles from Rapid City, SD
(605) 578-2535
(800) 800-8000
www.deadwoodSuper8.com

■ **Hotel:** 51 rooms, $45-$130

■ **Restaurant(s):** Pizzeria

Overall Payout: 95-97%

■ **Games Available:** Slots $1, Slots $5, Slots Nickel, Slots Quarter

Tin Lizzie Gaming

555 Main St.
Deadwood, SD 57732
(605) 578-1715
(800) 643-4490

Free live entertainment

■ **Games Available:** Blackjack, Slots

Wild Bill Bar

608 Main St.
Deadwood, SD 57732
(605) 578-2177

■ **Games Available:** Slots

Wild West Winners Casino

622 Main St.
Deadwood, SD 57732
(605) 578-1100
(888) 880-3835
www.heartofdeadwood.com/WildWest/

■ **Restaurant(s):** Wild Bill Steakhouse

Casino includes 10 buildings, three bars and the building where Wild Bill Hickok may have been shot.

■ **Games Available:** Slots

Wooden Nickel Casino

9 Lee St.
Deadwood, SD 57732
(605) 578-1952

■ **Restaurant(s):** Lee St. Station Café

■ **Games Available:** Slots

TEXAS

Kickapoo Lucky Eagle Casino

7777 Lucky Eagle Drive
Eagle Pass, TX 78852
(888) 255-8259
info@casino.kickapootribe.com
www.kickapooluckyeaglecasino.com

■ **Games Available:** Bingo, Blackjack, Poker, Slots

WASHINGTON

7 Cedars Casino

270756 Hwy. 101
Sequim, WA 98382
(360) 683-7777
(800) 4-LUCKY-7
info@7cedarscasino.com
www.7cedarscasino.com

■ **Restaurant(s):** Salish Room Restaurant

Live music and comedy.

■ **Games Available:** Bingo, Blackjack, Craps, Keno, Poker, Roulette, Slots

Big Al's Casino

12715 4th Ave.
West Everett, WA 98204
(425) 347-1669
(877) 244-2577
Fax: (425) 347-8910
www.wa-bigalscasino.com

Casino has 15 table games.

Live bands on weekends.

■ **Games Available:** 3-card poker, Blackjack, Lucky Ladies, Pai Gow, Pull-tab games, Spanish 21

Chewelah Casino

2555 Smith Rd.
Chewelah, WA 99109
(509) 935-6167
(800) 322-2788

Open 24 hours on weekends. RV Park with 20 spaces available.

Entertainment on special occasions.

■ **Games Available:** Blackjack, Craps , Pai Gow, Roulette, Slots - 400

Clearwater Casino

P.O. Box 1210
Suquamish, WA 98392
Near Seattle
(360) 598-6889
(800) 375-6073
www.clearwatercasino.com

■ **Restaurant(s):** Agate Pass Café

Live entertainers, karaoke.

■ **Games Available:** Bingo, Blackjack, Slots

Cleopatra's Cable Bridge Casino

101 S. Gum St.
Kennewick, WA 99336
(509) 585-9246
Fax: (509) 586-7926
Restaurant(s): Sports Bar
12 table games, 36 pull-tab games.

■ **Games Available:** Blackjack, Let It Ride, Lucky Ladies, Poker, Pull-tab games - 36, Spanish 21

Cleopatra's Club Casino

8418 Gage Blvd.
Kennewick, WA 99336
(509) 374-3289
Fax: (509) 374-3349
12 table games, 12 pull-tab games.

■ **Games Available:** Blackjack, Let It Ride, Poker, Pull-tab games - 12, Spanish 21

Cleopatra's Wild Goose Casino

1600 Carrier St.
Ellensburg, WA 98926
(509) 925-LUCK

Fax: (509) 962-5522
■ **Restaurant(s):** Sports Bar.
12 table games, 15 pull-tab games.
■ **Games Available:** Blackjack, Let It Ride, Lucky Ladies, Pull-tab games - 15, Spanish 21

Cleopatra's Wild Grizzly Casino

902 Ash St.
Kelso, WA 98626
(360) 423-6630
Fax: (360) 423-6608
■ **Restaurant(s):** Fine dining.
12 table games, 14 pull-tab games.
■ **Games Available:** 3-card poker, Blackjack, Let It Ride, Pull-tab games - 14 , Spanish 21

Coulee Dam Casino

515 Birch St.
Coulee Dam, WA 99116
(800) 556-7492
www.colvillecasinos.com
■ **Games Available:** Blackjack, Slots - 150

Double Eagle Spokane Casino

P.O. Box 961
Chewelah, WA 98232
(509) 935-4406
■ **Games Available:** Blackjack, Roulette, Slots

Legends Casino

580 Fort Rd.
Toppenish, WA 98948
(509) 865-8800
■ **Games Available:** Keno, Poker, Slots

Little Creek Casino

91 West State Route 108
Shelton, WA 98584-9270
15 miles from Olympia, Wash.
(360) 427-7711
(800) 667-7791
www.little-creek.com
50,000 square feet
Restaurant(s): Two restaurants: Creek Side Café; Legends fine dining.
Lounge and headliner acts
■ **Games Available:** Bingo - 400, Craps - 1, Keno - 1, Pai Gow - 2, Poker - 5, Roulette - 1, Slots - 345

Lucky Eagle Casino

12888 188th Ave. SW
Rochester, WA 98579
20 miles south of Olympia, Wash.
(360) 273-2000
(800) 720-1788
www.luckyeagle.com
■ **Restaurant(s):** Grand Buffet, Golden Eagle Prime Rib & Steak House, Center Stage Grill and Cabaret, Sidewalk Deli
Banquet Facilities, Catering, Live Weekend Entertainment, Boxing, Concerts, 1,100 Seat Event Center
Concerts, boxing, comedy
■ **Games Available:** $3 to $500, 3-card poker Bingo, Craps - 2, Keno, Let It Ride - 2, Pai Gow - 2, Roulette - 2, Slots $1, Slots Nickel, Slots Quarter

Casino entrance at the Lucky Eagle Casino in Rochester, Wash.

Mill Bay Casino

455 E. Wapato Lake Rd.
Manson, WA 98831
(800) 648-2946
www.colvillecasinos.com
■ **Restaurant(s):** Coyote Café
Casino has 11 table games.
■ **Games Available:** Blackjack, Craps, Roulette,
Slots - 400

Muckleshoot Casino

2402 Auburn Way S.
Auburn, WA 98002
Between Seattle and Tacoma
(800) 804-4944
www.muckleshootcasino.com
700,000 square feet
■ **Restaurant(s):** Five restaurants: Pisces
Seafood Buffet; Kookaburra's (fine dining); Oasis
Sushi Bar; Island Deli; Muckleshoot Restaurant.
More than 70 table games; 1,500 slot machines;
on-site bingo hall.
Live bands every night -- free admission.
Overall Payout: 93-97%
■ **Games Available:** Bingo, Blackjack $5,
Craps, Keno, Pai Gow, Roulette, Slots - 1500

Northern Quest Casino

100 N. Hayford Road
Airway Heights, WA 99001
10 minutes west of downtown Spokane
(509) 242-7000
info@northernquest.net
www.northernquest.net
■ **Restaurant(s):** River's Edge Buffet
Casino has 24 table games.
■ **Games Available:** Blackjack, Craps , Keno,
Poker, Roulette, Slots - 425

Okanogan Bingo-Casino

41 Appleway Rd.
Okanogan, WA 98841
(800) 559-4643
www.colvillecasinos.com
■ **Games Available:** Bingo, Blackjack, Slots -
160

Quinalt Beach Resort & Casino

78 State Route 115
Ocean Shores, WA 98569
(888) 461-2214
inquiries@quinaultbchresort.com
www.quinaultbchresort.com
■ **Hotel:** 159 rooms, $109-up
16,000 square feet
■ **Restaurant(s):** Emily's Restaurant, Sidewalk
Bistro.
Hotel has a spa. Casino has 30 table games.
■ **Games Available:** Blackjack, Craps , Keno,
Pai Gow, Roulette, Slots - 200

Red Wind Nisqually Olympia Casino

12819 Elm Highway
Olympia, WA 98513
(360) 412-5000
■ **Restaurant(s):** Blue Camas
■ **Games Available:** Blackjack, Craps, Roulette,
Slots - 250

Skagit Valley Casino Resort

5984 N. Darrk Lane
Bow, WA 98232
70 miles north of Seattle
(800) 895-3423
www.svcasinoresort.com
Hotel: 103 rooms, $69-up
64,000 square feet
Restaurant(s): Moon Beach Grille, Marketplace
Buffet and Grille, Northern Lights Deli.

Entertainment in the Pacific Showroom

■ **Games Available:** Blackjack, Craps, Keno, Let It Ride, Pai Gow, Roulette, Slots - 600

Swinomish Casino and Bingo

12885 Casino Drive
Anacortes, WA 98221
(360) 293-2691
info@swinomishcasino.com
www.swinomishcasino.com

■ **Restaurant(s):** 2 Salmon Café

Live music and comedy are featured.

■ **Games Available:** Bingo, Blackjack, Craps, Keno, Let It Ride, Pai Gow, Poker, Race book, Roulette, Slots

Tulalip Casino

6410 33rd Ave. NE
Marysville, WA 98271
North of Seattle
(360) 651-111
(888) 272-111
www.tulalipcasino.com

■ **Reservations:** (360) 659-5270

■ **Restaurant(s):** Prince of Whales Restaurant, Quil Deli.

Music and comedy in Bourbon Street Bar and Cabaret Lounge.

■ **Games Available:** Baccarat, Bingo, Blackjack, Craps, Keno , Poker, Roulette, Slots

Two Rivers Casino

6228-B Hwy. 25 South
Davenport, WA 99122
(509) 722-4000
(800) 722-4031
www.tworiverscasinoandresort.com

Resort has an RV park and a 200-slip marina on Lake Roosevelt.

■ **Games Available:** Slots, Blackjack, Craps, Roulette

Wizards Casino

15739 Ambaum Blvd. SW
Burien, WA 98166
10 minutes from Seattle International Airport
(206) 444-6100
www.wizards-casino.com
8,500 square feet

* **Games Available:** 3-card poker, Blackjack $3, Let It Ride, Lucky Ladies, Pai Gow, Spanish 21

WISCONSIN

Bad River Casino

P.O. Box 39
Odanah, WI 54861
10 miles east of Ashland, Wis.
(715) 682-7121
Fax: (715) 682-7149
bobp@badriver.com
www.badriver.com
■ **Hotel:** 50 rooms, $45-$85
■ **Reservations:** (800) 795-7121
■ **Games Available:** Blackjack - 5, Slots - 500

Ho-Chunk Casino & Bingo

S3214 Hwy. 12
Baraboo, WI 53913
Near Wisconsin Dells
(800) 746-2486
www.ho-chunk.com
■ **Hotel:** 250 rooms
86,000 square feet
■ **Restaurant(s):** Four restaurants: Copper Oak Steakhouse, Wo-Zha-Wa Restaurant, Stand Rock Buffet, Sunrise Cliffs Café.
200,000 square foot convention center, fitness center, aquatic center.
Concerts in Main Ballroom
■ **Games Available:** Bingo, Blackjack - 72, Slots - 1200

Hole in the Wall Casino

P.O. Box 98
Danbury, WI 54830
1 hours south of Superior, Wis., 1 1/2 hours north of Twin Cities
(715) 656-3444
(800) BET-UWIN
www.wisconsingaming.com

■ **Hotel:** 46 rooms, $40-$50
■ **Restaurant(s):** Loose Change Café
35-site RV park.
Live bands on weekends.
■ **Games Available:** Blackjack $2, Slots - 315

Isle Vista Casino

Highway 13
P.O. Box 1167
Bayfield, WI 54814
90 miles from Duluth-Superior
(715) 779-3712
(800) 226-8478
■ **Games Available:** Blackjack, Slots

Lake of the Torches Casino-Bingo

P.O. Box 550
Highway 47
Lac du Flambeau, WI 54538
12 miles west of Minocqua/Woodruff, Wis.
(800) 25-TORCH
www.lakeofthetorches.com
■ **Hotel:** 103 rooms
■ **Reservations:** (888) 599-9200
■ **Games Available:** Bingo, Blackjack - 16, Slots - 600

LCO Casino Lodge

13767W Cty. Rd. B
Hayward, WI 54843
(715) 634-5643
(800) LCO-CASH
Fax: (715) 634-6806
admin@lcocasino.com
www.lcocasino.com

■ **Hotel:** 54 rooms, $49-$100

Indoor pool, exercise room, convention facilities for 400.

Bands and entertainers

■ **Games Available:** Bingo, Blackjack $2 - 8, Keno, Slots - 600

Little Turtle Hertel Express & Casino

5384 State Road 70
Hertel, WI 54845
(715) 349-5658
www.stcroixcasino.com/hertle

■ **Games Available:** Slots - 99

Majestic Pines

W9010 Highway 54 East
Black River Falls, WI 54615
Four miles east of Black River Falls
(715) 284-9098
(800) 657-4621
Hotel: 60 rooms
16,000 square feet

■ **Reservations:** (888) 625-8668

■ **Restaurant(s):** Buffet daily for lunch and dinner; Deli/ snack bar open during casino hours

Discounts available with Player's Club Card.

■ **Games Available:** Bingo - 480, Blackjack $3 to $200 - 12, Slots $1 - 273, Slots $5 - 8, Slots Nickel - 35, Slots Quarter - 273

Menominee Casino Bingo Hotel

P.O. Box 760
Keshena, WI 54135
Five miles north of Shawano, Wis.
(800) 343-7778
www.menomineecasinoresort.com

■ **Hotel:** 100 rooms
33,000

■ **Restaurant(s):** Forest Island Restaurant
60-site RV park.

Entertainers including Paul Revere and the Raiders, Williams and Ree, Coasters and Platters.

■ **Games Available:** Bingo, Blackjack - 12, Slots - 837

A 100-room hotel is a haven for travelers to Menominee Casino-Bingo-Hotel in Keshena, Wis.

Mohican North Star Casino & Bingo

W12180 County Road A
Gresham, WI 54128
18 miles west of Shawano, Wis.
(800) 952-0195
marketing@mohican.com
www.mohican.com/casino

18-hole golf course with banquet hall and clubhouse.

Concerts, entertainers such as Willie Nelson and Brenda Lee.

■ **Games Available:** Bingo, Blackjack - 20, Slots - 837

Oneida Bingo & Casino

2020 Airport Drive
Green Bay, WI 54313
Across from Green Bay's Austin Straubel
  International Airport
(920) 494-4500
(800) 238-4263
casino@oneidanation.org
www.oneidabingoandcasino.net

■ **Hotel:** 301 rooms, $50-$125

■ **Reservations:** (800) 333-3333

■ **Restaurant(s):** The Gathering Cafeteria, Three Sisters Buffet, Shenandoah Restaurant.

Oneida Smoke Shop, Woodland Gift Shop, free parking, shuttle bus.

Entertainers including Alice Cooper, Cheap Trick, the Doobie Brothers, Gallagher, Kenny Rogers, Poison.

■ **Games Available:** Bingo, Blackjack - 46, Slots - 2800

_____

Potawatomi Bingo - Northern Lights Casino

Highway 32
P.O. Box 430
Wabeno, WI 54566
75 miles north of Green Bay, Wis.
(715) 473-2021
(800) 487-9522
Fax: (715) 473-6104
northernlights@ez-net.com
www.cartercasino.com

■ **Hotel:** 99 rooms

■ **Reservations:** (800) 777-1640

Indoor pool and whirlpool, adjoining convenience store.

■ **Games Available:** Bingo, Blackjack - 8, Slots

_____

Potawatomi Bingo Casino

1721 W. Canal St.
Milwaukee, WI 53233
(414) 645-6888
(800) PAYS BIG
natalio@paysbig.com
www.paysbig.com/potawatomi.html

■ **Restaurant(s):** Fire Pit Grill, Bya wi se nek Buffet, Dream Dance Restaurant

Entertainers including Bobby Vinton, Joan Rivers, Smokey Robinson, Dionne Warwick in Northern Lights Theater.

■ **Games Available:** Bingo, Blackjack - 24, Slots - 1000

Rainbow Casino and Bingo

949 Cty. Trunk G
Nekoosa, WI 54457
(715) 886-4560
(800) 782-4560
www.rbcwin.com

■ **Restaurant(s):** Rainbow Grille

Smoke and Gift Shop.

■ **Games Available:** Bingo, Blackjack $3 - 12, Slots - 600

_____

St. Croix Casino & Hotel

777 Highway 8/63
Turtle Lake, WI 54889
90 miles northeast of Twin Cities
(800) UGO-UWIN
Stcroix@stcroixcasino.com
www.stcroixcasino.com

■ **Hotel:** 166 rooms, $55-$120

■ **Restaurant(s):** Me-Ki-Noc Restaurant, TLC Buffet, Snack Bar

Pool, exercise room.

■ **Games Available:** Bingo, Blackjack $3 - 24, Slots - 1100

WEST VIRGINIA

Mountaineer Race Track and Gaming Resort

P.O. Box 358
Chester, WV 26034
North of Wheeling
(800) 80-40-HOT
info@mtrgaming.com
www.mtrgaming.com/homepage.html

■ **Hotel:** 101 rooms

■ **Reservations:** (800) 489-8192

■ **Restaurant(s):** Riverfront Buffet, Outdoor Café, Gatsby Dining Room, Big Al's Deli & Pizzeria.

New hotel and convention center scheduled to be completed in 2002, in addition to The Lodge at Mountaineer, 18-hole golf course, spa and fitness center.

Live horse racing year-round, plus simulcasting of other races. Entertainment in the Speakeasy Gaming Saloon and the Lighthouse Lounge. Concerts featuring stars such as Paul Anka, Kenny Rogers, Anne Murray.

■ **Games Available:** Slots

The Mountaineer's new hotel and convention center opened in 2002.

ILLINOIS

Alton Belle Casino

219 Piasa
Alton, IL 62002
25 minutes from St. Louis
(800) 711-GAME
www.argosycasinos.com

■ **Restaurant(s):** Captain's Table Buffet, Key West Bar, Outfitters Grill, La Cantina.

Free admission, free parking.

Headliners include Lesley Gore.

■ **Games Available:** 3-card poker - 2, Blackjack - 20, Craps - 2, Let It Ride - 1, Roulette - 2, Slots $1 - 200, Slots 50 cents - 50, Slots Nickel - 250, Slots Quarter - 350

Casino Queen

200 Front St.
East St. Louis, IL 62201
(800) 777-0777
www.casinoqueen.com

■ **Hotel:** 157 rooms, $49-up

■ **Restaurant(s):** Queen's Courtyard Buffet, the Royal Table, Gazebo Café.

Hotel has indoor pool, exercise room, banquet rooms.

An RV Park is also available.

■ **Games Available:** Blackjack - 29, Craps - 4, Let It Ride - 2, Mini-baccarat - 1, Poker - 4, Roulette - 4, Slots - 1200

Empress Casino Hotel

2300 Empress Drive
Joliet, IL 60436
(888) 4EMPRESS
www.argosycasinos.com

■ **Hotel:** 102 rooms

■ **Restaurant(s):** Steakhouse Alexandria, Café Casablanca, Marrakech Market Buffet.

Empress Hotel has been remodeled and features indoor pool, whirlpool, sundeck. RV Resort also available. Casino has 30 table games.

Entertainment on Pavilion Stage.

■ **Games Available:** 3-card poker, Baccarat, Craps, Mini-baccarat, Roulette, Slots - 1100

Grand Victoria Casino Elgin

250 S. Grove Ave.
Elgin, IL 60120
(888) 508-1900
www.grandvictoria-elgin.com

■ **Restaurant(s):** Buckinghams, Grand Victoria Buffet, Deli on Grove, Fox & Hounds.

■ **Games Available:** Baccarat - 1, Blackjack - 29, Craps - 6, Poker - 4, Roulette - 5, Slots - 1000

An 80,000 square foot pavilion is part of the complex at the Grand Victoria Casino.

Harrah's Joliet Casino & Hotel

151 N. Joliet St.
Joliet, IL 60432
(815) 740-7800
www.harrahs.com/our

■ **Hotel:** 204 rooms

■ **Reservations:** (800) HARRAHS

■ **Restaurant(s):** Van Buren's Restaurant, Union Station Buffet, Winning Streak Stadium Café, Club Cappuccino.

Fitness center, gift shop.

Live entertainment in pavilion.

■ **Games Available:** Baccarat, Blackjack, Craps, Let It Ride, Roulette, Slots - 1100

Harrah's Metropolis Casino

100 E. Front St.
Metropolis, IL 62960
Across from Paducah, Ky.
(800) 929-5905
www.harrahs.com/our_casinos/met/index.html
36,000 square feet

■ **Restaurant(s):** Fresh Market Square Buffet, Fresh Market Express, Range Steakhouse.

Casino has 25 table games. Amerihost Inn across the street from the riverboat has 120 rooms.

■ **Games Available:** Blackjack, Craps , Let It Ride, Mini-baccarat, Roulette, Slots - 1100

Hollywood Casino-Aurora

49 W. Galena Blvd.
Aurora, IL 60506
40 miles west of Chicago
(630) 801-1234
(800) 888-7777
www.hollywoodcasinoaurora.com
32,000 square feet

■ **Restaurant(s):** Four restaurants: Fairbanks Steak House, 7 Fortunes Chinese, Epic Buffet, Louie Dombrowski's.

44 table games, Hollywood Casino Studio Store, meeting and banquet facilities.

Superstar entertainment including Bill Cosby, Paul Anka, Engelbert Humperdinck, Tom Jones, Aretha Franklin and The Beach Boys.

■ **Games Available:** Blackjack $10 - 23, Craps, Poker, Roulette, Slots - 1100

Horseshoe Casino Hammond

P.O. Box 2789
Joliet, IL 60434
15 minutes from downtown Chicago
(219) 473-7000
(866) 711-SHOE
www.horseshoe.com

■ **Restaurant(s):** Jack Binion's Steak House, Village Square Deli, Lake Michigan Deli Company.

■ **Games Available:** Slots - 1700, Table games

Jumer's Casino

1735 1st Ave.
Rock Island, IL 61201
180 miles west of Chicago
(309) 793-4200
(800) 477-7747
Fax: (309) 793-4206
vip@jumerscri.com
www.jumerscri.com
35,000 square feet

■ **Restaurant(s):** Effie Afton Tugboat Restaurant

Five floors on two permanently moored riverboats. Xtra Club cash back.

Live music on Top of the Rock.

Overall Payout: 93%

■ **Games Available:** Blackjack $2 - 13, Craps - 2, Poker, Roulette - 2, Slots $1, Slots $5, Slots Nickel, Slots Quarter

Jumer's Casino Rock Island

Blackjack dealers get ready for bettors at Jumer's Casino Rock Island.

Par-A-Dice Hotel Casino

21 Blackjack Blvd.
East Peoria, IL 61611
(800) PARADICE
www.par-a-dice.com

■ **Hotel:** 208 rooms, $49-up

■ **Reservations:** (800) 547-0711

■ **Restaurant(s):** Broadway Buffet, Boulevard Grille, Nelson's Deli, Flappers, The Lounge.

■ **Games Available:** Blackjack, Craps , Let It Ride, Roulette, Slots - 1100

INDIANA

Argosy Casino & Hotel Lawrenceburg

777 Argosy Parkway
Lawrenceburg, IN 47025
20 minutes from downtown Cincinnati
(888) ARGOSY-7
www.argosycasinos.com/property/cincinnati
■ **Hotel:** 300 rooms, $69-up
4,000 passenger capacity
■ **Restaurant(s):** Bogarts' Grill, Passport Café, The Outpost, The Chartroom, Riviera Café, Dockside Deli.
Monthly headliner shows. Live entertainment in The Chartroom.
■ **Games Available:** Slots - 2000, Table games - 97

Belterra Casino Resort

777 Belterra Drive
Belterra, IN 47020
(888) BELTERRA
www.belterracasino.com
■ **Hotel:** 308 rooms, $59-up
38,000 square feet
■ **Restaurant(s):** Belterra Buffet, The Reef, Fireside Steak House, Seafood Bar, Rockwell's Café, The Deli.
The 18-hole Belterra Golf Club is available. Hotel has a shopping pavilion and a spa. Riverboat has 55 table games.
CenterStage Showroom has entertainers including Ronnie Milsap.
■ **Games Available:** 3-card poker, Blackjack, Craps, Let It Ride, Pai Gow, Slots - 1350, Spanish 21

Blue Chip Casino

2 Easy St.
Michigan City, IN 46360
60 miles from Chicago
(888) 879-7711

www.bluechip-casino.com
■ **Hotel:** 188 rooms
37,000 square feet
■ **Restaurant(s):** Blue Chip Buffet, The Grille on Easy Street, Jackpot Deli
Swimming pool, workout room at hotel.
Live music on weekends
■ **Games Available:** Blackjack $5 - 29, Craps - 5, Poker - 3, Roulette - 3, Slots $1 - 473, Slots $10 - 5, Slots $100 - 3, Slots $25 - 16, Slots $5 - 49, Slots 50 cents - 82, Slots Nickel - 251, Slots Quarter - 632

Caesars Indiana Casino Hotel

11999 Avenue of the Emperors
Elizabeth, IN 47117
20 minutes from Louisville, 90 minutes from
  Lexington
(888) ROMAN-4U
www.caesarsindiana.com
Hotel: 503 rooms, $69-$199
Reservations: (866) ROMANS-1
Restaurant(s): Eight restaurants: Portico, Legends, Villa Buffet, Cleo's Coffee and More, Aroma Café, Movie Casino Deli, Music Casino Deli, Bistro Italiano.
World's largest riverboat casino. Shopping at Emperors Essentials, Roman Rituals and Jewelry Kiosk. Hotel has indoor pool, 24-hour room service, fitness center. Free admission, free valet parking. Golf course opened in fall of 2002.
Stars who have appeared include Tony Bennett, Gladys Knight, Sinbad, Don Rickels, Tony Orlando, Chubby Checker, Bob Newhart and Johnny Rivers.
Overall Payout: 93.12%
■ **Games Available:** Blackjack - 85, Craps - 14, Keno, Pai Gow - 3, Poker - 10, Roulette - 10, Slots $1 - 560, Slots $10 - 22, Slots $100 - 6, Slots $20 - 11, Slots $5 - 70, Slots $500 - 2, Slots 50 cents - 170, Slots Nickel - 480, Slots Quarter - 1174

Caesars Sports Casino

Burning of Rome Casino

Cleopatras High Limit Casino

The elaborate Burning of Rome Casino is part of Roman décor at Caesars Indiana.

Caesars Indiana Casino Hotel features a 450-foot riverboat.

Casino Aztar

421 N.W. Riverside Drive
Evansville, IN 47708
800-DIAL-FUN
www.casinoaztar.com
■ **Hotel:** 250 rooms, $89-$375
Riverboat holds 2,700 passengers
■ **Restaurant(s):** Cavanaugh's, River City Grille, Corky's Ribs & BBQ, Riverview Buffet, Sidewalk Café.
Entertainment in Hoosiers Lounge.
■ **Games Available:** 3-card poker, Blackjack, Craps, Let It Ride, Poker, Roulette, Slots

Grand Victoria Casino and Resort

600 Grand Victoria Drive
Rising Sun, IN 47040
45 minutes from Cincinnati
(812) 438-1234
(800) GRAND-11
www.hyatt.com
■ **Hotel:** 200 rooms
40,000 square feet
■ **Restaurant(s):** Steakhouse, buffet.
Resort includes a spa, indoor pool, conference center and an 18-hole golf course. Casino has 80 table games.
■ **Games Available:** Baccarat - 1, Blackjack - 26, Craps - 8, Roulette - 4, Slots - 1300

Harrah's East Chicago

1 Showboat Place
East Chicago, IN 46312
20 minutes east of Chicago.
(219) 378-3000
(800) HARRAHS
www.harrahs.com
■ **Hotel:** 293 rooms
53,000 square feet
■ **Restaurant(s):** French Quarter Room, Fresh Market Square Buffet, Winning Streaks Bar & Grill, Club Cappuccino, High Voltage Grille.
A 293-room hotel tower opened in late 2001. Casino has 60 table games.

Live entertainment on Pavilion Stage.

■ **Games Available:** Blackjack, Craps, Let It Ride, Poker - 15, Slots - 2000

Majestic Star Casino

1 Buffington Harbor Drive
Gary, IN 46406
25 minutes from Chicago
(219) 977-7932
www.majesticstar.com

■ **Restaurant(s):** Harbor Steakhouse, Skyline Buffet, Jackpot Java, Harbor Treats, Shou Ki Sushi Bar, Miller Pizza Co.

Casino has 50 table games.

Live entertainment in Buffington Harbor's Lakeshore Lounge.

■ **Games Available:** 3-card poker, Baccarat, Blackjack, Craps, Let It Ride, Pai Gow, Roulette, Slots - 1500, Spanish 21

Trump Casino Hotel

1 Buffington Harbor Drive
Gary, IN 46406
25 miles from Chicago
(219) 977-7017
(888) 21-TRUMP
www.trumpindiana.com

■ **Hotel:** 300 rooms

■ **Restaurant(s):** Café Casino, Jackpot Java, Crystal Room, Skyline Buffet, Top Deck Deli, Lakeside Room, Harbor Steakhouse, Shou Ki Noodle Sushi Bar.

Hotel has indoor pool, exercise room.

■ **Games Available:** Blackjack, Craps, Mini-baccarat, Pai Gow, Poker, Roulette, Slots - 1400

IOWA

Ameristar Casino Council Bluffs

2200 River Road
Council Bluffs, IA 51501
(712) 328-8888
(877) 462-7827
www.ameristarcasinos.com

■ **Hotel:** 160 rooms, $70-$275

37,000 square feet

■ **Restaurant(s):** Waterfront Grill, The Veranda Buffet, Amerisports Bar, Prairie Mill Café and Bakery.

Iowa's largest riverboat received Four-Diamond award from AAA. Hotel features fitness center, pool and spa, gift shop, valet service, 24-hour room service, parking garage. Casino has 46 table games.

Star Arena on the riverfront features live outdoor entertainment on summer weekends. Entertainers featured in the Ballroom and in Amerisports Bar and Casino Mainstage.

■ **Games Available:** 3-card poker - 2, Blackjack - 27, Craps - 5, Let It Ride - 1, Pai Gow - 3, Roulette - 4, Slots - 1500

For visitors with a taste for luxury, plush suites are available at the Ameristar Casino in Council Bluffs, Iowa.

Belle of Sioux City Casino

100 Larson Park Road
Sioux City, IA 51102
(800) 424-0080
www.argosycasinos.com

12,000 square feet

■ **Restaurant(s):** Jackpots Grille and Buffet, Upper Deck Eatery.

■ **Games Available:** Blackjack, Craps , Poker, Roulette, Slots - 400

The Belle of Sioux City, which holds 1,500 passengers, takes a cruise on the Mississippi River.

Catfish Bend Casino

P.O. Box 471
Fort Madison, IA 52627
This riverboat cruises from Fort Madison from May to October and docks at Burlington from November to April.
(319) 372-2946
(800) 372-2946
Fax: (319) 372-9949
info@catfishbendcasino.com
www.catfishbendcasino.com

Diamond Jo Casino

Third Street
Dubuque, IA 52004
800-Lucky Jo
www.diamondjo.com
■ **Restaurant(s):** HighSteaks Restaurant,
Lighthouse Grill.
■ **Games Available:** Blackjack, Craps , Let It
Ride, Roulette, Slots - 640

Harrah's Council Bluffs

One Harveys Blvd.
Council Bluffs, IA 51501
(712) 329-6000
(800) HARRAHS
Fax: (712) 329-6491
www.harrahs.com
■ **Hotel:** 251 rooms
20,000 square feet
■ **Restaurant(s):** Beverlee's, Mr. G's Lounge,
Aces Diner, Ultimate Buffet
Health club, spa and salon opened in 2002. Casino
has 46 table games.
DJ music, karaoke, dance lessons.
■ **Games Available:** Blackjack, Craps , Pai Gow
Roulette, Slots - 1200, Spanish 21

Isle of Capri Bettendorf

1800 Isle Parkway
Bettendorf, IA 52722
(888) 782-9582
www.isleofcapricasino.com/Bettendorf/
■ **Hotel:** 256 rooms
■ **Restaurant(s):** Farraddays' Restaurant,
Calypso's Buffet.
Hotel has indoor pool, fitness center, convention
center with 9,600 square foot ballroom. Casino
has 38 table games.
Entertainers include Jerry Reed, Hotel California.
■ **Games Available:** Blackjack, Craps , Let It
Ride, Poker, Roulette, Slots - 1000

Isle of Capri Marquette

P.O. Box 460
Marquette, IA 52158
(800) THE-ISLE
www.isleofcapricasino.com/Marquette/
■ **Hotel:** 23 rooms, $59-up
■ **Restaurant(s):** Calypso's Seafood Buffet,
Tradewinds Marketplace.
■ **Games Available:** Blackjack, Craps , Let It
Ride, Poker, Roulette, Slots - 675

Lakeside Casino and Resort

777 Casino Drive
Osceola, IA 50213
(641) 342-9511
(877) 477-5253
■ **Hotel:** 60 rooms
■ **Restaurant(s):** The Landing Steakhouse,
Wheelhouse Buffet
Iowa's newest riverboat opened in 2000. The casi-
no has 40 tables.
■ **Games Available:** 3-card poker, Blackjack,
Craps, Let It Ride, Roulette, Slots - 850

Mississippi Belle II

P.O. Box 1234
Clinton, IA 55732
(319) 243-9000
(800) 457-9975
■ **Games Available:** Blackjack, Craps, Poker,
Roulette, Slots

Rhythm City Casino

West River Drive
Davenport, IA 52801
(800) 262-8711
www.rhythmcitycasino.com
■ **Restaurant(s):** Hit Parade Buffet, Rock
Around the Clock Diner.
Blackhawk Hotel is available nearby.
n Games Available: Blackjack, Craps, Let It Ride,
Pai Gow, Roulette, Slots - 1000, Spanish 21

LOUISIANA

Argosy Casino Baton Rouge

103 France St.
Baton Rouge, LA 70802
Adjacent to Sheraton Convention Center Hotel.
(800) 676-4847
www.argosycasinos.com
■ **Hotel:** 300 rooms
29,000 square feet
■ **Reservations:** (800) 325-3535
■ **Restaurant(s):** Le Marche, Riverview Sports Bar, Butler's Pantry Deli.
Live entertainment on weekends.
■ **Games Available:** Blackjack, Craps, Let It Ride, Mini-baccarat, Roulette, Slots - 800

Bally's Casino New Orleans

1 Stars and Stripes Blvd.
New Orleans, LA 70126
(800) 57-BALLY
www.ballysno.com
Belle of Orleans has 30,000 square feet
■ **Restaurant(s):** Great American Buffet, Liberty Bell Deli & Bakery.
Casino has 34 table games.
■ **Games Available:** 3-card poker - 1, Blackjack - 17, Craps - 3, Let It Ride - 1, Mini-baccarat - 3, Pai Gow - 2, Poker - 4, Roulette - 2, Slots $1 - 201, Slots $100 - 1, Slots $5 - 27, Slots 50 cents - 60, Slots Nickel - 201, Slots Quarter - 703

Bally's Casino in New Orleans features the city's trademarks - jazz and Cajun food.

Boomtown Casino New Orleans

P.O. Box 1385
Harvey, LA 70059
15 minutes from downtown New Orleans
(800) 366-7711
www.boomtowncasinos.com
30,000 square feet
■ **Restaurant(s):** Bayou Market Buffet, Pier 4 Restaurant and Oyster Bar, Bayou Market Express.
Casino has 50 table games
■ **Games Available:** Blackjack, Craps, Let It Ride, Mini-baccarat, Poker, Roulette, Slots - 1500

Casino Magic Bossier City

300 Riverside Drive
Bossier City, LA 71111
(877) 8-MAGIC8
www.casinomagicbossier.com
■ **Hotel:** 188 rooms
Restaurant(s): Randolph's, The Buffet, The Café.
Casino has 40 table games.
■ **Games Available:** Blackjack, Craps, Let It Ride, Mini-baccarat, Roulette, Slots - 1000

Casino Rouge

1717 River Road North
Baton Rouge, LA 70802
(800) 44-ROUGE
www.casinorouge.com
■ **Restaurant(s):** Capital Bistro, International Marketplace Buffet, Quizno's.
Casino has 44 table games.
Live music in Rhythms Lounge.
■ **Games Available:** 3-card poker, Blackjack, Craps, Let It Ride, Poker, Roulette, Slots - 1000

Harrah's Lake Charles

505 N. Lakeshore Drive
Lake Charles, LA 70601
Two hours east of Houston
(337) 437-1500
www.harrahs.com
30,000 square feet in two casinos

■ **Restaurant(s):** Island Buffet, Island Terrace Restaurant, Louisiana Café, Bong Sen, Pepper Rose.

■ **Games Available:** Blackjack, Craps , Let It Ride, Pai Gow Roulette, Slots - 1600

Harrah's Shreveport

315 Clyde Fant Parkway
Shreveport, LA 71101
(318) 424-7777
(800) HARRAHS
www.harrahs.com

■ **Hotel:** 514 rooms

■ **Restaurant(s):** Pepper Rose Café, International Buffet, Aromas, Fiore, Fortunes Bar & Lounge.

Grand Ballroom has 18,000 square feet. Hotel has spa and fitness center.

Live entertainment at Fortunes Bar & Lounge.

■ **Games Available:** 3-card poker, Blackjack, Craps, Let It Ride, Mini-baccarat, Roulette, Slots - 1100

Harrah's Shreveport has 514 guest rooms and suites available in its 23-story hotel tower.

Hollywood Casino-Shreveport

451 Clyde Fant Parkway
Shreveport, LA 71101
(877) 602-0711
www.hollywoodcasinoshreveport.com

■ **Hotel:** 403 rooms, $110-$155

■ **Reservations:** (877) 602-0711

■ **Restaurant(s):** Four restaurants: Fairbanks Steakhouse, Hollywood Diner, Epic Buffet, Cinema Café.

All-suites hotel, spa, Hollywood Casino Studio Store.

Lounge acts at the Celebrity Club Show Lounge.

■ **Games Available:** Blackjack - 39, Craps - 8, Mini-baccarat, Poker, Roulette, Slots - 1400

Horseshoe Casino & Hotel

711 Horseshoe Blvd.
P.O. Box 71111
Bossier City, LA 71111
(800) 895-0711
www.horseshoe.com/

■ **Hotel:** 606 rooms

30,000 square feet

■ **Restaurant(s):** Jack Binion's Steak House, Four Winds Restaurant, Oak Creek Café Grille, Village Square Buffet.

Horseshoe Casino & Hotel in Bossier City, the tallest hotel between Dallas and Atlanta, has 606 luxury suites in its 26-story tower.

Entertainers including Willie Nelson, the Doobie Brothers and Merle Haggard perform in the Riverdome.

The 26-story hotel has 606 luxury suites as well as four restaurants. The casino has 50 table games.

■ **Games Available:** Slots 1600, Blackjack, Craps, Roulette, Poker, Mini-Baccarat, Let It Ride, 3-card poker

Isle of Capri Bossier City

711 Isle of Capri Blvd.
Bossier City, LA 71111
(800) THE-ISLE
www.isleofcapricasino.com/Bossier_City/

■ **Hotel:** 310 rooms

30,000 square feet

■ **Restaurant(s):** Farraddays' Restaurant, Calypso's Seafood Buffet, Tradewinds Marketplace.

Hotel features outdoor pool, fitness center, Eno's Playhouse for children, Fantasy Island Arcade and 10,500 square feet of meeting space. Casino has 47 table games.

Caribbean Cove Showroom has entertainment.

■ **Games Available:** Blackjack, Craps , Mini-baccarat, Pai Gow, Poker, Roulette, Slots - 1050

Isle of Capri Lake Charles

100 Westlake Ave.
Westlake, LA 70669
(800) THE-ISLE
www.isleofcapricasino.com/Lake_Charles/
48,900 square feet

■ **Restaurant(s):** Farraddays' Restaurant, Calypso's Seafood Buffet, Lucky Wins & Tradewinds Café, Kitt's Kitchen and Rum Mill.

New all-suite hotel has opened.

■ **Games Available:** Slots, Table games

Treasure Chest Casino

5050 Williams Blvd.
Kenner, LA 70065
Near New Orleans
(504) 443-8000
(800) 298-0711
www.treasurechestcasino.com

■ **Restaurant(s):** Bobby G's, Treasure Island Buffet.

New poker room opened in December 2001.

Caribbean Showroom offers live entertainment.

■ **Games Available:** 3-card poker, Blackjack, Craps, Let It Ride, Mini-baccarat, Poker, Roulette Slots

MISSISSIPPI

Ameristar Casino Hotel Vicksburg

4146 Washington St.
Vicksburg, MS 39180
(601) 638-1000
(800) 700-7770
www.ameristarcasinos.com/corporate/vbfacts/
■ **Hotel:** 168 rooms, $40-up
42,000 square feet
■ **Restaurant(s):** Waterfront Grill, Veranda Buffet, Bottleneck Blues Bar
Hotel has pool and spa. Casino has 34 table games.
Bottleneck Blues Bar, which opened in 2001, features live music.
■ **Games Available:** Blackjack, Craps , Let It Ride, Poker - 7 Roulette, Slots - 1300

Bally's Casino Tunica

1450 Bally's Blvd.
Robinsonville, MS 38664
South of Memphis
(800) 38-BALLY
www.ballysms.com
■ **Hotel:** 235 rooms
40,000 square feet

Bally's Casino in Tunica is just south of Memphis.

■ **Restaurant(s):** Cornucopia Buffet Restaurant, Delta Levee Buffet.
Hotel has a pool. Casino has 40 table games.
Bonkerz Comedy Club, plus live entertainment in The Saloon six nights a week.
■ **Games Available:** Blackjack, Let It Ride, Poker, Slots

Guests relax in the pool at Bally's Casino Tunica, which features a 20-acre entertainment complex.

Bayou Caddy Casino

Lake Ferguson Waterfront
Greenville, MS 38701
(800) WIN-MORE
Hotel: 98 rooms
28,000 square feet
Casino has 20 table games.
■ **Games Available:** Slots - 600, Table games - 20

Boomtown Casino Biloxi

676 Bayview Ave.
Biloxi, MS 39530
(228) 435-7000
(800) 627-0777

www.boomtownbiloxi.com

33,000 square feet

■ **Restaurant(s):** Main Street Rotisserie & Grill, Boomtown Buffet and Bakery.

■ **Games Available:** Blackjack - 18, Craps - 2, Pai Gow - 4, Roulette - 2, Slots - 1100

Casino Magic Bay St. Louis

711 Casino Magic Drive
Bay St. Louis, MS 39520
East of New Orleans.
(228) 467-9257
(800) 5-MAGIC5
www.casinomagic.com/bay/

■ **Hotel:** 200 rooms

Restaurant(s): Randolph's, The Bridges Clubhouse Grill, Bienville's Bay Buffet, Café Magic.

RV Park has 100 spaces. The Bridges 18-hole golf course was designed by Arnold Palmer. Casino has 37 table games.

Entertainment ranges from Pat Boone to Ray Price to Engelbert Humperdinck.

■ **Games Available:** Blackjack, Craps , Let It Ride, Mini-baccarat, Pai Gow, Roulette, Slots - 1100

Casino Magic Biloxi

195 Beach Blvd.
Biloxi, MS 39530
(228) 386-4600
(800) 5-MAGIC-5
www.casinomagic.com/biloxi/index.htm

■ **Hotel:** 378 rooms

■ **Restaurant(s):** Savannah's, The Deli, The Buffet.

Hotel has an indoor pool/atrium, spa, health club and salon. Casino has 35 table games.

A variety of revues are offered.

■ **Games Available:** 3-card poker, Blackjack, Craps, Mini-baccarat, Pai Gow, Roulette, Slots - 1300

Copa Casino

P.O. Box 1600
Gulfport, MS 39502
(800) WIN-COPA
thecopacasino.com

■ **Restaurant(s):** Uncle Floyd's Barbecue, Cabana Cafe.

Free live entertainment

■ **Games Available:** Blackjack, Craps , Let It Ride, Roulette, Slots - 825, Spanish 21

Fitzgeralds Casino Tunica

711 Lucky Lane
Robinsonville, MS 38664
(800) 766-LUCK
Fax: (662) 363-3579
www.fitzgeraldstunica.com

■ **Hotel:** 507 rooms

■ **Restaurant(s):** Limericks Steakhouse, Shamrock Café, Sports Pub, Castle Court Buffet.

Casino has 30 table games.

■ **Games Available:** 3-card poker, Blackjack, Craps, Let It Ride, Poker, Roulette, Slots - 1200

Gold Strike Casino Resort

1010 Casino Center Drive
Robinsonville, MS 38664
15 miles south of Memphis
(888) 24K-STAY
www.goldstrikemississippi.com

■ **Hotel:** 1200 rooms, $69-up

50,000 square feet

■ **Restaurant(s):** Chicago Steakhouse, Atrium Café, Courtyard Buffet.

Hotel has pool, spa, workout room, business center, 30,000 square feet of convention facilities. Casino has 40 table games.

Millennium Theatre has entertainment Thursdays through Saturdays with entertainers including Cheap Trick, Eddie Money and Engelbert Humperdinck..

■ **Games Available:** 3-card poker, Blackjack, Craps, Let It Ride, Poker - 5, Roulette, Slots - 1400

Grand Casino Biloxi

265 Beach Blvd.
Biloxi, MS 39530
(800) WIN-2WIN
866-4-BILOXI
www.grandbiloxi.com

■ **Hotel:** 1000 rooms, $29-$179

135,000 square feet

■ **Restaurant(s):** Nine restaurants: LB's
Steakhouse, Seafood Buffet, Islandview Café,
Market Place Buffet, Brulo's Seafood Restaurant,
Roxy's Diner, Mississippi Long Bar Gaming Hall
and Saloon, Chopstix Restaurant, Noodle Bar, The
Creamery, Cabana Bar

Casino has 111 table games, 3,000 slots and a
poker room. Hotel has Bellissimo Spa and Salon,
Kid's Quest and Grand Arcade game room. Grand
Bear 18- hole Jack Nicklaus-designed golf course
available. Grand Advantage II Charter Boat is
available.

Biloxi Grand Theater hosts entertainers including
Pat Benatar, Gladys Knight, the Commodores,
Jetho Tull and Alabama. Backstage Nightclub and
Mississippi Long Bar also have entertainment.

■ **Games Available:** Baccarat, Blackjack,
Craps, Let It Ride, Pai Gow, Poker, Roulette,
Slots - 3000

Grand Casino Gulfport

3215 W. Beach Blvd.
Gulfport, MS 39501
75 miles from Mobile, 75 miles from New
  Orleans
866-GULFPORT
(800) WIN-7777
www.grandgulfport.com

■ **Hotel:** 1000 rooms, $29-$179

105,000 square feet

■ **Restaurant(s):** 10 restaurants and bars: LB's
Steakhouse, New Orleans Bistro, Murano's Italian
Restaurant, Market Place Buffet, Magnola's, Nifty
50's, Java Grande, Oasis Lobby Bar, Cabana Bar,
Sports Bar.

Casino has 2,300 slots, 84 table games and a
poker room. Oasis Resort and Casino Hotel has
Bellissimo Spa and Salon, Kid's Quest kids activity center and Grand Arcade game room and meeting space. Grand Bear 18-hole Jack Nicklaus golf
course available

The 2,500 seat outdoor Grand Pavilion and
Voodoo Groove Nightclub feature headliners, live
bands, boxing and sporting events.

■ **Games Available:** Baccarat, Blackjack,
Craps, Let It Ride, Pai Gow, Poker, Roulette, Slots
- 2300

Grand Casino Biloxi has 1,000 rooms in its two hotel towers.

Famed golfer Jack Nicklaus designed the Grand Bear Golf Course.

Grand Casino Tunica

13615 Old Highway 61 North
Robinsonville, MS 38664
South of Memphis
(866) 4-TUNICA
www.grandtunica.com

■ **Hotel:** 1353 rooms, $29-up

140,000 square feet

■ **Restaurant(s):** LB's Steakhouse, Grand Buffet, Big Sky Steakhouse, Murano's.

Three hotels -- Grand Casino Hotel, Veranda Resort, Terrace Hotel Resort -- are available. Hotels have a spa, outdoor pool, exercise rooms, sauna. Casino has 160 table games. RV Resort has 200 spaces. Cotton Woods Golf Course available.

The 2,500-seat events center features entertainers including Alabama, the Temptations and Lee Greenwood as well as boxing.

■ **Games Available:** Blackjack, Craps , Poker, Roulette, Slots - 3000

A craps table offers fun for patrons in the sprawling 140,000 square foot casino at Grand Casino Tunica.

Harrah's Tunica

1100 Casino Strip Blvd.
Robinsonville, MS 38664
(662) 363-7777
(800) HARRAHS
www.harrahs.com

■ **Hotel:** 201 rooms

150,000 square feet

■ **Restaurant(s):** Bourbon Street Bistro, Fresh Market Square Buffet, Harrah's Steak House, Club Cappucchino.

River Bend Links 18 hole golf course available. Casino has 20 table games.

■ **Games Available:** Blackjack, Craps , Let It Ride, Roulette, Slots - 1200

Harrah's Vicksburg

1310 Mulbery St.
Vicksburg, MS 39180
(601) 636-3423
(800) 843-2343
www.harrahs.com/our

36,000 square feet

■ **Restaurant(s):** Fresh Market Square Buffet, The Range Steakhouse, Coca Cola Café.

■ **Games Available:** 3-card poker, Blackjack, Craps, Roulette, Slots - 750

Hollywood Casino-Tunica

1150 Casino Strip Blvd.
Robinsonville, MS 38664
35 miles from Memphis
(662) 357-7700
www.hollywoodtunica.com

■ **Hotel:** 506 rooms

54,000 square feet

■ **Restaurant(s):** Fairbanks Steakhouse and Bar, Hollywood Diner, Epic Buffet, Safari Bar, Box Office Bar

50 gaming tables, 14,000 square foot ballroom, collection of movie memorabilia, 123 space RV Park, River Bend Links Golf Course, indoor pool and hot tub.

■ **Games Available:** Blackjack, Craps , Poker, Roulette, Slots - 1500

Horseshoe Casino-Tunica

1020 Casino Center Drive
Robinsonville, MS 38664
35 miles from Memphis
(800) 303-7463
www.horseshoe.com

■ **Hotel:** 505 rooms

■ **Restaurant(s):** Jack Binion's Steak House, Yasmin's Asian Restaurant, Café Sonoma, Village Square Buffet.

Entertainers including Dwight Yoakam, the Beach Boys and Meat Loaf perform in Bluesville.

The 26-story hotel has 311 luxury suites and 194 deluxe rooms as well as four restaurants. The casino has 70 table games.

■ **Games Available:** Slots - 2000, Blackjack, Craps, Roulette , Poker

Horseshoe Casino in Tunica boasts a 14-story hotel tower with 311 suites.

Imperial Palace Biloxi

850 Bayview Ave.
Biloxi, MS 39533
(228) 436-3000
www.ipbiloxi.com

■ **Hotel:** 1086 rooms, $40-up

70,000 square feet

■ **Reservations:** (800) 634-6441

■ **Restaurant(s):** Crown Room, Ming Terrace, Bahia's, Teahouse, Seahouse, Pizza Palace, Emperor's Buffet, Graveyard Grill, Embers Steakhouse, Betty's Café, Burger Palace.

The hotel includes Spa Caribe, outdoor pool, retail shops, Ippy's Fun Zone video arcade and a convention center. Floating casino has 50 table games.

Entertainment includes Bonkerz Comedy Club and six movie theaters.

■ **Games Available:** 3-card poker, Blackjack, Craps, Let It Ride, Pai Gow, Roulette, Slots - 1600

Isle of Capri Biloxi

151 Beach Blvd.
Biloxi, MS 39530
80 miles east of New Orleans
(800) THE-ISLE
www.isleofcapricasino.com/Biloxi/

■ **Hotel:** 370 rooms

32,000 square feet

■ **Restaurant(s):** Farradday's, Calypso's Seafood Buffet, Tradewinds Marketplace.

Hotel has outdoor pool, fitness center, 15,000 square feet of meeting space.

Live entertainment in the Caribbean Atrium

■ **Games Available:** Blackjack, Craps , Let It Ride, Poker, Roulette, Slots - 1180

Isle of Capri Natchez

P.O. Box 820668
Vicksburg, MS 39182
(888) 782-9582
www.isleofcapricasino.com/Natchez/

■ **Hotel:** 143 rooms

■ **Restaurant(s):** Farraddays' Restaurant, Calypso's Seafood Buffet.

Hotel has pool and fitness center.

■ **Games Available:** Blackjack, Craps, Roulette, Slots - 700

Isle of Capri Tunica

1600 Isle of Capri Blvd.
Robinsonville, MS 38664
(800) THE-ISLE
www.isleofcapricasino.com/Tunica/

■ **Hotel:** 227 rooms

■ **Restaurant(s):** Farraddays' Restaurant, Calypso's Seafood Buffet, Tradewinds Marketplace.

Caribbean Cove Showroom and Flamingo Bay Theatre have entertainment.

■ **Games Available:** Slots, Table games

Isle of Capri Vicksburg

P.O. Box 820668
Vicksburg, MS 39180
(800) 946-4753
www.isleofcapricasino.com/Vicksburg

■ **Hotel:** 122 rooms
32,000 square feet

■ **Restaurant(s):** Farraddays' Restaurant, Calypso Seafood Buffet, Tradewinds Marketplace

■ **Games Available:** Slots, Table games

Lighthouse Point Casino

199 N. Lakefront Rd.
Greenville, MS 38701
(800) 878-1777

■ **Hotel:** 157 rooms
22,000 square feet

■ **Games Available:** 3-card poker, Blackjack, Craps, Roulette, Slots - 800, Slots Nickel

President Casino Broadwater Resort

2110 Beach Blvd.
Biloxi, MS 39531
(228) 385-3500
(800) THE-PRES
Fax: (228) 385-4102
www.presidentbroadwater.com

■ **Hotel:** 500 rooms, $60-up
38,000 square feet

■ **Restaurant(s):** Audree's Fine Dining, President's Buffet, Oyster House.

Resort has three pools, 10 tennis courts, an 18-hole golf course and a marina.

■ **Games Available:** 3-card poker, Blackjack, Craps, Let It Ride, Pai Gow, Poker, Roulette, Slots - 950

Rainbow Hotel Casino

1380 Warrenton Road
Vicksburg, MS 39180
(800) 503-3777
www.rainbowcasino.com

■ **Hotel:** 89 rooms, $40-up

■ **Restaurant(s):** Rainbow Buffet

■ **Games Available:** Blackjack, Craps, Roulette, Slots - 1000

Sam's Town Tunica

1477 Casino Strip Resorts Blvd.
Robinsonville, MS 38664
South of Memphis
(800) 456-0711
www.samstowntunica.com

■ **Hotel:** 850 rooms

■ **Restaurant(s):** The Great Buffet, Corky's BBQ Buffet, Twain's Casual Fine Dining.

Hotel features pool, hot tub, gym and sauna, Emporium Shops and convention facilities. RV Park is available. River Bend Links Golf Course is 18-hole links-style course.

1600-seat River Palace Entertainment Center, features B.B. King, George Jones, George Carlin.

■ **Games Available:** Blackjack, Craps, Keno, Let It Ride, Pai Gow, Poker, Roulette, Slots

Sheraton Casino and Hotel

1107 Casino Center Drive
Robinsonville, MS 38664
(662) 363-4900
Fax: (662) 363-1677
Hotel: 133 rooms
31,000 square feet
Restaurant(s): Landing Buffet and Rotisserie, Hemmings River Club, Chips Snack Bar and Deli Lounge.
■**Games Available:** Slots, Table games

Treasure Bay Casino Resort

1980 Beach Blvd.
Biloxi, MS 39532
(800) PIRATE-9
www.treasurebay.com
■ **Hotel:** 262 rooms, $79-up
41,000 square feet
■ **Restaurant(s):** Lafitte's Feast Buffet, Rogue's Gallery, Buccaneer Brewery Restaurant, Captain's Quarters.
Casino has 28 table games.
Free entertainment nightly at Scalawag's Showbar.
■ **Games Available:** 3-card poker, Blackjack, Craps, Pai Gow Roulette, Slots

MISSOURI

Ameristar Casino St. Charles

1260 South Main St.
P.O. Box 720
St. Charles, MO 63302
Near St. Louis
(800) 325-7777
www.ameristarcasinos.com
115,000 square feet

■ **Restaurant(s):** Buffet, steakhouse, deli

Expanded in mid-2002 to 115,000 square feet and 104 table games. Cabaret lounge, arcade and gift shop were also added.

■ **Games Available:** Poker - 12, Slots - 3000, Table games - 104

Argosy Casino Kansas City

777 N.W. Argosy Parkway
Riverside, MO 64150
(816) 746-3140
www.argosycasinos.com
30,000 square feet

■ **Restaurant(s):** Constellations, Eclipse Bar & Grill, Sundial Café, Deli.

Casino has 40 table games.

■ **Games Available:** 3-card poker, Blackjack, Craps, Let It Ride, Pai Gow, Roulette, Slots - 1100, Spanish 21

Casino Aztar-Caruthersville

P.O. Box 1135
Caruthersville, MO 63830
(573) 333-6000
(800) 679-4945
info@casinoaztarmo.com
www.aztarcasino.com

■ **Restaurant(s):** Corky's Ribs & BBQ.

Casino has 20 table games.

■ **Games Available:** 3-card poker, Blackjack, Craps Let It Ride, Roulette, Slots - 700

Harrah's North Kansas City

1 Riverboat Drive
North Kansas City, MO 64116
(816) 472-7777
www.harrahs.com

■ **Hotel:** 200 rooms

■ **Restaurant(s):** The Range, Fresh Market Square Buffet, Café Andreotti, Winning Streaks Stadium Café.

Hotel has pool, exercise room, sauna, gift shop, 10,000 square foot ballroom. Mardi Gras Casino has added 30,000 square foot second floor.

Live entertainment in the Pavilion.

■ **Games Available:** Blackjack, Craps, Let It Ride, Mini-baccarat, Pai Gow, Roulette, Slots - 1000

Isle of Capri Boonville

1000 Isle of Capri Blvd.
Boonville, MO 65233
(800) THE-ISLE
www.isleofcapricasino.com/Boonville/
28,000 square feet

■ **Restaurant(s):** Farraddays' Restaurant, Calypso's Seafood Buffet, Tradewinds Marketplace.

The latest Isle of Capri opened in December 2001. A retail and entertainment center are featured. The casino has 35 table games.

■ **Games Available:** Slots - 900, Table games

Isle of Capri Kansas City

1800 E. Front St.
Kansas City, MO 64120
(816) 855-7777
(800) 946-8711
www.isleofcapricasino.com/Kansas_City/

■ **Restaurant(s):** Farraddays' Restaurant, Calypso's Buffet, Island O'Aces, Caribbean Cove, Tradewinds Marketplace.

■ **Games Available:** Blackjack, Craps, Roulette, Slots

President Casino

Lacredes Landing
800 N. First St.
St. Louis, MO 63102
Downtown St. Louis
(314) 622-1111
(800) 772-3647
www.presidentcasino.com

■ **Games Available:** Blackjack $10 - 15, Craps - 3, Keno - 10, Pai Gow - 1, Poker - 15, Roulette - 3, Slots - 1250

St. Jo Frontier Casino

777 Winners Circle
St. Joseph, MO 64505
One hour north of Kansas City's airport.
(816) 279-5514
(800) 888-2WIN
sjfc@stjocasino.com
www.stjocasino.com

■ **Restaurant(s):** Jesse's Steakhouse, Express Buffet.

Casino has 16 table games.

■ **Games Available:** 3-card poker, Blackjack, Craps, Let It Ride, Poker, Roulette, Slots - 502, Spanish 21

WASHINGTON

Emerald Queen Casino

2102 Alexander Ave.
Tacoma, WA 98421
(888) 831-7655
www.emeraldqueen.com

■ **Restaurant(s):** Lafayette's, Chinese Cuisine, Buffet.

Entertainers including Willy Nelson, Gladys Knight and Engelburt Humperdink perform in Emerald Showroom. More entertainment in lounges.

■ **Games Available:** Baccarat, Blackjack, Craps, Pai Gow Roulette, Slots - 850, Spanish 21

ARIZONA

Rillito Park

4502 N. First Ave.
Tucson, AZ 85718
(520) 293-5011
Quarter horse racing in February and March.

Turf Paradise

1501 West Bell Rd.
Phoenix, AZ 85023
14 miles northwest of downtown Phoenix
(602) 942-1101
Fax: (602) 588-2002
www.turfparadise.com
■ **Restaurant(s):** Clubhouse Restaurant, Turf Club.
Live horse racing October through May, Fridays through Tuesdays. Simulcasting of other races available daily.

Yavapai Downs

P.O. Box 26557
Prescott Valley, AZ 86312
(928) 445-0408
Fax: (520) 445-0408
Live horse races from late May through early September. Simulcasting available daily.

ARKANSAS

Oaklawn Park

2705 Central Ave.
Hot Springs, AR 71902
(800) OAKLAWN
winning@oaklawn.com
www.oaklawn.com
■ **Restaurant(s):** Carousel Terrace, Oyster Bar,
  Post Parade, Pony Express Grill

Live horse racing from late January through April.
  Simulcasting of other races daily.

CALIFORNIA

Bay Meadows

2600 S. Delaware St.
San Mateo, CA 94402
20 miles south of San Francisco
(650) 574-RACE
Live horse races March through mid-June,
September through early November.

_____

Cal Expo Race Track

1600 Exposition Way
Sacramento, CA 95865
(916) 263-7893
Fax: (916) 263-7887
cxporace@cwo.com
www.capitolracing.com
■ **Reservations:** (916) 920-5131
■ **Restaurant(s):** Turf Club

Free parking.

Harness racing from late October through
February. Simulcasting available.

_____

Del Mar Thoroughbred Club

2260 Jimmy Durante Blvd.
Del Mar, CA 92014
20 miles north of San Diego
(858) 755-1141
877-LETSBET
www.dmtc.com
■ **Reservations:** (858) 792-4272
■ **Restaurant(s):** Clubhouse Terrace Restaurant,
Café Del Sol, Stretch Run Grill

Live thoroughbred racing mid July through early
September. Simulcasting available.

Fairplex Park

1101 W. McKinley Ave.
Pomona, CA 91769
30 miles east of downtown Los Angeles
(909) 623-3111
Fax: (909) 865-3602
www.fairplex.com
■ **Hotel:** 247 rooms
■ **Restaurant(s):** Top of the Park Restaurant,
Paddock Grill and Bar.

Sheraton Suites Fairplex Hotel has 247 suites,
pool, spa, restaurant.

Live thoroughbred and quarter horse racing during
Los Angeles County Fair in September.
Simulcasting available year-round.

_____

Ferndale Race Track

1250 Fifth St.
Ferndale, CA 95536
(707) 786-9511
Fax: (707) 786-9450
Ten days of live horse racing in August during
Humboldt County Fair.

_____

Fresno Race Track

1121 S. Chance Ave.
Fresno, CA 93702
(559) 650-3247
Fax: (559) 650-3226
Eleven days of live horse racing during county fair
in October.

Golden Gate Fields

1100 Eastshore Highway
Albany, CA 94706
In Berkeley, eight miles from Oakland.
(707) 786-9450
help@baymeadows.com
■ www.ggfields.com
Restaurant(s): Turf Club, Top of the Stretch

Live thoroughbred races on Wednesday through
  Sundays in January through March and
  November through December. Simulcasting of
  other tracks available.

Hollywood Park Race Track

*Hollywood Park, just 11 miles from downtown Los Angeles, has
hosted horse races since 1938.*

Hollywood Park Racetrack

1050 South Prairie Ave.
Inglewood, CA 90306-0369
Three miles from Los Angeles International
  Airport
(310) 419-1500
Fax: (310) 671-4460
www.hollywoodpark.com
240 acres
Restaurant(s): Whittingham's Pub and Deli;
  Longshots Sports Bar.

See listing for Hollywood Park Casino for details.

Live horse racing from late April-late July and
  from early November-early December. Also
  simulcasting from other race tracks.

Los Alamitos Race Course

4961 E. Katella Ave.
Los Alamitos, CA 90720
(714) 820-2800
Fax: (714) 236-4503
larace@losalamitos.com
www.losalamitos.com
Restaurant(s): The Vessels Club, Turf Terrace
  Dining Room
Free parking.

Live thoroughbred and quarter horse racing year-
  round on Thursdays, Fridays, Saturdays,
  Sundays. Harness racing from January through
  April. Simulcasting available.

Los Alamitos Race Course

*Horses speed by Schwanie's Grill at the Gap, Los Alamitos' new
restaurant in front of the turn for home.*

*Jockeys push their thoroughbreds at Hollywood Park, one of
many California tracks.*

San Joaquin County Fair

1658 S. Airport Way
Stockton, CA 95206
(209) 466-5041
Ten days of live horse racing during county fair in
June.

Santa Anita Park

285 W. Huntington Drive
Arcadia, CA 91066
14 miles from downtown Los Angeles
(626) 574-7223
www.santaanita.com
■ **Restaurant(s):** Turf Terrace, Americana
Room, FrontRunner Restaurant,

Live thoroughbred racing Wednesdays through
Sundays in January through April, also late
December. Simulcasting available.

Santa Rosa Race Track

1350 Bennett Valley Road
Santa Rosa, CA 95402
(707) 524-6340
(800) 454-7223
Live horse racing during Sonoma County Fair in
July and August. Simulcasting of other tracks
available in Jockey Club.

Solano Race Track

900 Fairgrounds Drive
Vallejo, CA 94585
(707) 644-4401
Fax: (707) 642-7947
12 days of live thoroughbred and quarter horse
racing in July during Solano County Fair.

COLORADO

Arapahoe Park

26000 East Quincy Ave.
Aurora, CO 80046
(303) 690-2400
Arapahoe@Wembleyusa.com
www.wembleyusa.com/arapahoe/
Free parking

Live horse racing from June through August.
Simulcasting available.

DELAWARE

Delaware Park Racetrack & Slots

777 Delaware Park Blvd.
Stanton, DE 19804
(800) 41-SLOTS
programs@delpark.com
www.delpark.com
Restaurant(s): Terrace Dining Room, Racing
  Legends, On a Roll Deli.

Free admission and free parking.

Live Arabian horse racing from May through
  November. Simulcasting is available daily.

■ **Games Available:** Slots - 2000

Dover Downs

1131 N. DuPont Highway
Dover, DE 19901
(302) 674-4600
Fax: (302) 741-8986
www.doverdowns.com
■ **Hotel:** 240 rooms
■ **Reservations:** (866) 4-RESERV
■ **Restaurant(s):** Dover Downs Deli, Winner's
  Circle Grand Buffet, Garden Café.

Dover Downs Hotel & Conference Center opened
  in 2002. Facilities also include NASCAR race
  track, 80,000 square foot casino with 2,000 slot
  machines.

Harness racing from November through April.
  Simulcasting available.

■ **Games Available:** Slots - 2000

Harrington Raceway

15 West Rider Road
Harrington, DE 19952
(302) 398-RACE
(888) 88-SLOTS
Harness racing from late April through early July
  and September through October. Simulcasting of
  other races is available daily. Entertainment at
  Carousel Lounge of Midway Slots & Simulcast.

■ **Games Available:** Slots - 1151

FLORIDA

Calder Race Course

21001 NW 27th Ave.
Miami, FL 33056
Next to Pro Player Stadium in Miami.
(305) 625-1311
customerservice@calderracecourse.com
www.calderracecourse.com
Seating for 15,000

■ **Restaurant(s):** Calder's Clubhouse Dining Room, Turf Club, food court

Calder Hall of Fame.

Live horse racing May through December, Fridays through Tuesdays. Simulcasting available.

Gulfstream Park

901 S. Federal Highway
Hallandale, FL 33009
(954) 454-7000
(800) 771-TURF
www.gulfstreampark.com

■ **Restaurant(s):** Royal Palm Dining Room, Royal Palm Terrace, Rooftop Bar and Grill, Turf Club, snack bars and delis.

Live horse racing January through April. Also offers a concert series. Simulcasting of races from other tracks.

Hialeah Park

2200 E. Fourth Ave.
Hialeah, FL 33011
Five minutes north of Miami's airport.
(305) 885-8000
(800) HIALEAH
www.hialeahpark.com

■ **Restaurant(s):** Citation Room, Turf Club, Galleria.

Live thoroughbred horse racing from mid-March through late May. Simulcasting of other races available.

Pompano Park Racing

1800 S.W. 3rd St.
Pompano Park, FL 33069
(954) 972-2000

■ **Restaurant(s):** Patten's Top of the Park Restaurant, Patten's Place Easy Does It.

Poker room. Free grandstand admission and free parking.

Harness racing Monday, Wednesday, Friday and Saturday nights. Simulcasting of other races daily.

■ **Games Available:** Poker

Tampa Bay Downs

P.O. Box 2007
Oldsmar, FL 34677
Eight miles west of Tampa
(813) 855-4401
(800) 200-4434
www.tampadowns.com
Track opened in 1926. Clubhouse was remodeled in 2000.

Live thoroughbred racing December through April, simulcasting from other tracks year-round.

IDAHO

Les Bois Park

5610 Glenwood Rd.
Boise, ID 83714
(208) 376-RACE
Fax: (208) 378-4032
www.lesboispark.org
■ **Reservations:** (208) 376-3985

■ **Restaurant(s):** Turf Club, Clubhouse
Restaurant

Free parking

Live racing Wednesday and Saturday nights,
Sunday afternoons May through August.
Simulcasting from 30 other tracks daily year-
round.

ILLINOIS

Arlington Park

2200 W. Euclid
Arlington Heights, IL 60006
Near O'Hare Airport north of Chicago
(847) 385-7500
Fax: (847) 385-7251
www.arlingtonpark.com
■ **Restaurant(s):** Million Room, Paddock Pub, Cobey's Food Court, Hearth Grill.
Free parking
Live horse racing June through October.

Balmoral Park

26435 S. Dixie Highway
Crete, IL 60417
South of Chicago
(708) 672-1414
Fax: (708) 672-5932
info@balmoralpark.com
www.balmoralpark.com
■ **Restaurant(s):** Balmoral Club Dining Room, concession stands
Free admission and parking.
Live harness racing year-round on Tuesdays, Thursdays, Saturdays, Sundays. Simulcasting of other races daily.

Fairmount Park

9301 Collinsville Road
Collinsville, IL 62234
(618) 345-4300
fmtpark@fairmountpark.com
www.fairmountpark.com
■ **Restaurant(s):** Black Stallion Room, Top of the Turf, First Turn Café.
Live thoroughbred racing. Simulcasting of other races available daily.

Hawthorne Race Course

3501 S. Laramie
Cicero, IL 60804
(708) 780-3700
hawthorneracecourse.com
35,000 capacity
Free admission and free parking.
Live thoroughbred racing from May through mid-June and November and December. Simulcasting available.

Maywood Park

8600 W. North Ave.
Maywood, IL 60153
10 miles south of O'Hare Field, north of Chicago
(708) 343-4800
Fax: (708) 343-2564
info@maywoodpark.com
www.maywoodpark.com
■ **Restaurant(s):** Winner's Circle Dining Room, Favorites Bar & Grill.
Free parking.
Harness racing year-round on Monday, Wednesday and Friday nights. Simulcasting from other tracks available daily.

Sportsman's Park

3301 Laramie Ave.
Cicero, IL 60804
South of Chicago near Midway Airport
(708) 652-2812
www.sportsmanspark.com
Live horse racing Fridays through Tuesdays in March through May. Simulcasting of other races available.

INDIANA

Hoosier Park

4500 Dan Patch Circle
Anderson, IN 46013
(765) 642-RACE
(800) 526-RACE
Fax: (765) 644-0467
info@hoosierpark.com

www.hoosierpark.com
■ **Restaurant(s):** Homestretch Restaurant
Free parking
Live horse racing Thursdays through Mondays from late September through December. Simulcasting every day except Tuesdays.

IOWA

Prairie Meadows

1 Prairie Meadows Drive
Altoona, IA 50009
Northeast of Des Moines
(515) 967-1000
(800) 325-9015
www.prairiemeadows.com

■ **Restaurant(s):** Champions Restaurant
Live thoroughbred, quarter horse and harness racing late April through late October. Simulcasting of other race tracks available. Concerts by national touring acts held frequently.
■ **Games Available:** Slots - 1500

KANSAS

Eureka Downs

210 N. Jefferson St.
Eureka, KS 67045
(316) 583-5528
Fax: (316) 583 5381
Live quarter horse racing Saturdays, Sundays and
  holidays May through early July.

Woodlands Racetracks

9700 Leavenworth Rd.
Kansas City, KS 66109
13 miles from Kansas City, Mo.
(913) 299-9797
(800) 695-RACE
Fax: (913) 299-9804
info@woodlandskc.com
woodlandskc.com

■ **Horse track:** 20,000 capacity; dog track:
  7,000 cap

■ **Restaurant(s):** Kennel Club, Turf Club

Live horse racing in October, November. Live dog
  racing year-round. Open for year-round simulcasting of horse and greyhound races from
  around the U.S.

*The Woodlands in Kansas features horse and grey-
hound tracks.*

KENTUCKY

Bluegrass Downs

150 Downs Drive
Paducah, KY 42001
(270) 444-7117
Fax: (270) 442-1993
Free parking.
Harness racing Fridays, Saturdays and Sundays
  from late August to late September. Opened in
  1998.

Churchill Downs

700 Central Ave.
Louisville, KY 40208
Four miles from downtown Louisville
(502) 636-4470
www.kentuckyderby.com
48,500 grandstand capacity
■ **Restaurant(s):** Eclipse Dining Room and
  Terrace, Silks Restaurant, Skye Terrace, Central
  Avenue Deli.
Derby Museum
Live thoroughbred racing from late April to early
  July, then in November. Home of the famous
  Kentucky Derby.

Keeneland

4201 Versailles Road
P.O. Box 1690
Lexington, KY 40588-1690
6 miles from downtown Lexington
(859) 254-3412
(800) 456-3412
Fax: 859) 255-2484
www.keeneland.com
900 acres
■ **Restaurant(s):** Three restaurants: Lexington
  Room, Kentucky Room, Equestrian Room.
Live racing in April and October. Simulcasting
  from other race tracks.

Ellis Park Race Course

3300 U.S. Highway 41 North
P.O. Box 33
Henderson, KY 42419
120 miles west of Louisville, 150 miles north of
  Nashville
(812) 425-1456
(800) 333-8110
Fax: (812) 425-3725
www.ellisparkracing.com
■ **Restaurant(s):** Clubhouse Dining Room, Sky
  Theater Dining
Live racing early July through Labor Day.
  Simulcasting of racing at other tracks.

Thoroughbreds race toward the finish line at Ellis Park

Kentucky Downs

5629 Nashville Road
Franklin, KY 42135
35 miles north of Nashville
(270) 586-7778
North America's only all-turf race track.

Seven days of live horse racing in September.
  Year- round simulcasting of other race tracks.

The Red Mile

1200 Red Mile Road
Lexington, KY 40504
(859) 255-0752
Fax: (859) 231-0217
www.tattersallsredmile.com
■ **Restaurant(s):** Red Mile Clubhouse

Harness racing from late April through mid-June
  and early September through early October.
  Simulcasting of other races available year-
  round.

Thunder Ridge Racetrack

164 Thunder Rd.
Prestonsburg, KY 41653
(606) 886-7223
Fax: (606) 886-7225
Harness racing from late June through August.

Turfway Park

7500 Turfway Road
Florence, KY 41022
10 miles south of Cincinnati
(859) 371-0200
(800) 733-0200
www.turfway.com
■ **Restaurant(s):** Homestretch Restaurant
Free parking.

Live horse racing from January through April, in
  September and December. Simulcasting also
  available.

LOUISIANA

Delta Downs Racetrack & Casino

2717 Highway 3063
Vinton, LA 70668
Near Texas border
(337) 589-7441
www.deltadowns.com
■ **Restaurant(s):** Outlook Steakhouse, Triple Crown Buffet

Extensive renovations were made in 2001 to the racing facilities. The grandstand was completely renovated and a casino was added.

Live thoroughbred and quarter horse races from January through April. Quarter horse races from April through June. Simulcasting daily. Live entertainment in the Jockey Club.

■ **Games Available:** Slots

Evangeline Downs

Interstate 49
P.O. Box 90270
Lafayette, LA 70509
(337) 896-RACE
Fax: (337) 896-5445
info@evangelinedowns.com
www.evangelinedowns.com
Free parking.

Live horse racing from mid-April through Labor Day on Wednesday, Thursday, Friday, Saturday. Simulcasting available year-round.

Louisiana Fair Grounds Race Course

1751 Gentilly Blvd.
New Orleans, LA 70152
Near downtown New Orleans
(504) 944-5515
Fax: (504) 944-2511
www.fgno.com
145 acres
■ **Restaurant(s):** Clubhouse Dining Room, food court.

Free parking.

Live horse races from January through March and in December. Simulcasts of other races.

MAINE

Bangor Raceway

Main and Buck Streets
Bangor, ME 04402
(207) 990-2199
Fax: (207) 866-5793
3,500 grandstand capacity

Free admission and free parking.

Live harness racing from mid-May through mid-July.

Scarborough Downs

U.S. Route One
Scarborough, ME 04074
Eight miles from Portland, Maine
(207) 883-4331
Fax: (207) 883-1486
www.scarboroughdowns.com
■ **Restaurant(s):** Downs Club Restaurant

Harness racing from March through December. Simulcasting from other tracks daily.

MARYLAND

Laurel Park

Route 198
Laurel, MD 20725
20 miles from Washington, 20 miles from
  Baltimore
(301) 725-0400
www.pimlico.com
360 acres
■ **Restaurant(s):** Turf Club Dining Room,
  Tycoons, Sunny Jim's, Clocker's Corner

Free seating on weeknights, free parking.

Live thoroughbred racing on Wednesdays through
  Sundays from January through March.
  Simulcasting of other races daily.

Ocean Downs

10218 Racetrack Rd.
P.O. Box 11
Berlin, MD 21811
Four miles from Ocean City, MD, 150 miles from
  Baltimore
(410) 641-0600
www.oceandowns.com
168 acres, 5,100 capacity
Restaurant(s): Pacers Restaurant, Clubhouse Turn

Live racing late June through August. Simulcast
  of other races daily.

Pimlico Race Course

Hayward and Winner Avenues
Baltimore, MD 21215
(410) 542-9400
Fax: (410) 664-6645
www.pimlico.com
13,000 seating capacity
■ **Restaurant(s):** Terrace Dining Room, Hall of
  Fame Room, Triple Crown Room.

Home of the Preakness. Free parking.

Live horse racing April through mid-June,
  September. Simulcasting of other races available
  daily.

Rosecroft Raceway

6336 Rosecroft Drive
Ft. Washington, MD 20744
On the outskirts of Washington
(301) 567-4000
Fax: (301) 567-9267
www.rosecroft.com
■ **Restaurant(s):** Willy K's at Rosecroft

Free parking

Harness racing on Thursday, Friday and Saturday
  nights from February through the year.
  Simulcasting of other races daily.

MASSACHUSETTS

Plainridge Racecourse

301 Washington St.
Plainville, MA 02762
(508) 643-2500
Fax: (508) 643-4530
Free admission, parking

Harness racing mid-April through November.
   Track opened in 1999.

Suffolk Downs

111 Waldemar Ave.
East Boston, MA 02128
Near Logan Airport
(617) 567-3900
www.suffolkdowns.com

■ **Restaurant(s):** Terrace Dining Room,
   Legends, Deli Grill, Turf Club

Free parking.

Live horse races January through June, October
   through December. Simulcasting of other races
   available.

MICHIGAN

Great Lakes Downs

4800 S. Harvey St.
Muskegon, MI 49444
(231) 799-2400
(877) 800-4616
Fax: (231) 798-3120
glweb@greatlakesdowns.com
www.greatlakesdowns.com
Live thoroughbred racing from late April through
October. Simulcasting of other races available
Wednesdays through Saturdays.

Hazel Park Harness Raceway

1650 East Ten Mile Road
Hazel Park, MI 48030
12 miles north of Detroit
(248) 398-1000
Fax: (248) 398-5236
www.hollywoodgreyhound.com/tritrackhazel-
park.htm
■ **Restaurant(s):** Winners Circle

Harness racing from early April through October.
Simulcasting of other races available daily.

Jackson Raceway

200 W. Ganson St.
Jackson, MI 49204
(517) 788-4500
Fax: (517) 788-6772
Harness racing in April and May, also in
September and October.

Mount Pleasant Meadows

500 North Mission Road
Mount Pleasant, MI 48804
(989) 773-0012
Live quarter horse, thoroughbred and Arabian racing from May through September. Simulcasting
of other races available year-round.

Northville Downs

301 South Center Street
Northville, MI 48167
(248) 349-1000
Fax: (248) 348-8955
nvdowns@aol.com
www.northvilledowns.com
Grandstand capacity 3,000
■ **Restaurant(s):** Clubhouse Dining Room

Free admission and parking.

Harness racing year-round on Monday, Tuesday,
Thursday, Friday and Saturday. Simulcasting
available daily

Saginaw Harness Raceway

2701 East Genesee St.
Saginaw, MI 48601
(989) 755-3451
Fax: (989) 755-1300
casiala@journey.com
www.saginawraceway.com
Free parking.

Harness racing from early June through August.
Simulcasting of other races available daily.

Sports Creek Raceway

4290 Morrish Road
Swartz Creek, MI 48473
(313) 635-3333
Fax: (313) 635-9711
Free parking.

Harness racing from January through early April
and from mid-October through December.

MINNESOTA

Canterbury Park

1100 Canterbury Road
Shakopee, MN 55379
25 minutes from Minneapolis-St. Paul
(952)445-7223
(800) 340-6361
cbypark@canterburypark.com
www.canterburypark.com

355 acres

■ **Restaurant(s):** Park Restaurant, Ubetcha! Bar & Grill, King's Carvery buffet.

Card Club with 43 tables is open 24 hours a day. Free parking.

Live horse racing from mid-May through Labor Day. Simulcasting of other races available.

■ **Games Available:** Poker - 43

NEBRASKA

Columbus Racetrack

822 15th St.
Columbus, NE 68601
(402) 564-0133
www.agpark.com
Live thoroughbred racing from late July through
   mid- September on Fridays, Saturdays, Sundays.
   Simulcasting available year-round on weekends.

Fonner Park

700 E. Stolley Park Road
Grand Island, NE 68802
(308) 382-4515
Fax: (308) 384-2753
fonnerpark@aol.com
www.fonnerpark.com
Free parking.

Live thoroughbred racing from mid-February to
   mid- May. Year-round simulcasting from other
   race tracks seven days a week. Also features
   Keno Casino and Sports Lounge.

■ **Games Available:** Keno

Nebraska State Fair Park

1800 State Fair Park Drive
Lincoln, NE 68508
(402) 473-4100
Fax: (402) 473-4114

NEW HAMPSHIRE

Rockingham Park

1 Rockingham Park Blvd.
Salem, NH 03079
30 miles from Boston
(603) 898-2311
www.rockinghampark.com

■ **Restaurant(s):** Lou Smith Dining Room, Sports Club.

Bingo hall has 700 capacity.

Live horse racing from June through September. Simulcasting available year-round.

■ **Games Available;** Bingo

NEW JERSEY

Freehold Raceway

130 Park Ave.
Freehold, NJ 07728
(732) 462-3800
Fax: (732) 462-3807
www.freeholdraceway.com
■ **Restaurant(s):** Renaissance Dining Room

Free admission, free parking.

Trotters and pacers racing from August through
May. Simulcasting for other races available daily
year- round.

Garden State Park

P.O. Box 1906
Cherry Hill, NJ 08034
Six miles from Philadelphia
(856) 488-8400
Fax: (856) 488-3778
Harness racing from September through mid-
December.

Meadowlands Racetrack

50 Route 120
East Rutherford, NJ 07073
(201) 843-2446
www.thebigm.com
Restaurant(s): The Hambletonian Room, Pegasus,
Terraces.

Free parking.

Live harness racing from January through early
August. Simulcasting available daily.

Monmouth Park

175 Oceanport Ave.
Oceanport, NJ 07757
(732) 222-5100
www.monmouthpark.com
Live horse racing from mid-May through August
on Wednesdays through Sundays. Simulcasting
available year-round.

NEW MEXICO

Downs at Albuquerque

201 California NE
Albuquerque, NM 87198
(505) 266-5555
www.abqdowns.com
15,000 seat grandstand
■ **Restaurant(s):** The Jockey Club

Casino has 300 slots.

Live horse racing late March through June.
   Simulcasting available.

Overall Payout: 92%

■ **Games Available:** Slots $1 - 36, Slots $5 - 6,
   Slots Nickel - 117, Slots Quarter - 129

Sunland Park & Slots

P.O. Box 1
Sunland Park, NM 88063
(505) 589-1131
sunlandinfo@sunland-park.com
www.sunland-park.com
■ **Restaurant(s):** Rileys' Restaurant, Turf Club,
   Poor Albert's, Jackpot Grill.

Live quarter horse and thoroughbred racing from
   November through April. Simulcasting available
   daily. Concerts held occasionally.

■ **Games Available:** Slots - 600

Ruidoso Downs

P.O. Box 449
Ruidoso Downs, NM 88346
(505) 378-4431
info@ruidownsracing.com
www.btkcasino.com
Billy the Kid Casino
■ **Restaurant(s):** Ruidoso Downs Race Track &
   Casino Buffet, Billy the Kid's Fort Stanton Bar
   & Grill.

Live horse racing late May through Labor Day.
   Summer concert series.

■ **Games Available:** Slots - 300

SunRay Park and Casino

39 Road 5568
Farmington, NM 87401
(505) 566-1200
Fax: (505) 326-4292
www.sunraygaming.com
■ **Restaurant(s):** Legends Bar & Grill

Live horse racing from late September through
   November. Simulcasting is available.

■ **Games Available:** Slots - 300

NEW YORK

Aqueduct

110-00 Rockaway Blvd.
Jamaica, NY 11417
Near JFK Airport in New York City
(718) 641-4700
www.nyra.com/Aqueduct
■ **Restaurant(s):** Equestris Restaurant, Man 'O
War Room, Big "A" Grill, food court.

Live thoroughbred racing from January through
March and late October through December.
Simulcasting of other races available.

Batavia Downs

8315 Park Rd.
Batavia, NY 14020
585-343-3750
After closing in 1998, Batavia Downs reopened
for off- track betting in 2002 and planned to
begin live harness racing in late July 2002.

Belmont Park

2150 Hempstead Turnpike
Elmont, NY 11003
East of New York City
(516) 488-6000
cserv@nyrainc.com
www.nyra.com/belmont
■ **Restaurant(s):** Garden Terrace Dining Room,
Paddock Dining Room, Belmont Café, food
court.

Home of the Belmont Stakes.

Live thoroughbred racing from early May through
July and early September through October.
Simulcasting of other races available.

Buffalo Raceway

5600 McKinley Parkway
Hamburg, NY 14075
(716) 649-1280
Fax: (716) 649-0033
www.buffaloraceway.com
Harness racing on Wednesdays, Fridays, Saturdays
from late January through early December.
Simulcasting of other races available.

Finger Lakes Race Track

P.O. Box 25250
Farmington, NY 14425
20 miles from Rochester
(716) 924-3232
www.fingerlakesracetrack.com
■ **Restaurant(s):** Terrace Dining Room,
Paddock Room.

Live horse racing from early April to early
December on Fridays through Tuesdays.
Simulcasting available.

Historic Track-Goshen

44 Park Place
Goshen, NY 10924
(914) 294-5333
Harness racing in early July.

Monticello Raceway

Raceway Road
P.O. Box 5013
Monticello, NY 12701
90 miles northwest of New York City
(845) 794-4100
Fax: (845) 794-0523
SFW@FCC.NET
www.monticelloraceway.com
■ **Restaurant(s):** Track Dining Room

Slot machines coming in November 2002.

Live harness racing year-round. Simulcasts of other races.

Saratoga

Union Avenue
Saratoga Springs, NY 12866
(518) 584-6200
cserv@nyrainc.com
www.nyra.com/saratoga/
50,000 capacity

■ **Restaurant(s):** Turf Terrace Dining Room, At the Rail Pavilion, Carousel Restaurant, Porch Terrace, Club Terrace.

Live thoroughbred racing from late July through Labor Day. Harness racing 140 days a year. Simulcasting of other races available.

Vernon Downs

14 Ruth St.
Vernon, NY 13476
(315) 829-2201
(877) 777-8559
Fax: (315) 829-4384
www.vernondowns.com
■ **Hotel:** 175 rooms
■ **Restaurant(s):** Gold Cup Restaurant

Vernon Country Suites Hotel.

Harness racing from late April through November. Simulcasting available from other tracks daily. Special events include snocross and motorcycle racing, music concerts and rodeos.

Younkers Raceway

810 Central Ave.
Yonkers, NY 10704
(914) 968-4200
Fax: (914) 968-1121
Harness racing year-round. Simulcasting available.

OHIO

Beulah Park

3664 Grant Ave.
Grove City, OH 43123
Near Columbus
(614) 871-9600
Fax: (614) 871-0433
Live horse racing from January through May.
  Simulcasting of other races available daily.

Lebanon Raceway

665 N. Broadway St.
Lebanon, OH 45036
(513) 932-4936
www.thelebanonraceway.com
Free admission and parking.

Harness racing from January through May and
  from late September through December.

Northfield Park

10705 Northfield Road
Northfield, OH 44067
Cleveland-Akron area
(330) 467-4101
Fax: (330) 468-2628
NfldPark@aol.com
www.northfieldpark.com
■ **Restaurant(s):** Clubhouse Dining Room,
  Northfield Grille

More than $10 million in renovations have been
  completed.

Year-round harness racing on Mondays,
  Wednesdays, Fridays, Saturdays. Open for
  simulcasting daily.

Raceway Park

5700 Telegraph Road
Toledo, OH 43612
(419) 476-7751
Fax: (419) 476-7979
Free parking.

Harness racing from mid-March through mid-
  December.

River Downs

6301 Kellogg Ave.
Cincinnati, OH 45230
Four miles east of Cincinnati
(513) 232-8000
Fax: (513) 232-1412
johne@riverdowns.com
www.riverdowns.com
■ **Restaurant(s):** Turf Terrace

Free admission, free parking.

Live thoroughbred racing mid-April through
  Labor Day. Simulcasting of other races daily.

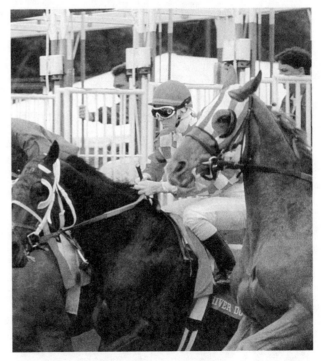

Horses burst from the starting gate at River Downs in Cincinnati.
Photo by Longshot Photo

Scioto Downs

6000 South High St.
Columbus, OH 43207
(614) 491-2515
(800) 723-6967
www.sciotodowns.com
Grandstand capacity 3,500

■ **Reservations:** (614) 491-2784

■ **Restaurant(s):** Clubhouse Restaurant, Outdoor Patio

Harness racing from early May through September. Simulcasting of other races daily.

Thistledown

21501 Emery Road
North Randall, OH 44128
Southeast of Cleveland
(216) 662-8600
(800) 289-9956
Fax: (216) 662-5339
tdownweb@hotmail.com
www.thistledown.com

■ **Restaurant(s):** Paddock Bar-B-Que

Live horse racing from late March through December. Simulcasting of other races daily. Summer concert series is featured.

Blue Ribbon Downs

3700 West Cherokee
Sallisaw, OK 74955
100 miles southeast of Tulsa
(918) 775-7771
Fax: (918) 775-5805
brd@blueribbondowns.net
www.blueribbondowns.net
Restaurant(s): Turf Club

Live horse racing February through November.
  Simulcasting of other races daily.

Fair Meadows at Tulsa

21st and Gale
P.O. Box 4735
Tulsa, OK 74159
100 miles from Oklahoma City
(918) 743-7223
Fax: (918)743-8053
Racing@fairmeadows.com
www.fairmeadows.com

Live horse racing June through August.
  Simulcasts of other races.

Remington Park

1 Remington Place
Oklahoma City, OK 73111
(405) 424-1000
www.remingtonpark.com
■ **Restaurant(s):** Eclipse Restaurant

Live horse racing from April through early June,
  August through December. Simulcasting from
  other tracks available.

Will Rogers Downs

20900 S. 4200 Road
Claremore, OK 74017
25 miles from Tulsa
(918) 343-5900
www.willrogersdowns.com
■ **Restaurant(s):** Turf Club Restaurant

Live horse racing Fridays through Mondays in
  April and May. Simulcasting available
  Wednesdays through Mondays.

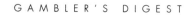

PENNSYLVANIA

Penn National Race Course

P.O. Box 32
Grantville, PA 17028
(717) 469-2211
fredDL@pngaming.com
www.pennnational.com
■ **Restaurant(s):** Mountainview Terrace Dining
Room

Live horse racing Wednesday through Saturday
nights year-round. Simulcasting available.

Pocono Downs

1280 Highway 315
Wilkes-Barre, PA 18702
(570) 825-6681
Fax: (570) 823-9407
JohnZ@pngaming.com
www.poconodowns.com
Grandstand capacity 3,000
■ **Reservations:** (570) 830-9738
■ **Restaurant(s):** Pacers Clubhouse

Harness racing from April through October on
Saturday, Sunday, Monday, and Tuesday.
Simulcasting available daily.

Philadelphia Park Turf Club

7 Penn Center
1635 Market St.
Philadelphia, PA 19103
Philadelphia Park Turf Clubs have five locations
in the Philadelphia area: Center City, South
Philadelphia, Upper Darby, Valley Forge and
Brandywine
(215) 246-1556
www.philadelphiapark.com
■ **Restaurant(s):** Sportsview Bar & Grill

Philadelphia Park Turf Clubs feature simulcasting
and wagering on thoroughbred and harness
races.

The Meadows

Box 499
Meadow Lands, PA 15347
(724) 225-9300
www.latm.com/meadows
16,000 track capacity
■ **Reservations:** (412) 563-1224

Free admission and parking.

Harness racing from January through December.
Simulcasts of other tracks available.

Lone Star Park

1000 Lone Star Parkway
Grand Prairie, TX 75050
Dallas/Fort Worth area
(972) 263-PONY
(800) 795-RACE
www.lonestarpark.com
■ **Restaurant(s):** Silks Dining Room

Live thoroughbred races from April through July
and quarter horse races from October through
November. Simulcasting of races from other
tracks available.

Manor Downs

9211 Hill Lane
Austin, TX 78714
(512) 272-5581
www.manordowns.com
■ **Restaurant(s):** Turf Club

Quarter horse races from February through mid-
April; thoroughbreds from late April through
May. Simulcasting available daily except
Tuesdays.

Retama Park

1 Retana Parkway
Selma, TX 78154
20 miles north of San Antonio
(210) 651-7000
www.retamapark.com
20,000 capacity grandstand
■ **Restaurant(s):** Terrace Dining, Sports Bar

Live quarterhorse racing in April through June;
thoroughbred racing from August through

October. Simulcasting other races daily.
Entertainment includes concerts, clowns, face
painters, pony rides, petting zoos.

*Horses round the turn at Retama Park in San
Antonio*

Sam Houston Race Park

7575 North Sam Houston Pkwy. West
Houston, TX 77064
(281) 807-8700
General@shrp.com
www.shrp.com
20,000 capacity
■ **Restaurant(s):** Winner's Circle Restaurant,
Quarter Post Café

Live thoroughbred racing from January through
March, quarter horses from July through Labor
Day, and thoroughbreds from November through
December. Simulcasting of other races daily.

VIRGINIA

Colonial Downs Racetrack

10515 Colonial Downs Parkway
New Kent, VA 23124
25 miles from Richmond, 20 miles from
 Williamsburg
(804) 966-7223
codowns@erols.com
www.colonialdowns.com
10,000 capacity grandstand

■ **Restaurant(s):** Jockey Club Dining Room,
 Turf Club Restaurant

Colonial Downs has the widest turf course in
 North America and the second largest dirt track
 in the U.S.

Thoroughbred racing in June and July, harness
 racing in October. Simulcasting of other races
 available.

WASHINGTON

Emerald Downs

2300 Emerald Downs Drive
Auburn, WA 98001
(253) 288-7000
(888) 931-8400
www.emdowns.com
■ **Reservations:** (253) 288-7711
■ **Restaurant(s):** Rainier Restaurant
Free parking.
Live horse racing from mid-April to mid-
 September. Simulcasting available.

Walla Walla Race Track

9th and Orchard
Walla Walla, WA 99362
(509) 527-3247
Live horse racing in early May and early
 September.

WEST VIRGINIA

Charles Town Races & Slots

U.S. Route 340
Charles Town, WV 25414
60 minutes from Baltimore.
(800) 795-7001
www.ctownraces.com

■ **Restaurant(s):** Sundance Café, Premiere Buffet, Skyline Terrace Dining Room.

Live horse racing Wednesday through Saturday nights, Sunday afternoons. Simulcasting available.

■ **Games Available:** Slots

Mountaineer Park

P.O. Box 358
Chester, WV 26034
(800) 80-40-HO
info@mtrgaming.com
www.mtrgaming.com/homepage.html

■ **Restaurant(s):** Riverfront Buffet, Outdoor Café, Gatsby's Dining Room, Mountaineer Clubhouse & Terrace Dining Room.

Also includes casino, golf course, resort. See listing under Casinos.

Live horse racing from January through early December on Saturdays through Tuesdays. Simulcasting of other race tracks available.

WYOMING

Wyoming Downs

10180 Highway 89N
Evanston, WY 82930
80 miles east of Salt Lake City
(307) 789-0511
(866) 681-RACE
wyhr@phoenixleisure.com
www.wyomingdowns.com

■ **Hotel:** 113 rooms

■ **Restaurant(s):** Clocker's Corner

Free parking. Hotel is High Country Inn.

Live horse races on Saturdays and Sundays from late June through late August. Simulcasting available. Off- track betting at 1936 Harrison Drive, Evanston; 621 SE Wyoming Blvd., Casper; 507 E. 16th St., Cheyenne; and 1549 Elk St., Rock Springs.

ALABAMA

Mobile Greyhound Park

P.O. Box 43
Theodore, AL 36590
(334) 653-5000
Fax: (334) 653-9185
info@mobilegreyhoundpark.com
www.mobilegreyhoundpark.com

Live greyhound racing Monday through Saturday nights and Monday, Wednesday and Saturday matinees year- round. Simulcasting available.

Victoryland Greyhound Racing

P.O. Box 128
Shorter, AL 36075
Off I-85 between Montgomery and Tuskegee
(334) 727-0540
(800) 688-2946
Fax: (334) 727-0737
www.victoryland.com
12,000 capacity grandstand

Live greyhound racing plus simulcasts of races at other tracks.

■ **Games Available:** Slots - 300

ARIZONA

Apache Greyhound Park

2551 West Apache Trail
Apache Junction, AZ 85220
East of Phoenix
(602) 982-2371
Free admission and parking
Live greyhound racing from November through March. Simulcasting available.

Phoenix Greyhound Park

3801 E. Washington St.
Phoenix, AZ 85036
Near Sky Harbor Airport
(602) 273-7181
www.phoenixgreyhoundpark.com
Grandstand admission and parking are free.
Live greyhound racing year-round. Simulcasting and off-track betting available.

Tucson Greyhound Park

2601 S. Third Ave.
Tucson, AZ 85713
(520) 884-7576
www.tucdogtrak.com
3,000 capacity
Free admission and free parking.
Live greyhound racing year-round nightly except Mondays. Simulcasting of other races daily.

ARKANSAS

Southland Greyhound Park

1550 North Ingram Blvd.
West Memphis, AR 72301
10 minutes from downtown Memphis
(870) 735-3670
(800) 467-6182

Fax: (870) 732-8335
www.southlandgreyhound.com

■ **Restaurant(s):** Kennel Club, Winner's Edge.

Live racing year-round: Matinees - Monday, Wednesday, Saturday; Evenings: Monday, Tuesday, Thursday, Friday, Saturday. Simulcasting available.

COLORADO

Cloverleaf Kennel Club

P.O. Box 88
Loveland, CO 80539
(970) 667-6211
Live greyhound racing from February through May.

Mile High Greyhound Racing

6200 Dahlia
Commerce City, CO 80022
(303) 288-1591
milehigh@wembleyusa.com
www.wembleyusa.com/milehigh
■ **Restaurant(s):** Wembley Club Restaurant
Free parking.

Live greyhound racing from January through early February, then June through December, Monday through Saturday afternoons and Saturday nights. Simulcasting of other races available.

Pueblo Greyhound Park

3215 Lake Ave.
Pueblo, CO 81004
(719) 566-0370
Fax: (303) 289-1640
Pueblo@Wembleyusa.com
www.wembleyusa.com/pueblo
Free parking
Live racing January through March on Tuesday through Saturday nights and Sunday matinees. Simulcasting available.

Rocky Mountain Greyhound Park

P.O. Box 7229
Colorado Springs, CO 80933
(719) 632-1391
(800) 444-7297
Live greyhound racing from April through December.

CONNECTICUT

Plainfield Greyhound Park

Interstate 395
P.O. Box 205
Plainfield, CT 06374
(800) RACES ON
www.trackinfo.com/pl/

Free admission and free parking.

Live racing year-round, with matinees Sunday, Tuesday, Wednesday, Thursday, Saturday as well as Friday and Saturday nights. Simulcasting available daily.

Shoreline Star Greyhound Park

255 Kossuth St.
Bridgeport, CT 06608
(203) 576-1976
(888)GO-DOG-GO
ssgreyhound@mindspring.com
www.shorelinestar.com

■ **Restaurant(s):** Shoreline Terrace, Paddock Grille.

Free admission and free parking.

Live greyhound racing from May through October. Simulcasting of other races is available daily. Also available is simulcasting of jai alai matches.

FLORIDA

Daytona Beach Kennel Club

U.S. Highway 92
Daytona Beach, FL 32114
(904) 252-6484
www.dbkennelclub.com

■ **Restaurant(s):** The Pavilion, Cabaret Deli

Live greyhound racing year-round. Simulcasting of other races available. Poker room is featured.

■ **Games Available:** Poker

Derby Lane - St. Petersburg

10490 Gandy Blvd.
St. Petersburg, FL 33702
(727) 812-3339
www.derbylane.com

■ **Restaurant(s):** Derby Club Restaurant, coffee shop.

Live greyhound racing from January through June, nightly except Sundays, with matinees Mondays, Wednesdays and Saturdays. Simulcasting available daily.

■ **Games Available:** Poker

Ebro Greyhound Park

Highways 79 and 20
Ebro, FL 32437
15 minutes north of Panama City
(850) 234-3943
www.ebrogreyhoundpark.com

Live greyhound racing from February through October. Simulcasting of other races available.

Flagler Dog Track Sports and Entertainment Center

401 NW 38th Court
P.O. Box 350940
Miami, FL 33135
Five minutes from downtown Miami.
(305) 649-3000
www.flaglerdogs.com

■ **Restaurant(s):** Sports bar

Free admission. Domino and pool tables. Flea market with 400 booths every weekend.

Live dog racing from June 1-Nov. 30 every night; matinees Tuesday, Thursday, Saturday. Simulcasts of other races daily.

■ **Games Available:** Poker

Hollywood Greyhound Track

831 N. Federal Highway
Hallandale, FL 33009
1 mile east of I-95
(954) 924-3200
www.hollywoodgreyhound.com
■ **Restaurant(s):** Dog House Sports Bar and Grill

Sports Bar offers 100 TVs. Flea market every weekend year-round. Billiards tables, poker tables.

Live racing nightly Dec. 1 to end of May, matinees Tuesday, Thursday, Saturday. Simulcasting from other racetracks daily.

■ **Games Available:** Poker

Jacksonville Greyhound Racing

1440 N. McDuff Ave.
Jacksonville, FL 32254
(904) 680-DOGS
www.jaxkennel.com

Live greyhound racing from early June through Labor Day. Simulcasting of other races available.

Naples Fort Myers Greyhounds

10601 Bonita Beach Road
P.O. Box 2567
Bonita Springs, FL 34135-2567
Between Fort Myers and Naples.
(941) 992-2411
naplesftmyersdog@aol.com
www.naplesfortmyersdogs.com
Free admission.

Live racing year-round, seven days a week from Dec. 26 through Easter. Five or six days live racing the remainder of the year. Simulcasting of other races daily.

■ **Games Available:** Poker

Orange Park Kennel Club

455 Park Ave.
Orange Park, FL 32073
(904) 646-0001
www.jaxkennel.com
Live greyhound racing from early September through May, daily except Tuesdays. Simulcasting of other races available.

Palm Beach Kennel Club

1111 North Congress Ave.
West Palm Beach, FL 33409
(561) 683-2222
www.pbkennelclub.com
■ **Restaurant(s):** The Paddock Restaurant
Free parking.

Live greyhound and simulcasting available year-round with daily matinees and racing Monday, Wednesday, Thursday, Friday and Saturday evenings. Poker room has 30 tables.

■ **Games Available:** Poker - 30

Pensacola Greyhound Park

Highway 98 West at Dog Track Road
Pensacola, FL 32575
(850) 455-8595
(800) 345-3997
www.pensacolagreyhoundpark.com
■ **Restaurant(s):** Kennel Club
Free parking

Live racing year-round nightly Wednesday through Saturday, matinees on Saturday and Sunday. Simulcasting available.

Sanford Orlando Kennel Club

301 Dog Track Rd.
Longwood, FL 32750
North of Orlando
(407) 831-1600
www.orlandogreyhoundracing.com

■ **Restaurant(s):** Two clubhouse dining areas.

Live greyhound racing year-round Monday through Saturday nights and Monday, Wednesday and Saturday matinees. Simulcasting available daily.

Sarasota Kennel Club

5400 Bradenton Rd.
Sarasota, FL 34234
(941) 355-7744
www.orlandogreyhoundracing.com

■ **Restaurant(s):** Two clubhouse dining areas.

Free parking.

Live greyhound racing from late December through April on Monday through Saturday nights and Monday, Wednesday, Friday and Saturday matinees. Simulcasting available daily.

Seminole Greyhound Park

2000 Seminola Blvd.
Casselberry, FL 32707
(407) 699-4510
Live greyhound racing in May and June.

Tampa Greyhound Track

8300 N. Nebraska Ave.
Tampa, FL 33674
(813) 932-4313
Fax: (813) 932-5048
www.tampadogs.com

Live greyhound racing from July through December. Simulcasting available.

■ **Games Available:** Poker

IOWA

Dubuque Greyhound Park and Casino

1855 Greyhound Park Drive
Dubuque, IA 52004
At the Iowa-Wisconsin border.
(319) 582-3647
(800) 373-3647
brianc@dgpc.com

www.dgpc.com
■ **Restaurant(s):** Winners Restaurant
Live greyhound racing from May through October. Simulcasting of other races available. Casino has 600 slot machines.
■ **Games Available:** Slots - 600

KANSAS

Wichita Greyhound Park

1500 E 77th St. North
Valley Center, KS 67147
(316) 755-4000
(800) 872-2894
geninfo@wgpi.com

www.wgpi.com
Free admission and free parking.
Live greyhound racing year-round daily except Tuesdays. Simulcasting of other races available daily.

MASSACHUSETTS

Raynham-Taunton Greyhound Park

1958 Broadway
Raynham, MA 02767
(508) 824-4071
general@rtgp.com
www.rtgp.com

■ **Restaurant(s):** Club 1, Terrace Dining Room.
Free parking.
Live greyhound racing year-round. Simulcasting available. Live entertainment in the Promenade Lounge.

NEW HAMPSHIRE

Hinsdale Greyhound

688 Brattleboro Road
Hinsdale, NH 03451
(603) 336-5382
(800) NH-TRACK
Fax: (603) 336-5477
info@hinsdalegreyhound.com
www.hinsdalegreyhound.com

Free admission and free parking.
Live greyhound races Wednesday through Sunday afternoons and Saturday nights.

Lakes Region Greyhound Park

Route 106
Belmont, NH 03220
15 miles from Concord, N.H.
(603) 267-7778
Fax: (603) 267-7667

■ **Restaurant(s):** Dog House sports bar; Dining Room trackside.
Shopping malls, golf courses and ski slopes in the area.

Seabrook Greyhound Park

P.O. Box 219
Seabrook, NH 03874
55 minutes from Boston
(603) 474-3065
www.seabrookgreyhoundpark.com

■ **Restaurant(s):** Kennel Club Dining
Free parking.
Live greyhound racing year-round Tuesday through Sunday afternoons and Friday and Saturday nights. Simulcasting available daily.

OREGON

Multnomah Greyhound Park

NE 223rd Ave & Glisan
Wood Village, OR 97070
(503) 667-7700
mgp@multnomahgreyhoundpark.com

www.ez2winmgp.com
Free admission, free parking.
Live greyhound racing from May through October.
Simulcasting available daily.

RHODE ISLAND

Lincoln Park

1600 Louisquisset Pike
Lincoln, RI 02865
5 miles north of Providence
(800) 720-PARK
www.lincolnparkri.com
75,000 square feet

■ **Restaurant(s):** Queen of Clubs, Cityscapes Pub
& Café, Blackjack Bar & Café, food court.

Free grandstand and clubhouse admission, free
parking, open year-round.
Live greyhound races and simulcasts of other races.
Oldies concerts, dinner theater.
Overall Payout: 92-94%
■ **Games Available:** Keno - 963, Slots 10 cents -
67, Slots Nickel - 157, Slots Quarter - 1476

TEXAS

Corpus Christi Greyhound Race Track

5302 Leopard St.
Corpus Christi, TX 78408
129 miles to San Antonio, 225 miles to Houston
(361) 289-9333
(800) 580-RACE
ccgrt@aol.com
www.corpuschristidogs.com
3,500 capacity

■ **Restaurant(s):** Buffet Fridays and Saturdays.

Races nightly Wednesday-Saturday; matinees Wednesday, Friday, Saturday, Sunday. Simulcasts of other races daily.

Gulf Greyhound Park

P.O. Box 488
La Marque, TX 77568
30 miles south of Houston
(409) 986-9500
(800) ASK-2WIN
gulfpark@gulfgreyhound.com
www.gulfgreyhound.com
14,000 capacity at track

■ **Restaurant(s):** Horizon Clubhouse

World's largest greyhound operation.

Live greyhound racing year-round. Simulcasting available daily.

WISCONSIN

Dairyland Greyhound Park

5522 104th Ave.
Kenosha, WI 53144
South of Milwaukee near Illinois border
(262) 657-8200
(800) 233-3357
Fax: (262) 657-8231
www.dairylandgreyhoundpark.com
12,500 capacity
Live greyhound racing year-round. Simulcasting of other races available.

Geneva Lakes Greyhound Track

1600 E. Geneva St.
P.O. Box 650
Delavan, WI 53115
70 miles north of Chicago, 30 miles south of Milwaukee
(262) 728-8000
(800) 477-4552
www.genevagreyhounds.com
Live greyhound racing Friday and Saturday night, matinees on Tuesday, Thursday, Saturday, Sunday. Simulcasting of other races daily.

WEST VIRGINIA

Tri-State Greyhound Park

P.O. Box 7118
Cross Lanes, WV 25356
(304) 776-1000
Live greyhound racing year-round. Simulcasting available.

Wheeling Downs

1 S. Stone St.
Wheeling, WV 26003
(877) WIN-HERE
www.wheelingdowns.com

■ **Restaurant(s):** Terrace Dining Room, Islander Buffet

Live greyhound racing year-round. Simulcasting available daily.

■ **Games Available:** Keno, Slots - 1400

FLORIDA

Dania Jai-Alai

301 E. Dania Beach Blvd.
Dania Beach, FL 33004
(954) 927-2841
Fax: (954) 920-9095
genlmgr@betdania.com
www.dania-jai-alai.com

Free parking.

Jai-Alai year-round nightly Tuesdays through
Saturdays; matinees Tuesday, Saturdays, Sundays.
Simulcasting of jai-alai, horse racing and harness
racing daily.

■ **Games Available:** Poker

*Dania Jai-Alai, which opened in 1953 in Florida, has seating
for 5,600 fans as well as simulcasting betting, restaurants,
and a sports bar. Annual attendance is more than 500,000.*

Ft. Pierce Jai-Alai

1750 South Kings Highway
Fort Pierce, FL 34945
(561) 464-7500
(800) Jai-Alai
www.jaialai.net

■ **Restaurant(s):** Pelota Pub, Courtside Club.

Live jai-alai matches. Simulcasting of jai-alai and
horse and greyhound races daily.

Miami Jai-Alai

3500 N.W. 37th Ave.
Miami, FL 33142
(305) 633-6400
www.fla-gaming.com/miami/

■ **Restaurant(s):** Courtview Clubhouse
Restaurant.

Year-round live jai-alai, matinees daily except
Tuesdays, and Wednesday, Friday and Saturday
nights. Simulcasting of jai-alai and horse racing
available daily.

■ **Games Available:** Poker

Ocala Jai-Alai

4601 NW Hwy 318
Orange Lake, FL 32681
(352) 591-2345
Fax: (352) 591-4306
www.ocalajaialai.com

Live jai-alai available as well as simulcasting of
jai-alai and horse and dog racing.

Orlando Jai-Alai

6405 S. Highway 17-92
Casselberry, FL 32730
(407) 339-6221
www.orlandojaialai.com

Live jai-alai on Monday, Thursday, Friday and
Saturday nights, and Thursday and Saturday afternoons. Simulcasting of jai-alai and horse races
daily.

RHODE ISLAND

Newport Grand Jai-Alai
150 Admiral Kalbfus Road
Newport, RI 02840
(401) 849-5000
www.newportgrand.com
Restaurant(s): Grand Grille

Free admission and free parking.

Live jai-alai from March through October.
Simulcasting available daily of jai-alai and horse races.

■ **Games Available**: Slots - 775

FLORIDA

Celebrity Cruises

1050 Caribbean Way
Miami, FL 33132
(305) 262-6677
(800) 242-6374

Gambling is available on many of the Celebrity cruise ships.

■ **Games Available:** Blackjack, Craps , Poker, Roulette, Slots

Discovery Cruises

1850 Eller Drive
Fort Lauderdale, FL 33316
(305) 597-0336
(800) 866-8687
www.discoverycruiseline.com

Cruises to Grand Bahama, with casino aboard.

■ **Games Available:** Blackjack, Craps, Poker, Roulette, Slots - 200

Horizon's Edge Casino Cruises - Riviera Beach

Riviera Beach Marina
Riviera Beach, FL 33404
(800) LUCKY32
Fax: (561) 840-9689
www.horizonsedge.com

Restaurant(s): Palmer's on the Horizon.

Live musical entertainment.

■ **Games Available:** Blackjack - 8, Craps - 1, Let It Ride - 1, Roulette - 2, Slots - 200

Palm Beach Princess Casino

777 East Port Rd.
Riviera Beach, FL 33404
(561) 845-SHIP
(800) 841-SHIP
www.pbcasino.com
15,000 square feet
Restaurant(s): Royal Palm Restaurant

Live entertainment is featured. Cruises are scheduled seven days a week.

■ **Games Available:** Blackjack - 17, Craps - 2, Let It Ride - 2, Poker - 8, Roulette - 2, Slots

SeaEscape Cruises

3045 N. Federal Highway
Landmark Building 7
Ft. Lauderdale, FL 33306
Island Adventure sails from Port Everglades in Ft. Lauderdale, Terminal One, across from Ft. Lauderdale Convention Center.
(954) 453-3333
(877) SEA-ESCA
www.seaescape.com

■ **Hotel:** 130 rooms

1,100 capacity

125 cabins, 5 suites available.

Day cruises Tuesday through Sunday, night cruises daily. Live entertainment.

■ **Games Available:** Blackjack - 25, Craps - 2, Let It Ride - 1, Mini-baccarat - 1, Pai Gow - 1, Poker - 2, Roulette - 2, Slots - 300

Sterling Casino Lines

101 George King Blvd., Suite 3
Cape Canaveral, FL 32920
35 minutes from Orlando.
(800) ROLL-7-11
www.sterlingcasinolines.com

1,800 capacity

■ **Restaurant(s):** Two complimentary buffets. Free parking, no admission fee. Casino has 50 table games.

Ships sails twice a day. Legends in Concert show is featured entertainment.

■ **Games Available:** Blackjack - 50, Craps - 8, Keno, Roulette - 4, Slots - 1000

SunCruz Casinos

647 E. Dania Beach Blvd.
Dania Beach, FL 33004
(954) 929-3880
Fax: (954) 929-3830
www.suncruzcasino.com

SunCruz casino boats operate in Key Largo, Hollywood, Jacksonville, Port Canaveral, John's Pass and Daytona Beach, Fla., and in Myrtle Beach, S.C.

■ **Games Available:** Blackjack, Craps, Poker, Roulette, Slots

Vegas West Casino Cruises

Hilton Pier
Key West, FL 33040
(305) 295-7775
vegaswest@kwest.net

Daily cruises are available.

■ **Games Available:** Blackjack, Craps, Poker, Roulette, Slots - 72

GEORGIA

Emerald Princess Cruises

1701 Newcastle St.
Brunswick, GA 31520
(912) 265-3558
(800) 842-0115
info@emeraldprincesscasino.com
www.emeraldprincesscasino.com

Daily cruises to international waters. Live entertainment.

■ **Games Available:** Blackjack - 8, Craps, Poker, Roulette, Slots - 130

MASSACHUSETTS

Horizon's Edge Casino Cruises

76 Marine Blvd.
Lynn, MA 01905
(781) 581-7733
(800) LUCKY32
Fax: (781) 581-2777

feedback@horizonsedge.com
www.horizonsedge.com

Restaurant(s): Palmer's on the Horizon.

Entertainers include comedians and musicians.

■ **Games Available:** Slots - 200, Table games - 13

TEXAS

Fantasea Casino Cruises

Texas City Dike
Texas City, TX 77590
(409) 945-0808
www.fantaseacasino.com
Gaming ship sails out of Texas City
Cruises on Friday and Saturday nights, Saturday and Sunday afternoons.

■ **Games Available:** Blackjack - 4, Craps, Poker, Roulette, Slots - 100

Texas Treasure Casino Cruise - Corpus Christi

225 Highway 361 South
Port Arkansas, TX 78373
30 minutes from downtown Corpus Christi
(800) 472-5215
www.txtreasure.com
Casino has 28 table games.
Ship sails twice daily.

■ **Games Available:** Blackjack, Craps, Let It Ride, Mini-baccarat, Roulette, Slots - 460

Texas Treasure Casino Cruise - Freeport

Route 288 South
Freeport, TX 77541
50 minutes from South Houston
(800) 472-5215
www.txtreasure.com
Casino has 21 table games.
Ship sails daily.

■ **Games Available:** Blackjack, Craps, Mini-baccarat, Roulette, Slots - 320

ALABAMA

Mobile Greyhound Park - www.mobilegreyhound-park.com

Victoryland Greyhound Racing - www.victoryland.com

ARKANSAS

Oaklawn Park - www.oaklawn.com

Southland Greyhound Park - www.southlandgrey-hound.com

ARIZONA

Apache Gold Casino Resort - www.apachegoldcasi-noresort.com

BlueWater Resort and Casino - www.bluewaterfun.com

Bucky's Casino - www.buckyscasino.com

Casino Arizona - www.casinoaz.com

Cliff Castle Casino - www.cliffcastle.com

Desert Diamond Casino - www.desertdiamondcasi-no.net

Fort McDowell Casino - www.fortmcdowellcasino.com

Gila River Casino Vee Quiva - www.wingilariver.com

Golden Hasan Casino - www.desertdiamondcasino.net

Harrah's Ak-Chin Casino Resort - www.harrahs.com/our_casinos/akc/ index.html

Hon-Dah Casino Resort - www.hon-dah.com

Paradise Casino - www.paradisecasinoyuma.com

Phoenix Greyhound Park - www.phoenixgreyhound-park.com

Tucson Greyhound Park - www.tucdogtrak.com

Turf Paradise - www.turfparadise.com

Wild Horse Pass Casino - www.wingilariver.com

Yavapai Casino - www.buckyscasino.com

CALIFORNIA

Barona Casino - www.barona.com

Cache Creek Indian Bingo and Casino - www.cachecreek.com

Cal Expo Race Track - www.capitolracing.com

California Grand Casino - www.calgrandcasino.com

Casino Pauma - www.casinopauma.com

Cher-Ae Heights Casino - www.cher-ae-heights-casino.com

Chumash Casino - www.chumashcasino.com

Colusa Casino - www.colusacasino.com

Commerce Casino - www.commercecasino.com

Crystal Park Casino Hotel - www.crystalparkcasino.com

Del Mar Thoroughbred Club - www.dmtc.com

Fairplex Park - www.fairplex.com

Fantasy Springs Casino - www.fantasyspringsresort.com

Feather Falls Casino - www.featherfallscasino.com

Gold Country Casino - www.gold-country-casino.com

Golden Gate Fields - www.ggfields.com

Hollywood Park Casino - www.playhpc.com

Hollywood Park Racetrack - www.hollywoodpark.com

Jackson Rancheria - www.jacksoncasino.com

Konocti Vista Casino - www.kvcasino.com

Los Alamitos Race Course - www.losalamitos.com

Lucky 7 Casino - www.lucky7casino.com

Mono Wind Casino - www.monowind.com

Pala Casino - www.palacasino.com

Palace Indian Gaming Center - www.thepalace.net

Pechanga Entertainment Center - www.pechanga.com

San Manuel Indian Bingo and Casino - www.san-manuel.com

Santa Anita Park - www.santaanita.com

Soboba Casino - www.soboba.net

Spotlight 29 Casino - www.spotlight29casino.com

Sycuan Casino & Resort - www.sycuancasino.com

Twin Pine Casino - www.twinpine.com

Valley View Casino - valleyviewcasino.com

Viejas Casino - www.viejas.com

Win-River Casino Bingo - www.win-river.com

COLORADO

Arapahoe Park - www.wembleyusa.com/arapahoe/

Black Hawk Casino by Hyatt - www.blackhawkcasinobyhyatt.com

Brass Ass Casino - www.midnightrose.com

Colorado Central Station - www.coloradocentralsta-tion.com

Double Eagle Casino - www.decasino.com

Famous Bonanza Casino - www.famousbonanza.com

Fitzgeralds Casino Black Hawk - www.fitzgeralds.com

Imperial Casino Hotel - www.imperialcasinohotel.com

Isle of Capri Black Hawk - www.isleofcapricasino.com/Black_Hawk/

J.P. McGill's Hotel Casino - www.midnightrose.com

Mardi Gras Casino - www.mardigrasbh.com

Midnight Rose Hotel and Casino - www.mid-nightrose.com

Mile High Greyhound Racing - www.wembleyusa.com/milehigh

Palace Hotel & Casino - www.palacehotelcasino.com
Pueblo Greyhound Park -
　www.wembleyusa.com/pueblo
Riviera Black Hawk - www.theriviera.com/blackhawk
Sky Ute Casino - www.skyutecasino.com
The Lodge Casino at Black Hawk - www.thelodge-casino.com

CONNECTICUT

Foxwoods Resort - www.foxwoods.com
Mohegan Sun - www.mohegansun.com
Plainfield Greyhound Park - www.trackinfo.com/pl/
Shoreline Star Greyhound Park -
　www.shorelinestar.com

DELAWARE

Delaware Park Racetrack & Slots - www.delpark.com
Dover Downs - www.doverdowns.com

FLORIDA

Brighton Seminole Bingo and Gaming -
　www.seminoletribe.com
Calder Race Course - www.calderracecourse.com
Dania Jai-Alai - www.dania-jai-alai.com
Daytona Beach Kennel Club -
　www.dbkennelclub.com
Derby Lane - St. Petersburg - www.derbylane.com
Discovery Cruises - www.discoverycruiseline.com
Ebro Greyhound Park - www.ebrogreyhoundpark.com
Flagler Dog Track Sports and Entertainment Center
　- www.flaglerdogs.com
Ft. Pierce Jai-Alai - www.jaialai.net
Gulfstream Park - www.gulfstreampark.com
Hialeah Park - www.hialeahpark.com
Hollywood Greyhound Track -
　www.hollywoodgreyhound.com
Horizon's Edge Casino Cruises - Riviera Beach -
　www.horizonsedge.com
Jacksonville Greyhound Racing - www.jaxkennel.com
Miami Jai-Alai - www.fla-gaming.com/miami/
Miccosukee Indian Casino - www.miccosukee.com
Naples Fort Myers Greyhounds -
　www.naplesfortmyersdogs.com
Ocala Jai-Alai - www.ocalajaialai.com
Orange Park Kennel Club - www.jaxkennel.com
Palm Beach Kennel Club - www.pbkennelclub.com
Palm Beach Princess Casino - www.pbcasino.com

Pensacola Greyhound Park -
　www.pensacolagreyhoundpark.com
Sanford Orlando Kennel Club -
　www.orlandogreyhoundracing.com
Sarasota Kennel Club - www.orlandogreyhoundrac-ing.com
SeaEscape Cruises - www.seaescape.com
Seminole Gaming Palace - www.seminoletribe.com
Sterling Casino Lines - sterlingcasinolines.com
Tampa Bay Downs - www.tampadowns.com
Tampa Greyhound Track - www.tampadogs.com

GEORGIA

Emerald Princess Cruises -
　www.emeraldprincesscasino.com

IDAHO

Clearwater River Casino - www.crcasino.com
Coeur D'Alene Casino - www.cdacasino.com
It'Se Ye-Ye Casino - www.crcasino.com
Kootenai River Inn & Casino - www.koote-nairiverinn.com
Les Bois Park - www.lesboispark.org
Shoshone Bannock Casino - www.sho-ban.com

ILLINOIS

Alton Belle Casino - www.argosycasinos.com/proper-ty/st_louis
Arlington Park - www.arlingtonpark.com
Balmoral Park - www.balmoralpark.com
Casino Queen - www.casinoqueen.com
Empress Casino Hotel -
　www.argosycasinos.com/property/joliet/joliet_home.
Fairmount Park - www.fairmountpark.com
Grand Victoria Casino - www.grandvictoria-elgin.com
Harrah's Joliet Casino & Hotel -
　www.harrahs.com/our_casinos/jol/index.html
Harrah's Metropolis - www.harrahs.com/our_casi-nos/met/index.html
Hawthorne Race Course - hawthorneracecourse.com
Hollywood Casino-Aurora -
　www.hollywoodcasinoaurora.com
Horseshoe Casino Hammond - www.horseshoe.com
Jumer's Casino - www.jumerscri.com
Maywood Park - www.maywoodpark.com
Par-A-Dice Hotel Casino - www.par-a-dice.com
Sportsman's Park - www.sportsmanspark.com

INDIANA

Argosy Casino & Hotel Lawrenceburg - www.argosycasinos.com/property/ cincinnati

Belterra Casino Resort - www.belterracasino.com

Blue Chip Casino - www.bluechip-casino.com

Caesars Indiana Casino Hotel - www.caesarsindiana.com

Casino Aztar - www.casinoaztar.com

Grand Victoria Casino and Resort - www.hyatt.com

Harrah's East Chicago - www.harrahs.com/our_casinos/ech/index.html

Hoosier Park - www.hoosierpark.com

Majestic Star Casino - www.majesticstar.com

Trump Casino Hotel - www.trumpindiana.com

IOWA

Ameristar Casino Council Bluffs - www.ameristarcasinos.com/corporate/cbfacts

Belle of Sioux City Casino - www.argosycasinos.com/property/sioux_city/ sioux_ci

Bluffs Run Casino - www.harrahs.com/our_casinos/hbr/index.html

Catfish Bend Casino - www.catfishbendcasino.com

Diamond Jo Casino - www.diamondjo.com

Dubuque Greyhound Park and Casino - www.dgpc.com

Harrah's Council Bluffs - www.harrahs.com/our_casinos/cou/index.html

Isle of Capri Bettendorf - www.isleofcapricasino.com/Bettendorf/

Isle of Capri Marquette - www.isleofcapricasino.com/Marquette/

Meskwaki Bingo Casino Hotel - www.Meskwaki.com

Prairie Meadows - www.prairiemeadows.com

Rhythm City Casino - www.rhythmcitycasino.com

Winnavegas Casino - www.winnavegas-casino.com

KANSAS

Golden Eagle Casino - www.goldeneaglecasino.com

Harrah's Prairie Band - www.harrahs.com/our_casinos/top/index.html

Wichita Greyhound Park - www.wgpi.com

Woodlands Racetracks - woodlandskc.com

KENTUCKY

Churchill Downs - www.kentuckyderby.com

Ellis Park Race Course - www.ellisparkracing.com

Keeneland - www.keeneland.com

The Red Mile - www.tattersallsredmile.com

Turfway Park - www.turfway.com

LOUISIANA

Argosy Casino Baton Rouge - www.argosycasinos.com/property/baton_rouge/ baton_r

Bally's Casino New Orleans - www.ballysno.com

Boomtown Casino New Orleans - www.boomtowncasinos.com

Casino Magic Bossier City - www.casinomagic-bossier.com

Casino Rouge - www.casinorouge.com

Cypress Bayou Casino - www.cypressbayou.com

Delta Downs Racetrack & Casino - www.deltadowns.com

Evangeline Downs - www.evangelinedowns.com

Grand Casino Coushatta - www.gccoushatta.com

Harrah's New Orleans - www.harrahs.com/our_casinos/nor/index.html

Harrah's Shreveport - www.harrahs.com/our_casinos/shr/index.html

Hollywood Casino-Shreveport - www.hollywoodcasinoshreveport.com

Horseshoe Casino Hotel Bossier City - www.horseshoe.com

Isle of Capri Bossier City - www.isleofcapricasino.com/Bossier_City/

Isle of Capri Lake Charles - www.isleofcapricasino.com/Lake_Charles/

Louisiana Fair Grounds Race Course - www.fgno.com

Paragon Casino Resort - www.grandcasinoavoyelles.com

Treasure Chest Casino - www.treasurechestcasino.com

MAINE

Scarborough Downs - www.scarboroughdowns.com

MARYLAND

Laurel Park - www.pimlico.com

Ocean Downs - www.oceandowns.com

Pimlico Race Course - www.pimlico.com

MASSACHUSETTS

Horizon's Edge Casino Cruises -
www.horizonsedge.com
Raynham-Taunton Greyhound Park - www.rtgp.com
Suffolk Downs - www.suffolkdowns.com

MICHIGAN

Chip-In's Island Resort & Casino - www.chipincasi-
no.com
Great Lakes Downs - www.greatlakesdowns.com
Greektown Casino - greektowncasino.net
Hazel Park Harness Raceway - www.hollywoodgrey-
hound.com/ tritrackhazelpark.htm
Kewadin Casino Christmas - www.kewadin.com
Kewadin Casino Hessel - www.kewadin.com
Kewadin Casino Manistique - www.kewadin.com
Kewadin Casino Sault Ste. Marie -
www.kewadin.com
Kewadin Casino St. Ignace - www.kewadin.com
Leelanau Sands Casino - www.casino2win.com
Little River Casino - www.littlerivercasinos.com
MGM Grand Detroit - detroit.mgmgrand.com
Motor City Casino - www.motorcitycasino.com
Northville Downs - www.northvilledowns.com
Ojibwa Casino & Resort I - www.ojibwacasino.com
Ojibwa Casino & Resort II - www.ojibwacasino.com
Saginaw Harness Raceway -
www.saginawraceway.com
Soaring Eagle Casino & Resort -
www.soaringeaglecasino.com
Turtle Creek Casino - www.casino2win.com
Victories Casino - www.victories-casino.com

MINNESOTA

Black Bear Casino - www.blackbearcasinohotel.com
Canterbury Park - www.canterburypark.com
Fond-du-Luth Casino - www.fondduluthcasino.com
Fortune Bay Resort Casino - www.fortunebay.com
Grand Casino Hinckley - www.grandcasinosmn.com
Grand Casino Mille Lacs - www.grandcasinosmn.com
Grand Portage Lodge & Casino - www.grand-
portagemn.com
Jackpot Junction Casino Hotel - www.jackpotjunc-
tion.com
Mystic Lake Casino Hotel - www.mysticlake.com
Northern Lights Casino -
www.northernlightcasino.com
Palace Bingo & Casino - www.palacecasinohotel.com
Seven Clans Red Lake - www.redlakegaming.com

Seven Clans Thief River Falls -
www.redlakegaming.com
Seven Clans Warroad Casino -
www.redlakegaming.com
Shooting Star Casino - www.starcasino.com
Treasure Island Casino -
www.treasureislandcasino.com

MISSISSIPPI

Ameristar Casino Hotel Vicksburg - www.ameristar-
casinos.com/corporate/ vbfacts/
Bally's Casino Tunica - www.ballysms.com
Beau Rivage Resort & Casino - www.beaurivage.com
Boomtown Casino Biloxi - www.boomtownbiloxi.com
Casino Magic Bay St. Louis -
www.casinomagic.com/bay/
Casino Magic Biloxi -
www.casinomagic.com/biloxi/index.htm
Copa Casino - thecopacasino.com
Fitzgeralds Casino Tunica -
www.fitzgeraldstunica.com
Gold Strike Casino Resort - www.goldstrikemississip-
pi.com
Grand Casino Biloxi - www.grandbiloxi.com
Grand Casino Gulfport - www.grandgulfport.com
Grand Casino Tunica - www.grandtunica.com
Harrah's Tunica -
www.harrahs.com/our_casinos/tun/index.html
Harrah's Vicksburg -
www.harrahs.com/our_casinos/vic/index.html
Hollywood Casino-Tunica -
www.hollywoodtunica.com
Horseshoe Casino Tunica - www.horseshoe.com
Imperial Palace Biloxi - www.ipbiloxi.com
Isle of Capri Biloxi -
www.isleofcapricasino.com/Biloxi/
Isle of Capri Lula - www.isleofcapricasino.com/Lula/
Isle of Capri Natchez -
www.isleofcapricasino.com/Natchez/
Isle of Capri Tunica -
www.isleofcapricasino.com/Tunica/
Isle of Capri Vicksburg -
www.isleofcapricasino.com/Vicksburg
Palace Casino Resort - www.palacecasinoresort.com
President Casino Broadwater Resort -
www.presidentbroadwater.com
Rainbow Hotel Casino - www.rainbowcasino.com
Sam's Town Tunica - www.samstowntunica.com
Silver Star Hotel & Casino -
www.silverstarresort.com
Treasure Bay Casino Resort - www.treasurebay.com

MISSOURI

Ameristar Casino Hotel Kansas City - www.ameristarcasinos.com/corporate/ kcfacts/

Ameristar Casino St. Charles - www.ameristarcasinos.com/corporate/scfacts

Argosy Casino Kansas City - www.argosycasinos.com/property/kansas_city

Casino Aztar-Caruthersville - www.aztarcasino.com

Harrah's North Kansas City - www.harrahs.com/our_casinos/nkc/ location_home.html

Harrah's St. Louis - www.harrahs.com/our_casinos/stl/index.html

Isle of Capri Boonville - www.isleofcapricasino.com/Boonville/

Isle of Capri Kansas City - www.isleofcapricasino.com/Kansas_City/

President Casino - ww.presidentcasino.com

St. Jo Frontier Casino - www.stjocasino.com

MONTANA

Gran Tree Inn - www.bestwestern.com/grantreeinn

Fonner Park - www.fonnerpark.com

NEBRASKA

Columbus Racetrack - www.agpark.com

Rosebud Casino - www.rosebudcasino.com

NEVADA

Aladdin Resort - www.aladdincasino.com

Alamo Travel Center - www.thealamo.com

Arizona Charlie's - www.arizonacharlies.com/west

Arizona Charlie's East - www.arizonacharlies.com/east

Atlantis Casino Resort - www.atlantiscasino.com

Avi Resort and Casino - www.avicasino.com

Baldini's Sports Casino - www.baldinissportscasino.com

Bally's Las Vegas - www.ballyslv.com

Barcelona Hotel and Casino - www.barcelonalasvegas.com

Bellagio - www.bellagio.com

Best Western Mardi Gras Inn - www.bestwestern.com

Binion's Horseshoe - www.binions.com

Boomtown Hotel Casino - www.boomtowncasinos.com

Bordertown Casino - www.statelinecasinos.com

Boulder Station Casino - www.boulderstation.com

Buffalo Bill's Resort & Casino - www.primadonna.com

Burro Inn - www.burroinn.com

Cactus Petes Resort Casino - www.ameristarcasinos.com/corporate/cpfacts

Caesars Palace - www.caesars.com

Caesars Tahoe - www.caesars.com/tahoe

Cal-Neva Resort - www.calnevaresort.com

California Hotel Casino - www.thecal.com

Carson City Nugget - www.ccmotel.com

Carson Station Hotel and Casino - www.carsonstation.com

CasaBlanca Resort - www.casablancaresort.com

Casino Royale & Hotel - www.casinoroyalehotel.com

Castaways Hotel Casino - www.showboat-lv.com

Circus Circus - www.circuscircus.com

Circus Circus Reno - www.circusreno.com

Club Cal-Neva Casino - www.clubcalneva.com

Colorado Belle Hotel & Casino - www.colorado-belle.com

Commercial Casino - www.fh-inc.com

Days Inn Town Hall Casino - www.daysinntownhall.com

Edgewater Hotel & Casino - www.edgewater-casino.com

Eldorado Casino - www.eldoradocasino.com

Eldorado Casino Reno - www.eldoradoreno.com

Eureka Casino Hotel - www.eurekamesquite.com

Excalibur Hotel and Casino - www.excaliburlasvegas.com

Fernley Truck Inn Casino - www.truckinn.com

Fitzgeralds Casino Las Vegas - www.fitzgeralds.com

Fitzgeralds Casino Reno - www.fitzgeralds.com

Flamingo Las Vegas - www.flamingolasvegas.com

Flamingo Laughlin - www.laughlinflamingo.com

Fremont Hotel & Casino - www.fremontcasino.com

Gold Spike Hotel and Casino - www.goldspikehotelcasino.com

Gold Strike Hotel - www.nevadalanding.com

Golden Gate Hotel - www.goldengatecasino.net

Golden Nugget Hotel - www.goldennugget.com

Golden Nugget Laughlin - www.gnlaughlin.com

Golden Palm Casino - www.hojo.com/lasvegas01140

Green Valley Ranch Resort - www.greenvalleyranchresort.com

Hacienda Hotel & Casino - www.haciendaonline.com

Hard Rock Hotel Casino - www.hardrockhotel.com

Harrah's Lake Tahoe - www.harrahs.com/our_casinos/tah/index.html

Harrah's Las Vegas - www.harrahs.com/our_casinos/las/index.html

Harrah's Laughlin - www.harrahs.com/our_casinos/lau/index.html

Harrah's Reno - www.harrahs.com/our_casinos/ren/location_home.html

Harveys Lake Tahoe - www.harrahs.com/our_casinos/hlt/index.html

Holy Cow! Casino, Café, Brewery - www.holycowbrewery.com

Horizon Casino Resort - www.horizoncasino.com

Horseshu Hotel and Casino - www.ameristarcasinos.com/corporate/hsfacts

Hotel Nevada and Gambling Hall - www.hotelnevada.com

Hotel San Remo Casino & Resort - www.sanremolasvegas.com

Hyatt Regency Lake Las Vegas - www.lakelasvegas.hyatt.com

Imperial Palace - www.imperialpalace.com

Jailhouse Motel Casino - www.elyjailhouse.com

Jerry's Nugget - www.jerrysnugget.com

John Ascuaga's Nugget Casino Resort - www.janugget.com

JW Marriott - www.gowestmarriott.com/lasvegas

Key Largo Casino - www.keylargocasino.com

Lady Luck Casino Hotel - www.ladyluck.com

Lakeside Inn and Casino - www.lakesideinn.com

Las Vegas Club Casino Hotel - www.playatlvc.com

Las Vegas Hilton - www.lv-hilton.com

Luxor Las Vegas - www.luxor.com

Mahoney's Silver Nugget - www.mahoneyscasino.com

Main Street Station - www.mainstreetcasino.com

Mandalay Bay Resort & Casino - www.mandalay-bay.com

MGM Grand - www.mgmgrand.com

Mirage - www.mirage.com

Model T Casino - www.modelt.com

Monte Carlo Resort & Casino - www.monte-carlo.com

Nevada Landing - www.nevadalanding.com

Nevada Palace Hotel and Casino - www.nvpalace.com

New York New York Hotel & Casino - www.nynyhotelcasino.com

Oasis Resort Casino - www.oasisresort.com

Owl Club Bar and Restaurant - www.eurekaowlclub.com

Palace Station - www.palacestation.com

Palms Resort Casino - www.palms.com

Paris Las Vegas - www.parislasvegas.com

Peppermill Reno - www.peppermillreno.com

Peppermill Wendover - www.peppermillwendover.com

Pinion Plaza - www.pinonplaza.com

Pioneer Hotel & Gambling Hall - www.pioneerlaughlin.com

Plaza Hotel and Casino - www.plazahotelcasino.com

Primm Valley Resort and Casino - www.primmvalleyresorts.com

Railroad Pass Hotel & Casino - www.railroadpass.com

Ramada Express Hotel Casino - www.ramadaexpress.com

Red Garter Hotel & Casino - www.fh-inc.com/RedGarter/

Red Lion Casino - www.redlioncasino.com

Reno Hilton - www.renohilton.com

Rio All-Suite Hotel and Casino - www.harrahs.com/our_casinos/rlv/location_home.html

River Palms Resort - www.rvrpalm.com

Riverside Resort - www.riversideresort.com

Riviera Hotel Casino - www.theriviera.com

Saddle West Hotel, Casino and RV Resort - www.saddlewest.com

Sahara Hotel and Casino - www.saharavegas.com

Sam's Town Hotel & Gambling Hall - www.samstownlv.com

Santa Fe Station - www.stationsantafe.com

Si Redd's Oasis Resort - www.playandstay.com

Siena Spa Casino - www.sienareno.com

Silver Club - www.silverclub.com

Silver Legacy Resort - www.silverlegacyreno.com

Silverton Hotel, Casino, RV Park - www.silvertoncasino.com

Stagecoach Hotel & Casino - www.stagecoachhotel.com

Stardust Resort & Casino - www.stardustlv.com

Stockman's Casino - www.nvohwy.com/h/holinexp.htm

Stockmen's Hotel and Casino - www.fh-inc.com

Stratosphere Casino Hotel & Tower - www.stratospherehotel.com

Sundowner Hotel Casino - www.sundownercasino.com

Sunset Station - www.sunsetstation.com

Tahoe Biltmore Lodge and Casino - www.tahoebiltmore.com

Texas Station - www.texasstation.com

Topaz Lodge and Casino - www.enterit.com/topaz3338

Treasure Island at the Mirage - www.treasureisland.com

Tropicana Resort & Casino - www.tropicanalv.com

Tuscany Hotel Casino - www.tuscanylasvegas.com

Venetian Resort-Hotel-Casino - www.venetian.com

Westward Ho Casino - www.westwardho.com

Whiskey Pete's Hotel Casino - www.primadonna.com

Winners Casino - www.winnerscasino.com

NEW YORK

Akwesasne Mohawk Casino - www.mohawkcasino.com
Belmont Park - www.nyra.com/belmont
Buffalo Raceway - www.buffaloraceway.com
Finger Lakes Race Track - www.fingerlakesrace-track.com
Monticello Raceway - www.monticelloraceway.com
Saratoga - www.nyra.com/saratoga/
Turning Stone Casino - www.turning-stone.com
Vernon Downs - www.vernondowns.com

NORTH CAROLINA

Harrah's Cherokee Casino - www.harrahs.com/our_casinos/che/index.html

NORTH DAKOTA

Dakota Magic Casino - www.dakotamagic.com
Four Bears Casino - www.4bearscasino.com
Prairie Knights Casino & Resort - www.prairieknights.com
Sky Dancer Hotel & Casino - www.skydancercasino.com
Spirit Lake Casino & Resort - www.spiritlakecasino.com

OHIO

Lebanon Raceway - www.thelebanonraceway.com
Northfield Park - www.northfieldpark.com
River Downs - www.riverdowns.com
Scioto Downs - www.sciotodowns.com
Thistledown - www.thistledown.com

OKLAHOMA

Blue Ribbon Downs - www.blueribbondowns.net
Cherokee Casino - www.cherokeecasino.com
Fair Meadows at Tulsa - www.fairmeadows.com
Lucky Star Casino - luckystarcasino.org
Remington Park - www.remingtonpark.com
Will Rogers Downs - www.willrogersdowns.com

NEW HAMPSHIRE

Hinsdale Greyhound - www.hinsdalegreyhound.com
Rockingham Park - www.rockinghampark.com

Seabrook Greyhound Park - www.seabrookgreyhoundpark.com

NEW JERSEY

Atlantic City Hilton Casino Resort - www.hiltonac.com
Bally's Atlantic City - www.ballysac.com
Caesars Atlantic City - www.caesarsac.com
Claridge Casino Hotel - www.claridge.com
Freehold Raceway - www.freeholdraceway.com
Harrah's Atlantic City - www.harrahs.com/our_casinos/atl/index.html
Meadowlands Racetrack - www.thebigm.com
Monmouth Park - www.monmouthpark.com
Resorts Atlantic City - www.resortsac.com
Sands Casino Hotel - www.acsands.com
Showboat Atlantic City - www.harrahs.com/our_casinos/sac/location_home.html
Tropicana Casino and Resort-Atlantic City - www.tropicana.net
Trump Marina Hotel Casino - www.trumpmarina.com
Trump Plaza - www.trumpplaza.com
Trump Taj Mahal - www.trumptaj.com

NEW MEXICO

Camel Rock Casino - www.camelrockcasino.com
Cities of Gold Casino - www.citiesofgold.com
Dancing Eagle Casino - dancingeaglecasino.com
Downs at Albuquerque - www.abqdowns.com
Ohkay Casino Resort - www.ohkay.com
Ruidoso Downs - www.btkcasino.com
San Felipe's Casino - www.sanfelipecasino.com
Sandia Casino - www.sandiacasino.com
Santa Ana Star - www.santaanastar.com
Sky City Casino - www.skycitycasino.com
Sunland Park & Slots - www.sunland-park.com
SunRay Park and Casino - www.sunraygaming.com
Taos Mountain Casino - www.taosmountaincasino.com

OREGON

Chinook Winds Casino - www.chinookwindscasino.com
Indian Head Casino - www.kah-nee-taresort.com
Kla-Mo-Ya Casino - www.klamoya.com
Multnomah Greyhound Park - www.ez2winmgp.com
Seven Feathers Hotel & Casino Resort - 7feathers.com

Spirit Mountain Casino - www.spiritmountain.com
The Mill Casino - www.themillcasino.com
Wildhorse Resort and Casino - www.wildhorseresort.com

PENNSYLVANIA
Penn National Race Course - www.pennnational.com
Philadelphia Park Turf Club - www.philadelphiapark.com
Pocono Downs - www.poconodowns.com
The Meadows - www.latm.com/meadows

RHODE ISLAND
Lincoln Park - www.lincolnparkri.com
Newport Grand Jai-Alai - www.newportgrand.com

SOUTH DAKOTA
Best Western Hickok House - www.bestwestern.com
Bullock Hotel - www.heartofdeadwood.com/Bullock/
Dakota Connection - www.dakotaconnection.net
Dakota Sioux Casino - www.dakotasioux.com
Deadwood Dick's Saloon - www.deadwooddicks.com
Deadwood Gulch Resort - www.deadwoodgulch.com
First Gold Hotel & Gaming - www.firstgold.com
Four Aces Casino/Hampton Inn - www.fouracescasino.org
Gold Dust Gaming - www.golddustgaming.com
Grand River Casino - www.grandrivercasino.com
Gulches of Fun - www.gulchesoffun.com
McKenna's Gold Casino - www.deadwood.com/attractions/McKennas.html
Midnight Star - www.themidnightstar.com
Mineral Palace Hotel - www.mineralpalace.com
Miss Kitty's - www.heartofdeadwood.com/MissKittys/
Old Style Saloon # 10 - www.saloon10.com
Royal River Casino - www.royalrivercasino.com
Silverado Gaming Establishment & Restaurant - www.silveradocasino.com
Super 8 Lodge - www.deadwoodSuper8.com
Wild West Winners Casino - www.heartofdeadwood.com/WildWest/

TEXAS
Corpus Christi Greyhound Race Track - www.corpuschristidogs.com
Fantasea Casino Cruises - www.fantaseacasino.com
Gulf Greyhound Park - www.gulfgreyhound.com
Kickapoo Lucky Eagle - www.kickapooluckyeaglecasino.com

Lone Star Park - www.lonestarpark.com
Manor Downs - www.manordowns.com
Retama Park - www.retamapark.com
Sam Houston Race Park - www.shrp.com
Texas Treasure Casino Cruise - Corpus Christi - www.txtreasure.com
Texas Treasure Casino Cruise - Freeport - www.txtreasure.com

VIRGINIA
Colonial Downs Racetrack - www.colonialdowns.com

WASHINGTON
7 Cedars Casino - www.7cedarscasino.com
Big Al's Casino - wa-bigalscasino.com
Clearwater Casino - www.clearwatercasino.com
Coulee Dam Casino - colvillecasinos.com
Emerald Downs - www.emdowns.com
Little Creek Casino - www.little-creek.com
Lucky Eagle Casino - www.luckyeagle.com
Mill Bay Casino - www.colvillecasinos.com
Muckleshoot Casino - www.muckleshootcasino.com
Northern Quest Casino - www.northernquest.net
Okanogan Bingo-Casino - www.colvillecasinos.com
Quinalt Beach Resort & Casino - www.quinaultbchresort.com
Skagit Valley Casino Resort - www.svcasinoresort.com
Swinomish Casino and Bingo - www.swinomishcasino.com
Tulalip Casino - www.tulalipcasino.com
Wizards Casino - www.wizards-casino.com

WEST VIRGINIA
Charles Town Races & Slots - www.ctownraces.com
Mountaineer Park - www.mtrgaming.com/homepage.html
Mountaineer Race Track and Gaming Resort - www.mtrgaming.com/ homepage.html
Wheeling Downs - www.wheelingdowns.com

WISCONSIN
Bad River Casino - www.badriver.com
Dairyland Greyhound Park - www.dairylandgreyhoundpark.com

Geneva Lakes Greyhound Track - www.genevagreyhounds.com

Ho-Chunk Casino & Bingo - www.ho-chunk.com

Hole in the Wall Casino - www.wisconsingaming.com

Lake of the Torches Casino-Bingo - www.lakeofthetorches.com

LCO Casino Lodge - www.lcocasino.com

Little Turtle Hertel Express & Casino - www.stcroixcasino.com/hertle

Menominee Casino Bingo Hotel - www.menomineecasinoresort.com

Mohican North Star Casino & Bingo - www.mohican.com/casino

Oneida Bingo & Casino - www.oneidabingoandcasino.net

Potawatomi Bingo - Northern Lights Casino- www.cartercasino.com

Potawatomi Bingo Casino - www.paysbig.com/potawatomi.html

Rainbow Casino and Bingo - www.rbcwin.com

St. Croix Casino & Hotel - www.stcroixcasino.com

WYOMING

Wyoming Downs - www.wyomingdowns.com

Gambling Books

Quick, name a gambling topic. Chances are, for whatever topic came to mind, there has been a book written about it – or a dozen, or two dozen books.

Nearly everyone who has had an unbeatable formula to break the bank at baccarat, slots, craps or roulette has set that valuable information down on paper and published it.

A vast array of books are available, from dozen-page paperbacks with tables on blackjack formulas to coffee table hardcovers with slick photos of race horses. Prices range from a dollar or two up to $100.

Well-known authors who have written several books on virtually every casino game include Frank Scoblete, John Patrick, Stanford Wong, Henry Tamburin, and Mike Caro.

And, for beginners, there are books for the "clueless," for "dummies," for "idiots," and for "absolute beginners."

Horse racing and dog racing have their own libraries of books that focus on the science of handicapping. And there's an extensive list of books on beating the sports odds.

Travelers also benefit from a long list of books dealing with Las Vegas, Atlantic City, and other popular destinations.

Books in print, and the remaining copies of those out of print, are readily available at a number of stores and online sources. Gambler's Book Shop in Las Vegas, which supplied the following extensive library to us, has one of the largest collections. It can be reached at (800) 522-1777 or (800) 634-6243, or by e-mail at info@gamblersbook.com. Prices are subject to change.

Here is a sampling of the books available on gambling topics:

Baccarat books

72 Days at the Baccarat Table, by Erick St. Germain, 300 pages, 5x8 plastic spiralbound. 1995. $24.95

Baccarat Battle Book, by Frank Scoblete, 214 pages, paperbound, 1999. $12.95

Baccarat Fair and Foul, by Professor Hoffman, 80 pages,

paperbound, originally published in 1891. $2.95

Baccarat for the Clueless, by John May, 144 pages, paperbound, 1998. $12

Baccarat Made Simple, by David Vernon, 24 pages, 8 x 11 plastic paperbound, 1994. $9.95

Baccarat: Playing to Win, by Tony Korfman, 48 pages, paperbound. $3.50

Baccarat System Tester, by Baccarat International, 248 pages, in 8 x 11 spiralbound, 1992. $29.95

The Basics of Winning Baccarat, by Avery Cardoza, 59 pages, paperbound, 1992. $4.95

The Effects of Marked Cards in a Baccarat Game, by George Joseph, 45 pages, paperbound, 1986. $25

Facts of Baccarat, by Walter I. Nolan, 48 pages, paperbound, 1976. $1.50

How to Play and Win at Casino Baccarat, by Ray Kane, 32 pages, paperbound, 1997. $4.95

Lyle Stuart on Baccarat, by Lyle Stuart, 272 pages, paperbound, revised in 1997. $20

Power Baccarat 2, by Byron F. Hebert, 241 pages, paperbound, 2000. $19.95

Q's Baccarat Winning Strategies: Vol. II, by John Qui, (No Volume I printed),122 pages, paperbound, 1997. $26.99

So You Wanna Be a Gambler- Baccarat, by John Patrick, 248 pages, paperbound, 1985. $14.95

Winning at Baccarat, by Mike McGuire, 111 pages, paperbound, 1994. $9.95

Winning Baccarat Strategies, by Henry Tamburin and Dick Rahm, 96 pages, paperbound, 1983. $19.95

Blackjack Books

All About Blackjack, by John Gollehon, 57 pages, paperbound, 1993. $4.99

Archer Method of Winning at 21, by John Archer, 204 pages, paperbound, 1973. $10.

Armada Strategies for Spanish 21, by Frank Scoblete, $12.95

Basic Blackjack, by Stanford Wong, 5 x 8 paperbound, 224 pages, 1995 $14.95

The Basics of Winning Blackjack, by J. Edward Allen, 57 pages, paperbound, 1992. $4.95

Beat the Dealer (Blackjack), New Fortune Series, 16 pages, paperbound, 1970. $1

Beat the 1-Deck Game, by Arnold Snyder, 64 pages, paperbound, 1987. $10

Beat the 2-Deck Game, by Arnold Snyder, 64 pages, paperbound, 1987. $10

Beat the 4-Deck Game, by Arnold Snyder, 64 pages, paperbound, 1987. $10

Beat the 6-Deck Game, by Arnold Snyder, 64 pages, paperbound, 1987. $10

Beat the 8-Deck Game, by Arnold Snyder, 64 pages, paperbound, 1987. $10

Beat the Dealer, by Edward O. Thorp, Ph.D., 220 pages, paperbound, 1966. $11

Best Blackjack, by Frank Scoblete, 283 pages, paperbound, 1996. $14.95

Beyond Counting, by James Grosjean, 223 pages, paperbound, 2000. $39.95

Blackbelt in Blackjack (Playing 21 as a Martial Art), by Arnold Snyder, 124 pages, paperbound, 1997. $19.95

Blackjack and the Law, by Nelson Rose and Robert A. Loeb, 245 pages, paperbound, 1998. $24.95

Blackjack Attack, by Don Schlesinger, 345 pages, indexed, 2000. $19.95

Blackjack Autumn, by Barry Meadow, 351 pages, hardbound, 1999. $27.95. Paperbound, $14.95

Blackjack, Blackjack, Blackjack, by Robert Neuzil, 83 pages, paperbound, 1993. $9.95

Blackjack Bluebook, by Fred Renzey, 180 pages, paperbound, 1996. $14

Blackjack Blueprint: How to Operate a Blackjack Team, by Rick "Night Train" Blaine, 94 pages, 8x11 format, paperbound, 2000. $39.95

Blackjack Decision Tables, by Tempe Publishers, 32 pages, paperbound, 1984. $6.95

Blackjack Essays, by Mason Malmuth, 238 pages, paperbound, 1996. $19.95

Blackjack for the Clueless, by Walter Thomason, originally titled *The Ultimate Blackjack Book,* now revised.156 pages, paperbound, 1998. $12

Blackjack for Winners, by Scott Frank, 136 pages, paperbound, 1993. $11.95

Blackjack: How to Play Like an Expert, by R.W. Frawley, 8 x11 format, 32 pages, paperbound, 1993. $4.95

Blackjack in the Zone, by Rick "Night Train" Blaine, 54 pages, 8x11 format, paperbound, 2000. $19.95

Blackjack for Blood, by Bryce Carlson, 247 pages, paperbound, 1994. Revised, 2000. $19.95

Blackjack Magic, by Richard G. Sievers, 129 pages 8x11 spiralbound format. 1996. $22.50

Blackjack – Playing to Win, by Tony Korfman, 49 pages, paperbound, 1985. $3.50

Blackjack Reality, by David Morse, 112 pages, spiralbound, 1998. $34.95

Blackjack Secrets, by Stanford Wong, indexed, 256 pages, paperbound, 1993. $14.95

Blackjack (Take the Money & Run), by Henry Tamburin, indexed, 148 pages, paperbound, 1994. $11.95

Blackjack Strategy, by Michael Benson, 176 pages, paperbound, 2001. $11.95

Blackjack the Smart Way, by Richard Harvey, 288 pages, paperbound, 2000. $19.95

Blackjack Tracker, by Bob Hubby, 200 pages, spiralbound, 2000. $29.95

Blackjack Wisdom, by Arnold Snyder, 204 pages, paperbound, 1997. $19.95

Blackjack Your Way to Riches, by Richard Albert Canfield, 213 pages, paperbound, 1995. $14.95

Blackjack's Winning Formula, by Jerry Patterson, 244 pages, paperbound, 1982. $9.95

Blackjack X-Count 2000, by J.C. Moore, 53 pages, spiralbound, 2000. $14.95

Burning the Tables in Las Vegas, by Ian Andersen, 354 pages, hardbound, 1999. $27.95

Card Counting for the Casino Executive, by Bill Zender, 138 pages, in 8x11 plastic spiralbound, 1990. $20

Casino Blackjack: Strategy and Game Plan, by Ron Modica, 73 pages, Spiralbound. 1998. $14.95

Casino Tournament Strategy, by Stanford Wong, 256 pages, paperbound, 1997. $29.95

Cheating at Blackjack Squared, by Dustin D. Marks, indexed, 202 pages, paperbound, 1996. $24.95

Complete Book of Blackjack, by T.J. Reynolds, 204 pages, paperbound, 1998. $14.95

The DHM Blackjack System, by D.H. Mitchell, 30 pages, paperbound, 1995. $14.95

Expert Strategy for Spanish Blackjack, by Lenny Frome, 10 pages, paperbound, 1996. $4.95

Fundamentals of 21, by Mason Malmuth and Lynne Loomis, 66 pages, paperbound, 1993. $3.95

Fundamentals of Blackjack, by Carlson Chambliss & Tom Roginski, indexed, 232 pages paperbound, 1990. $12.95

Gambling Times Guide to Blackjack, by Stanley Roberts, indexed, 255 pages, paperbound, 1984. $12.95

Get the Edge Blackjack, by John May, 167 pages, indexed, paperbound, 2000. $13.95

Hi-Opt II System for Winning at Casino Blackjack, by Julian Braun and Lance Humble, 20 pages, 8x11, stapled, 1976 originally, but revised six times, the latest in 1997. $39.95

Hit and Run!, How to Beat Blackjack as a Way of Life, by Arnold Bruce Levy, $14.95

How to Detect Casino Cheating at Blackjack, by Bill Zender, 164 pages, paperbound, 1999. $19.95

Honest to Goodness Blackjack, by G. D. Sheneman, 79 pages, 5x8 spiralbound, 1996. $10

John Auston's World's Greatest Blackjack Simulation Charts, Red Seven Count Simulation, The K-O Count, The Zen Count, Omega II Count, each $14.95

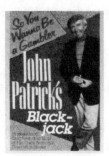

John Patrick's Blackjack, by John Patrick, 208 pages, paperbound, 1991. $14.95

Julian's No-Nonsense Guide to Winning Blackjack, by John F. Julian, 112 pages, paperbound, 1992. $16.95

Ken Uston on Blackjack (Secrets of Winning at 21' by the $5,000,000 Man), by Ken Uston, 212 pages, paperbound, 1986. $12.95

Knock-Out Blackjack, by Olaf Vancura & Ken Fuchs, Revised 1998 with additional chapters, paperbound, 180 pages. $17.95

Las Vegas Blackjack Diary, by Stuart Perry, 214 pages, paperbound, 1997. $19.95

Low Stakes Blackjack, by John Sharpe, 87 pages, paperbound, 1994. $9.95

Millionaire Blackjack, by Dean A. Johnston, 345 pages, indexed, paperbound, 2001. $24.95

Million Dollar Blackjack, by Ken Uston, 332 pages, paperbound, 1981. $18.95

The Morons of Blackjack, by King Scobe, 115 pages, paperbound, 1992. $16.95

Multi-Level Betting Only Count, by Fred Lite, 30 pages, paperbound, 1988. $10

The Over-Under Report, by Arnold Snyder, 18 pages, paperbound, 1989. $29

Playing Blackjack as a Business, by Lawrence Revere, 177 pages, paperbound, 1969. $16.95

Power Blackjack, by Bryan Thibodeaux, 80 pages, paperbound, 1991. $10

Professional Blackjack, by Stanford Wong, includes 8-page glossary; four pages of references; a 3-page index. 348 pages, paperbound, 1994. $19.95

Progression Blackjack, by Donald Dahl, 153 pages, paperbound, 1995. $12.95

Read the Dealer, by Steve Forte, 82 pages, paperbound, 1986. $40

Sklansky Talks Blackjack, by David Sklansky, 140 pages, paperbound, 1999. $19.95

The Silver Fox Blackjack System, by Ralph Stricker, 79 pages, in 8 x 11, plastic spiralbound. Revised in 1997. $29.95

So You Wanna Be a Gambler! Card Counting, by John Patrick, 370 pages, paperbound, 1986. $19.95

The Theory of Blackjack (6th Ed.-1998), by Peter Griffin, indexed, 262 pages, paperbound, $12.95

Twenty-First Century Blackjack, by Walter Thomason, 186 pages, paperbound, 1999. $12.95

Two Books on Blackjack, by Ken Uston, 1979, $7.95

Winning at Blackjack, by NFS, 47 pages, paperbound, 1991. $1

Winning Blackjack for the Non-Counter, by Avery Cardoza, 55 pages, paperbound, 1992. $12.95

Winning Blackjack for the Serious Player, by Edwin Silberstang, 183 pages, paperbound, 1993. $12.95

World's Greatest Blackjack Book, by Lance Humble and Carl Cooper, 432 pages, paperbound, 1980. $11.95

Caribbean Stud Poker Books

Basics of Winning Caribbean Stud Power and Let It Ride, by J. Edward Allen, 56 pages, paperbound, 1996. $4.95

Bold Card Play, by Frank Scoblete, indexed, 151 pages, paperbound. $12.95

Everything You Always Wanted to Know About Caribbean Stud Poker, by Woody Dorsey, 8 pages, paperbound, 1994. $2.95

Expert Strategy for Caribbean Stud Poker, by Ira and Elliot Fromme, 13 pages, paperbound. Revised, 1996. $5.95

Winning Caribbean Stud Poker and Let It Ride, by Avery Cardoza, $12.95

Casino Books

101 Casino Gambling Tips, by John Marchel, 158 pages, paperbound. $14.95

The 101 Most Asked Questions About Las Vegas and Casino Gambling, by George Joseph, 186 pages, paperbound, 2000. $14.95

109 Ways to Beat the Casino, by Walter Thomason, 133 pages, paperbound, 2000. $13.95

Absolute Beginner's Guide to Gambling, by Robert J. Hutchinson, indexed, 316 pages, paperbound, 1996. $6.99

Atlantic City: Behind the Tables, by John Alcamo, 233 pages, paperbound, 1991. $5.95

American Casino Guide, by Steve Bourie, 440 pages, paperbound. $14.95

American Mensa Guide to Casino Gambling, by Andrew Brisman, paperbound, 272 pages, 1999. $17.95

Beating the Casinos at Their Own Game, by Petyer Svoboda, indexed (with glossary), 278 pages, paperbound, 2001. $19.95

Be A Winner, by Gaming Council, 64 pages, paperbound. 1994. $2.95

Beating the Casino's Big Six Wheel, by R. Carl Cohen, 34 pages, paperbound, 1987. $5.95

Beat the House, by Frederick Lembeck, 183 pages, paperbound, 1995. $12.95

Beyond Counting, by James Grosjean, 223 pages, paperbound, 2000. $39.95

The Book Casino Managers Fear the Most!, by Marvin Karlins Ph.D., 246 pages, paperbound, 1998. $7.99

Budget Gambling, by John Gollehon, 256 pages, paperbound, 1999. $14.99

Caro on Gambling, by Mike Caro, 188 pages, paperbound, 1984. $6.95

Casino Answer Book, by John Grochowski, 236 pages, paperbound, 1998. $12.95

Casino Cafeteria, by Stephen Kuriscak, 96 pages, paperbound, 1992. $20

Casino Fun Facts, by John Gollehon, 98 pages, paperbound, 2001. $5.99

Casino Gambling, by Bob Trebor, 101 pages, paperbound, 1997. $21.95

Casino Gambling: A Winner's Guide, by Jerry L. Patterson, 235 pages, paperbound, 2000. $13.95

Casino Gambling: Winning Techniques, by Jerry L. Patterson, 240 pages, paperbound, 1982. $10

Casino Gambling Behind the Tables, by John Alcamo, 234 pages, paperbound, 1997. $7.99

Casino Gambling for the Clueless, by Darwin Ortiz, previously titled *Darwin Ortiz on Casino Gambling*, 268 pages, paperbound, 1999. $14.95

Casino Gambling the Smart Way, by Andrew N.S. Glazer, 254 pages, indexed, paperbound, 1999. $14.99

Casino Games (A Golden Guide), by Bill Friedman, 160 pages, paperbound, revised 1996. $6.49

Casino Games II, by John Gollehon, 178 pages, paperbound, 1997. $6.99

Casino Games Made Easy, by Victor H. Royer, 319 pages, paperbound, 1999. $12.95

Casino Secrets, by Barney Vinson, 280 pages, paperbound, 1997. $14.95

The Complete Idiot's Guide to Gambling Like a Pro, by Susan Spector with Stanford Wong, indexed, 320 pages, paperbound, 1996. $18.95

The Confident Gambler, by John Gollehon, 177 pages, paperbound, 2000. $6.99

The Encyclopedia of Gambling, by R. Carl Sifakis, 340 pages, paperbound, 1990. $19.95

The Everything Casino Gambling Book, by George Mandos, 274 pages, paperbound, 1998. $12.95

Experts' Guide to Casino Games, Walter Thomason, editor, 249 pages, paperbound, 1997. $16.95

For Winners Only, by Peter J. Andrews, 133 pages, paperbound, 1996. $18.95

The Gambler's Bible, by M.C. Fisk, 214 pages, paperbound. 1996. $5.95

The Gambler's Guide to the World, by Jesse May, indexed, 307 pages, 2000. $17.50

The Gambler's Playbook, by Avery Cardoza, 122 pages, paperbound, 1991. $4.95

Gambling and Taxes III, by Frank Sutherland, 58 pages, paperbound, 1994. $9.95

Gambling for Dummies, by Richard Harroch, Lou Krieger and Arthur Reber, 338 pages, paperbound, 2002. $21.99

Gambling for a Living, by David Sklansky & Mason Malmuth, 250 pages, paperbound. 1997. $24.95

Gambling Times Guide to Casino Games, by Len Miller, 162 pages, paperbound, 1983. $5.95

Gambling Know-How, by Irv Sutton, 64 pages, paperbound, 1980. $2.95

Gambling Scams, by Darwin Ortiz, 262 pages, paperbound, 1984. $12.95

The Gambling Times Guide to European and Asian Games, by Syd Helprin, 223 pages, paperbound, 1986. $7.95

Gambling with the Best of Them, by Tex Sheahan, 8x11 format, 147 pages, spiralbound, 1994. $16.95

Gaming (Cruising the Casinos), by John Grochowski, 182 pages, paperbound, 1996. $11.95

Gaming Card Set, by Instructional Services, 10 plastic cards. $10.95

Gambling's Greatest Secrets Revealed, by B.J. Berry, 100 pages, paperbound, 2000. $29.95

Getting the Best of It, by David Sklansky, 248 pages, paperbound, 1992. $29.95

Guerrilla Gambling, by Frank Scoblete, illustrated, indexed, 339 pages, paperbound, 1993. $12.95

Henry Tamburin on Casino Gambling (The Best of the Rest), by Henry Tamburin, 224 pages, paperbound, 1998. $15.95

How to Gamble in a Casino, by Tom Ainsley, 224 pages, paperbound, 1979. $10

How to Win, by Mike Goodman, 302 pages, paperbound, 1963. $6.99

How to Win at Casino Gaming Tournaments, by Haven Earle Haley, 178 pages, paperbound, 1986. $8.95

How to Win at Gambling, by Avery Cardoza, 312 pages, paperbound, 1991. $12.95

I Did It!, by John Tippin with Lance Tominaga, 150 pages, paperbound, 2001. $16.95

KISS Guide to Gambling, by John Marchal. $19.95

Las Vegas Behind the Tables, by Barney Vinson, 240 pages, paperbound, 1988. $6.99

Lifestyles of a High Roller, by Phyllis Wolff, 247 pages, paperbound, 1991. $5.95

The Money Spinners, by Jacques Black, 201 pages, paperbound, 1998. $13.95

The New Gambler's Bible, by Arthur S. Reber, indexed, 384 pages, paperbound, 1996. $18

Pay the Line, by John Gollehon, 144 pages, paperbound, 1988. $5.95

Play Smart and Win, by Victor H. Royer, 272 pages, paperback, 1994. $11

Playboy's Book of Games, by Edwin Silberstang, 528 pages, paperbound, 1979. $8.95

Playboy's Guide to Casino Gambling, by Edwin Silberstang, 448 pages, hardbound, 1980. $15.95

The Professional Gambler's Handbook, by Weasel Murphy, 143 pages, paperbound. 1997. $18

The Quotable Gambler, by Paul Lyons, 326 pages, hardbound, 1999. $20

Reference Guide to Casino Gambling, by Henry Tamburin, indexed, 153 pages, paperbound, 1996. $11.95

Scarne's New Complete Guide to Gambling, by John Scarne, 872 pages, paperbound. 1961. $20

Secrets of the New Casino Games, by Marten Jensen, 144 pages, paperbound, 2000. $14.95

Silberstang's Encyclopedia of Games & Gambling, by Edwin Silberstang, indexed, 541 pages, paperbound, 1996. $17.95

Smart Casino Gambling (2nd edition), by Olaf Vancura, Ph.D., 384 pages, paperbound, 1999. $24.95

Smart Casino Play, by Edwin Silberstang, 64 pages, paperbound, 1976. $4.95

Taking the Edge, by R. Martin Allen, 64 pages, paperbound, 1981. $2.95

The Tax Guide for Gamblers (4th ed.), by Roger Roche and Yolanda Smulik Roche, 102 pages, paperbound, 1998. $29.95

The Ten Best Casino Bets, by R. Henry Tamburin, 82 pages, paperbound, 1983. $3.95

Thrifty Gambling, by John G. Brokopp, 153 pages, paperbound. $13.95

The Unofficial Guide to Casino Gambling, by Basil Nestor, $15.95

You Can Bet on It! Vol. 1: Casino Games, by Larry Grossman, 200 pages, paperbound, 1984. $14.95

What Casinos Don't Want You to Know, by John Gollehon, 180 pages, paperbound, 1999. $6.99

Winner Take All, by John Gollehon, 213 pages, paperbound, 1994. $6.99

Winner's Guide to Casino Gambling, by Edwin Silberstang, 363 pages, paperbound, revised 1997. $14.95

Winner's Guide to Casino Gambling, by Roger Gros, 256 pages paperbound, illustrated, 2000. $12.95

Winning at Casino Gambling, by Lyle Stuart, 320 pages, paperbound, 1995. $18

Winning at Casino Gaming, by Rouge et Noir, 150 pages, spiralbound 8x11 format, 2000. $35

Winning Casino Play, by Avery Cardoza, 150 pages, paperbound, 1994. $7.95

Winning Tips for Casino Games, by John Grochowski, 144 pages, paperbound, 1995. $4.99

Yes, You Can Win, by Bob Stupak, 149 pages, illustrated, paperbound, 1992. $5.95

CRAPS BOOKS

7 Heavy Dice Strategy, by Leonard J. Strong, 69 pages, paperbound, 1993. $19.95

50 Years at the Crap Table, by Malcolm Jay, 131 pages, paperbound. $12

72 Hours at the Crap Table, by B. Mickelson, 126 pages, paperbound. 1978. $6.95

All About Craps, by John Gollehon, 57 pages, paperbound,1998. $4.99

The Basics of Winning Craps, by J. Edward Allen, 56 pages, paperbound.1972. $4.95

Beat the Craps Out of the Casinos, by Frank Scoblete, 152 pages, paperbound, 1991. $9.95

The Captain's Craps Revolution!, by Frank Scoblete, 153 pages, paperbound, 1995. $21.95

Casino Craps: Strategies for Reducing the Odds Against You, by Robert R. Roto, 126 pages, paperbound, 1999. $12

Casino Craps for the Winner (revised), by Avery Cardoza, 120 pages, paperbound, 1998. $9.95

Casino Craps is a Vicious $$ Devouring Game, by Zeke Feinberg, 78 pages, paperbound. 1992. $9.95

Collecting Casino Dice, by George Martin, 108 pages, paperbound, 1986. $6.95

Commando Craps and Blackjack, by John Gollehon, 178 pages, paperbound, 1997. $10.99

Conquering Casino Craps, by John Gollehon, 178 pages, paperbound, 1997. $6.99

Craps Answer Book, by John Grochowski, 126 pages, paperbound, 2001. $13.95

Craps - A Smart Shooter's Guide, by Thomas Midgley, 200 pages, paperbound, 1980. $12.95

Craps for the Clueless, by John Patrick, 138 pages, paperbound, 1999. $12

Craps Made Easy (A Craps Handbook), by Steve Kirol, 119 pages, paperbound, 1999. $9.95

Craps: Playing for the Money, by David Medansky, 120 pages, paperbound, 2001. $19.95

Craps – Playing to Win, by Tony Korfman, 49 pages, paperbound, 1985. $3.50

Craps - Pressing Your Luck, by Robert Spira, 31 pages, paperbound, 1982. $3

Crapshooting Made Simple and Easy, by Roy "Kansas" Downs, 45 pages, 8 x 11 format, 1994. $10

Craps - Secrets of Professionals, by Pascal, 30 pages, paperbound, 1988. $14.95

Craps Strategy, by Michael Benson, 116 pages, paperbound, 2001. $14.95

Craps System Tester, by Erick St. Germain, 292 pages, 8x11 plastic spiralbound, 1994. $24.95

Craps: Take the Money and Run, by Henry Tamburin, 127 pages, paperbound, 1996. $11.95

Dealing the Game of Craps, by Stephen F. Porrino, 169 pages, spiralbound, 2001. $50

The Dice Doctor (revised), by Sam Grafstein, 146 pages, paperbound, 1990, reprinted in 2001. $19.95

Dice Illustrated, by Thomas Michaels, 187 pages, paperbound, 2001. $19.95

Dice: Squares, Tops, and Shapes, by Burton Williams, 104 pages, paperbound, 1982. $7.95

Dicertations, by C. Josef Mennec, 64 pages, paperbound, 1980. $6.95

Eleven Craps Strategies, by Tempe Publishing, 33 pages, paperbound, 1985. $5.95

Exploding the Myth About Craps, by Zeke Feinberg, 17 pages, paperbound, 1992. $5.95

Forever Craps, by Frank Scoblete, 172 pages, paperbound, 2000. $13.95

Fundamentals of Craps, by Mason Malmuth and Lynne Loomis, 70 pages, paperbound (pocket size), 1995. $3.95

Gamble to Win: Craps, by R.D. Ellison, 245 pages, paperbound, 2001. $14.95

The Gambling Times Guide to Craps, by N. B. Winkless, Jr., 138 pages, paperbound. 1981. $9.95

A Guide to Craps Lingo, by Chris Fagans and David Guzman, 78 pages, paperbound, 2000. $9.95

Hot Dice-How To Leave A Winner, by Jack Kiely, 32 pages, 8x11 format, paperbound. 1986. $4.95

How to Make Your Living Playing Craps, by Larry Edell, indexed, 112 pages, paperbound, 1996. $19.95

How to Win at Craps, by Frank Hanback, 192 pages, paperbound, 1986. $4.95

Learn How to Play Craps and Win, by Jimmy Jordan, 35 pages, paperbound. $7.95

Master Craps with Einstein (formerly Craps with Einstein), by Mickey Day, 125 pages, 8 x 11 paperbound. Newly revised for 1998. $19.95

Mastering Craps, by Tony Badillo, 192 pages, paperbound, 1996. $19.95

The New Easy Way to Win at Craps, by Bill Jones, 59 pages, paperbound, 1977. $12

Playboy's Guide to Casino Gambling: Vol. 1: Craps, by Edwin Silberstang, 199 pages, paperbound, 1980. $7.95

Play Craps and Win Big, by Glen (Sully) Sullivan, 28 pages, paperbound, 1989. $8.95

Pre-Setting Dice, by Zeke Feinberg, illustrated. 128 pages, paperbound, 1972. $20

Scarne on Dice, by John Scarne, 496 pages, paperbound, 1974. $20

So You Wanna Be a Gambler: Craps, by John Patrick, 324 pages, paperbound, 1991. $19.95

The Ultimate Dice Book, by Mike McGuire, 76 pages, 8x11 format, paperbound, 1984. $12

What You Wanted to Know About Craps, by Hugh Heritage, illustrated, 216 pages, paperbound, 1993. $5.95

Winning at Crap$, by Dr. Lloyd T. Commins, 90 pages, paperbound, 1965. $10

Winning at Craps, by Richard F. Schulte, 138 pages, paperbound, 1993. $9.95

Winning Casino Craps, by Edwin Silberstang, 141 pages, paperbound, 1965. $15

Winning Craps for the Serious Player, by J. Edward Allen, 182 pages, paperbound, 1993. $14.95

You Can Earn Each Hour $12 to $24 or More Playing Casino Craps, by Zeke Feinberg 205 pages, paperbound, 1994. $15

KENO BOOKS

Basics of Winning Keno, by J. Edward Allen, 60 pages, paperbound, 1995. $4.95

Beating Video Keno, by M.G. Davis, 40 pages, paperbound, 1997. $10

Complete Guide to Winning Keno, by David Cowles, 267 pages, paperbound, 1996. $14.95

The Facts of Keno, by Walter I. Nolan, 109 pages, paperbound, 1984. $4.95

It's a Pleasure to Win at Keno, by New Fortune Series, 24 pages, paperbound, 1970. $1

Keno and Your Calculator, by Robert Spira, 17 pages, paperbound, 1980. $2.50

Keno: The Art of Playing and Winning, by Harry Stinson, 32 pages, 8x11 format, paperbound, 1989. $4.95

Keno-Playing to Win, by Tony Korfman, 49 pages, paperbound, 1985. $3.50

Keno Winning Ways, by Wayne McClure, 217 pages, hardbound, 1979. $6.95

Lottery and Keno Winning Strategies, by Wayne McClure, 150 pages, paperbound, 1979. Revised in 1991. $14.95

Sophisticated Keno (New Fortune Series), by Computerized Systems Inc., 36 pages, paperbound, 1970. $1

LET IT RIDE BOOKS

A Basic Strategy for Let It Ride, by L.R. Brooks, 17 pages 8x11 format, stapled, 1994. $6.95

Expert Strategy for Let It Ride, by Lenny Frome, 10 pages, paperbound. Revised 1996 $4.95

Let It Ride: Optimal Strategy, by Dr. Edward Gordon, 17 pages 8x11 format, stapled. 1994. $4.95

Mastering the Game of Let It Ride, by Stanley Ko, 41 pages, paperbound, 1997. $7.95

PAI GOW BOOKS

Billy Woos's Pai-Gow Poker II (Revised), by Bill Walsh, 44 pages, paperbound, 1988. $8.95

Caro's Professional Pai Gow Poker Report, by Mike Caro, 34 pages, paperbound, 1986. $19.95

How to Play Pai-Gow Poker, by Dr. George R. Allen. $6.95

Optimal Strategy for Pai Gow Poker, by Stanford Wong, 52 pages, 8x11 format, paperbound, 1992. $14.95

Pai Gow (Chinese Dominoes), by Michael Musante, 78 pages, paperbound, 1981. $8.95

Pai Gow Poker: Understanding Procedures and Strategies, by Bill Zender, 83 pages, paperbound, 1991. $20

Pai Gow Without Tears, by Bill Zender, 80 pages, 8 x 11, paperbound, 1989. $20

PAN BOOKS

The Complete Book of Pan, by Howard Scott Warshaw, 1990. $19.95

Pan, by Murray M. Sheldon, 130 pages, paperbound, 1969. $7.50

Pan - the Gambler's Card Game, by Mac James, 109 pages, hardbound, 1979. $9.95

Pan Statistics, by Jim Mann, 11 pages, paperbound, 1997. $10

POKER BOOKS

101 Tournament Hands: Hold 'em, by D. H. Sherer, 97 pages, spiralbound, 1999. $14.95

A Friendly Game?, by Bert Morris, 106 pages, paperbound, 1997. $17.95

Archer Method: Winning at Poker, by John Archer, indexed, 158 pages, paperbound, 1978. $10

Awesome Profits, by George "Profit" Elias, 380 pages, paperbound, 1993. $29.95

Basic Records I (How Am I Doing?), by Edwin "Tony" Wuehle, 20 pages, paperbound. 1988. $2

Basics of Winning Poker, by J. Edward Allen, 64 pages, paperbound, 1992. $4.95

The Best of Cappalletti on Omaha, by Mike Cappelletti, 106 pages, 8 x 11 paperbound. 1990. $14.95

Big Book of Poker Slang, by John Vorhaus, 42 pages, paperbound, 1996. $7.95

Book of Tells: The Body Language of Poker, by Mike Caro, 50 pages of new material, new photo illustrations, 352 pages, paperbound, 2000. $24.95

Cappelletti on Omaha, by Mike Cappelletti, 69 pages, paperbound, 1990. $16.95

Card Player Digest, 7x 10 format, paperbound, 1995. $29.95

Caro's 11 Days to 7 Stud Success, by Mike Caro, 20 pages, paperbound, 1993. $19.95

Caro's 12 Days to Hold 'Em Success, by Mike Caro, 28 pages, paperbound. 1990. $19.95

Caro's Fundamental Secrets of Poker, by Mike Caro, indexed, 6 x 9 format, 150 pages, paperbound. 1996. $9.95

Caro's Guide to Doyle Brunson's Super/System, by Mike Caro, illustrated, 86 pages, stapled and plasticbound. $19.95

Caro's Professional Hold 'Em Report, by Mike Caro, 40 pages, 1988. $19.95

Caro's Professional 7-Stud Report, by Mike Caro, 32 pages, paperbound. 1989. $19.95

Complete Book of Hold 'Em Poker, by Gary Carson, 313 pages, paperbound, 2001. $14.95

Cowboys, Gamblers & Hustlers, by Byron Cowboy Wolford, 343 pages, paperbound, 1977. $19.95

Casino Poker Without Fear, by Gary Oliver, 54 pages, 5 x 8 plastic spiralbound, 1996. $8.95

Champion of Champions, by Don Jenkins, 214 pages, paperbound, 1981. $8.95

Championship Hold 'Em, by T.J. Cloutier and Tom McEvoy, 320 pages, photos & illustrations. $39.95

Championship No-Limit Pot Limit Hold 'Em, by T.J. Cloutier & Tom McEvoy, 209 pages, paperbound, 1997. $39.95

Championship Omaha Poker, by T.J. Cloutier and Tom McEvoy, $39.95

Championship Stud (7-Card Stud, Stud 8/Better, Razz), by Max Stern, Tom McEvoy, Linda Johnson, illustrated, 224 pages, paperbound, 1998. $29.95

Chinese Poker: 13 Card Pai Gow Poker, by Don Smolen, 32 pages, spiralbound, 1994. $24.95

Complete Poker Room, by Chuck Ferry, 96 pages, paperbound, 1998. $19.95

Crazy Pineapple (High-Low Split), by Skip Rhode and John Toms, 8x11 format, 88 pages, plastic spiralbound, 1994. $19.95

Education of a Poker Player, by Herbert O. Yardley, 140 pages, paperbound. $12.95

Foolproof (a 30-Day Training Program To Hold 'em Success), by Richard Allen, 75 page workbook, 221 pages, 8x11 spiralbound, 1998. $49.95

Free Money, by Michael Wiesenberg, 332 pages, paperbound, 1984. $8.95

Fundamentals of Poker, by Mason Malmuth and Lynne Loomis, 66 pages, paperbound. 1993. $5.95

Gambling for a Living, by David Sklansky & Mason Malmuth, 250 pages, paperbound. 1997. $24.95

Gentleman Gambler, by "Oklahoma" Johnny Hale, 227 pages, paperbound, 1999. $14.95

Getting the Best of It, by David Sklansky, 248 pages, paperbound, 1992. $29.95

The Greatest Book of Poker for Winners, by George Epstein, 296 pages, paperbound, 2001. $24.95

The Hand I Played, by David Spanier, 246 pages, paperbound, 2001. $18.95

High-Low Split Poker for Advanced Players, by Ray Zee, 331 pages, paperbound, 1994. $34.95

Hold 'Em Excellence, by Lou Krieger, indexed and illustrated, 169 pages, paperbound. 1996. $19.95

Hold 'Em's Odds Book, by Mike Petriv, 207 pages, paperbound, 1996. $24.95

Hold 'Em Poker, by David Sklansky, 110 pages, paperbound, 1996. $19.95

Hold 'Em Poker Bible (A Poker Classic), by Dick Davis, 277 pages, paperbound, 1995. $21.95

Hold 'Em Poker in a Nutshell, by J.C. Moore, 44 pages, spiralbound, 1993. $14.95

Hold 'Em Split (Eight or Better for Low), by John Payne, 8x11 format, 145 pages, paperbound, 1990. $24

How to Play Winning Poker, by Avery Cardoza, revised in 1999 with 50 additional pages, 159 pages, paperbound. $12.95

How to Win at Poker, by Terence Reese and Anthony T. Watkins, indexed, 146 pages, paperbound, 1964. $10

How to Win at Stud Poker, by James Wickstead, 158 pages, paperbound, 1976. $7.95

Improve Your Poker, by Bob Ciaffone, 220 pages, paperbound, 1997. $25

Inside the Poker Mind, by John Feeney, indexed, 274 pages, paperbound. $24.95

John Patrick's Casino Poker, by John Patrick, 204 pages, paperbound, 1996. $17.95

Language of Poker, by George Percy, 98 pages, paperbound, 1988. $12

Liars Poker: A Winning Strategy, by John Archer, 64 pages, paperbound, 1982. $4.95

Life is a Game of Poker, by Jim (Cowboy) Childers, 102 pages, paperbound, 1999. $14.95

The Little Book of Poker, by David Spanier, 170 pages, paperbound, $8.95

Low Limit 7-Card Stud Casino Strategy, by Gary Oliver, 27 pages, spiralbound, 1991. $6.95

Mastering the Game of Three Card Poker, by Stanley Ko, $6.95

Memoirs of a Poker Player, by H.C. Byler Jr., 116 pages, paperbound, 2001. $12.42

Middle Limit Hold 'Em Poker, by Bob Ciaffone and Jim Brier, 332 pages, paperbound, 2001. $25

Ms Poker…Up Close and Personal, by Susie Isaacs, 246 pages, paperbound, 1999. $19.95

Money Poker, by Mr. X as told to Walter Gibson, 210 pages, paperbound, 1983. $9.95

More Hold 'Em Excellence, by Lou Krieger, 221 pages, paperbound, revised and expanded in 1999. $19.95

New Poker Games, by Mike Caro, 156 pages, paperbound, 1984. $5.95

No Fold 'Em Hold 'Em, by D. R. Sherer, 109 pages, paperbound, 1997. $19.95

Official Dictionary of Poker, by Michael Wiesenberg, 274 pages, paperbound, 2000. $14.95

Official Rules, Regulations, Procedures Manual for Poker, by Ron Cramer, 74 pages, paperbound, 1998. $9.95

Omaha Hi-Lo Poker (Eight or Better), by Shane Smith, 61 pages, paperbound, 1996. $17.95

Omaha Hold 'Em Poker, by Bob Ciaffone, 106 pages, paperbound, 2000. $20

Omaha Poker in a Nutshell, by J.C. Moore, 38 pages, spiralbound, 1993. $14.95

Omaha Split 8 or Better for Low, by John Payne, 64 pages, paperbound, 1992. $18

Pineapple Hold 'Em, by Brian Smith, 80 pages, paperbound, 1995. $6.95

Playing Low Limit Hold 'Em, by Bob Turgeon, 90 pages, paperbound. $11.95

Play Poker, Quit Work, Sleep Til Noon, by John Fox, 343 pages, paperbound, 1977. $14.95

Play Poker to Win, by W.J. Florence, 139 pages, 1980. $2.50

Play Winning Poker, by Jack King, 64 pages, paperbound, 1974. $2.95

Poker by Hardison, 63 pages, paperbound, 1914. $2.95

Poker Essays, by Mason Malmuth, three volumes, $24.95 each

Poker! (Las Vegas Style), by Bill "Bulldog" Sykes, 224 pages, paperbound, 1992. $9.95

Poker: America's Game, by George Percy, 152 pages, paperbound, 1988. $19.95

Poker: Bets, Bluffs, and Bad Bets, by A. Alvarez, 128 pages, hardbound, 2001. $29.95

Poker Expertise Through Probability, by Robert Riley, 186 pages, spiralbound, 1997. $34.95

Poker for Dummies, by Lou Krieger and Richard D. Harroch, indexed, illustrated, 298 pages, paperbound, 2000. $16.99

Poker: How To Win at the Great American Game, by David Daniel, 399 pages, hardbound, 1997. $24.95

Poker Humor (A Collection of Poker Wit), by Gary Oliver, 96 pages, paperbound. 1993. $5.95

Poker Odds, by Frank R. Wallace, 15 pages, paperbound, 1968. $.60

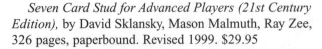

Poker Playing to Win, by Tony Korfman, 42 pages, paperbound, 1985. $3.50

Poker-The Small Limit Game, by Scotty Barclay, 48 pages, paperbound, 1980. $2.95

Poker to Win, by Al Smith, 64 pages, paperbound, 1931. $2.95

Poker Tournament Strategy, by "Sylvester Suzuki," 180 pages, paperbound, 1998. $19.95

Poker Tournament Tips from the Pros-2001 Millennium Edition, by Shane Smith, 114 pages, paperbound. $19.95

Pokerfarce and Pokertruth, by Ray Michael B., $19.95

Pot-Limit and No-Limit Poker, by Bob Ciaffone and Stewart Reuben, 220 pages paperbound, 1997. $25

Pro Poker Playbook, by John Vorhaus, 173 pages, paperbound, 1995. $19.95

Professional Poker Dealer's Handbook, by Donna Harris/Dan Paymar/Mason Malmuth, 180 pages, paperbound, 1998. $19.95

The Secret to Winning Big in Tournament Poker, by Ken Buntjer, 192 pages, paperbound, 1994. $49.95

Poker, Gaming, and Life, by David Sklansky, 205 pages, paperbound, 1997. $24.95

The P$ychology of Poker P$ymplified, by David Whalen, 158 pages, paperbound, 1997. $19.95

The Psychology of Poker, by Alan N. Schoonmaker, Ph.D., 329 pages, indexed, paperbound, 2000. $24.95

The Railbird, by Rex Jones, 157 pages, paperbound, 1984. $6.95

Read 'Em and Laugh, by Max Shapiro, 150 pages, paperbound, 1995. $19.95

Robert's Rules of Poker, by Bob Ciaffone, 71 pages, spiralbound, 2001. $9.95

Rules of Neighborhood Poker, by Stewart Wolpin, indexed, 356 pages, paperbound, 1990. $6.95

Secrets of Winning Poker, by Tex Sheahan, 200 pages, paperbound, 1993. $14.95

7-Card Stud (A Complete Course In Winning at Medium and Lower Limits), by Roy West, 154 pages, paperbound, 1996. $24.95

Serious Poker, by Dan Kimberg, indexed, 318 pages, paperbound. $12.95

Seven Card Stud for Advanced Players (21st Century Edition), by David Sklansky, Mason Malmuth, Ray Zee, 326 pages, paperbound. Revised 1999. $29.95

Seven-Card Stud Split (8 or Better for Low), by John Payne, 39 pages, in 8x11 plastic spiralbound format, 1990. $14.95

Seven Card Stud Poker, by Konstantin Othmer, 258 pages, paperbound, 1996. $25

Seven Card Stud-The Waiting Game, by George Percy, 80 pages, spiralbound, 1979. $8.95

Silberstang's Guide to Poker, by Edwin Silberstang, 124 pages , paperbound, 1985. $7.95

Stud Poker Blue Book, by George H. Fisher, 64 pages, paperbound, 1934. $2.95

Super/System (A Course in Poker Power), by Doyle Brunson, 604 pages, hardbound, 1978. $50

Tales Out of Tulsa, by Bobby (The Owl) Baldwin, 167 pages, paperbound, 1984. $6.95

Texas Hold 'Em Poker with Begin to Win (CD), by G. Ed Conly, $32

Total Poker, by David Spanier, indexed, 252 pages, 1995. $14.95

Texas Hold 'Em Flop Types, by Mort Badiza-degan, illustrated and indexed, 149 pages, 8x11plastic spiralbound, 1999. $24.95

Tournament Poker, by Tom McEvoy, 344 pages, paperbound, 1997. $39.95

Wacky Side of Poker, by Ralph Wheeler and Friends, 176 pages, paperbound. $9.95

When to Hold 'Em and When to Fold 'Em, by William Edwin Barnes, paperbound, 2001, $24.95.

Win at Poker, by Jeff Rubens, 218 pages, hardbound, 1968. $7.95

Winner's Guide to Casino Poker, by Edwin Silberstang, 310 pages, paperbound, 2000. $5.99

Winner's Guide to Texas Hold 'Em, by Ken Warren, 210 pages paperbound, 1996. $14.95

Winning Low Limit Hold 'Em 2nd Edition, by Lee Jones, 198 pages, paperbound, 2000. $24.95

Winning Poker for the Serious Player, by Edwin Silberstang, 224 pages, paperbound. 1996. $12.95

Winning Poker Systems, by Norman Zadeh, 208 pages, paperbound, 1974. $10

Winning Secrets of a Poker Master, by J.D. McEvoy, 8x11 format, 32 pages, paperbound. 1986. $4.95

Wins, Places and Pros, by Tex Sheahan, 137 pages, paperbound, 1984. $6.95

World Poker Diary, 128 pages, paperbound, 2000. $18.95

Zen and the Art of Poker, by Larry Phillips, 175 pages, paperbound, 1999. $12.95

Hold 'Em Poker for Advanced Players (21st Edition), by David Sklansky & Mason Malmuth, 332 pages, paperbound. Revised, 1999. $29.95

Theory of Poker, by David Sklansky, 242 pages, paperbound, 1994. $29.95

Winning Concepts in Draw and Lowball, by Mason Malmuth, 380 pages, paperbound. 1993. $24.95

ANDY NELSON POKER BOOKS

Poker: 101 Ways to Win. $17.95

Poker: Hold 'Em (Book One). $8.95

Poker: Hold 'Em (Advanced). $8.95

Poker: Intermediate Hold 'Em. $8.95

Poker: Seven Ways to Win. $8.95

Poker: Seven More Ways to Win. $8.95

Poker: A Winner's Guide. $11.95

Poker: Omaha. $8.95

Poker: Omaha High/Low Split Book One. $8.95

Poker: Omaha High/Low Split Intermediate. $8.95

Poker: 7-Card Stud (Hi-Lo Split, 8 or Better) Book One. $8.95

Poker: 7-Card Stud (Hi-Lo Split, 8 or Better) Intermediate. $8.95

ROULETTE BOOKS

Action Roulette, by NFS, 24 pages, paperbound, 1970. $1

All About Roulette, by John Gollehon, 58 pages, paperbound, 1985. $4.99

The Basics of Winning Roulette, by J. Edward Allen, 58 pages, paperbound, 1993. $4.95

Basic Roulette, by Bert Walker, 80 pages, paperbound, 1982. $4.95
Beating the Wheel, by Russell Barnhart, 216 pages, paperbound, 1992. $14.95

Get the Edge at Roulette, by Christopher Pawlecki, 229 pages, paperbound, 2001. $13.95

How to Beat the Casino at Roulette, by Professor Garland, 112 pages, paperbound, 1996. $12.95

How to Find and Wager on Biased Roulette Wheels, by M. Pascual with Dennis Wilsef, 51 pages 8x11 format, spiralbound, 1996. $35

Playing Roulette as a Business, by R.J. Smart, 165 pages, paperbound, 1996. $12.95

Roulette Eurotester, by Erik St. Germain, 180 pages, paperbound, 2000. $22

Roulette: Playing to Win, by Tony Korfman, 49 pages, paperbound, 1987. $3.50

Roulette Recorder, by LA Crews, three versions, 20 pages, paperbound, 2001. $2 each

Roulette Wheel Study, by Ron Shelley, 124 pages spiralbound, 1992. $50

Roulette System Tester, by Erik St. Germain, 299 pages, plastic spiral-bound, 1995. $24.95

Secrets of Winning Roulette, by Marten Jensen, 201 pages, paperbound, 1998. $16.95

Secrets of Winning Casino Roulette, by Lawrence Lowrey, 32 pages 8x11 format, paperbound, 1988. $4.95

Spin Roulette Gold, by Frank Scoblete, indexed, 229 pages, paperbound, 1997. $14.95

Thirteen Against the Bank, by Norman Leigh, 203 pages, paperbound, 1991. $14.95

Winning at Roulette, by New Fortune Series, 28 pages, paperbound, 1970. $1

SLOT MACHINE BOOKS

All About Slots and Video Poker, by John Gollehon, 60 pages, paperbound, 1985. $4.99

Basics of Winning Slots, by J. Edward Allen, 62 pages, paperbound, 1984. $4.95

Break the One-Armed Bandits, by Frank Scoblete, 178 pages, paperbound, 1994. $9.95

Don't Play the Slot Machines...Until You Read This Book, by Michael D. Geller, 125 pages, paperbound, 2001. $12

John Patrick's Slots, by John Patrick, 228 pages, paperbound, 1994. $19.95

Las Vegas Slot Clubs, by Charles W. Lund, 2000. $19.95

Lucky Slots, by Jack Kiely, 32 pages, paperbound, 1997. $4.95

Robbing the One-Armed Bandits, by Charles W. Lund, 258 pages, paperbound, 2000. $19.95

Secrets of Modern Slot Playing, by Larry Mak, Revised December 1999, paperbound. $9.95

Slot Expert's Guide for Playing Slots, by John Robison, 19 pages, 2000. $9.95

Slots for the Clueless, by John Patrick, 174 pages, paperbound, 2001. $12.95

Slots: Playing to Win, by Tony Korffman, 42 pages, pocket-size paperback, 1985. $3.50

Slot Machine Answer Book, by John Grochowski, 165 pages, paperbound, 1999. $12.95

Slot Machine Mania, by Dwight & Louise Crevelt, 243 pages, paperbound, 1988. $6.99

Slot Machine Strategy, by MacIntyre Symms, 143 pages, paperbound, 2001. $14.95

Slot Play: Build Your Own Jackpot (Revised), by Carlene Cole, 204 pages, paperbound. $9.95

Slot Smarts, by Claude Halcombe, 157 pages, paperbound, 1996. $12

VIDEO POKER

Deuces Wild Video Poker, by Bob Dancer, 45 pages, 8 x 11 spiralbound, 1996. $10

9-6 Jacks or Better Video Poker, by Bob Dancer, 27 pages, 8 x 11 spiralbound, 1996. $10

10-7 Double Bonus Video Poker, by Bob Dancer, 26 pages, 8 x 11 spiralbound, 1996. $10

America's National Game of Chance, by Lenny Frome and Maryann Guberman, 200 pages, paperbound, 1992. $19.95

Basics of Winning Video Poker, by J. Edward Allen, 54 pages, paperbound, 1990. $4.95

Beating the Poker Slot Machines, by Carl Cohen, 36 pages, paperbound, 1981. $4.95

Beating Video Keno, by M.G. Davis, 40 pages, paperbound, 1997. $10

Beginner's Best Shot at Video Poker, by Bob Maxwell, 96 pages, paperbound, 1995. $7.95

Best of Video Poker Time, by Dan Paymar, 76 pages, paperbound, Vol. 1, $19.95. Vol. 2, $24.95

Expert Strategy for 5-Deck Frenzy, by Lenny Frome, 8 pages, paperbound, 1997. $3.95

Expert Video Poker for Atlantic City, by Lenny Frome, 47 pages, paperbound, 1992. $7.95

Expert Video Poker for Las Vegas, by Lenny Frome, 47 pages, paperbound, 1992. $9.95

Fundamentals of Video Poker, by Mason Malmuth and Lynne Loomis, 68 pages, paperbound, 1995. $3.95

John Patrick's Video Poker, by John Patrick, 320 pages, paperbound, 2001. $14.95

Las Vegas Video Poker Buffet, by Lenny Frome, 12 pages, paperbound, 1991. $6.95

Professional Video Poker, by Stanford Wong, 159 pages, paperbound, 1993. $14.95

Secrets of Winning at Video Poker, by Hugh McKenna, 32 pages, paperbound, 1990. $4.95

The Undeniable Truth About Video Poker, by Rob Singer, 125 pages, indexed, paperbound, 2000. $19.95

Victory at Video Poker, by Frank Scoblete, 281 pages, indexed, paperbound, 1995. $12.95

Video Poker Anomalies and Anecdotes, by Dan Paymar, 40 pages, paperbound, 1998. $5.95

Video Poker Answer Book, by John Grochowski, $13.95

Video Poker for Profit, by Marty Mendelsohn, 55 pages, paperbound, 1998. $9.95

Video Poker Mania, by Dwight and Louise Crevelt, 140 pages, paperbound, 1991. $5.99

Video Poker Optimum Play, by Dan Paymar, 1998. $19.95

Win at Video Poker, by Roger Fleming, 158 pages, paperbound, 1993. $12

Winning Strategy for Video Poker, by Lenny Frome, 120 pages, paperbound, Revised 1997. $15.95

RACING BOOKS
GREYHOUND RACING

1001 Ways You Can Win at Greyhound Racing, by John Brasswell, 1992, $35

Advanced Handicapping Rules & Reasons, by Don Casey, 16 pages, paperbound. $10

Advanced Handicapping Secondary Marks, by Dan Casey, 21 pages, paperbound. $10

The Brenner System, by Fred Brenner, 160 pages, paperbound, 1978. $40

Class Rating Races, by Don Casey, 14 pages, paperbound. $10

Gambling Times: Greyhound Racing, by William McBride, 198 pages, paperbound, 1984. $9.95

Gone to the Dogs, by Ron Duval, 66 pages, paperbound, 1988. $14.95

Greyhound Betting for Profit, by Ross Hamilton, 64 pages, paperbound, 1989. $7.95

Greyhound Gold, by C.Y. Chen, 114 pages, paperbound, 1979. $20

The Greyhound Handicapper, by Earl Adams, 70 pages, paperbound, 1994. $8.50

Greyhound Handicapping, by Richard Weiss, 85 pages, paperbound, 1994. $30

Greyhound Money Management for the '90s, by Dan Casey, pages, paperbound, $10

How to Analyze a Race, by Dan Casey, 20 pages, paperbound. $10

How to Beat the Dog Races!, by Bill McBride, 8x11, 175 pages, paperbound, 1999 $18.95

How to Bet Like a Pro at Dog Tracks, by John Page, 39 pages, paperbound. $10

How to Hit Big Trifectas, by Peter Maxim, 48 pages, paperbound. $10

How You Can Wager and Win, by John Brasswell, 1993. $4.95

How You Can Win Like a Pro II, by John Brasswell, 40 pages, paperbound, 1992. $4.95

Let's Go to the Greyhound Races, by Gold Enterprises, 79 pages, paperbound, 1980. $9.95

Making Money with Lower Grade Races, by Dave Farr, 38 pages, paperbound. $10

Making Money with Quinielas and Exactas, by Carl Kirsch, 47 pages, paperbound. $10

Off the Leash, by David Heer, 92 pages, paperbound, 1993. $6.95

Playing the Dogs and Winning, by Jim Saide, 129 pages, paperbound, 1985. $12.95

Pro-Am Quinella Strategy, by Dan Casey, 26 pages, paperbound. $10

Quick Way to Pick Winning Greyhounds, by Bill Mays, 35 pages, paperbound. $10

Secrets to Winning at Greyhound Racing, by John G. Brasswell, 103 pages, spiralbound, 1996. $35

Special Trifecta Plays, by Art Cross, 20 pages, paperbound. $10

Ten Minute Handicapping, by Gary Freeman, 64 pages, paperbound. $15

Winning Daily Doubles and Pick 3's, by Scott Perry, 42 pages, paperbound. $10

Winners Guide to Greyhound Racing, by Professor Jones, 88 pages, paperbound, 1993. $9.95

Winning Consistently at the Greyhound Races, by J.J. "Clocker" Clarkin, 32 pages, paperbound, 1987. $4.95

The Winning Greyhound Formula, by Dan Casey, 40 pages, paperbound. $15

Winning Greyhound Handicapping, by Brian Mason, 78 pages, paperbound. $15

Winning Quiniela Doubles, by Ross Hauer, 24 pages, paperbound. $10

Winning Simulcast Races, by Mike Smith, 32 pages, paperbound. $10

Winning Superfectas, by Fran Stuart, 22 pages, paperbound. $10

Winning Trifectas at Dog Tracks, by Lee Hardesty, 46 pages, paperbound. $10

Winning Twin Trifectas and Tri-Supers, by Jack Mead, 30 pages, 8x11, paperbound. $10

HARNESS RACING BOOKS

ABC's of Pari-Mutuel Wagering, by John Berry, 40 pages, paperbound, 1987. $4

Betting Winners, by Don Valliere, 173 pages, paperbound, 1981. $9.95

The Evil Side of a Racetrack, by Micael John Horak, 154 pages, hardbound, 1994. $30

Handicapping Beyond the Basics, by Jerry Connors, 8x11 format, 80 pages, paperbound, 1985. $3.50

Handicapping Beyond the Basics II, by Jerry Connors, 8x11 format, 103 pages, paperbound. $5

Harness Handicapping the Computer Way, by Howard Berenbon, 70 pages, spiralbound. copyright 1995, published in 1999. $19.95

Harness Racing Angles, by Al Stanley, 60 pages, paperbound, 1995. $39.95

Harness Racing Gold, by Prof. Igor Kusyshyn, 160 pages, paperbound, 1979. $14.95

The Kentucky Harness Horse, by Ken McCarr, 130 pages, hardbound, 1978. $4.95

Picking Winners at Harness Races, by Paul Goodwin, 8x11 format, 32 pages, paperbound, 1987. $4.95

Professional Harness Betting, by Barry Meadow, 303 pages, 1988. $198

Selecting the Standardbred, by Robert Perosino, 8x11 format, 221 pages, paperbound. 1994. $29.95

Stanley's Law, by Al Stanley & Sam Dragich, 132 pages, paperbound, 1980. $9.95

Still Hooked on Harness Racing, by Donald P. Evans, 254 pages, hardbound, 1978. $9.95

Success at the Harness Races, by Barry Meadow, 180 pages, paperbound, 1967. $7

QUARTER HORSE RACING BOOKS

Exacta Betting, Gil Morgan and Herb Morgan, 115 pages, paperbound, 1979. $11.95

Quarter Horse Racing, by American Quarter Horse Association, illustrated, 32 pages paperbound, 1986. 50 cents

Speed and the Quarter Horse, by Nelson C. Nye, indexed, 356 pages, hardbound, 1973. $17.95

Training Quarter Horses, by Don Essary, indexed, 243 pages, hardbound,1980. $14.95

THOROUGHBRED HORSE RACING BOOKS

2001 Pars Plus, by David E. Schwartz, 130 pages, paperbound, 2001. $100

American Racing Manual, by Racing Form, 1,600 pages, hardbound, 2001. $60

Modern Pace Handicapping, by Tom Brohamer, 315 pages, hardbound, 2000. $29.95

Handicapper's Condition Book, by James Quinn, 208 pages, hardbound, 2000. $29.95

21st Century in Handicapping, by Dick Mitchell, 255 pages, paperbound, 1999. $39.95

25 Ways to Beat the Horses, by Walter B. Gibson, 140 pages, indexed. $8.95

150 Blue Ribbon Winning Systems, by GBC Staff, 64 pages, paperbound, 1979. $4.95

150 More Blue Ribbon Winning Systems, by GBC Staff, 64 pages, paperbound, 1979. $4.95

Advanced Winning Analysis, by Ken Lempenau, 20 pages, 1995. $19.95

Ainslie's Complete Guide to Thoroughbred Racing, by Tom Ainslie, 348 pages, paperbound, 1986. $14

All About Horseracing and Winning Handicapping, by Eric Ryan, 40 pages, paperbound, 1976. $2.50

Anatomy of a Race Meet, by Jim Selvidge, 42 pages, paperbound, 1990. $14.95

The Angle Emporium!, by RPM Information Systems, 8x10 format, 88 pages plus 38 pages of appendix examples, spiralbound, 1996. $29.95

Bankroll Control, by M. Pascual, 8x11 format, 118 pages, spiralbound, 1987. $35

Barry Meadow Special Reports on Thoroughbred Handicapping, set of nine reports, 1996. $29

Beating the Daily Double, Exacta, Q, Tri, etc., by Bert Norman, 8x11 format, 60 pages, paperbound, 1987. $24.95

The Best of Bert Norman, (Secrets of a Professional Handicapper), by Bert Norman, 130 pages, 8 x 11, spiralbound, 1994. $39.95

Betting and Beating the Exotics, by Jerry Samovitz, 8x11 format, 88 pages, spiralbound. 1995. $34

Betting Horses to Win, by Les Conklin, 182 pages (including glossary), paperbound. 1954. $10

Betting Cheap (Broken Down) Claimers, by David Powers, 8x11 format, 56 pages, paperbound, 1996. $29.95

Betting Thoroughbreds (2nd Rev Ed.), by Steve Davidowitz, 347 pages, paperbound. 1995. $16.95

Bet with the Best, by Daily Racing Form, 249 pages, hardbound. $29.95

Beyer on Speed, by Andrew Beyer, 239 pages, paperbound, 1993. $15

Beyer Positive Elimination Method, by Jeff Goldstein, 10 pages 8x11 format, spiralbound, 1995. $29.95

Body Language Columns, by Trillis Parker, 8x11 spiralbound, 1992. $19.95

Body Language of Horses, by Tom Ainslie & Bonnie Ledbetter, 208 pages, hardbound. 1980. $20

Breeder's Cup, by Jay Privman, 200 pages, hardbound, large format, 2001. $50

Bringing Home the Jackpots, by Jerry Samovitz, 70 pages, 8 x 11 paperbound, 1999. $38

Broodmare Sire Rankings (4th Ed.), by The Maiden Man, 86 pages, 8x11 binder format. 1995. $25

California Trainer Profile, by Jeff Goldstein, 183 pages 8 x 11 spiralbound. (Seasonal), $29.95

Calibration Handicapping, by Jim Lehane, 118 pages, 8x11 format, paperbound, 2000. $45.45

C&O's Greatest Hits, Vol. 1, by Mark Cramer and Bill Olmsted, 168 pages, paperbound. 1996. $35

Claims, by Ed Bain, Covers tracks in So. Calif, NY, MD, and KY. Paperbound. Seasonal. $88.88

Layoffs, by Ed Bain, 8x11 spiralbound, 2001. $88.88

Champions, by The Racing Form, 421 pages, illustrated, hardbound. $75

Complete Guide to Racetrack Betting, by David Rosenthal, 162 pages, paperbound, 1986. $9.95

Complete Idiot's Guide to Betting on Horses, by Sharon B. Smith, $16.95

Crushing the Cup, by Jim Mazur and Peter Mallett, 2001. $21.95

Debut Trainer Guide 2000, by Mike Helm and Jay Helm, 64 pages, paperbound, 2000. $30

Debut Winners of 1999, by Mike Helm, 29 pages, paperbound, 2000. $25

Dowst Revisited, by Ron Thacker, 72 pages, paperbound, 1977. $2.95

Dutching Made Simple, by Jim Giordano, six pages, paperbound, 1993. $6.95

Eleven Winning Exacta Situations, by Mark Cramer, 102 pages, paperbound, 1991. $49

Exacta Expose, by Douglas Railey, 182 pages, paperbound, 1992. $29.95

Exotic Overlays, by Bill Heller, 221 pages, paperbound, 1996. $14.95

Exotic Wagering Formulas, by Thomas C. Walters, 77 pages, paperbound, 2000. $19.95

Exploring Pedigree: Handicapping's Newest Frontier, by Mike Helm, 217 pages, paperback, 1994. $29.95

Fast and Fit Horses, by Bob Heyburn, 158 pages, paperbound, 1988. $9.95

Fast Track to Thoroughbred Profits, by Mark Cramer, 184 pages, paperbound 1984. $8.95

Finding Hot Horses, by Vincent Reo, 135 pages, paperbound, 1993. $12

The First Century, by Joe Hirsch, 215 pages, hardbound, 1996. $29.95

Glossary of Thoroughbred Racing, by Frank M.Briggss, Sr., 166 pages, paperbound, 1985. $9.95

Great Betting Systems, by Norman Dash, 186 pages, hardbound, 1968. $4.95

Great Horse Racing Mysteries, by John McEvoy, indexed and illustrated, 264 pages, hardbound, 2001. $24.95

The Gulfstream Handicapper 2002, by Jim Mazur, spiralbound. $21.95

Handicap! Finding the Key Horse, by David Christopher and Albert Beerhower, 172 pages, paperbound, 1992. $12.95

Handicapping for Winners, by Boots Baker, 31 pages, magazine format. $3

Handicapping in Cyberspace, by George Kaywood, 239 pages, spiralbound, 2000. $29.95

Handicapping Magic, by Michael Pizzolla, 433 pages, paperbound, 2000. $34.95

Handicapping Speed, by Charles Carroll, 234 pages, paperbound, 1996. $14.95

Handicapping the Flats and Trots, by Don Zamarelli, 40 pages, paperbound, 1970. $3

Handicapping Trainers, by John Whitaker, 152 pages, paperbound, 1990. $12.95

Hold Your Horses, by James Selvidge, 174 pages, paperbound, 1976. $6.95

Horse Market Analysis, by David E. Schwartz, 58 pages, stapled, 2001. $29.95

Horse Power: Politics of the Turf, by Christopher Hill, indexed, 283 pages, hardbound, 1988. $40

The Horsemen, by Jack Engelhard, 22 pages, hardbound, 1974. $5.95

Horseracing: Playing to Win, by Jimmy Kizzire, 41 pages, paperbound. $2.95

Horses Talk-It Pays to Listen, by Trillis Parker, 99 pages, paperbound, 1989. $19.95

Sire Ratings 2001-2002, by Mike Helm, 98 pages, paperbound, 2001. $35

How to Beat the Horses, by Mike Fiore, 209 pages, hardbound, 1977. $25

How to Pick Winning Horses, by Bob McKnight, 192 pages, paperbound, 1963. $5

How to Profit from Pars, by Gordon Pine, 66 pages, paperbound. $29.95

How to Win at Horseracing, by Robert V. Rowe, 200 pages, paperbound, 1990. $12.95

How to Win at the Races, by Sam Lewin with Frederick Klein, 205 pages, paperbound. 1969. $5

How You Can Beat the Races, by Jack Kananagh, 222 pages, paperbound. $5

Inside the Claiming Game, by Steve Collison, 101 pages, spiralbound, 1998. $39.95

Inside Racing Angles, by Bill Hogan, 71 pages, booklet paperbound. $5

Krazy Koncepts, by Jeff Goldstein, 68 pages, 8 x 11 plastic spiralbound, 1996. $29.95

Las Vegas Parlay Tables, by Huey Mahl, 32 pages, paperbound, 1975. $2.95

Laughing in the Hills, by Bill Barich, 228 pages, paperbound, 2000. $14

Lightning in a Jar, by W. Cothran Campbell, 310 pages, hardbound, 2000. $29.95

Maiden Manifesto, by David Powers, 74 pages, 8x11 format, spiralbound, 1996. $29.95

Maiden Stats 2001, by Bloodstock Research Services, 300 pages, paperbound, 2000. $99.95

The Match Up, by Jim "The Hat" Bradshaw, 120 pages paperbound, 1996. $30

Modern Impact Values, by Michael E. Nunamaker, 160 pages, spiralbound, 2000. $99.99

Money Management, by James Selvidge, 144 pages, spiralbound, 1993. $19.95

Money Secrets at the Racetrack, by Barry Meadow, 142 pages, paperbound, 1990. $24.95

Oaklawn Handicapper 2002, by Jim Mazur, spiralbound. $29.95

Official Kentucky Derby Quiz Book, by Randall Baron and Philip von Borries, 159 pages, paperbound. 1986. $7.95

Olmsted's Trainer Guide 2000-01, Bill Olmsted, 131 pages, paperbound, pocket format, 2000. $60

The Only Trifecta Wagering Book You'll Ever Need, by David Powers, 8x11 format, 31 pages, spiralbound, 1994. $29.95

Out of the Red into the Black, by Jerry Samovitz, 8 x 11 format, 41 pages, paperbound, 1993. $19

Overlay Handicapping, by Tim Maas, 74 pages, spiralbound, 1997. $40

Overlay, Overlay, by Bill Heller, 228 pages, paperbound, 1990. $9.95

Own and Race Claiming Horse, by Peter Filipovich, 85 pages, paperbound, 1994. $12.95

Pari-Mutuel Betting, by James Hillis, 69 pages, paperbound, 1976. $4.95

Payday at the Races, by Les Conklin, 208 pages, paperbound, 1953. $7

Physicality Handicapping Made Easy, by Joe Takach, manuscript format, 2001. $19.95

Picking Winners, by Andrew Beyer, 226 pages, paperbound, 1975. $15

Players Guide to Nevada Racebooks 1999-2000 Edition, by Barry Meadow, 100 pages. $29.95

Postures, Profiles and Performance, by Joe Takach, 139 pages, 8 x 11 format, 1993. $29.95

Power Handicapping, by Dave Powers, 60 pages, spiralbound, 2000. $35

Prime Collection, by Joe Takach, 137 pages, paperbound, 1993. $29.95

Prime Collection II, by Joe Takach, 70 pages, spiralbound, 1993. $29.95

Probability – Odds Line & Optimal Dutching Programs, by Michael J. Pascual, 8x11 format, 10 pages, spiralbound, 1988. $14.95

Pro Rated Longshots, by Al Smallman, 24 pages, paperbound, 2001. $20

The Race Fixers, by James Selvidge, 119 pages, spiralbound, 1991. $19.95

The Race is Pace, by Huey Mahl, 126 pages, paperbound, 1983. $7.95

Racetrack Betting: The Professor's Guide to Strategies, by Peter Asch and Richard Quandt, 195 pages, paperbound, 1986. $20.95

Racing Maxims & Methods of "Pittsburgh Phil," by Edward W. Cole, 126 pages, paperbound, 1974. $7.95

Rare Stakes, by Graham Sharpe, illustrated, 144 pages, paperbound, 1986. $5.95

Razoo at the Races, by Gary West, 202 pages, paperbound, 1999. $15

Real-Life Handicapping, by Dave Litfin, 189 pages paperbound, 1997. $25

The Right Blood, by Carole Case, indexed, 241 pages, hardbound, 2000. $26

The Right Horse, by William Murray, indexed, 196 pages, hardbound, 1997. $17.95

The Santa Anita Analyst, by David Powers, 105 pages, spiralbound, 1998. $29

The Santa Anita Handicapper 2002, by Jim Mazur, spiralbound, 8x11 format. $29.95

The Saratoga Handicapper, by Jim Mazur with John Angelo, 111 pages, paperbound. $21.95

Seabiscuit, by Laura Hillebrand, indexed, 399 pages, hardbound, 2001. $24.95

Search for the Winning Horse, by Richard Sasuly, 241 pages hardbound, 1979. $9.95

Secrets of the Pick Six, by Barry Meadow, 44 pages, paperbound, 1994. $29.95

Sire Ratings 2000, by Mike Helm, 85 pages, paperbound. $35

Situation Handicapping, by Joe Takach, 158 pages, paperbound, 1991. $32.95

Smart Choices, by Craig Victor, 108 pages, paperbound, 1982. $9.95

Something Else of Great Value, by Dick Herter, 8x11 format, 25 pages, paperbound, 1987. $3

They're Off (Horse Racing at Saratoga), by Edward Hotaling, 368 pages, hardbound. 1995. $45

Thinking Man II, by Katcha Goodwon, 350 pages, paperbound, 1990. $9.95

The Thoroughbred Bloodlines Manual, by Arthur Gindick, 143 pages, spiralbound, 1997. $29.95

The Top 52, by Len Czyzniejewski, 118 pages, spiralbound, 2000. $39

The Tote Board is Alive and Well, by Milt Gaines, 144 pages, paperbound, 1981. $12.95

Trackfacts, by Dan DiPleco, 170 pages, paperbound, 1997. $24.95

Training Thoroughbred Horses, by Preston M. Burch, 122 pages, hardbound, 1992. $19.95

Trip Tips, by Joe Takach, 140 pages, paperbound, 1994. $29.95

Turf Moms, by Dave Evans, spiralbound, 2000. $60
Value Handicapping, by Mark Cramer, 160 pages, paperbound 1998. $25

Wagering to Win!, by M. Paul Andersen, 182 pages, paperbound, 1995. $19.95

Winning at the Track, by David Christopher, 201 pages, paperbound,1987. $9.95

The Winning Horseplayer, by Andrew Beyer, 192 pages, paperbound, 1983. $14

Winning in the `90s, by Joe Takach, 201 pages, paperbound, 1990. $34.95

Winning Strategies and the Ready Horse, by Joe Takach, 204 pages, paperbound, 1992. $36.95

Winning with the Thoroughbreds, by Joseph Mitlitello, 283 pages, paperbound, 1994. $14.95

Wire `Em And Win, by Denny Border, 119 pages, paperbound, 1995. $12.95

Workouts and Maidens, by Vincent Reo, 165 pages, paperbound, 1994. $11.95

Women in Racing, by John and Julia McEvoy, 285 pages, hardbound, illustrated, 2001. $19.95

World Encyclopedia of Horseracing, by George Ennor and Bill Mooney, Indexed, hardbound, 224 pages, hardbound, 2001. $45

Woulda, Coulda, Shoulda, by Dave Feldman with Frank Sugano, 279 pages, paperbound, 1989. $12.95

The Wrong Horse, by William Murray, 224 pages, paperbound, 1992. $10.95

SPORTS BETTING BOOKS

The Basics of Winning Sports Betting, by Avery Cardoza, 45 pages, paperbound, 1991. $4.95

Betting Angles and Money Management, by Dave Barr, 32 pages, 8x11 manuscript format, 1990. $19.95

Betting the Line, by Richard O. Davies and Richard G. Abram. $24.95

The Book on Bookies, by James Jeffries as told to Charles Oliver, 128 pages, paperbound, 2000. $18

The Chicago Sports Barroom Analyst, by Bob Logan, 243 pages, paperbound, 1988. $9.95

The Complete Fantasy Sports Handbook, by Casey Moore, 8x11 format, 110 pages, paperbound, 1995. $19.95

How to Win Betting on College Basketball, by Pro Sports, 97 pages, spiralbound. $29.95

How to Win Betting on Pro Basketball, by Pro Sports, 155 pages, spiralbound. $29.95

Insights into Sports Betting, by Bob McCune, 295 pages, spiralbound, 1993. $29.95

John Patrick's Sports Betting, by John Patrick, 320 pages paperbound, 1996. $29.95

The Odds, by Chad Millman, 260 pages, hardbound, $26

Plug-in Parlay Systems, by Mickey Day, 56 pages, spiralbound, 1999. $11.95

Sports Betting 101, by Arne K. Lang, 190 pages, paperbound, 1992. $19.95

Sports Book Management, by Michael Roxborough & Mike Rhoden, 128 pages, paperbound, 1998. $35

The Theory and Practice of Las Vegas Style Sports Betting, by Marty Mendelsohn, 112 pages, paperbound, 1997. $14.95

Winning Strategies of Football Handicapping, by Bruce Marshall and the Gold Sheet Staff, 64 pages, paperbound. $24.95

TheWise-Guy's Bible, by Tony (Sonny) Daniels, 8x11 format, 321 pages, paperbound. 1993. $24.95

You Can Bet on It! Vol. 2: Sports Betting, by Larry Grossman, 200 pages, paperbound, 1994. $14.95

LAS VEGAS BOOKS

The 101 Most Asked Questions About Las Vegas and Casino Gambling, by George Joseph, 186 pages, paperbound. 2000. $14.95

101 Things You Gotta Love About Las Vegas, by Ed Atchinson with illustrations by Jim Day, 1998, $5.95

24/7: Living It Up and Doubling Down in the New Las Vegas, by Andres Martinez, 329 pages, hardbound, 1999. $25. Paperbound, $13.95

Access Las Vegas 2000, by Ed Atchinson with illustrations by Jim Day, 140 pages, paperbound. $19

Black Steps in the Desert Sands, A Chronicle of African-Americans' Involvement in the Growth of Las Vegas, Nevada, by Everett Louis Overstreet, 238 pages, 2000. $20

Boulder City Nevada, by Martin Booth, 128 pages, paperbound, 2000. $18.99

Buildings of Nevada, by Julie Nicoletta, indexed, 312 pages, hardbound, 2000. $45

The Cheapskate's Guide to Las Vegas, by Connie Emerson, 202 pages, paperbound, 1998. $9.95

Chip-Wrecked in Las Vegas, by Barney Vinson, 392 pages, paperbound, 1994. $19.95

Complete Idiot's Travel Guide to Las Vegas, by Rick Garman, 238 pages, paperbound. $15.95

Cult Vegas, by Mike Weatherford, 247 pages, paperbound, 2001. $19.95

Don't Get Ripped Off in Las Vegas, by Word to the Wise Publications, 48 pages, paperbound, 2000. $2.95

Experience Las Vegas, 544 pages, paperbound, 1998. $19.95

Fodor's 2000 Las Vegas, Reno Taho, illustrated (with maps), indexed, 193 pages, paperbound, 1999. $14.50

Frommer's 2002 Las Vegas, by Mary Herczog, 308 pages, paperbound, 2002. $18.99

The Frugal Gambler, by Jean Scott, indexed, 240 pages, paperbound, 1998. $12.95

In Nevada, by David Thompson, indexed, illustrated, 329 pages, hardbound. $27.50

Irreverent Guide to Las Vegas, by Jordan Simon for Frommer's, illustrated, indexed, 242 pages, paperbound, 2000. $12.99

Las Vegas (4th Edition), by Deke Castleman, indexed, 297 pages, paperbound, 1996. $18.95

Las Vegas Agenda, by Joyce Wiswell, indexed, 200 pages, paperbound, 1995. $14.95

Las Vegas: As It Began – As It Grew, by Stanley W. Paher, indexed, 180 pages, paperbound, 1971. $29.95

Las Vegas Fun Facts, by John Gollehon, 96 pages, paperbound, 2000. $5.99

Las Vegas Guide, by Ed Kranmar and Avery Cardoza, indexed, 224 pages, paperbound. 1997. $13.95

Las Vegas Trivia, by John Gollehon, 185 pages, paperbound, 2000. $6.99

Las Vegas With Love, by Dorothy Rice, 192 pages, hardbound, 2001. $85

The Money and the Power, by Sally Denton, indexed, illustrated.479 pages, hardbound, 2001. $26.95

Nevada, by Deke Castleman, 344 pages, photos, illustrations, indexed, paperbound, 2000. $21

A Short History of Las Vegas, by Barbara and Myrick Land, illustrated,1999. $15.95

The Real Las Vegas: Life Beyond the Strip, edited by David Littlejohn, 306 pages, hardbound, 1999. $30

Super Casino, by Pete Earley, indexed, 396 pages, hardbound, 1999, $26.95. Paperbound, $7.50

The Unofficial Guide to Las Vegas 2002, by Bob Sehlinger with Deke Castleman, 504 pages, paperbound, 2002. $16.99

Gambling Publications

Whether gaming enthusiasts are looking for advice or information to plan gambling excursions, they have a wealth of publications that can help.

A half-dozen publications focus on that gambling mecca, Las Vegas, including two daily newspapers and magazines such as Las Vegas Insider and Las Vegas Life. Others, such as Las Vegas Weekly and What's On Las Vegas Guide are widely distributed in the Las Vegas area.

Other regional publications include Midwest Gaming & Travel, Southern Gaming and Destinations, and Atlantic City Insider.

Horse racing buffs can consult American Turf Monthly, The Horseman or Thoroughbred Times.

And a large number of online publications have sprung up, covering topics from poker to bingo.

Here is a selection of periodicals and online magazines that cover gambling topics:

American Turf Monthly, monthly, www.american-turf.com, 306 Broadway, Lynbrook, NY 11563, $29 per year.

Atlantic City Insider, monthly, www.casinocenter.com, (800) 969-0711, $49 per year.

Bingo & Gaming News, monthly, www.bingogamingnews.com, (707) 451-4646, 349 Flagstone Court, Vacaville, CA 95687, free distribution in California, Oregon, Nevada.

The Blood-Horse, weekly, www.bloodhorse.com, (800) 582-5604, $89 per year.

Card Player Magazine, www.cardplayer.com, (702) 871-1720, 3140 S. Polaris Avenue #8 Las Vegas, NV 89102, $59 per year.

Casino Player, monthly, www.casinocenter.com, (800) 969-0711, 5240 S. Eastern Ave., Las Vegas, NV 89119, $24 a year.

Chance Magazine, bimonthly, www.chancemag.com, 888-CHANCE8, $21.99 per year.

Gambling Newsletter, weekly, www.gamblingnewsletter.com, free by e-mail.

GameRoom Magazine, monthly, www.gameroommagazine.com, (732) 739-1955, PO Box 41, Keyport, NJ 07735, $33 per year.

Gaming Today, weekly, www.gamingtoday.com, (702) 798-1151, P.O. Box 93116, Las Vegas, NV 89193, $180 per year.

The Horseman, weekly, www.harnessracing.com, 800-860-8199, P.O. Box 8480, Lexington, KY 40533, $80 per year.

Jackpot! Magazine, Southern edition and Delta edition, biweekly, www.jackpotmagazine.com, (228) 832-7004, 15487 Oak Lane Suite 200J, Gulfport, MS 39503, $50 per year.

Las Vegas Insider, monthly, www.lasvegasinsider.com, 2385 E. Windmill #303, Las Vegas, NV 89123, $45 per year.

Las Vegas Life, monthly, www.lvlife.com, (702) 990-2440, 2290 Corporate Circle Dr. Suite 250, Henderson, NV 89074, $14.95 per year.

Las Vegas Review-Journal, daily newspaper, www.lvrj.com, (702) 383-0211, 1111 W. Bonanza Road, P.O. Box 70, Las Vegas, NV 89125.

Las Vegas Sporting News, weekly, www.lvsn.com, (800) 325-8259, $97 per year.

Las Vegas Sun, daily newspaper, www.lasvegassun.com, (702) 383-0400, W. Bonanza Road, Las Vegas, NV 89106.

Las Vegas Weekly, weekly, www.lasvegasweekly.com, P.O. Box 230657, Las Vegas, NV 89123, available free in Las Vegas.

Midwest Gaming & Travel, www.midwestgamingandtravel.com, monthly, (507) 835-1662, 409 Tenth St., Waseca, MN, $24 per year.

Internet magazines

BingoGamingnews.com

BlackJackMagazine.com

Blackjack Review, www.bjrnet.com

CasinoDetroit.net

CasinoMagazine.com

CasinoGaming.com

CasinoMonthly.com

PlayerMagazine.com

Gamblersguide.net

GamblingMagazine.com

GamersMagazine.com

GamingMagazine.com

Handicapping.com

HorseracingMagazine.com

OnlineCasinoNews.com

PlayersEdge.com

Rolling Good Times, www.rgtonline.com

Winneronline.co

Native American Casino, monthly, www.nacasino.com, (888)265-2188, 3256 Rosecrans St., San Diego, CA 92110, $69.95 per year.

Poker Digest, bimonthly, www.casinocenter.com, (800) 969-0711, $69 per year.

Showbiz Weekly, weekly, www.showbiz.vegas.com, (800) Showguide, Henderson, NV, available in Las Vegas.

Southern Gaming and Destinations, quarterly, www.southerngaming.net, (502) 583-0330, 640 S. Fourth St., Louisville, KY, $3 per issue (free to members of Southern Gaming Players' Club).

Strictly Slots, monthly, www.casinocenter.com, (800) 969-0711, $24 per year.

Thoroughbred Times, weekly, www.thoroughbredtimes.com, (859) 260-9800, 496 Southland Drive, Lexington, KY 40503, $89 per year.

Today in Las Vegas, weekly, www.todayinlv.com, (702) 385-2737, Las Vegas, available in Las Vegas.

What's On Las Vegas Guide, biweekly, (702) 891-8811, Las Vegas, available in Las Vegas.

Where Las Vegas, monthly, 500 S. Rancho Drive, Suite 7, Las Vegas, NV 89106, $30 per year.

Computer Software

A home computer can be a valuable tool in learning more about gaming. It can also be a research assistant that helps you compile statistics to help improve your chances in sports or racing wagers.

Some of the computer programs available can also act as training aids in learning how to play blackjack or other games. And there's the pure fun of dealing yourself a few winning hands whenever you like.

Most of this software and its prices were compiled from the Gambler's Book Shop online catalog (http://www.gamblersbookclub.com/, phone 1-800-522-1777 & 1-800-634-6243). Software is also available from a variety of other sources.

GENERAL GAMBLING

Bicycle Card Games (Windows), CD-ROM, $17.95

Bicycle Casino Games 1.5 (Windows), CD-ROM, $17.95

The Dice Man's Backgrounds and Screen Savers, $9.95

High Stakes Gambling, by Nintendo, $16.99

Hoyle Casino 2001 (Windows or Mac), CD-ROM, $24.95

BLACKJACK

Blackjack 6, 7, 8, by Stickysoft, CD-ROM. $59.95

Bjedge, by Stanford Wong, spreadsheet. $19.95

Blackjack Master Course for Windows with Practicum, by Ne Plus Ultra. $39.95

Cheating at Blackjack 2000 (Interactive), by Dustin Marks, CD. $49.95

Blackjack Risk Manager, by John Auston, CD-ROM. $69.95

Blackjack Trainer, by Conjelco. $75

Blackjack Vision, by Shiloh Research Systems. $79.95

Casino Verite Blackjack, by Qfit. $90

Masque Blackjack, by Masque. $19.95

Party Blackjack, by Stanford Wong. $49.95

Professional Blackjack Analyzer, by Stanford Wong, CD. $149.95

Smart Cards, by Extreme Blackjack. $59.95

Statistical Blackjack Analyzer, by Karel Janecek, Conjelco. $159.95

Tournament Blackjack, by Stanford Wong, $49.95

CRAPS

Craps Sim II Interactive Version, by Conjelco. $34.95

Craps Sim Pro 2.0 Professional Version Simulator, by Conjelco. $79.95

POKER

Caribbean Stud Poker Pro for Windows, by Masque. $19.99

Poker Wiz, by David Daniel and Ricardo Pessanha. $49.95

Statking, by Tod Levi, CD. $29.95

Turbo Texas Hold 'Em for Windows, by Wilson Software. $89.95

Tournament Texas Hold 'Em, by Wilson Software. $59.95

Turbo Omaha High-Low Split for Windows, by Wilson Software, $89.95

Turbo Omaha High: Windows, by Wilson Software, $89.95

Turbo Seven Card Stud for Windows, by Wilson Software, $89.95

Turbo Seven Card Stud 8 or Better for Windows, by Wilson Software. $89.95

World Series of Poker Adventure, by Masque. $29.99

SPORTS

2001 PDS Baseball Handicapping Software, by The Sports Judge. $89.95

Baseball Logs on Disk, by Phil Erwin/Baseball Insight. $24.95

Data on Disk: NFL, by Davler Sports. $200

Data on Disk: College Football, by Davler Sports. $200

Davler NBA Basketball Data: 11 Years, by Davler Sports, $200

The Optimizer, by Mike Orkin, football data patterns, four years, $125. Eight years, $225

PDS College Basketball Handicapping and Statistics, The Sports Judge (Windows). $89.95

PDS College Football Handicapping System, The Sports Judge (Windows). $89.95

PDS Pro Football Handicapping System, The Sports Judge (Windows). $89.95

PDS Pro Basketball Handicapping and Statistics, The Sports Judge (Windows). $89.95

PDS Pro Hockey Handicapping and Statistics, The Sports Judge (Windows). $89.95

THOROUGHBRED RACING

PDS ThoroughBred Software, by The Sports Judge. $89.95

Thoroughbred Handicapper, by Educated Guess. $39.95

VIDEO POKER

Multiplay Video Poker with Blackjack and Spanish Blackjack, by Masque Publishing, $24.99

Masque Video Poker Strategy Pro, by Lenny Frome w/ Masque Publishing, $29.99

Winpoker, by Bob Dancer presents WinPoker by Zamzow Software Solutions, $30

Video Poker Strategy Master, by TomSki. $29.95

Video Poker Tutor, by Panamint, $30

Gambling Videos

For gamblers who prefer to learn by watching the masters, there is a host of instructional videos available.

Some of gaming's biggest names, including John Patrick, Henry Tamburin, Mike Caro and Bob Dancer, demonstrate the art of playing casino games and viewers can follow along. Even actor Telly Savalas got into the act as the host of a video on blackjack.

Blackjack players can learn how to count cards and manage their money, while poker players can learn the intricacies of when the hold 'em and when to fold 'em. Other videos focus on craps, roulette and Pai Gow.

For players who like big events, there's none bigger than the famous World Series of Poker at Binion's Hotel and Casino. A series of videos capturing annual highlights of this marathon of poker stars is available.

This list of videos and prices was compiled from the Gambler's Book Shop online catalog (http://www.gamblersbookclub.com/, phone 1-800-522-1777 & 1-800-634-6243). Videos are also available from a variety of other sources.

BACCARAT

Best Bets at Roulette, Baccarat & Craps, by Casino Masters, 58 minutes. $29.95

John Patrick's Baccarat, by John Patrick. $39.95

BLACKJACK

The ABC's of Winning Blackjack, by Telly Savalas/Blue Chip Productions, 55 minutes. $19.95

Blackjack: 21 for the 21st Century, by Jim Schian. $19.95

Blackjack – Deal Me In, by Henry Tamburin/Magic, Inc., 90 minutes. $19.95

The Business of Blackjack, by Howard Collier, 40 minutes. $29.95

Cheating at Blackjack, by Casino Research Development, Inc., 43 minutes. $49.95

Gambling Protection Series (three volumes on cheating at cards, marked cards, etc.), $49.95 each

John Patrick's Basic Blackjack. $39.95

John Patrick's Advanced Blackjack (Card Counting Course). $39.95

Winning at Casino Blackjack, by Strategic Play Productions, 30 minutes. $19.95

Winning Blackjack Level I: Basic Strategy and Money Management, by Casino Masters, 47 minutes. $29.95

Winning Blackjack Level II: Card Counting for Extra Profit, by Casino Masters, 40 minutes. $29.95

Winning Blackjack Level III: Advanced Professional Techniques, by Casino Masters, 90 minutes. $29.95

CASINO GAMES

How to Deal Casino Games: A Video Series, by Joe Janik & Larry Smith, 10 videos on baccarat, blackjack, poker, craps, roulette and pai gow. $40 each

Interactive Roulette Casino Gambling Kit, $19.95

John Patrick's Beginners Craps. $39.95

John Patrick's Intermediate Craps. $39.95

John Patrick's Basic Roulette. $39.95

John Patrick's Caribbean Stud/Let It Ride. $39.95

John Patrick's Charting the Tables. $39.95

John Patrick's Pai Gow Poker. $39.95

Craps – Rolling to Win, by Henry Tamburin, 90 minutes. $19.95

Dice with Ken Yerike, 40 minutes. $50

Learn to Play the California Games, by Hollywood Park, 30 minutes. $10

Pai Gow: Chinese Dominoes, by Michael Musante and Kam Chau. $100

Play to Win!: The Insider's Guide to Casino Gambling, Presented by the Las Vegas Hilton, $14.95

Roulette Spinning to Win, by Henry Tamburin, 30 minutes. $19.95

Winning at Video Poker, by Lenny Frome-Strategic Play Productions, 45 minutes, $24.95

POKER

Annual World Series of Poker, series of annual highlights of Binion's Hotel and Casino Poker Tournament. $14.95 to $39.95 each

Caro's Major Poker Seminar, by Mike Caro, 60 minutes. $24.95

Caro's Power Poker Seminar, by Mike Caro, 60 minutes. $39.95

Caro's Pro Poker Tells, by Mike Caro, 90 minutes. $59.95

How to Beat Winning Hold 'Em Players, by Ben Tracy and Joe Marks, 56 minutes. $49.95

John Patrick's 7-Card Stud Poker. $39.95

Learning to Deal Poker Like a Professional, by Shiloh Productions, 53 minutes. $39.95

Poker for All, by Steve Fox, 45 minutes. $19.95

Sklansky: The Seminar, by Ben Tracy & Joe Marks Production, 67 minutes. $29.95

Sklansky: The Video, by Ben Tracy & Joe Marks Production, 90 minutes. $59.95

VIDEO POKER

9/6 Jacks or Better Video Poker, by Bob Dancer, 60 minutes. $29.95

10/7 and 9/6 Double Bonus Video Poker, by Bob Dancer, 60 minutes. $29.95

Deuces Wild Video Poker, by Bob Dancer, 60 minutes. $29.95

Getting the Most Of Slot Clubs, by Jeffrey Compton, 60 minutes. $29.95

Secrets of A Video Poker Winner, by Bob Dancer, 60 minutes. $29.95

Getting the Most Of Slot Clubs, by Jeffrey Compton, 60 minutes. $29.95

Home Gambling Supplies

Gambling enthusiasts who can only get to Las Vegas once or twice a year or to their local casino once or twice a month can quench their thirst for their favorite games right in their own homes.

There's a wide variety of gaming equipment available, from poker tables for that weekly card game in the den to full-fledged craps tables.

Slot machines are popular for both players and collectors. Modern slot machines and video poker machines start at about $1,000 and go up to the $3,000 range. And some of the older models are prized as antiques by collectors, costing well in excess of $3,000.

Note that slot machines are not legal in some states and other states have rules regulating their use. In some places, only antique machines are legal.

Home players can set up a Vegas style casino game using green felt game layouts. All the trimmings, from card decks to chips to dice, are readily available. More sophisticated play is possible using authentic roulette wheels or full-sized gaming tables.

Collectors enjoy chasing chips from casinos, some active and some long since out of business. Some of these chips can actually fetch more than their face value and they make colorful displays.

A sampling of home gambling items was furnished by Gamblers General Store of Las Vegas (800) 322-2447, which also publishes a catalog listing several thousand items. It also lists items on its Web site: Gamblersgeneralstore.com. Prices are subject to change.

SLOT MACHINES

Bally electronic slot machines, 5 cents and 25 cents machines, fruit reel, $1,595 and up.

Bally's Money Honey, rebuilt, 25 cents machine, $2,495.

IGT Series "S" and "S+" electronic slot machines, $1,795 to $1,995.

Bally "EM-type" electromechanical slot machines, $999 to $1,595.

IGT Players Edge and Players Edge Plus video draw poker machines, 5 cents, 25 cents and $1, $1,695 and up.

IGT video poker machines, several versions, $1,795 to $2,495.

Antique slot machines, several versions, $2,995 and up.

Remanufactured Mills machines, 25 cents, several versions, $2,995 to $3,295.

Slot machine stands and bases, $99 and up.

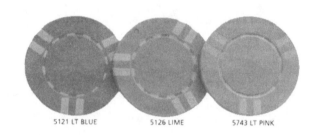

5121 LT BLUE   5126 LIME   5743 LT PINK

CHIPS

Three-spot insert chips, 17 colors available, $42 per 100.

Six-stripe chips, 17 colors available, $42 per 100.

Card symbol chips, with gold foil embossing of denominations, $42 per 100.

Dragon chips, can be embossed with company logo, initials, or design, 6 cents each plain or 10 cents each stamped.

Mermaid chips, $15 per 100.

Diamond chips, $22 per 100.

CHIP COLLECTING SUPPLIES

Acrylic chip display frame, $19.95.

Chip holder keychain, $3.95.

Air-tight holders for collectible chips, 60 cents each.

Hardwood chip display frame, 12-chip capacity, $39.95.

CHIP CASES AND TRAYS

Mahogany interior chip case, 300 chip capacity, $94.95.

Cherrywood chip box, 250 capacity, $129.95.

Vinyl chip case, 200 capacity, $23.95.

Chip carousel, 300 capacity, $79.95.

Deluxe chip tray, 400 capacity, $15.95.

Poker chip tray with storage for two decks, 360 capacity, $24.95.

BLACKJACK SUPPLIES

Twenty-one game table, formica top with padded arm rest, $995.

Aluminum chip tray with 12 tubes and locks, $175.

Twenty-one conversion bar, $1,995.

Portable blackjack table with chip tray, $699.

Money paddle of clear lucite, $8.95.

Casino dealing shoe, four deck, $95.

Home-style casino game layouts for craps, blackjack, roulette, baccarat, or pai gow poker, green felt, $29.95 each.

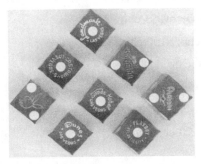

CRAPS SUPPLIES

Craps table, 12 foot size, $4,395.

Craps table, 8 foot size, $3,995.

Dice sticks made of rattan, $23.95 to $30.95.

Dice, set of five, $9.95 to $10.50.

Collector dice, from Dunes, Landmark, Sands, or Hacienda, set of five, $15.

Home-style craps layout, green felt, $29.95.

ROULETTE SUPPLIES

Roulette table, 54" by 102", $2,495.

32-inch casino roulette wheel, wood, $6,750.

16-inch roulette wheel, plastic, $44.95.

Roulette ball, $6 each.

Roulette crown marker, $9.95.

Roulette chip rack, wrap-around style, $65.

Roulette layout, rubberbacked cloth, $175.

POKER SUPPLIES

Poker table, hardwood, seats eight, $365.

Poker table, 84" oblong double metal pedestal, $1,095.

Chip tray with locking cover, $175.

Dealer's Choice portable gaming table top for card table, $99.95.

BINGO SUPPLIES

Bingo cage, ping pong ball capacity, $129.95.

Box of 100 cards, $225.

Plastic spotters, 300 per box, $3.95.

Single roll tickets, $4.95.

Dauber, $1.25.

Let's Play Bingo set with 25 cards, $34.95.

CARDS

Bee Diamondback design cards, $2.95 per deck.

Kem Galaxy, Club or Arrow cards, two-deck set, $18.95.

Plastic-coated Hoyle cards, $1.99 per deck.

Bicycle cards, $2.85 per deck.

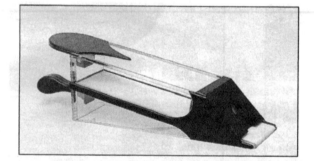

CASINO EQUIPMENT

Money wheel, 60" with metal post stand, $2,995.

Baccarat dealing shoe, eight deck, $159.95.

Pai Gow layout, mali cloth, $75.

Pai Gow dominos, $29.95.

Pai Gow dice, set of three, $6.50.

Change apron, black nylon with six pockets, $49.95.

Big Six clapper, leather with felt tip, $39.95.

Baccarat chip tray, 1,200 chip capacity, walnut finish, $650.

Red dog for red dog game, $3.95.

COLLECTOR'S CASINO CHIPS

Bally's, $5 Englebert Humperdinick chip, $18.

Binion's Horseshoe, 25-cent chip, $90.

Bonanza Club, $100 chip, $40.

California Club, $100 chip, $35.

Coin Castle, $5 chip, $120.

Cowboy Gene's, $25 chip, $160.

Dunes, $500 Baccarat, $75.

Dunes, 10-cent chip, $65.

El Rancho, $100 chip, $95.

Foxy's Firehouse, $25 chip, $140.

Frontier Club, $5 chip, $120.

Gay 90's, $1 chip, $55.

Hacienda, $25 chip, $185.

Honest John's, $25 chip, $70.

Hotel Nevada, $100 chip, $24.

Jockey Club, $500 chip, $22.

Jolly Trolley, $100 chip, $55.

Last Frontier, $25 chip, $55.

Mint Hotel, $25 chip, $80.

New Brown Derby, $1 chip, $65.

Overland, Reno, $100 chip, $35.

Sahara, $100 chip, $18.

Silver City, $5 chip, $55.

Sundance, $1 chip, $10.

Union Plaza, 70-cent chip, $12.

Online Casinos

Off-Shore Gaming Association Casinos

Bet World Wide, www.betworldwide.com, (800) 316-0066, based in Costa Rica, 27 games java.

Casino on Net, www.entercasino.com, (268) 460-8425 (fax), based in Antigua, 1996, six games download.

GameDay, www.gamedaysportsbook.com, (800) 769-5633, based in Curacao, 1999, four games Java.

Global Wager, www.globalwager.com, (800) 432-0736, based in Costa Rica, eight games java or download.

GoTo Casino, www.gotocasino.com, (888) 333-PLAY, based in Costa Rica, 1997, 10 games CD or java.

Nasa Casino International, www.nasacasino.com, (888) 999-2387, based in Costa Rica, eight games java.

On-Line Casino, www.on-linecasino.com, (800) 430-6763, based in Costa Rica, 1998, three versions of seven games download or java.

Omni of the Caribbean, www.omnicasino.com, (888) 477-2239, eight games CD or download.

Players Bet, www.playersbet.com, (800) 432-0624, based in Costa Rica, 27 games java or download.

Sands of the Caribbean, www.carsands.com, (888) 872-2238, 40 games CD or download.

SBG Global, www.sbgglobal.com/osga, (800) 422-2108, based in Costa Rica, seven games download.

Sportbook.com, www.sportbook.com, (800) WIN-CASH, based in Costa Rica, eight games Java.

Toucan Casino, www.toucancasino.com, (888) 771-9079, based in Costa Rica, seven games java.

Non-member online casino sites:

00 Casino (888) 685-7619

1 King (888) 872-2238

1 Lucky Gambler (888) 685-7619, Antigua.

1 Royal Flush (888) 872-2238

1 World Casino No Phone

100 Black Rhino (888) 685-7619

123 Casino & Sportsbook (888) 881-1123, Grenada.

2001 Casino & Sportsbook (877) 491-6963, Costa Rica

21 BlackJack (888) 872-2238

22ndCenturyCasino (888) 685-7619, St. Kitts.

2BetOn.com No number

3D Blackjack (888) 872-2238

3D Roulette (888) 872-2238

3D Slots (888) 872-2238

3D Craps (888) 872-2238

4 Cherrys Casino (888) 685-7619, Antigua.

5 High Cards Casino (888) 685-7619, St. Kitts.

5th Avenue Casino (888) 685-7619

5th Avenue Online Casino & Sportsbook (888) 685-7619, Antigua.

7Palms (800) 606-3093, Curacao, 1996.

88 Fortune Casino & Sportsbook (888) 685-7619, Antigua.

AAA Gambling.com

AAAA Casino (888) 685-7619, Antigua.

A1 Vegas

Abbey Southport Casino   (888) 685-7619, UK.

ABC Islands Sports (800) 605-5893 or (800 605-5894), Curacao.

Abetz International Sportsbook and Casino (800) 403-3417

Abracadabra Online Casino

Abyss Casino

Ace City Casino

Ace In The Hole No Number

Aces Casino (888) 685-7619

Aces Club Casino (888) 685-7619

Aces Gold Casino & Sportsbook (800) 256-7157

Acropolis Internet Casinos

Action Magic Casino

Active Gaming (800) 867-4659

Adult Club Casino

Akira Casino

Air 777 Casino

Aladden Casino

Aladdin's Casino

Alibaba Casino

All American Sportsbook (888) 827-7119 or
    (888) 827-7120

All Nude Gaming

All Sports Bets No number

All Sports Casino (888) 492-6886

All Sports Casino 2 (888) 685-7619

All Star Sportsbook (888) 462-5788

All World Sportsbook & Internet Casino (800) 922-
    2201, 2000, Curacao.

AlphaCasino

Aloha Casino & Sportsbook (800) 352-2733

Alps Casino

Amazon Casino

America Jackpot (888) 872-2238

American Casino (888) 872-2238

American Craps (888) 872-2238

American Lottery Casino

American Poker (888) 872-2238

Amsterdam Casino

Ancient Man Casino

Andromeda Casino

Anime Casino

Apollo Casino (888) 685-7619

Arcade Casino

Arrowhead Sportsbook Casino (800) 409-5078
    Canada (800) 495-5553

Ascot Casino

Astrobet Space Casino

Asia Casino & Sportsbook (888) 685-7619

Asian Casino (888) 872-2238

Atlantic City Casino (888) 872-2238

Atlantic Interbet

Atlantis Casino & Sportsbook

Atlantis Star Casino

Australian Casino (888) 872-2238

Avalon Casinos

Avatar Casino

Aztec Gaming (888) 685-7619

Aztec Sportsbook (888) 685-7619

Aztec Gold Casino

Azure Coast Casino

Bali Casino (800) 352-2758

Bedrock Gaming (888) 685-7619

Belmont Sportsbook & Casino (800) 916-3217

Best Bet Sports (888) 386-4049

Best Craps (888) 872-2238

Bet2Win (888) 685-7619, Antigua.

Bet & Win Online Sportsbook No Number

Bet Green (800) 413-9065, Costa Rica, 2000

Bet the Globe (888) 685-7619

Bet With The Champ (888) 685-7619

betmaker (888) 238-2238, Costa Rica, now
    SportingbetUSA

BetShop (011) 44 7000 693 555

Big Book & Casino, The (888) 278-9199, Licensed
    Costa Rica 1999

Big Daddy Sportsbook (888) 283-6186 or (888)386-
    4049 International 011 506 280 9076

Big Deal Casino (877) 725-6708

Black Tie Casino & Sportsbook (888) 685-7619

Blackjack Emporium No Number

Blackjack Time No Number

Bookie's Cafe (800) 835-0243

British Casino (888) 872-2238

Bubba's Casino & Sportsbook (877) 752-9282

Bugsy Online Casino (888) 257-7738

Bulls' n Bears Casino (888) 248-4710

Cabana Casino No Number

Caesars Gold No Number

Canadian Casino (888) 872-2238

Capitol Casino (888) 894-0936

Caribbean Cyber Online Casino (800) 446-3018

Caribbean Gold Casino No Number

Caribbean Island On-Line Casino, The No Number

Caribbean Offshore Action (888) 521-9438

Casares 011(506) 442 - 2898.

Cash City Casino 888 685-7619

Casino 21 No Number

Casino 8 Online (888) 872-2BET

Casino Alitalia No Number

Casino and Sports No Number

Casino Araneum No Number

Casino Atlantis (888) 685-7619

Casino Australia No Number

Casino Bahamas No Number

Casino Bar No Number

Casino Bellissimo (888) 338-6391

Casino Bet (800) 214 1788

Casino Cabaret No Number

Casino Cafe (800) 835-0249

Casino Caribe No Number

Casino Circuit No Number

Casino CoCo No Number

Casino Crystal No Number

Casino Curacao (504) 561-6566

Casino des Champs Elysees No Number

Casino Domain No Number

Casino Earth No Number

Casino Fantasy No Number

Casino Fortune No Number

Casino Grande No Number

Casino Hollywood (888) 872-2238

Casino Inn No Number

Casino Internationale Curaçao (888)-872-2BET

Casino Jetset No Number

Casino King Tut (888) 685-7619

Casino Kingdom No Number

Casino Magique (877) 412-2917

Casino Manhattan No Number

Casino Monte Carlo (888) 872-2238

Casino Net Gambling

Casino New York (888) FANATIK

Casino of the Kings (888) 685-7619

Casino On Air (888) 685-7619

Casino Pacific 011 (506) 442 - 3084

Casino Paradis (888) 257-7738

Casino Pirata No Number

Casino Regal (888) 872-2238

Casino San Fran No Number

Casino Sanctuary (888) 535-8222

Casino Silk Road No Number

Casino Titanic No Number

Casino Toronto No Number

Casino Treasure Island (888) 244-8647

Casino Vega No Number

Casino VR No Number

Casino Wild West (888) 596-5666

Casino World (888) 872-2238

CasinoXO (888) 465-7646

CasinoClique - Online Casino & Sportsbook (888) 685-7619

Casinos Australasia No Number

Casinos Happywin International No Number

Casinos of the South Pacific No Number

Casinos of the World No Number

Centrebet Sports Betting No Number

Challenge Casino (877) 502-7124, Antigua.

Champion Casino & Sportsbook (888) 685-7619

Chicago Betting (800) 310-1885

Classic Casino (888) 685-7619

Cloud Casino (888) 873-5972, Costa Rica, 2000

Club 8 Casino & Sportsbook (888) 685-7619

Club Casino No Number

Club Monte Carlo No Number

Club Rio Casino (888) 685-7619

Code Casino No Number, Belize

Constellation Casino No Number

Cowboy Casino (877) 296-6417

Crazy Horse Online Casino No Number

Crystal Casino (888) 685-7619

Cyber City Casino No Number

Cyber Cosmos Casino (888) 244-8647

Cyber Slot Tournament No Number

Cyber-Vegas No Number

Cyberbetz (888) 268-8888, Dominica, 1998

Cyberbookie No Number

CyberCardShark's Casino & Sportsbook (888) 685-7619

Cyberspace Casino Tech Ltd No Number

Cyberspades 888) 872-2BET

Cybersportsbook and Casino (888) 685-7619

Delta Poker Club No Number

Desperado Casino No Number

Diamond Club Casino (888) 880-0807

DOR-Cino No Number

e777 Casino & Sportsbook (888) 685-7619

Easy Life Casino & Sportsbook (888) 685-7619

Easy Rider Casino (888) 338-6392

Easy Rollers Casino & Sportsbook (888) 685-7619

EChecks Casino, Grenada

Egyptian Casino & Sportsbook (888) 685-7619

Eiffel Casino & Sportsbook No Number

El San Juan Casino No Number

Elite Casino & Sportsbook (888) 685-7619

Emerald Beach Casino (888) 607-0630

English Harbour Casino (888) 368-8809

Enterbet.com (800) 432-2878

European Union Casino (888) 685-7619

Eurovegas Casino (888) 872-2238

EZ Bets Sportsbook (800) 660-9261

Fairbet Casino No Number

Fair Deal Casino (800) 769-5651, Web TV Compatible

Fashion Casino No Number

Festival Casino No Number

First Live Casino No Number

FiveStar Casino (877) 296-6418

Flam Casino No Number

Flamingo Club Online Casino (888) 257-7738

Flying Dragon Casino (888) 248-4710

Four Aces Casino (877) 250-5542

Free Chips Casino & Sportsbook (800) 867-4659

Funscape's Casino Royale No Number

Future Bet No Number

GalaxiWorld No Number

Gamblecom (888) 685-7619

GambleNet (610) 941-0305

Gamblers Palace Casino & Sportsbook (800) 535-8108

Gambling Palace (888) 872-2238

Game Gate (212) 616-5151

Gametime Casino

Gamesville No Number

Gaming Club Casino (888) 872-2238

Global Betting (888) 872-2238

Go Casino (888) 338-6058

Gold Beach Plaza No Number

Gold Club Casino (888) 853-3720

Gold Key Casino No Number

Gold Nugget Online Casino (888) 338-6391

Gold Tiger Casino (888) 244-8647

Golden Bets (877) 582-5997, Costa Rica, 1999

Golden Dragon Online Casino (888) 338-6391

Golden Garden Casino No Number

Golden Jackpot Casino No Number

Golden Palace Online Casino (888) 217-5648

Golden Pyramid Internet Casino (888) 714-9770

Golden Star Casino, Costa Rica, 2000

Golden Wager Casino & Sportsbook (800) 352-4082

Gold Medal Sports (800) 209-4632, Curacao, 1996.

GoldMine Casino No Number

GoldRush Casino No Number

Good Luck Club No Number

Grand Dominican Online Resort and Casino No Number

Grand Gambler No Number

Grand Online Casino (888) 257-7738

Grand Prix Sportsbook & Casino (888) 854-5654

Grand Riviera Online Casino (888) 338-6391

Hall of the Emperors Casino (888) 685-7619

Happy Win Casino No Number

Hawaiian Casino & Sportsbook (888) 685-7619

High Roller Casino (888) 685-7619

HomeBookie.com Sportsbook & Casino (888) 685-7619

Hot Gambling (888) 872-2238

I-Sportsbook (888) 685-7619

Iceberg Casino No Number

Imperial Dragon Casino (888) 338-6058

iNetBet Casino (877) 465-7359

InstaCash Casino (800) 584-4860

interBet Casino No Number

InterCasino (888) 872-2238

InterKeno 011 506 442-2898

Internet Casinos No Number

Intertops Online Sports Betting (877) 412-2915

Island Casino (800) 511-4844

Israel Casino Foreign Language (Hebrew)

Jackpot 7 Casino (888) 685-7619

Jackpot City (888) 677-8162

Jackpot Palace (888) 561-2098

Java Casino (888) 685-7619

Jetset Casino No Number

Kenny Rogers Casino No Number

King Solomon's Online Casino (800) 886-7249

King Tut's Casino (877) 524-4677

Kings Casino No Number

Kings Club Casino (888) 685-7619

Kinky Casino (888) 685-7619

Kosher Casino (888) 338-6391

La Cruise Virtual Poker No Number

Las Vegas At Home Casino (888) 685-7619

Las Vegas Casino (888) 872-2238

Las Vegas City Casino No Number

Las Vegas from Home (800) 665-3119

Las Vegas Gambling No Number

Lasseters Online No Number

Liberty Casino (888) 253-9566

LuckMasters No Number

Lucky Dragons (888) 363-3362, Costa Rica, 1999

Lucky Jackpot (888) 872-2238

Lucky Land (800) 549-2515

Lucky Nugget Casino (888) 677-8180

Lucky's Casino and Sportsbook (888) 228-2221

Majestic International Casino (877) 491-6964

MaPau Online Casino (888) 349-3571

Mardigras Dollars Slot Machine (800) 675-3267

Mayan Casino & Sportsbook (888) 685-7619

Megabahis Casino No Number

Megaplay (800) 549-2191

Merlin Casino (888) 685-7619

Metro Casino

Metro Gaming No Number

Miami Beach Casino (888) 349-3571

Micro Casino (888) 872-2238

Millennium Casino (800) 824-1637

Money Plays Casino (888) 685-7619

Monte Cristo Casino No Number

Mustang Casino No Number

MySportsbook (888) 685-7619

Mystic Dunes (888) 253-9078

NASA SportsBook (888) 973-1514

Net Poker No Number

Nevada Casino (888) 872-2238

New York Casino (888) 819-7924

Nierfield's Internet Casino No Number

Night Casino (888) 872-2238

NYC Casino (888) 326-2845

Oasis Casino (800) 922-4515

Old Glory Casino (888) 248-4710

Online Vegas (888) 257-7738

Orient Express Casino (888) 248-4710

Oscar Casino (888) 633-2128

OZ Gaming (888) 685-7619

Pachinko Casino Foreign Language, nothing in English

Pacific Princess Online 888 338-6391

Pagoda Casino No Number

Palace of Isis Casino (888) 685-7619

Palms Casino, The

Paramount Casinos

Paris Casino & Sportsbook (888) 685-7619

Parisian Casino

Piggs Peak Casino

Pirate Island Casino & Sportsbook (888) 685-7619

Place My Bet

Place That Bet

Place Your Betz (888) 685-7619

Planet City Casino

Planet Luck Casino

Planet Poker

Planet Rock Casino

Platinum Casino

Play Big Casino

Players Lounge

Players Only Sportsbook & Casino (800) 388-0456

PlayStar Casino

PlayStar Casino

Playstar Online Casino

Poker Jackpot (888) 872-2238

Polo Casino & Sportsbook (888) 685-7619

Prairie Meadows

Prestige Casino (877) 233-7686, Antigua, 2000.

Primadonna Casino Resorts

Queen of Lust Casino & Sportsbook

Quick Draw Casino

Racing Casino (888) 685-7619

Ramses Valley of the Kings Casino

Raquel's Casino (888) 685-7619

Real Casino

Rich Bitch Casino (888) 685-7619

Rio International (800) 809-3246

Ritz Casino (888) 872-2238

River Belle Casino

Rock n Roll Casino and Sports Book (888) 685-7619

Rodeo Casino (888) 685-7619

Rodney Dangerfield's Place (888) 685-7619

Rosie's Chalk Island Sportsbook & Casino (800) 248-4115

Royal Dynasty Casino

Royal Flush (888) 872-2238

Royal Island Casino & Sportsbook No Number

Royal Magic Casino

Russian Casino (888) 872-2238

S.S. Casino

Safari Casino

Sharky's (888) 363-3362, Costa Rica, 1998.

Showdown Casino

Showgirls Casino

SilverStar Casino & Sportsbook

Six Shooter Online Casino

Sky High Online Casino

SlotsVegas Casino & Sportsbook (888) 860-4110

Southern Belle Casino & Sportsbook (888) 228-2221

Sportbet.com (800) 214-1788

Sportfanatik (888) 685-7619

Sporting Casino (888) 685-7619

Sportingbet.com (877) 620-9013

Star Online Casino

Starluck Casino

Starz Casino

Sultan Casino

Sunset Casino (888) 287-6317, Antigua.

Super Casino

Super Craps (888) 872-2238

Superbet Casino & Sportsbook (888) 685 7619

Supermoney (888) 872-2238

Tangiers Casino

Teasers Palace (888) 685-7619

Texas Casino (888) 333 PLAY

The Big Casino

The Boathouse Casino

The Cyber Casino & Sportsbook (888) 685-7619

The Gambler

the Royal Magic Street

The Sands of the Caribbean

The Stadium Casino

The Virtual Slot Machine

TheOnlineCasino & Sportsbook (888) 860-4110

Titanic Casino & Sportsbook (888) 685-7619

Top Bet Casino

Tradewinds Virtual Casino (800) 467-7678

Treasure Hunter Casino

Triple Win Online Gambling

Tropical Casino

Tropical Island Casino (888) 685-7619

Trump Card Casino

Twinkling Star Casino

US Sports Casino

USA Casino

USA Jackpot

VegasUSA

Video Poker Palace

VIP Casino, Web TV Compatible

VIP Sports (800) 606-3576

Virtual Gaming Technologies, Inc.

Virtual Island Casino

Virtual Vegas

Virtual Wagering (888) 685-7619, Antigua.

Viva Casino

Wallstreet Casino (800) 485-4092

Wild Jack Casino No Number

Wild West Frontier Casino (888) 685-7619

William Hill Casino (888) 872 2238, Licensed in the UK.

Win City Casino (888) 685-7619, Antigua.

Win Win Casino No number

Winning Worlds Casino No Number

Winward Casino & Sportsbook No Number

World Bet Casino (888) 685-7619, Antigua.

World Charity Casino (888) 685-7619, Antigua.

World Games Casino & Sportsbook (888) 685-7619, Antigua.

World Race Tracks No Number

World Wide Vegas

Worldwide Casino No Number, Costa Rica.

Worldwide Gamble (888) 685-7619, Antigua.

WWCasino (888) 217-5648

Yellowcab Casino_ (888) 217-5648

Your Casino (888) 872-2238

Online Sports Books

Off Shore Gaming Association Sports Books

Badlands, **www.badlands.co.cr/**, (800) 291-3359, based in Costa Rica, 1999.

Betmaker, **www.betmaker.com**, (800) 644-6405, based in Curacao, 1996.

Bettors Trust, **www.bettorstrust.com**, (866) 867-BETS, based in Costa Rica, 1997.

Bet World Wide, **www.betworldwide.com**, (800) 316-0066, based in Costa Rica, 2000.

The Big Book, **www.thebigbook.com**, (877) 960-5400, based in Costa Rica, 1995.

BoDog Sports Book & Casino, **www.bodog.com**, (888) 263-0000, based in Costa Rica, 1995.

Empress Gaming, **www.empressgaming.com**, (888) 564-4345, based in Costa Rica, 1995.

First Fidelity Deposit Trust, **www.youwager.com**, (800) YOUWAGER, based in Costa Rica, 1994.

Gameday, **www.gamedayhelp.com/osga/**, (800) 769-5633, based in Curacao, 1999.

Gibraltar Sports, **www.bettherock.com**, (800) 582-1381, based in Costa Rica, 1995.

Global Wager, **www.globalwager.com**, (800) 432-0736, based in Costa Rica, 2000.

GoTo Casino, **www.gotocasino.com**, (888) 333-PLAY, based in Costa Rica, 1997.

Grand Central Sports, **www.gcsports.com**, (800) 213-3370, based in Margarita Island, 1997.

Infinity Sports International, **www.betoninternet.com**, (877) 919-4263, based in Costa Rica, 1994.

Jaguar Sports, **www.jagsportsbet.com**, (877) 275-6278, based in Costa Rica, 1995.

Malibu Sportsbook & Casino, **http://betmalibu.co.cr/**, (800) 387-9208, based in Costa Rica, 1995.

Mega Sportsbook International, **www.betmega.com**, (888) 535-8830, based in Margarita Island, 2000.

Millennium Sports, **www.millsports.com**, (866) 444-4263, based in Costa Rica, 1995.

MVP Sports Superbook and Casino, **www.mvpbets.com**, (866) 687-1687, based in Costa Rica, 1995.

Nasa Sports International, **www.betonsports.com**, (888) 999-2387, based in Costa Rica, 1991.

Omni Casino & Sports Book, **www.omnicasino.com**, (888) 477-2239, based in Antigua, 1997.

On-Line Casino, **www.on-linecasino.com**, (800) 430-6763, based in Costa Rica, 1997.

Payoffs Plus, **www.payoffsplus.com**, (888) 492-4377, based in Costa Rica, 1997.

Players Bet, **www.playersbet.com**, (800) 432-0624, based in Costa Rica, 1998.

Players Super Book, **www.players-sb.com**, (888) 771-9075, based in Costa Rica, 1998.

Prestige Sports International, **www.prestigesports.co.cr**, (800) 429-5153, based in Costa Rica, 1998.

Post Time Sports, **www.post-time.com**, (888) BET-POST, based in Antigua, 1996.

Regency Casino & Sports Book, **www.regency.co.cr**, (800) 274-8313, based in Costa Rica, 1997.

Rock Island Sports, **www.rockislandsports.com**, (866) 488-7625, based in Costa Rica, 1997.

SBG Global Sportsbook and Online Casino, **www.sbgglobal.com**, (800) WINNER4, based in Costa Rica, 1991.

Seven Palms Sports Book & Casino, **www.seven-palms.com**, (800) 606-3093, based in Curacao, 1998.

SportBet, **www.sportbet.com**, (800) 214-1788, based in Costa Rica, 1996.

Sportbook.com, **www.sportbook.com**, (888) WIN-CASH, based in Costa Rica, 1996.

Wager World Wide, **http://sports.wagerworldwide.com**, (866) WWW-BETS, based in Nicaragua, 1999.

World Sports Exchange, **www.wsex.com**, (888) 498-8227, based in Antigua, 1996. World Wide Tele Sports, www.betswwts.com, (800) 238-9987, based in Antiqua, 1991.

VIP Sports, **www.vipsports.com**, (800) 769 5685, based in Curacao, 1996.

Virtual Bookmaker, **www.virtualbookmaker.com**, (888) 771-9079, based in Costa Rica, 1998.

V-Wager, **www.v-wager.com**, (888) 771-9080, based in Costa Rica, 1998.

Non-members of the Off Shore Gaming Association:

00 Casino

1Bet (888)741-0290, Costa Rica

1 Lucky Gambler (888) 685-7619, Antigua

Black Rhino Sporting Club (888) 685-7619, Antigua

123 Casino & Sportsbook (888) 881-1123, Grenada

2001 Casino & Sportsbook (877) 491-6963, Costa Rica

22ndCenturyCasino (888) 685-7619, St. Kitts

2BetOn.com, Antigua

4 Cherrys Casino (888) 685-7619, Antigua

5 Dimes Sportsbook and Casino (800) 305-3517

5 High Cards Casino and Sportsbook (888) 685-7619, St. Kitts

5th Avenue Casino & Sportsbook (888) 685-7619, Antigua

88 Fortune Casino & Sportsbook (888) 685-7619, Antigua

AAAA Casino (888) 685-7619, Antigua

Abbey Southport Casino (888) 685-7619, UK

ABC Islands Sports (800) 605-5893 or (800) 605-5894, Licensed in Costa Rica, 1995

Aces Sportsbook (888) 675 ACES, Antigua

Aces Club Casino

Aces Gold Casino & Sportsbook (800) 256-7157, Curaco

Active Gaming (800) 867-4659, Curaco

All Aboard Casino (888) 527-2982

All American Sportsbook (888) 827-7119, Costa Rica

All Sports Bets, Costa Rica

All Sports Casino (888) 492-6886

All Sports Casino 2 (888) 685-7619

All Star Sportsbook (888) 462-5788, Margarita Island

All World Sportsbook & Casino (800) 922-2201, Curacao, 2000

Aloha Casino & Sportsbook (800) 352-2733

Asia Casino & Sportsbook (888) 685-7619

Aztec Sportsbook (888) 685-7619

Bali Casino (800) 352-2758

Bedrock Gaming (888) 685-7619, Antigua

Belmont Sportsbook & Casino (800) 388-0456, Venezuela

Bet & Win Online Sportsbook +43 5522 83 292, Licensed in Austria, 1998

Bet Ehorse (800) 416-2838, Costa Rica, Horse Racing Only

Bet Eurosport (888) 387-6060, Costa Rica, 2000

Bet FC, United Kingdom, 2001, Soccer book

Bet Green (800) 413-9065, Costa Rica, 2000

Bet the Globe (888) 685-7619, St. Kitts

Bet With The Champ (888) 685-7619 Bet2Day (888) 818-8258, Antigua

Betanything (800) 582-5881, Costa Rica, 2000

Betquick.com, Costa Rica, 2000

BetShop +44 7000 693 555, UK

Bet Virtual Sportsbook International (BetVSI) (888) 771-9079, Costa Rica, 1998

Big Daddy Sportsbook (888) 283-6186, Costa Rica

Blue Marlin (888) 292-7491, Costa Rica

Bookie's Cafe (800) 835-0243, Antigua

Bowman International (888) BOWMANS, Isle of Manchester, UK, 1985

British Caribbean Sports (800) 259-8406, Costa Rica

Bubba's Casino & Sportsbook (877) PLAY BUBBA, Antigua

Canbet (800) 399-8063, Australia

Carib Sportsbook Inc. (800) 611-7000, Antigua

Caribbean Offshore Action (888) 521-9438, Costa Rica

Casablanca (800) 689-2600, Costa Rica, 1996

Cascade Sportsbook (877) 614-8726, Costa Rica, 2000

Casino and Sports (888) 685-7619, Antigua

Casino Atlantis (888) 685-7619, Dominica

Casino Bet (800) 214-1788, 1997

Casino Cafe (800) 835-0249, Curacao

Casino Curacao 1998

Casino Fortune (888) 349-3571, Antigua, 1997

Casino King Tut (888) 685-7619, Antigua

Casino New York

Casino of the Kings (888) 685-7619, Antigua

Casino On Air (888) 685-7619

Casino Titanic (888) 685-7619

CasinoClique - Online Casino & Sportsbook (888) 685-7619, Antigua

CasinoSports (800) 313-1436, Costa Rica

Centrebet Sports Betting +61 8 8955 5800, Australia, 1992

Champion Casino & Sportsbook (888) 685-7619, St. Kitts

Chicago Betting (800) 310-1885, Costa Rica

City Index 0171 861 5000, UK, 1984, Spread wagering only

Classic Casino (888) 685-7619, St. Kitts

Cloud Casino (888) 873-5972, Costa Rica, 2000

Club 8 Casino & Sportsbook (888) 685-7619, Antigua

Club Rio Casino (888) 685-7619, Venezuela

Coastal Sportsbook (888) 854-5982, Costa Rica

Costa Rica International Sports (CRIS) (800) 596-8946, Costa Rica

Cyberbetz (888) 268-8888, Dominica, 1998

Cyberbookie, Costa Rica

Cybersportsbet (888) 685-7619, Antigua

Cybersportsbook and Casino (888) 685-7619, Antigua

Desert Palace (888) 685-7619, Antigua

Diamond Sports and Race Book (877) 223-8374, Costa Rica, 1995

Dunes Sports (877) 600-9116, Costa Rica, 1999

e777 Casino & Sportsbook (888) 685-7619

Easybets (877) 880-3983, Antigua, 1997, formerly in Ireland

Easy Life Casino & Sportsbook (888) 685-7619, Antigua

Easy Rollers Casino & Sportsbook (888) 685-7619, Antigua

Easybets (800) 660-9261, Dominican Republic, 1997

E Baseball Betting (866) 244-2387, Costa Rica

Egyptian Casino & Sportsbook (888) 685 7619, Dominica

Eiffel Casino & Sportsbook (888) 685 7619, Antigua

Elite Casino & Sportsbook (888) 685 7619, St. Kitts

Emerald Palms Casino and Sportsbook

Enterbet.com (800) 432-2878, Costa Rica, 1998

European Union Casino (888) 685-7619, Antigua

EuroSports Casino & Sportsbook (888) 685-7619

EZ Sportsbook (888) 675-2237, Venezuela

EZ Bets Sportsbook (888) 685-7619, Antigua

Fair Deal Sports (800) 769-5651, Curacao, 1997

Five Card Charlie's (800) 414-5523, Curacao, 1997

Free Chips Casino & Sportsbook (800) 867-4659, Curacao

Gamble USA (800 471-4530, Costa Rica, 1998

Gamblecom (888) 685-7619, Antigua

Gamblers Palace Casino & Sportsbook (800) 535-8108, Costa Rica

Gambling Place (888) 685-7619, Antigua

Globet International Sports Betting Ltd, UK

Go Win Casino (888) 685-7619

Gold Medal Sports (800) 209-4632, Curacao, 1996

GoldRush Casino

Grand Prix Sportsbook & Casino (888) 854-5654, Licensed in Costa Rica, 1999

Guardian Guaranty (800) 624-2521, Costa Rica

Hall of the Emperors Casino

Hampton Casino (800) 305-1000

Hawaiian Casino & Sportsbook, Dominica

Heritage Sportsbook (800) 800-7777, Costa Rica

High Roller Casino (888) 685-7619, Antigua

HomeBookie.com Sportsbook & Casino (888) 685-7619, Antigua

Horizon Sports (800) 284-5737, Costa Rica

Horizon International (888) 319-0996, St. Maarten, 2000

I-Sportsbook (888) 685-7619, Antigua

Ibet (800) 432-5402

InetSportsBook (888) 386-4049, Costa Rica, 1996

Instant Action Sports (800) 366-7866, Costa Rica

Interbet International +44 87 0747 0646, UK

InterCasino (888) 872-2238, Antigua,1996

International All Sports Limited, Australia

International Sports Betting Service +44 (171) 354 9434, UK, Belgium, 1976

Intertops Online Sports Betting (877) 412 2915, Antigua, 1992

Interwetten Wien +43 1 (774) 647 711, Austria, 1989

Island Casino (800) 511-4844, Costa Rica, 1996

Israel Casino

Jackpot 7 Casino (888) 685-7619, St. Kitts

Java Casino (888) 685-7619

Jazz Casino & Sportsbook (800) 830-2695, Costa Rica

Kings Club Casino (888) 685-7619, Antigua

Las Palmas (877) 527-7256, Costa Rica, 2000

Las Vegas Club Casino & Sportsbook

Las Vegas from Home (888) 685-7619, Antigua

Loose Lines (800) 475-8259, St. Maarten

Majestic International Casino (877) 491-6964

MaPau Online Casino (888) 349 3571, Carribean, South Africa, 1991

Mayan Casino & Sportsbook (800) 206-7030, Costa Rica

Mega Sports (800) 000 380, Australia

Merlin Casino (888) 685-7619, Antigua

Metro Gaming

Miami Beach Casino (888) 349-3571, Carribean, South Africa, 1997

Money Plays Casino (888) 685-7619, Antigua

MVP Sportsbook (888) 771-9076, Costa Rica

MySportsbook (888) 685-7619, Antigua

NASA Sportsbook (800) 973-1514, Costa Rica

New York Casino (888) 819-7924, Antigua

NYC Sportsbook (800) 996-5152, Antigua, Venezuela

Oasis Casino (800) 922-4515, Licensed in Curacao

Offshore Wagering International (800) 897-2865, Costa Rica

Olympic Sports (888) 327 8238, Jamaica

Online Sports Bet (888) 283-6186, Costa Rica

Option Sports (800) 305-4011, Costa Rica, 2000

OZ Gaming

Palace of Isis Casino (888) 685-7619, Antigua

Paradise Sports Book (888) 283-6186

Paris Casino & Sportsbook (888) 685-7619, Dominica

Parlay Teaser.com (888) 283-6186, Costa Rica

Pirate Island Casino & Sportsbook (888) 685-7619, Dominica

Pinnacle Sportsbook (800) 484-3333, Licensed in Curacao 1994

Place My Bet

Place That Bet

Place Your Betz (888) 685-7619, Antigua

Players Offshore (888) 685-7619, Venezuela

Players Only Sportsbook & Casino (800) 388-0456, Antigua

Polo Casino & Sportsbook (888) 685-7619, Antigua

Premiere League (888) 221-2288, Antigua, 1998

Queen of Lust Casino & Sportsbook

Quick Pay Sports, Costa Rica

Racing Casino (888) 685-7619, Antigua

Raquel's Casino (888) 685-7619

Rio International (800) 809-3246, Costa Rica, 1997

Ritz Casino (888) 685-7619, Venezuela

Rock n Roll Casino and Sports Book (888) 685-7619, Dominica

Rodney Dangerfield's Place (888) 685-7619, Antigua

Rosies Chalk Island Casino (800) 248-4115, St. Kitts

Royal Island Casino & Sportsbook (877) 615-8726, Costa Rica

Royal Sports (800) 557-6710, Licensed in Curacao

Royal St. Kitts (888) 284-5803, St. Kitts

Russian Casino

Sharky's Sportsbook (888) 363-3362, Costa Rica, 1998

Skybook (888) SKYBOOK, Costa Rica

SlotsVegas Casino & Sportsbook (888) 860-4110

Southern Belle Casino & Sportsbook (888) 228-2221

Sporting Casino (888) 685 7619, Romania

Sporting Index USA (888) 230-5484, UK, 1992

Sportingbet.com (877) 620-9013, Alderny, British Isles, 1999

Sports Bettors Paradise (888) 283-6186, Costa Rica

Sportsbook.com (800) 996-5152, Antigua, St Kitts, Germany, Canada, Venezuela, Italy

Sports InterAction (888) 922-5575, in Kahnawake Mohawk Territory, Canada

Sports Offshore (SOS) (800) PLAYLEGAL, Antigua, 1996

Sports-Market.com (800) 721-8885, Curacao, 1996

SportsBetting.com (888) 685-7619, Antigua

SportsNetBet (888) 283-6186, Costa Rica

SSP International +44 (171) 354 9434, UK, Belgium, 1976

Superbet Casino & Sportsbook (888) 685-7619, Licensed in Venezuela

Teasers Palace (888) 685-7619

TeleSportsBet (877) 543-7150, Costa Rica, 1999

Texas Casino (888) 333 PLAY, Costa Rica, 1998

The Cyber Casino & Sportsbook (888) 685-7619, Antigua

The TAB of NSW

TheOnlineCasino & Sportsbook (888) 860-4110

Titanic Casino & Sportsbook

Top Bet Casino (888) 685-7619, St. Kitts

Tradewinds Virtual Casino (800) 467-7678, Is now Go Sports.

Tropical Island Casino (888) 685-7619, St. Kitts

Ultimate Sports Betting (888) 283-6186, Costa Rica

Vegas International (877) 779-3427, Costa Rica, 1999

Vegas Way (800) 334-6573, Margarita Island

Victor Chandler (877) 9VICTOR, Licensed in Gibraltar, Spain.

Virtual Wagering (888) 685-7619, Antigua

Wagerstreet (888) 628-2873, Kahnawake Mohawk Territory, Canada

Wall Street Superbook (800) 485-4092, Licensed in Curacao, 1998.

William Hill (800) 322-6250 Licensed in the UK.

Win City Casino (888) 685-7619, Antigua

Winners Hill (800) 891-7794, 1996

Winning Worlds Casino

WIT Sportsbook (800) 262-7857, Costa Rica, 2000

World Bet Casino (888) 685-7619, Antigua

World Charity Casino (888) 685-7619, Antigua

World Games Casino & Sportsbook (888) 685-7619, Antigua.

World Sportsbook (888) 685-7619, Antigua.

World Wager

WorldBet SportBook

World Wide Bet (888) 685-7916, St. Kitts

Worldwide Casino Costa Rica.

Worldwide Gamble (888) 685-7619, Antigua

Ya Bet (877) 509-2238, Curacao, 1999.

State Lotteries

ARIZONA

Fantasy 5: Players with all five numbers win $50,000.

Pick 3: Daily. Top prize, $500.

The Pick: Weekly. Six numbers plus Pick number.

Powerball: Five numbers plus Powerball (multi-state)

CALIFORNIA

Daily 3:

Fantasy 5: (daily)

Daily Derby: To win the grand prize, ticket-holders must match in exact order the winning race time and the first, second and third place horses. Lesser prizes are given to ticket-holders who correctly match other horses or race times.

SuperLottoPlus: Weekly. Five numbers plus SuperLotto number.

Big Spin: Prizes awarded on weekly TV show.

COLORADO

Cash 5: Drawings Monday, Tuesday, Wednesday, Thursday, Friday and Saturday nights.

Lotto: Weekly, six numbers.

Powerball: Five numbers plus Powerball (multi-state)

CONNECTICUT

Midday Play 3 Lottery: Daily.

Midday Play 4 Lottery: Daily.

Evening Play 3: Daily.

Evening Play 4: Daily.

Lotto: Weekly, six numbers.

Cash 5: Daily.

Powerball: Five numbers plus Powerball (multi-state)

DELAWARE

Midday Pick 3: Daily.

Midday Pick 4: Daily.

Evening Pick 3: Daily.

Evening Pick 4: Daily.

Powerball: Five numbers plus Powerball (multi-state)

Rolldown: Five numbers, always pays a jackpot (multi-state)

DISTRICT OF COLUMBIA

Midday Pick 3: Daily.

Midday Pick 4: Daily.

Evening Pick 3: Daily.

Evening Pick 4: Daily.

Quick Cash Game: Six numbers.

Hot Five: Daily.

Powerball: Five numbers plus Powerball (multi-state)

FLORIDA

Cash 3: Daily.

Play 4: Daily.

Fantasy 5

Florida Lotto: Six numbers

Mega Money: Four numbers plus "MegaBall"

GEORGIA

Midday Pick 3

Midday Pick 4

Evening Pick 3

Evening Pick 4

Fantasy 5

IDAHO

Pick 3

Powerball: Five numbers plus Powerball (multi-state)

Wild Card: Five numbers plus playing card (multi-state)

Rolldown: Five numbers, always pays a jackpot (multi-state)

ILLINOIS

Pick Three-Midday

Pick Three-Evening

Pick Four-Midday

Pick Four-Evening

Big Game: Five numbers plus special number.

Little Lotto: Five numbers.

Lotto: Six numbers.

INDIANA

Daily Three-Midday

Daily Three-Evening

Daily Four-Midday

Daily Four-Evening

Lucky 5: Daily.

Hoosier Lotto: Six numbers.

Powerball: Five numbers plus Powerball (multi-state)

IOWA

Cash Game: Five numbers.

Pick 3

FreePlay Replay: Weekly, six numbers.

Powerball: Five numbers plus Powerball (multi-state)

Rolldown: Five numbers, always pays a jackpot (multi-state)

KANSAS

Pick 3: Daily

Winners Take All: weekly, five numbers.

Kansas Cash: Six numbers.

Powerball: Five numbers plus Powerball (multi-state)

KENTUCKY

MIDDAY

Pick 3:

Pick 4:

EVENING

Pick 3:

Pick 4:

Cash Ball: Weekly, four numbers plus Cash Ball number.

Powerball: Five numbers plus Powerball (multi-state)

LOUISIANA

Louisiana Lottery

Pick 3: Maximum prize $500

Pick 4: Maximum prize $5,000

Cash Quest: Four numbers.

Lotto: Six numbers

Powerball: Five numbers plus Powerball (multi-state)

Rolldown: Five numbers, always pays a jackpot (multi-state)

MAINE

Pick 3: Daily

Pick 4: Daily.

Win Cash: Weekly, six numbers.

Powerball: Five numbers plus Powerball (multi-state)

MARYLAND

Midday Pick 3

Midday Pick 4

Evening Pick 3

Evening Pick 4

Big Game: Five numbers plus Big Game number.

Cash-in-Hand: seven numbers.

Lotto: Six numbers.

MASSACHUSETTS

Big Game: Five numbers plus special number.

Numbers: Four numbers.

Mass Cash: Five numbers.

Megabucks: Six numbers.

MassMillions: Six numbers and a bonus number.

MICHIGAN

Midday Daily Lottery

Midday Daily-4

Daily 3

Daily 4

Rolldown: Five numbers.

Keno: 22 numbers.

Big Game: Five numbers plus "Big Money Ball" number

Michigan Millions: Seven numbers.

MINNESOTA

Daily 3

Gopher 5: Five numbers plus Gopher number.

Powerball: Five numbers plus Powerball (multi-state)

Rolldown: Five numbers, always pays a jackpot (multi-state)

MISSOURI

Pick 3

Pick 4

ShowMe 5 Paydown: five numbers.

Lotto: Six numbers.

Powerball: Five numbers plus Powerball (multi-state)

MONTANA

Montana Cash: Five numbers.

Powerball: Five numbers plus Powerball (multi-state)

Wild Card: Five numbers plus playing card (multi-state)

Rolldown: Five numbers, always pays a jackpot (multi-state)

NEBRASKA

Pick 5

Powerball: Five numbers plus Powerball (multi-state)

Rolldown: Five numbers, always pays a jackpot (multi-state)

NEW HAMPSHIRE

Pick 3

Pick 4

Win Cash: Six numbers.

Megabucks: Six numbers plus Megabucks number.

Powerball: Five numbers plus Powerball (multi-state)

Rolldown: Five numbers, always pays a jackpot (multi-state)

NEW JERSEY

Pick 3

Pick 4

Big Game: Five numbers plus special number.

Jersey Cash 5

Pick 6 Lotto

Lotzee: Four numbers

NEW MEXICO

Pick 3

Road Runner Cash: Five numbers.

Powerball: Five numbers plus Powerball (multi-state)

NEW YORK

Pick 3

Win 4

Pick 10

Take 5

Lotto: Six numbers and a bonus number

OHIO

Midday Pick 3

Midday Pick 4

Evening Pick 3

Evening Pick 4

Buckeye 5

Super Lotto Plus: Six numbers plus special number

Kicker: Six numbers

OREGON

Pick 4

Win for Life: Four numbers.

Megabucks: Six numbers.

Powerball: Five numbers plus Powerball (multi-state)

PENNSYLVANIA

Pick 3

Pick 4

Cash 5

Super 6 Lotto

RHODE ISLAND

Pick 4

Money Roll: Four numbers

Powerball: Five numbers plus Powerball (multi-state)

SOUTH DAKOTA

Dakota Cash: Five numbers

Powerball: Five numbers plus Powerball (multi-state)

Wild Card: Five numbers plus playing card (multi-state)

Rolldown: Five numbers, always pays a jackpot (multi-state)

TEXAS

Pick 3

Cash 5

Lotto: Six numbers.

VERMONT

Pick 3

Pick 4

Win Cash: Six numbers.

Megabucks: Six numbers plus Megabucks number.

VIRGINIA

DAY DRAWING

Pick 3:

Pick 4:

Cash 5:

NIGHT DRAWING

Pick 3:

Pick 4:

Cash 5:

Big Game: Five numbers plus special number.

WASHINGTON

Pick 3

Lotto: Six numbers.

Keno: 20 numbers.

Lucky for Life: Four numbers.

Quinto: Five combination numbers/letters.

WEST VIRGINIA

Pick 3

Pick 4

Cash 25

Powerball: Five numbers plus Powerball (multi-state)

Rolldown: Five numbers, always pays a jackpot (multi-state)

WISCONSIN

Pick 3: Maximum prize: $500

Pick 4: Maximum prize: $5,000

Money Roll: Five numbers. Maximum prize: $500,000

SuperCash: Six numbers. Maximum prize: $250,000

Powerball: Five numbers plus Powerball (multi-state)

A Handbook for the K-12 Reading Resource Specialist

Related Titles of Interest

Reading in the Content Areas for Junior High and High School
Judith A. Cochran
ISBN: 0-205-13404-1

126 Strategies to Build Language Arts Abilities
Cathy Collins
ISBN: 0-205-13025-9

**A Green Dinosaur Day: A Guide for Developing Thematic Units in
   Literature-Based Instruction, K—6**
Patricia L. Roberts
ISBN: 0-205-14007-6

Language and Literacy Learning in Multicultural Classrooms
Leslie W. Crawford
ISBN: 0-205-13922-1